NEW YORK INSTITUTE
OF TECHNOLOGY LIBRARY

D0560731

The Incomparable Max

The Incomparable
MAX

A Collection of Writings of

SIR MAX BEERBOHM

NEW YORK INSTITUTE
OF TECHNOLOGY LIBRARY

045062

DODD, MEAD & COMPANY, *New York*

OLD WESTBURY LIBRARY

PR 6003
.E4A6
C.1

© Eva G. Reichmann, 1962
All rights reserved
No part of this book may be reproduced in any form
without permission in writing from the publisher
Library of Congress Catalog Card Number: 62-20642
Printed in the United States of America

The Fire and Whistler's Writing, reprinted from *Yet Again* by Max Beerbohm by permission of Alfred A. Knopf, Inc. Copyright 1951 by Alfred A.
Knopf, Inc. The Mote in the Middle Distance and Euphemia Clashthought,
reprinted from *A Christmas Garland* by Max Beerbohm. Reprinted by per-
mission of E. P. Dutton & Co., Inc. Enoch Soames and A. V. Laider, reprinted
from *Seven Men and Two Others* by Max Beerbohm. Copyright 1920 by
Max Beerbohm. Reprinted by permission of Brandt & Brandt. No. 2 The
Pines, Hosts and Guests, Quia Imperfectum, 'A Clergyman,' and William and
Mary, reprinted from *And Even Now* by Max Beerbohm. Copyright 1921 by
E. P. Dutton & Co., Inc. Renewal, 1949, by Max Beerbohm. A Note on the
Einstein Theory, London Revisited, A Small Boy Seeing Giants, The Top
Hat, Lytton Strachey, and H. B. Irving as a Young Man, reprinted from
Mainly on the Air by permission of Alfred A. Knopf, Inc. Copyright 1946 by
Max Beerbohm, 1957 by Elizabeth Beerbohm.

Contents

Contents

From *Around Theatres*

From *Yet Again*

From *A Christmas Garland*

From *Seven Men*

From *And Even Now*

Contents

From *Herbert Beerbohm Tree*

From *Mainly on the Air*

The Happy Hypocrite

Acknowledgments

The publishers are indebted to the following for permission to reproduce copyright material:

The Cambridge University Press (The Rede Lecture, 'Lytton Strachey'); Rupert Hart-Davis Ltd ('Duse at the Lyceum', 'A Cursory Conspectus of G. B. S.', 'Coquelin's Death', 'Henry Irving', 'Hamlet, Princess of Denmark', ' "Macbeth" ' – all from *Around Theatres*); The Bodley Head Ltd ('Dandies and Dandies', 'Diminuendo', 'King George the Fourth', 'The Pervasion of Rouge' from *The Works of Max Beerbohm*, and 'Some Words on Royalty', 'Groups of Myrmidons', 'A Cloud of Pinafores' from *More*); Messrs Hutchinson & Co. ('From a Brother's Standpoint' from *Herbert Beerbohm Tree*).

Introduction

Max was a keen Latinist. Mr. Wilkinson, his first school-master in Orme Square, gave him a love of Latin 'and thereby enabled me to write English *well*'. At Charterhouse what he liked was 'Latin prose, Latin verse and drawing caricatures'. So, when he grew up, he would write *egomet* in place of 'for myself' and would happily coin such compounds as 'inenubilable' and 'multiscience'.

As it is probable that one of the texts in use at Orme Square or Charterhouse, or both, was Caesar, *de Bello Gallico*, I am led to reflect that Max's literary career might be divided, like Caesar's Gaul, into three parts: first, the dramatic criticism, essays and tales published between 1894 and 1910; second, *Zuleika Dobson* and the later essays (1910 to 1935); third, the Rede Lecture and the broadcasts (1935 to 1955).

The purpose of such a trichotomy is not to expound any elaborate theory of stylistic development, but rather to emphasise how large a proportion of Max's writing belongs to the time before his marriage in 1910 and his subsequent, or consequent, retirement to Rapallo.

At any stage in his career Max loved to contemplate himself in retrospect. In 1895 he wrote in *Diminuendo*:
'I shall write no more. Already I feel myself to be a trifle outmoded. I belong to the Beardsley period. Younger men, with months of activity before them, with fresher schemes and notions, with newer enthusiasm, have pressed forward since then. *Cedo junioribus*'.
In 1921, when he refused to give any help to Bohun Lynch in his proposed biography:

'My gifts are small. I've used them very well and discreetly, never straining them: and the result is that I've made a charming little reputation.'

And in 1924, when he dedicated *Around Theatres*, a selection from his dramatic criticism, to Gordon Craig:

'I was at one time a dramatic critic . . . There the articles were . . . in *The Saturday Review*, week by week. And there were a great many of them. I went on for twelve whole years. On and on I went, doggedly, from the age of twenty-five to the age of thirty-seven. It seems incredible; but it is a fact.'

It is, moreover, a point to be remembered. Stress is so frequently laid upon the exquisite polish (the *limae labor*) of Max's essays and upon the comparative rarity of their appearance that his long years of journalistic apprenticeship are disregarded.

Gratitude for Max's willingness to make an anthology of his dramatic criticism should not be allowed to obscure the fact that nothing short of a complete study of his *Saturday Review* articles could illustrate the full range of his reflections on life and literature. Dramatic criticism was his primary duty; but drama, he said, gave him neither emotional nor intellectual pleasure and it was only in relation to the literary quality of a play that he felt any measure of self-confidence. Whenever he could, he would leave the middle path of drama and enjoy himself in the byways of contemporary literature.

Thus the dramatisation of *The Prisoner of Zenda* would lead him to compare Anthony Hope, favourably, with Robert Louis Stevenson ('Stevenson was always whittling and filing, embroidering and confectioning'); he admired Quiller-Couch's style, but found his *causerie* to be 'a very porcupine of quotations'; Hall Caine's melodrama led him to observe that 'the proper study of Manx kind is the Isle of Man'; *John Chilcote, M.P.* provoked a tribute to, and a delicious pastiche of, Sherlock Holmes ('I was at an impressionable age when he burst upon the world; and so he became a part of my life, and will never, I suppose, be utterly dislodged. I cannot pass through Baker Street, even now, without thinking of him.')

In 1907, the publication of Shaw's *Dramatic Opinions and Essays* gave him the opportunity of assessing the critical quality of his predecessor and also of enforcing what was, for him, a fundamental distinction:

'[Shaw's criticisms] were essentially journalism. Of course they were not journalistic in the sense of being written at random by a man without any cohesion of principle, endeavour, or style . . . Mr. Shaw wrote ever as one who had two thousand words or so of printed matter to wake the dead in. He made every word "tell" forcibly . . . But what distinguishes literature from journalism is not vigour and sharpness of expression: it is beauty of expression.'

Beauty of expression had been Max's aim from the time when, as a freshman at Merton, he had amused his tutor by his wish to attend Walter Pater's lectures; and when, a few weeks before his marriage in 1910, he wrote a valedictory *apologia* in *The Saturday Review*, he explained that his acute literary conscience made writing uphill work: 'to seem to write with ease and delight is one of the duties which a writer owes to his readers, to his art.'

Dr. Johnson, the moralist, held that it was always a writer's duty to make the world better; to Max, the artist, amelioration was not relevant. But he would be a harsh critic who would contend that the world of letters has not benefited by the beauty of his ordered prose. In one respect, at least, Johnson was at one with Max. He, too, had a literary conscience; for him, too, the act of writing was a burden.

Introduction

'I sat yesterday morning' he wrote in No. 134 of *The Rambler* 'employed in deliberating on which of the various subjects . . . I should bestow the paper of to-day . . . I grew every moment more irresolute . . . till at last I was awakened from this dream of study by a summons from the press.'

How warmly, on one of his Thursdays (the latest possible day for the writing of his *Saturday Review* article), would Max have sympathised with that confession. 'I wonder, Sir,' said Boswell to Johnson after his release from journalistic obligations 'you have not more pleasure in writing than in not writing.' 'Sir,' said Johnson, 'you *may* wonder.' To a similar expression of surprise, Max's reply would have been more polite, but it would have meant the same thing.

Free, in his Villino, of any summons from the press, Max could write, at stately intervals, on subjects of his own choice. Certain parodies which had appeared in *The Saturday Review* were revised and supplemented and *A Christmas Garland* (1912) stands as a supreme example of the critical value inherent in parody. For the good parodist is not one who simply makes fun of his author; he seeks rather to get inside the author's skin and it is significant that Max's best parodies are of those writers (Henry James, for instance) whom he most admired.

In *Seven Men* (1919) and *And Even Now* (1920) Max's powers as an essayist are seen at their highest. He remains a satirist and for snobs and humbugs his satire has a sting. But the youthful arrogance and impish mockery of the *Yellow Book* period have given place to a gentler urbanity and an enlarged sympathy—especially for the unfortunate. Although 'The Century of the Common Man' was a phrase at which Max shuddered, his heart went out to a variety of underdogs and in a spirit of what he called Tory Anarchism he expressed a strong desire to abolish domestic service. But it was the misfits and the failures of the literary world who evoked his fullest powers of sympathetic, if satirical, insight. Failure, he wrote, has always a certain dignity and on two failures, Enoch Soames and 'Savonarola' Brown, he has conferred immortality.

Enoch Soames might serve as a microcosm of Max's grace and skill in story-telling, in satire and in parody. It begins like a piece of autobiographical reminiscence of his early friendship with Will Rothenstein and of his introduction to Aubrey Beardsley, to the Bodley Head, to the domino room of the Café Royal and, indeed, to 'life'. Enter Soames. For the moment he seems to be actual, but Rothenstein avers that he is non-existent. Whether he is existent, or non-existent, or, as Max more charitably suggests, merely dim, he serves as the perfect subject, with his absinthe and his *Fungoids* and his ἀφορίσματα and his Catholic Diabolism, for Max's half-wistful, half-satirical retrospection of the Nineties.

'Savonarola' Brown was another unfortunate—unfortunate at the font (his Christian name was Ladbroke) and unfortunate at his end, being knocked over and killed by a motor-omnibus in Piccadilly Circus. But in this essay the play's the thing and the biographical sketch of Brown is but an introduction to his four-act torso of Renaissance tragedy. 'Here,' writes Max with that limpid, blue-eyed innocence which he assumed so easily, 'is a play that abounds in striking situations and I have searched it vainly for one line that does not scan.' Yet another unfortunate was 'A Clergyman.' Here the mock-solemnity is somehow more solemn than mocking. The nameless cleric, who was crushed by a single retort of Dr. Johnson at the Thrales' house in April 1778, haunted Max's memory and 'solicited his weak imagination.' I first read 'A Clergyman' when it was published in *The Owl* in

1919. At that time I had recently developed an enthusiasm for Johnson and for books about Johnson and that product of a weak imagination seemed to me to illuminate the Streatham scene with peculiar and convincing clarity.

But for me the most moving essay in *And Even Now* is 'William and Mary.' It is, in fact, a short story rather than an essay—the story of an idyllic marriage between 'a not greatly gifted' idealist and a gay, 'practical' girl who adored him. It is the simplest of stories about two ordinary people; but Max has given it an elegiac quality.

My own association with Max came much later. *Zuleika Dobson*, his one full-length novel, was published in 1911. Max had begun it years before in London, but, so long as he was a working journalist, he found it impossible to go on. Leisure enabled him to revise and complete it and he intimated to Will Rothenstein that it was rather a beautiful piece of work. As a story-teller, Max always inclined to fantasy and *Zuleika Dobson* was fantasy on a larger scale than that of *The Happy Hypocrite*. Max thought it beautiful because it commemorated and glorified Oxford; but it was the last paragraph of the book that haunted my memory and solicited my weak imagination. What happened to Zuleika after she had boarded the special train to Cambridge? My own conjectural answer, eventually given in 1941, brought me Max's *imprimatur* and, more important, his friendship. I first met him at the party given in honour of his seventieth birthday at the Players' Theatre on 24 August 1942. He was slightly overwhelmed, I think by the throng of friends and admirers, but he made a graceful little speech in reply to Desmond MacCarthy's tribute. He was living in the country at the time and said that old Gaffer Beerbohm would go back and tell the village all about it. In the following year he was induced to visit Cambridge and his Rede Lecture exemplified Mr. Behrman's apt remark that 'he made one aware of how beautiful spoken English can sound.' For his seventy-fifth birthday I offered him, with apologies to the shade of Dr. Johnson, a 'short song of congratulation':

> Undetected, five-and-seventy
>   Hurrying years at length are flown;
> Fame and leisure, friends in plenty,
>   Dear Sir Max, are now your own.
>
> Loos'd from editorial tether,
>   Free to satirise or write,
> Keen as rapier, light as feather,
>   Grant us still some rare delight.
>
> All the faithful Maximilians,
>   All disciples everywhere
> Relish your remarks to millions,
>   Spoken mainly on the air.
>
> Gratefully we beg to tender
>   Birthday greetings to the speaker,
> Greetings due from many a sender—
>   Not forgetting dear Zuleika.

I was flattered, of course, when Max wrote that he had learnt the lines by heart.

Between 1949 and 1955 I went several times to Rapallo. Perhaps the most notable visit was in 1952, when a small party assembled for luncheon at the inn at Montallegro and drank Max's health on his eightieth birthday. To sit with Max on the terrace of the Villino looking across the lovely bay, to linger among the misleading title-pages and extra-illustrations in his study, to listen, as he sat in the sunshine outside the inn at Montallegro, to stories of Henry James and John Davidson and Harley Granville-Barker and a host of others—this indeed was to know something of *la douceur de vivre*.

S. C. ROBERTS

Dandies and Dandies

How very delightful Grego's drawings are! For all their mad
perspective and crude colour, they have indeed the sentiment
of style, and they reveal, with surer delicacy than does any
other record, the spirit of Mr. Brummell's day. Grego guides
me, as Virgil Dante, through all the mysteries of that other
world. He shows me those stiff-necked, over-hatted, wasp-
waisted gentlemen, drinking Burgundy in the *Café des Milles
Colonnes* or riding through the village of Newmarket upon
their fat cobs or gambling at Crockford's. Grego's *Green
Room of the Opera House* always delights me. The formal way
in which Mlle. Mercandotti is standing upon one leg for the
pleasure of Lord Fife and Mr. Ball Hughes; the grave regard
directed by Lord Petersham towards that pretty little maid-a-
mischief who is risking her rouge beneath the chandelier; the
unbridled decorum of Mlle. Hullin and the decorous debau-
chery of Prince Esterhazy in the distance, make altogether a
quite enchanting picture. But, of the whole series, the most
illuminative picture is certainly the *Ball at Almack's*. In
the foreground stand two little figures, beneath whom, on
the nether margin, are inscribed those splendid words, *Beau
Brummell in Deep Conversation with the Duchess of Rutland.*
The Duchess is a girl in pink, with a great wedge-comb erect
among her ringlets, the Beau *très dégagé*, his head averse,
his chin most supercilious upon his stock, one foot advanced,
the gloved fingers of one hand caught lightly in his waistcoat;
in fact, the very deuce of a pose.

In all this, as in all known images of the Beau, we are struck

1

by the utter simplicity of his attire. The 'countless rings' affected by D'Orsay, the many little golden chains, 'every one of them slighter than a cobweb,' that Disraeli loved to insinuate from one pocket to another of his vest, would have seemed vulgar to Mr. Brummell. For is it not to his fine scorn of accessories that we may trace that first aim of modern dandyism, the production of the supreme effect through means the least extravagant? In certain congruities of dark cloth, in the rigid perfection of his linen, in the symmetry of his glove with his hand, lay the secret of Mr. Brummell's miracles. He was ever most economical, most scrupulous of means. Treatment was everything with him. Even foolish Grace and foolish Philip Wharton, in their book about the beaux and wits of this period, speak of his dressing-room as 'a studio in which he daily composed that elaborate portrait of himself which was to be exhibited for a few hours in the clubrooms of the town.' Mr. Brummell was, indeed, in the utmost sense of the word, an artist. No poet nor cook nor sculptor, ever bore that title more worthily than he.

And really, outside his art, Mr. Brummell had a personality of almost Balzacian insignificance. There have been dandies, like D'Orsay, who were nearly painters; painters, like Mr. Whistler, who wished to be dandies; dandies like Disraeli, who afterwards followed some less arduous calling. I fancy Mr. Brummell was a dandy, nothing but a dandy, from his cradle to that fearful day when he lost his figure and had to flee the country, even to that distant day when he died, a broken exile, in the arms of two *religieuses*. At Eton, no boy was so successful as he in avoiding that strict alternative of study and athletics which we force upon our youth. He once terrified a master, named Parker, by asserting that he thought cricket 'foolish.' Another time, after listening to a reprimand from the headmaster, he twitted that learned man with the asymmetry of his neckcloth. Even in Oriel he could see little charm, and was glad to leave it, at the end of his first year, for a commission in the Tenth Hussars. Crack though the regiment was—indeed, all the commissions were granted by the Regent himself—young Mr. Brummell could not bear to see all his brother-officers in clothes exactly like his own; was quite as deeply annoyed as would be some god, suddenly entering a restaurant of many mirrors. One day, he rode upon parade in a pale-blue tunic, with silver epaulettes. The Colonel, apologizing for the narrow system which compelled him to so painful a duty, asked him to leave the parade. The Beau saluted, trotted back to quarters and, that afternoon, sent in his papers. Henceforth he lived freely as a fop, in his maturity, should.

His *début* in the town was brilliant and delightful. Tales of his elegance had won for him there a precedent fame. He was reputed rich. It was known that the Regent desired his acquaintance. And thus, Fortune speeding the wheels of his cabriolet and Fashion running to meet him with smiles and roses in St. James's, he might well, had he been worldly or a weakling, have yielded his soul to the polite follies. But he passed them by. Once he was settled in his suite, he never really strayed from his toilet-table, save for a few brief hours. Thrice every day of the year did he dress, and three hours were the average of his every toilet, and other hours were spent in council with the cutter of his coats or with the custodian of his wardrobe. A single, devoted life! To White's, to routs, to races, he went, it is true, not reluctantly. He was known to have played battledore and shuttlecock in a moonlit garden with Mr. Previté and some other gentlemen. His elopement with a young Countess from a ball at Lady Jersey's was quite notorious. It was even whispered that he once, in the company of some friends, made as though he would wrench the knocker off the door of some shop. But these things he did, not, most certainly, for any exuberant love of life. Rather did he regard them as healthful exercise of the body and a charm against that dreaded corpulency which, in the end, caused his downfall. Some recreation from his work even the most strenuous artist must have; and Mr. Brummell naturally sought his in that exalted sphere whose modish elegance accorded best with his temperament, the sphere of *le plus beau monde*. General Bucknall used to growl, from the window of the Guards' Club, that such a fellow was only fit to associate with tailors. But that was an old soldier's fallacy. The proper associates of an artist are they who practise his own art rather than they who— however honourably—do but cater for its practice. For the rest, I am sure that Mr. Brummell was no lackey, as they have suggested. He wished merely to be seen by those who were best qualified to appreciate the splendour of his achievements. Shall not the painter show his work in galleries, the poet flit down Paternoster Row? Of rank, for its own sake, Mr. Brummell had no love. He patronized all his patrons. Even to the Regent his attitude was always that of a master in an art to one who is sincerely willing and anxious to learn from him.

Indeed, English society is always ruled by a dandy, and the more absolutely ruled the greater that dandy be. For dandyism, the perfect flower of outward elegance, is the ideal it is always striving to realize in its own rather incoherent way. But there is no reason why dandyism should be confused, as it has been by nearly all writers, with mere social life. Its contact with social life is, indeed, but one of the accidents of an art. Its influence, like the scent of a flower, is diffused unconsciously. It has its own aims and laws, and knows none other. And the only person who ever fully acknowledged this truth in æsthetics is, of all persons most unlikely, the author of *Sartor Resartus*. That anyone who dressed so very badly as did Thomas Carlyle should have tried to construct a philosophy of clothes has always seemed to me one of the most pathetic things in literature. He in the Temple of Vestments! Why

sought he to intrude, another Clodius, upon those mysteries
and light his pipe from those ardent censers? What were his
hobnails that they should mar the pavement of that delicate
Temple? Yet, for that he betrayed one secret rightly heard
there, will I pardon his sacrilege. 'A dandy,' he cried through
the mask of Teufelsdröck, 'is a clothes-wearing man, a man
whose trade, office and existence consists in the wearing of
clothes. Every faculty of his soul, spirit, purse, and person is
heroically consecrated to this one object, the wearing of clothes
wisely and well.' Those are true words. They are, perhaps,
the only true words in *Sartor Resartus*. And I speak with some
authority. For I found the key to that empty book, long ago,
in the lock of the author's empty wardrobe. His hat, that is
still preserved in Chelsea, formed an important clue.

But (behold!) as we repeat the true words of Teufelsdröck,
there comes Monsieur Barbey D'Aurevilly, that gentle
moqueur, drawling, with a wave of his hand, '*Les esprits qui ne
voient pas les choses que par leur plus petit côté, ont imaginé que le
Dandysme était surtout l'art de la mise, une heureuse et audacieuse
dictature en fait de toilette et d'élégance extérieure. Trés-certaine-
ment c'est cela aussi, mais c'est bien davantage. Le Dandysme est
toute une manière d'être et l'on n'est pas que par la côté matérielle-
ment visible. C'est une manière d'être entièrement composée de
nuances, comme il arrive toujours dans les sociétés très-vieilles et
très-civilisées.* It is a pleasure to argue with so suave a subtlist,
and we say to him that this comprehensive definition does not
please us. We say we think he errs.

Not that Monsieur's analysis of the dandiacal mind is
worthless by any means. Nor, when he declares that George
Brummel was the supreme king of the dandies and *fut le
dandysme même*, can I but piously lay one hand upon the brim
of my hat, the other upon my heart. But it is as an artist, and
for his supremacy in the art of costume, and for all he did to
gain the recognition of costume as in itself an art, and for that

superb taste and subtle simplicity of mode whereby he was able to expel, at length, the Byzantine spirit of exuberance which had possessed St. James's and wherefore he is justly called the Father of Modern Costume, that I do most deeply revere him. It is not a little strange that Monsieur D'- Aurevilly, the biographer who, in many ways, does seem most perfectly to have understood Mr. Brummell, should belittle to a mere phase that which was indeed the very core of his existence. To analyse the temperament of a great artist and then to declare that his art was but a part—a little part—of his temperament, is a foolish proceeding. It is as though a man should say that he finds, on analysis, that gunpowder is composed of potassium chloride (let me say), nitrate and power of explosion. Dandyism is ever the outcome of a carefully cultivated temperament, not part of the temperament itself. That *manière d'être, entièrement composée de nuances*, was not more, as the writer seems to have supposed, than attributory to Mr. Brummell's art. Nor is it even peculiar to dandies. All delicate spirits, to whatever art they turn, even if they turn to no art, assume an oblique attitude towards life. Of all dandies, Mr. Brummell did most steadfastly maintain this attitude. Like the single-minded artist that he was, he turned full and square towards his art and looked life straight in the face out of the corners of his eyes.

It is not hard to see how, in the effort to give Mr. Brummell his due place in history, Monsieur D'Aurevilly came to grief. It is but strange that he should have fallen into a rather obvious trap. Surely he should have perceived that, so long as Civilization compels her children to wear clothes, the thoughtless multitude will never acknowledge dandyism to be an art. If considerations of modesty or hygiene compelled every one to stain canvas or chip marble every morning, painting and sculpture would in like manner be despised. Now, as these considerations do compel every one to envelop himself in things made of cloth and linen, this common duty is confounded with that fair procedure, elaborate of many thoughts, in whose accord the fop accomplishes his toilet, each morning afresh, Aurora speeding on to gild his mirror. Not until nudity be popular will the art of costume be really acknowledged. Nor even then will it be approved. Communities are ever jealous (quite naturally) of the artist who works for his own pleasure, not for theirs—more jealous by far of him whose energy is spent only upon the glorification of himself alone. Carlyle speaks of dandyism as a survival of 'the primeval superstition, self-worship.' *'La vanité,'* are almost the first words of Monsieur D'Aurevilly, *'c'est un sentiment contre lequel toute le monde est impitoyable.'* Few remember that the dandy's vanity is far different from the crude conceit of the merely handsome man. Dandyism is, after all, one of the decorative arts. A fine ground to work upon is its first postulate. And the dandy cares for his physical endowments only in so far as they are susceptible of fine results. They are just so much to him as to the decorative artist is inilluminate parchment, the form of a white vase or the surface of a wall where frescoes shall be.

Consider the words of Count D'Orsay, spoken on the eve of some duel, 'We are not fairly matched. If I were to wound him in the face it would not matter; but if he were to wound me, *ce serait vraiment dommage!'* There we have a pure example of a dandy's peculiar vanity—'It would be a real pity!' They say that D'Orsay killed his man—no matter whom— in this duel. He never should have gone out. Beau Brummell never risked his dandyhood in these mean encounters. But D'Orsay was a wayward, excessive creature, too fond of life and other follies to achieve real greatness. The power of his predecessor, the Father of Modern Costume, is over us yet. All that is left of D'Orsay's art is a waistcoat and a handful of rings—vain relics of no more value for us than the fiddle of Paganini or the mask of Menischus! I think that in Carolo's painting of him, we can see the strength, that was the weakness, of *le jeune Cupidon*. His fingers are closed upon his cane as upon a sword. There is mockery in the inconstant eyes. And the lips, so used to close upon the wine-cup, in laughter so often parted, they do not seem immobile, even now. Sad that one so prodigally endowed as he was, with the three essentials of a dandy—physical distinction, a sense of beauty and wealth or, if you prefer the term, credit—should not have done greater things. Much of his costume was merely showy or eccentric, without the rotund unity of the perfect fop's. It had been well had he lacked that dash and spontaneous gallantry that make him cut, it may be, a more attractive figure than Beau Brummell. The youth of St. James's gave him a wonderful welcome. The flight of Mr. Brummell had left them as sheep without a shepherd. They had even cried out against the inscrutable decrees of fashion and curtailed the height of their stocks. And (lo!) here, ambling down the Mall with tasselled cane, laughing in the window at White's or in Fop's Alley posturing, here, with the devil in his eyes and all the graces at his elbow, was D'Orsay, the prince paramount who should dominate London and should guard life from monotony by the daring of his whims. He accepted so many engagements that he often dressed very quickly both in the morning and at nightfall. His brilliant genius would sometimes enable him to appear faultless, but at other times not even his fine figure could quite dispel the shadow of a toilet too hastily conceived. Before long he took that fatal step, his marriage with Lady Harriet Gardiner. The marriage, as we all know, was not a happy one, though the wedding was very pretty. It ruined the life of Lady Harriet and of her mother, the Blessington. It won the poor Count further still further from his art and sent him spinning here, there, and everywhere. He was continually at Clevedon, or Belvoir, or Welbeck, laughing gaily as he brought down our English partridges, or at

8

Crockford's, smiling as he swept up our English guineas from the board. Holker declares that, excepting Mr. Turner, he was the finest equestrian in London and describes how the mob would gather every morning round his door to see him descend, insolent from his toilet, and mount and ride away. Indeed, he surpassed us all in all the exercises of the body. He even essayed preëminence in the arts (as if his own art were insufficient to his vitality!) and was for ever penning impetuous verses for circulation among his friends. There was no great harm in this, perhaps. Even the handwriting of Mr. Brummell was not unknown in the albums. But D'Orsay's painting of portraits is inexcusable. The æsthetic vision of a dandy should be bounded by his own mirror. A few crayon sketches of himself—*dilectissimæ imagines*—are as much as he should ever do. That D'Orsay's portraits, even his much-approved portrait of the Duke of Wellington, are quite amateurish, is no excuse. It is the process of painting which is repellent; to force from little tubes of lead a glutinous flamboyance and to defile, with the hair of a camel therein steeped, taut canvas, is hardly the diversion for a gentleman; and to have done all this for a man who was admittedly a field-marshal . . .

I have often thought that this selfish concentration, which is a part of dandyism, is also a symbol of that *einsamkeit* felt in greater or less degree by the practitioners of every art. But, curiously enough, the very unity of his mind with the ground he works on exposes the dandy to the influence of the world. In one way dandyism is the least selfish of all the arts. Musicians are seen and, except for a price, not heard. Only for a price may you read what poets have written. All painters are not so generous as Mr. Watts. But the dandy presents himself to the nation whenever he sallies from his front door. Princes and peasants alike may gaze upon his masterpieces. Now, any art which is pursued directly under the eye of the public is always far more amenable to fashion than is an art with which the public is but vicariously concerned. Those standards to which artists have gradually accustomed it the public will not see lightly set at naught. Very rigid, for example, are the traditions of the theatre. If my brother were to declaim his lines at the Haymarket in the florotund manner of Macready, what a row there would be in the gallery! It is only by the impalpable process of evolution that change comes to the theatre. Likewise in the sphere of costume no swift rebellion can succeed, as was exemplified by the Prince's effort to revive knee-breeches. Had his Royal Highness elected, in his wisdom, to wear tight trousers strapped under his boots, 'smalls' might, in their turn, have reappeared, and at length—who knows? knee-breeches. It is only by the trifling addition or elimination, modification or extension, made by this or that dandy and copied by the rest, that the mode proceeds. The young dandy will find certain laws to which he must conform. If he outrage them he will be hooted by the urchins of the street, not unjustly, for he will have outraged the slowly constructed laws of artists who have preceded him. Let him reflect that fashion is no bondage imposed by alien hands, but the last wisdom of his own kind, and that true dandyism is the result of an artistic temperament working upon a fine body within the wide limits of fashion. Through this habit of conformity, which it inculcates, the army has given us nearly all our finest dandies, from Alcibiades to Colonel Br*b*z*n *de nos jours*. Even Mr. Brummell, though he defied his Colonel, must have owed some of his success to the military spirit. Any parent intending his son to be a dandy will do well to send him first into the army, there to learn humility, as did his archetype, Apollo, in the house of Admetus. A sojourn at one of the Public Schools is also to be commended. The University it were well to void.

Of course, the dandy, like any other artist, has moments

when his own period, palling, inclines him to antique modes.
A fellow-student once told me that, after a long vacation spent
in touch with modern life, he had hammered at the little gate
of Merton and felt of a sudden his hat assume plumes and an
expansive curl, the impress of a ruff about his neck, the dangle
of a cloak and a sword. I, too, have my Elizabethan, my
Caroline moments. I have gone to bed Georgian and awoken
Early Victorian. Even savagery has charmed me. And at
such times I have often wished I could find in my wardrobe
suitable costumes. But these modish regrets are sterile, after
all, and comprimend. What boots it to defy the conventions
of our time? The dandy is the 'child of his age,' and his best
work must be produced in accord with the age's natural influence. The true dandy must always love contemporary
costume. In this age, as in all precedent ages, it is only the
tasteless who cavil, being impotent to win from it fair results.
How futile their voices are! The costume of the nineteenth
century, as shadowed for us first by Mr. Brummell, so quiet,
so reasonable, and, I say emphatically, so beautiful; free from
folly or affectation, yet susceptible to exquisite ordering;
plastic, austere, economical, may not be ignored. I spoke of
the doom of swift rebellions, but I doubt even if any soever
gradual evolution will lead us astray from the general precepts
of Mr. Brummell's code. At every step in the progress of
democracy those precepts will be strengthened. Every day
their fashion is more secure, corroborate. They are acknowledged by the world. The barbarous costumes that in bygone
days were designed by class-hatred, or hatred of race, are
dying, very surely dying. The costermonger with his pearl-
emblazoned coat has been driven even from that Variety
Stage, whereon he sought a desperate sanctuary. The
clinquant corslet of the Swiss girl just survives at *bals costumés*.
I am told that the kilt is now confined entirely to certain of the
soldiery and to a small cult of Scotch Archaïcists. I have seen

11

men flock from the boulevards of one capital and from the avenues of another to be clad in Conduit Street. Even into Oxford, that curious little city, where nothing is ever born nor anything ever quite dies, the force of the movement has penetrated, insomuch that tasselled cap and gown of degree are rarely seen in the streets or colleges. In a place which was until recent times scarcely less remote, Japan, the white and scarlet gardens are trod by men who are shod in boots like our own, who walk—rather strangely still—in close-cut cloth of little colour, and stop each other from time to time, laughing to show how that they too can furl an umbrella after the manner of real Europeans.

It is very nice, this universal acquiescence in the dress we have designed, but, if we reflect, not wonderful. There are three apparent reasons, and one of them is æsthetic. So to clothe the body that its fineness be revealed and its meanness veiled has been the æsthetic aim of all costume, but before our time the mean had never been struck. The ancient Romans went too far. Muffled in the ponderous folds of a toga, Adonis might pass for Punchinello, Punchinello for Adonis. The ancient Britons, on the other hand, did not go far enough. And so it had been in all ages down to that bright morning when Mr. Brummell, at his mirror, conceived the notion of trousers and simple coats. Clad according to his convention, the limbs of the weakling escape contempt, and the athlete is unobtrusive, and all is well. But there is also a social reason for the triumph of our costume—the reason of economy. That austerity, which has rejected from its toilet silk and velvet and all but a few jewels, has made more ample the wardrobes of Dives, and sent forth Irus nicely dressed among his fellows. And lastly there is a reason of psychology, most potent of all perhaps. Is not the costume of to-day, with its subtlety and sombre restraint, its quiet congruities of black and white and grey, supremely apt a medium for the expression of modern

12

emotion and modern thought? The aptness, even alone, would explain its triumph. Let us be glad that we have so easy, yet so delicate, a mode of expression.

Yes! costume, dandiacal or not, is in the highest degree expressive, nor is there any type it may not express. It enables us to classify any 'professional man' at a glance, be he lawyer, leech or what not. Still more swift and obvious is its revelation of the work and the soul of those who dress, whether naturally or for effect, without reference to convention. The bowler of Mr. Jerome K. Jerome is a perfect preface to all his works. The silk hat of Mr. Whistler is a real *nocturne*, his linen a symphony *en blanc majeur*. To have seen Mr. Hall Caine is to have read his soul. His flowing, formless cloak is as one of his own novels, twenty-five editions latent in the folds of it. Melodrama crouches upon the brim of his *sombrero*. His tie is a Publisher's Announcement. His boots are Copyright. In his hand he holds the staff of *The Family Herald*.

But the dandy, innowise violating the laws of fashion, can make more subtle symbols of his personality. More subtle these symbols are for the very reason that they are effected within the restrictions which are essential to an art. Chastened of all flamboyance, they are from most men occult, obvious, it may be, only to other artists or even only to him they symbolize. Nor will the dandy express merely a crude idea of his personality, as does, for example, Mr. Hall Caine, dressing himself always and exactly after one pattern. Every day as his mood has changed since his last toilet, he will vary the colour, texture, form of his costume. Fashion does not rob him of free will. It leaves him liberty of all expression. Every day there is not one accessory, from the butterfly that alights above his shirt-front to the jewels planted in his linen, that will not symbolize the mood that is in him or the occasion of the coming day.

On this, the psychological side of foppery, I know not one so expert as him whom, not greatly caring for contemporary names, I will call Mr. Le V. No hero-worshipper am I, but I cannot write without enthusiasm of his simple life. He has not spurred his mind to the quest of shadows nor vexed his soul in the worship of any gods. No woman has wounded his heart, though he has gazed gallantly into the eyes of many women, intent, I fancy, upon his own miniature there. Nor is the incomparable set of his trousers spoilt by the perching of any dear little child upon his knee. And so, now that he is stricken with seventy years, he knows none of the bitterness of eld, for his toilet-table is an imperishable altar, his wardrobe a quiet nursery and very constant harem. Mr. Le V. has many disciples, young men who look to him for guidance in all that concerns costume, and each morning come, themselves tentatively clad, to watch the perfect procedure of his toilet and learn invaluable lessons. I myself, a lie-a-bed, often steal out, forgoing the best hours of the day abed, that I may attend that *levée*. The rooms of the Master are in St. James's Street, and perhaps it were well that I should give some little record of them and of the manner of their use. In the first room the Master sleeps. He is called by one of his valets, at seven o'clock, to the second room, where he bathes, is shampooed, is manicured and, at length, is enveloped in a dressing-gown of white wool. In the third room is his breakfast upon a little table and his letters and some newspapers. Leisurely he sips his chocolate, leisurely learns all that need be known. With a cigarette he allows his temper, as informed by the news and the weather and what not, to develop itself for the day. At length, his mood suggests, imperceptibly, what colour, what form of clothes he shall wear. He rings for his valet—'I will wear such a such a coat, such and such a tie; my trousers shall be of this or that tone; this or that jewel shall be radiant in the folds of my tie.' It is generally near noon that he reaches

the fourth room, the dressing-room. The uninitiate can
can hardly realize how impressive is the ceremonial there
enacted. As I write, I can see, in memory, the whole scene—
the room, severely simple, with its lemon walls and deep
wardrobes of white wood, the young fops, φιλομαθέστατοι τινες
τῶν νεανίσκων, ranged upon a long bench, rapt in wonder,
and, in the middle, now sitting, now standing, negligently,
before a long mirror, with a valet at either elbow, Mr. Le V.,
our cynosure. There is no haste, no faltering when once the
scheme of the day's toilet has been set. It is a calm toilet.
A flower does not grow more calmly.

Any of us, any day, may see the gracious figure of Mr. Le
V., as he saunters down the slope of St. James's. Long may
the sun irradiate the surface of his tilted hat! It is comfortable
to know that, though he die to-morrow, the world will not lack
a most elaborate record of his foppery. All his life he has kept
or, rather, the current valets have kept for him, a *Journal de
Toilette*. Of this there are now fifty volumes, each covering
the space of a year. Yes, fifty springs have filled his buttonhole with their violets; the snow of fifty winters has been less
white than his linen; his boots have outshone fifty sequences
of summer suns, and the colours of all those autumns have
faded in the dry light of his apparel. The first page of each
volume of the *Journal de Toilette* bears the signature of Mr.
Le V., and of his two valets. Of the other pages each is given
up, as in other diaries, to one day of the year. In ruled spaces
are recorded there the cut and texture of the suit, the colour
of the tie, the form of jewellery that was worn on the day the
page records. No detail is omitted and a separate space is set
aside for 'Remarks.' I remember that I once asked Mr. Le V.,
half in jest, what he should wear on the Judgment Day.
Seriously, and (I fancied) with a note of pathos in his voice,
he said to me, 'Young man, you ask me to lay bare my soul
to you. If I had been a saint I should certainly wear a light

15

suit, with a white waistcoat and a flower, but I am no saint, sir, no saint. . . . I shall probably wear black trousers or trousers of some very dark blue, and a frock-coat, tightly buttoned.' Poor old Mr. Le V.! I think he need not fear. If there be a heaven for the soul, there must be other heavens also, where the intellect and the body shall be consummate. In both these heavens Mr. Le V. will have his hierarchy. Of a life like his there can be no conclusion, really. Did not even Matthew Arnold admit that conduct of a cane is three-fourths of life?

Certainly Mr. Le V. is a great artist, and his supremacy is in the tact with which he suits his toilet to his temperament. But the marvellous affinity of a dandy's mood to his daily toilet is not merely that it finds therein its perfect echo nor that it may even be, in reflex, thereby accentuated or made less poignant. For some years I had felt convinced that in a perfect dandy this affinity must reach a point, when the costume itself, planned with the finest sensibility, would change with the emotional changes of its wearer, automatically. But I felt that here was one of those boundaries, where the fields of art align with the fields of science, and I hardly dared to venture further. Moreover, the theory was not easy to verify. I knew that, except in some great emotional crisis, the costume could not palpably change its aspect. Here was an *impasse*; for the perfect dandy—the Brummell, the Mr. Le V.—cannot afford to indulge in any great emotion outside his art; like Balzac, he has not time. The gods were good to me, however. One morning near the end of last July, they decreed that I should pass through Half Moon Street and meet there a friend who should ask me to go with him to his club and watch for the results of the racing at Goodwood. This club includes hardly any member who is not a devotee of the Turf, so that, when we entered it, the cloak-room displayed long rows of unburdened pegs—save where one hat shone. None but that illustrious dandy, Lord X., wears quite so broad a brim as this hat had. I said that Lord X. must be in the club.

'I conceive he is too nervous to be on the course,' my friend replied. 'They say he has plunged up to the hilt on to-day's running.'

His lordship was indeed there, fingering feverishly the sinuous ribands of the tape-machine. I sat at a little distance, watching him. Two results straggled forth within an hour, and, at the second of these, I saw with wonder Lord X.'s linen actually flush for a moment and then turn deadly pale. I looked again and saw that his boots had lost their lustre. Drawing nearer, I found that grey hairs had begun to show themselves in his raven coat. It was very painful and yet, to me, very gratifying. In the cloak-room, when I went for my own hat and cane, there was the hat with the broad brim, and (lo!) over its iron-blue surface little furrows had been ploughed by Despair.

King George the Fourth

They say that when King George was dying, a special form of prayer for his recovery, composed by one of the Archbishops, was read aloud to him and that His Majesty, after saying Amen 'thrice, with great fervour,' begged that his thanks might be conveyed to its author. To the student of royalty in modern times there is something rather suggestive in this incident. I like to think of the drug-scented room at Windsor and of the King, livid and immobile among his pillows, waiting, in superstitious awe, for the near moment when he must stand, a spirit, in the presence of a perpetual King. I like to think of him following the futile prayer with eyes and lips and then, custom resurgent in him and a touch of pride that, so long as the blood moved ever so little in his veins, he was still a king, expressing a desire that the dutiful feeling and admirable taste of the Prelate should receive a suitable acknowledgment. It would have been impossible for a real monarch like George, even after the gout had turned his thoughts heavenward, really to abase himself before his Maker. But he could, so to say, treat with Him, as he might have treated with a fellow-sovereign, in a formal way, long after diplomacy was quite useless. How strange it must be to be a king! How delicate and difficult a task it is to judge him! So far as I know, no attempt has been made to judge King George the Fourth fairly. The hundred and one eulogies and lampoons, irresponsibly published during and immediately after his reign, are not worth a wooden hoop in Hades. Mr. Percy Fitzgerald has published a history of George's reign, in which he has so

18

artistically subordinated his own personality to his subject, that I can scarcely find, from beginning to end of the two bulky volumes, a single opinion expressed, a single idea, a single deduction from the admirably-ordered facts. All that most of us know of George is from Thackeray's brilliant denunciation. Now, I yield to few in my admiration of Thackeray's powers. He had a charming style. We never find him searching for the *mot juste* as for a needle in a bottle of hay. Could he have looked through a certain window by the river at Croisset or in the quadrangle at Brasenose, how he would have laughed! He blew on his pipe, and words came tripping round him, like children, like pretty little children who are perfectly drilled for the dance, or came, did he will it, treading in their precedence, like kings, gloomily. And I think it is to the credit of the reading mob that, by reason of his beautiful style, all that he said was taken for the truth, without questioning. But truth after all is eternal, and style transient, and now that Thackeray's style is becoming, if I may say so, a trifle 1860, it may not be amiss that we should inquire whether his estimate of George is in substance and fact worth anything at all. It seems to me that, as in his novels, so in his history of the four Georges, Thackeray made no attempt at psychology. He dealt simply with types. One George he insisted upon regarding as a buffoon, another as a yokel. The fourth George he chose to hold up for reprobation as a drunken, vapid cad. Every action, every phase of his life that went to disprove this view, he either suppressed or distorted utterly. 'History,' he would seem to have chuckled, 'has nothing to do with the First Gentleman. But I will give him a niche in Natural History. He shall be King of the Beasts.' He made no allowance for the extraordinary conditions under which all monarchs live, none for the unfortunate circumstances by which George, expecially, was from the first hampered. He judged him as he judged Barnes Newcome and all the scoundrels he created.

Moreover, he judged him by the moral standard of the Victorian Age. In fact, he applied to his subject the wrong method, in the wrong manner, and at the wrong time. And yet every one has taken him at his word. I feel that my essay may be scouted as a paradox; but I hope that many may recognize that I am not, out of mere boredom, endeavouring to stop my ears against popular platitude, but rather, in a spirit of real earnestness, to point out to the mob how it has been cruel to George. I do not despair of success. I think I shall make converts. The mob is really very fickle and sometimes cheers the truth.

None, at all events, will deny that England stands to-day otherwise than she stood a hundred and thirty-two years ago, when George was born. To-day we are living a decadent life. All the while that we are prating of progress, we are really so deteriorate! There is nothing but feebleness in us. Our youths, who spend their days in trying to build up their constitutions by sport or athletics and their evenings in undermining them with poisonous and dyed drinks; our daughters, who are ever searching for some new quack remedy for new imaginary megrim, what strength is there in them? We have our societies for the prevention of this and the promotion of that and the propagation of the other, because there are no individuals among us. Our sexes are already nearly assimilate. Women are becoming nearly as rare as ladies, and it is only at the music-halls that we are privileged to see strong men. We are born into a poor, weak age. We are not strong enough to be wicked, and the Noncomformist Conscience makes cowards of us all.

But this was not so in the days when George was walking by his tutor's side in the gardens of Kew or of Windsor. London must have been a splendid place in those days—full of life and colour and wrong and revelry. There was no absurd press nor vestry to protect the poor at the expense of the rich and see that everything should be neatly adjusted. Every man had to shift for himself and, consequently, men were, as Mr. Clement Scott would say, manly, and women, as Mr. Clement Scott would say, womanly. In those days, a young man of wealth and family found open to him a vista of such licence as had been unknown to any since the barbatuli of the Roman Empire. To spend the early morning with his valet, gradually assuming the rich apparel that was not then tabooed by a hard sumptuary standard; to saunter round to White's for ale and tittle-tattle and the making of wagers; to attend a 'drunken *déjeuner*' in honour of '*la très belle Rosaline*' or the Strappini; to drive some fellow-fool far out into the country in his pretty curricle, 'followed by two well-dressed and well-mounted grooms, of singular elegance certainly,' and stop at every tavern on the road and curse the host for not keeping better ale and a wench of more charm; to reach St. James's in time for a random toilet and so off to dinner. Which of *our* dandies could survive a day of pleasure such as this? Which would be ready, dinner done, to scamper off again to Ranelagh and dance and skip and sup in the rotunda there? Yet the youth of that period would not dream of going to bed or ever he had looked in at Crockford's—*tanta lubido rerum*—for a few hours' faro.

This was the kind of life that young George found opened to him, when, at length, in his nineteenth year, they gave him an establishment in Buckingham House. How his young eyes must have sparkled, and with what glad gasps must he have taken the air of freedom into his lungs! Rumour had long been busy with the damned surveillance under which his childhood had been passed. A paper of the time says significantly that 'the Prince of Wales, with a spirit which does him honour, has three times requested a change in that system.' King George had long postponed permission for his son to appear at any balls, and the year before had only given it, lest he should offend the Spanish Minister, who begged it as a personal favour. I know few pictures more pathetic than that of George, then an overgrown boy of fourteen, tearing the childish frill from around his neck and crying to one of the Royal servants, 'See how they treat me!' Childhood has always seemed to me the tragic period of life. To be subject to the most odious espionage at the one age when you never dream of doing wrong, to be deceived by your parents, thwarted of your smallest wish, oppressed by the terrors of manhood and of the world to come, and to believe, as you are told, that childhood is the only happiness known; all this is quite terrible. And all Royal children, of whom I have read, particularly George, seem to have passed through greater trials in childhood than do the children of any other class. Mr. Fitzgerald, hazarding for once an opinion, thinks that 'the stupid, odious, German, sergeant-system of discipline that had been so rigorously applied was, in fact, responsible for the blemishes of the young Prince's character.' Even Thackeray, in his essay upon George III., asks what wonder that the son, finding himself free at last, should have plunged, without looking, into the vortex of dissipation. In Torrens' *Life of Lord Melbourne* we learn that Lord Essex, riding one day with the King, met the young Prince wearing a wig, and that the culprit, being sternly reprimanded by his father, replied that he had 'been ordered by his doctor to wear a wig, for he was subject to cold.' Whereupon the King, to vent the aversion he already felt for his son, or, it may have been, glorying in the satisfactory result of his discipline, turned to Lord Essex and remarked, 'A lie is ever ready when it is wanted.' George never lost this early ingrained habit of lies. It is to George's childish fear of his guardians that we must trace that extraordinary power of bamboozling his courtiers, his ministry, and his mistresses that distinguished him through his long life. It is characteristic of the man that he should himself have bitterly deplored his own untruthfulness. When, in after years, he was consulting Lady Spencer upon the choice of a governess for his child, he made this remarkable speech, 'Above all, she must be taught the truth. You know that I don't speak the truth and my brothers don't, and I find it a great defect, from which I would have my daughter free. *We have been brought up badly, the Queen having taught us to equivocate.*' You may laugh at the picture of the little chubby, curly-headed fellows learning to equivocate at their mother's knee, but pray remember that the wisest master of ethics himself, in his theory of ἕξεις ἀποδείκτιχαι, similarly raised virtues, such as telling the truth, to the level of regular accomplishments, and, before you judge poor George harshly in his entanglements of lying, think of the cruelly unwise education he had undergone.

However much we may deplore this exaggerated tyranny, by reason of its evil effect upon his moral nature, we cannot but feel glad that it existed, to afford a piquant contrast to the life awaiting him. Had he passed through the callow dissipations of Eton and Oxford, like other young men of his age, he would assuredly have lacked much of that splendid, pent vigour with which he rushed headlong into London life. He was so young and so handsome and so strong, that can we wonder if all the women fell at his feet? 'The graces of his person,' says one whom he honoured by an intrigue, 'the irresistible sweetness of his smile, the tenderness of his melodious, yet manly voice, will be remembered by me till every vision of this changing scene are forgotten. The polished and fascinating ingenuousness of his manners contributed not a little to enliven our promenade. He sang with exquisite taste, and the tones of his voice, breaking on the silence of the night, have often appeared to my entranced senses like more than mortal melody.' But besides his graces of person, he had a most delightful wit, he was a scholar who could bandy

quotations with Fox or Sheridan, and, like the young men of
to-day, he knew all about Art. He spoke French, Italian,
and German perfectly. Crossdill had taught him the violoncello. At first, as was right for one of his age, he cared more
for the pleasures of the table and of the ring, for cards and
love. He was wont to go down to Ranelagh surrounded by
a retinue of bruisers—rapscallions, such as used to follow
Clodius through the streets of Rome—and he loved to
join in the scuffles like any commoner. Pugilism he learnt
from Angelo, and he was considered by some to be a fine
performer. On one occasion, too, at an *exposition d'escrime*,
when he handled the foils against the *maître*, he 'was highly
complimented upon his graceful postures.' In fact, despite
all his accomplishments, he seems to have been a thoroughly
manly young fellow. He was just the kind of figure-head
Society had been long in need of. A certain lack of tone had
crept into the amusements of the *haut monde*, due, doubtless,
to the lack of an acknowledged leader. The King was not yet
mad, but he was always bucolic, and socially out of the
question. So at the coming of his son Society broke into a
gallop. Balls and masquerades were given in his honour
night after night. Good Samaritans must have approved when
they found that at these entertainments great ladies and
courtesans brushed beautiful shoulders in utmost familiarity,
but those who delighted in the high charm of society probably
shook their heads. We need not, however, find it a flaw in
George's social bearing that he did not check this kind of
freedom. At the first, as a young man full of life, of course
he took everything as it came, joyfully. No one knew
better than he did, in later life, that there is a time for laughing with great ladies and a time for laughing with courtesans.
But as yet it was not possible for him to exert influence.
How great that influence became I will suggest hereafter.

I like to think of him as he was at this period, charging

about, in pursuit of pleasure, like a young bull. The splendid
taste for building had not yet come to him. His father would
not hear of him patronizing the Turf. But already he was implected with a passion for dress and seems to have erred
somewhat on the side of dressing up, as is the way of young
men. It is fearful to think of him, as Cyrus Redding saw him,
'arrayed in deep-brown velvet, silver embroidered, with cut-
steel buttons, and a gold net thrown over all.' Before that
'gold net thrown over all,' all the mistakes of his after-life seem
to me to grow almost insignificant. Time, however, toned his
too florid sense of costume, and we should at any rate be
thankful that his imagination never deserted him. All the
delightful munditiæ that we find in the contemporary 'fashion-
plates for gentlemen' can be traced to George himself. His
were the much-approved 'quadruple stock of great dimensions,'
the 'cocked grey-beaver,' 'the pantaloons of mauve silk
negligently crinkled,' and any number of other little pomps
and foibles of the kind. As he grew older and was obliged to
abandon many of his more vigorous pastimes, he grew more
and more enamoured of the pleasures of the wardrobe. He
would spend hours, it is said, in designing coats for his friends,
liveries for his servants, and even uniforms. Nor did he ever
make the mistake of giving away outmoded clothes to his
valets, but kept them to form what must have been the finest
collection of clothes that has been seen in modern times. With
a sentimentality that is characteristic of him, he would often,
as he sat, crippled by gout in his room at Windsor, direct his
servant to bring him this or that coat, which he had worn ten or
twenty or thirty years before, and, when it was brought to him,
spend much time in laughing or sobbing over the memories
that lay in its folds. It is pleasant to know that George, during
his long and various life, never forgot a coat, however long
ago worn, however seldom.

But in the early days of which I speak he had not yet touched that self-conscious note which, in manner and mode of life, as well as in costume, he was to touch later. He was too violently enamoured of all around him, to think very deeply of himself. But he had already realized the tragedy of the voluptuary, which is, after a little time, not that he must go on living, but that he cannot live in two places at once. We have, at this end of the century, tempered this tragedy by the perfection of railways, and it is possible for our good Prince, whom Heaven bless, to waken to the sound of the Braemar bagpipes, while the music of Mdlle. Guilbert's latest song, cooed over the footlights of the Concerts Parisiens, still rings in his ears. But in the time of our Prince's illustrious great-uncle there were not railways; and we find George perpetually driving, for wagers, to Brighton and back (he had already acquired that taste for Brighton which was one of his most lovable qualities) in incredibly short periods of time. The rustics who lived along the road were well accustomed to the sight of a high, tremulous phaeton flashing past them, and the crimson face of the young prince bending over the horses. There is something absurd in representing George as, even before he came of age, a hardened and cynical profligate, an Elagabalus in trousers. His blood flowed fast enough through his veins. All his escapades were those of a healthful young man of the time. Need we blame him if he sought, every day, to live faster and more fully?

In a brief essay like this, I cannot attempt to write, as I hope one day to do, in any detail a history of George's career, during the time when he was successively Prince of Wales and Regent and King. Merely is it my wish at present to examine some of the principal accusations that have been brought against him, and to point out in what ways he has been harshly and hastily judged. Perhaps the greatest indignation against him was, and is to this day, felt by reason of his treatment of his two wives, Mrs. Fitzherbert and Queen Caroline. There are some scandals that never grow old, and I think the story of George's married life is one of them. It was a real scandal. I can feel it. It has vitality. Often have I wondered whether the blood with which the young Prince's shirt was saturate when Mrs. Fitzherbert was first induced to visit him at Carlton House, was merely red paint, or if, in a frenzy of love, he had truly gashed himself with a razor. Certain it is that his passion for the virtuous and obdurate lady was a very real one. Lord Holland describes how the Prince used to visit Mrs. Fox, and there indulge in 'the most extravagant expressions and actions—rolling on the floor, striking his forehead, tearing his hair, falling into hysterics and swearing that he would abandon the country, forgo the crown, &c.' He was indeed still a child, for Royalties, not being ever brought into contact with the realities of life, remain young for longer than other people. Cursed with a truly royal lack of self-control, he was unable to bear the idea of being thwarted in any wish. Every day he sent off couriers to Holland, whither Mrs. Fitzherbert had retreated, imploring her to return to him, offering her formal marriage. At length, as we know, she yielded to his importunity and returned. It is difficult indeed to realize exactly what was Mrs. Fitzherbert's feeling in the matter. The marriage must be, as she knew, illegal, and would lead, as Charles James Fox pointed out in his powerful letter to the Prince, to endless and intricate difficulties. For the present she could only live with him as his mistress. If, when he reached the legal age of twenty-five, he were to apply to Parliament for permission to marry her, how could permission be given, when she had been living with him irregularly? Doubtless, she was flattered by the attentions of the Heir to the Throne, but, had she really returned his passion, she would surely have preferred 'any other species of connection with His Royal Highness to one leading to so much misery and mischief.' Really to understand her marriage, one must look at the portraits of her that are extant. That beautiful and silly face explains much. One can well fancy such a lady being pleased to live after the performance of a mock-ceremony with a prince for whom she felt no passion. Her view of the matter can only have been social, for, in the eyes of the Church, she could only live with the Prince as his mistress. Society, however, once satisfied that a ceremony of some kind had been enacted, never regarded her as anything but his wife. The day after Fox, inspired by the Prince, had formally denied that any ceremony had taken place, 'the knocker of her door,' to quote her own complacent phrase, 'was never still.' The Duchesses of Portland, Devonshire and Cumberland were among her visitors.

How much pop-limbo has been talked about the Prince's denial of the marriage! I grant that it was highly improper to marry Mrs. Fitzherbert at all. But George was always weak and wayward, and he did, in his great passion, marry her. That he should afterwards deny it officially seems to me to have been utterly inevitable. His denial did her not the faintest damage, as I have pointed out. It was, so to speak, an official quibble, rendered necessary by the circumstances of the case. Not to have denied the marriage in the House of Commons would have meant ruin to both of them. As months passed, more serious difficulties awaited the unhappily wedded pair. What boots it to repeat the story of the Prince's great debts and desperation? It was clear that there was but one way of getting his head above water, and that was to yield to his father's wishes and contract a real marriage with a foreign princess. Fate was dogging his footsteps relentlessly. Placed as he was, George could not but offer to marry as his father willed. It is well, also, to remember that George was not ruthlessly and suddenly turning his shoulder upon Mrs. Fitzherbert. For some time before the British plenipotentiary went to fetch him a bride from over the waters, his name had been associated with that of the beautiful and unscrupulous Countess of Jersey.

Poor George! Half-married to a woman whom he no longer worshipped, compelled to marry a woman whom he was to hate at first sight! Surely we should not judge a prince harshly. 'Princess Caroline very *gauche* at cards,' 'Princess Caroline very *missish* at supper,' are among the entries made in his diary by Lord Malmesbury, while he was at the little German Court. I can conceive no scene more tragic than that of her presentation to the Prince, as related by the same nobleman. 'I, according to the established etiquette,' so he writes, 'introduced the Princess Caroline to him. She, very properly, in consequence of my saying it was the right mode of proceeding, attempted to kneel to him. He raised her gracefully enough, and embraced her, said barely one word, turned round, retired to a distant part of the apartment, and calling to me, said: "Harris, I am not well: pray get me a glass of brandy." ' At dinner that evening, in the presence of her betrothed, the Princess was 'flippant, rattling, affecting wit.' Poor George, I say again! Deportment was his ruling passion, and his bride did not know how to behave. Vulgarity—hard, implacable, German vulgarity—was in everything she did to the very day of her death. The marriage was solemnized on Wednesday, April 8th, 1795, and the royal bridegroom was drunk.

So soon as they were separated, George became implected with a morbid hatred for his wife, which was hardly in accord with his light and variant nature and shows how bitterly he had been mortified by his marriage of necessity. It is sad that so much of his life should have been wasted in futile strainings after divorce. Yet we can scarcely blame him for seizing upon every scrap of scandal that was whispered of his wife. Besides his not unnatural wish to be free, it was derogatory to the dignity of a prince and a regent that his wife should be living an eccentric life at Blackheath with a family of singers named

Sapio. Indeed, Caroline's conduct during this time was as indiscreet as ever. Wherever she went she made ribald jokes about her husband, 'in such a voice that all, by-standing, might hear.' 'After dinner,' writes one of her servants, 'Her Royal Highness made a wax figure as usual, and gave it an amiable pair of large horns; then took three pins out of her garment and stuck them through and through, and put the figure to roast and melt at the fire. What a silly piece of spite! Yet it is impossible not to laugh when one sees it done.' Imagine the feelings of the First Gentleman in Europe when the unseemly story of these pranks was whispered to him!

For my own part, I fancy Caroline was innocent of any infidelity to her unhappy husband. But that is neither here nor there. Her behaviour was certainly not above suspicion. It fully justified George in trying to establish a case for her divorce. When, at length, she went abroad, her vagaries were such that the whole of her English suite left her, and we hear of her travelling about the Holy Land attended by another family, named Bergami. When her husband succeeded to the throne, and her name was struck out of the liturgy, she despatched expostulations in absurd English to Lord Liverpool. Receiving no answer, she decided to return and claim her right to be crowned Queen of England. Whatever the unhappy lady did, she always was ridiculous. One cannot but smile as one reads of her posting along the French roads in a yellow travelling-chariot drawn by cart-horses, with a retinue that included an alderman, a reclaimed lady-in-waiting, an Italian count, the eldest son of the alderman, and 'a fine little female child, about three years old, whom Her Majesty, in conformity with her benevolent practices on former occasions, had adopted.' The breakdown of her impeachment, and her acceptance of an income, formed a fitting anti-climax to the terrible absurdities of her position. She died from the effects of a chill caught when she was trying vainly to force a way to her husband's coronation. Unhappy woman! Our sympathy for her is not misgiven. Fate wrote her a most tremendous tragedy, and she played it in tights. Let us pity her, but not forget to pity her husband, the King, also.

It is another common accusation against George that he was an undutiful and unfeeling son. If this was so, it is certain that not all the blame is to be laid upon him alone. There is more than one anecdote which shows that King George disliked his eldest son, and took no trouble to conceal his dislike, long before the boy had been freed from his tutors. It was the coldness of his father and the petty restrictions he loved to enforce that first drove George to seek the companionship of such men as Égalité and the Duke of Cumberland, both of whom were quick to inflame his impressionable mind to angry resentment. Yet, when Margaret Nicholson attempted the life of the King, the Prince immediately posted off from Brighton that he might wait upon his father at Windsor—a graceful act of piety that was rewarded by his father's refusal to see him. Hated by the Queen, who at this time did all she could to keep her husband and his son apart, surrounded by intriguers, who did all they could to set him against his father, George seems to have behaved with great discretion. In the years that follow, I can conceive no position more difficult than that in which he found himself every time his father relapsed into lunacy. That he should have by every means opposed those who through jealousy stood between him and the regency was only natural. It cannot be said that at any time did he show anxiety to rule, so long as there was any immediate chance of the King's recovery. On the contrary, all impartial seers of that chaotic Court agreed that the Prince bore himself throughout the intrigues, wherein he himself was bound to be, in a notably filial way.

There are many things that I regret in the career of George IV., and what I most of all regret is the part that he played in

the politics of the period. Englishmen to-day have at length
decided that Royalty shall not set foot in the political arena. I
do not despair that some day we shall place politics upon a
sound commercial basis, as they have already done in America
and France, or leave them entirely in the hands of the police,
as they do in Russia. It is horrible to think that, under our
existing *régime*, all the men of noblest blood and highest intellect should waste their time in the sordid atmosphere of the
House of Commons, listening for hours to nonentities talking
nonsense, or searching enormous volumes to prove that somebody said something some years ago that does not quite tally
with something he said the other day, or standing tremulous
before the whips in the lobbies and the scorpions in the con-
stituencies. In the political machine are crushed and lost all
our best men. That Mr. Gladstone did not choose to be a
cardinal is a blow under which the Roman Catholic Church
still staggers. In Mr. Chamberlain Scotland Yard missed its
smartest detective. What a fine voluptuary might Lord Rosebery have been! It is a platitude that the country is ruled best
by the permanent officials, and I look forward to the time when
Mr. Keir Hardie shall hang his cap in the hall of No. 10
Downing Street, and a Conservative working-man shall lead
Her Majesty's Opposition. In the lifetime of George, politics
were not a whit finer than they are to-day. I feel a genuine
indignation that he should have wasted so much of tissue in
mean intrigues about ministries and bills. That he should have
been fascinated by that splendid fellow, Fox, is quite right.
That he should have thrown himself with all his heart into the
storm of the Westminster election is most natural. But it is
awful inverideed to find him, long after he had reached man's
estate, indulging in back-stair intrigues with Whigs and
Tories. It is, of course, absurd to charge him with deserting
his first friends, the Whigs. His love and fidelity were given,
not to the Whigs, but to the men who led them. Even after

the death of Fox, he did, in misplaced piety, do all he could for
Fox's party. What wonder that, when he found he was
ignored by the Ministry that owed its existence to him, he
turned his back upon that sombre couple, the 'Lords G. and
G.,' whom he had always hated, and went over to the Tories?
Among the Tories he hoped to find men who would faithfully
perform their duties and leave him leisure to live his own
beautiful life. I regret immensely that his part in politics did
not cease here. The state of the country and of his own
finances, and also, I fear, a certain love that he had imbibed for
political manipulation, prevented him from standing aside.
How useless was all the finesse he displayed in the long-drawn
question of Catholic Emancipation! How lamentable his terror
of Lord Wellesley's rude dragooning! And is there not something pitiable in the thought of the Regent at a time of minis-
terial complications lying prone on his bed with a sprained
ankle, and taking, as was whispered, in one day as many as
seven hundred drops of laudanum? Some said he took these
doses to deaden the pain. But others, and among them his
brother Cumberland, declared that the sprain was all a sham.
I hope it was. The thought of a voluptuary in pain is very
terrible. In any case, I cannot but feel angry, for George's
own sake and that of his kingdom, that he found it impossible
to keep further aloof from the wearisome troubles of political
life. His wretched indecision of character made him an easy
prey to unscrupulous ministers, while his extraordinary diplomatic powers and almost extravagant tact, made them, in their
turn, an easy prey to him. In these two processes much of his
genius was spent untimely. I must confess that he did not quite
realize where his duties ended. He wished always to do too
much. If you read his repeated appeals to his father that he
might be permitted to serve actively in the British army against
the French, you will acknowledge that it was through no fault
of his own that he did not fight. It touches me to think that in

his declining years he actually thought that he had led one of
the charges at Waterloo. He would often describe the whole
scene as it appeared to him at that supreme moment, and refer
to the Duke of Wellington, saying, 'Was it not so, Duke?' 'I
have often heard you say so, your Majesty,' the old soldier
would reply, grimly. I am not sure that the old soldier was at
Waterloo himself. In a room full of people he once referred
to the battle as having been won upon the playing-fields of
Eton. This was certainly a most unfortunate slip, seeing that
all historians are agreed that it was fought on a certain field
situate a few miles from Brussels.

In one of his letters to the King, craving for a military
appointment, George urges that, whilst his next brother, the
Duke of York, commanded the army, and the younger
branches of the family were either generals or lieutenant-
generals, he, who was Prince of Wales, remained colonel of
dragoons. And herein, could he have known it, lay the right
limitation of his life. As Royalty was and is constituted, it is
for the younger sons to take an active part in the services, whilst
the eldest son is left as the ruler of Society. Thousands and
thousands of guineas were given by the nation that the Prince
of Wales, the Regent, the King, might be, in the best sense of
the word, ornamental. It is not for us, at this moment, to
consider whether Royalty, as a wholly Pagan institution, is not
out of place in a community of Christians. It is enough that
we should inquire whether the god, whom our grandfathers
set up and worshipped and crowned with offerings, gave grace
to his worshippers.

That George was a moral man, in our modern sense, I do
not for one moment pretend. It were idle to deny that he was
profligate. When he died there were found in one of his
cabinets more than a hundred locks of women's hair. Some of
these were still plastered with powder and pomatum, some
were mere little golden curls, such as grow low down upon a

girl's neck, others were streaked with grey. The whole of this collection subsequently passed into the hands of Adam, the famous Scotch henchman of the Regent. In his family, now resident in Glasgow, it is treasured as an heirloom. I myself have been privileged to look at all these locks of hair, and I have seen a *clairvoyante* take them one by one, and, pinching them between her lithe fingers, tell of the love that each symbolized. I have heard her tell of long rides by night, of a boudoir hung with grass-green satin, and of a tryst at Windsor; of one, the wife of a hussar at York, whose little lap-dog used to bark angrily whenever the Regent came near his mistress; of a milkmaid who, in her great simpleness, thought her child would one day be King of England; of an arch-duchess with blue eyes, and a silly little flautist from Portugal; of women that were wantons and fought for his favour, great ladies that he loved dearly, girls that gave themselves to him humbly. If we lay all pleasures at the feet of our Prince, we can scarcely hope that he will remain virtuous. Indeed, we do not wish our Prince to be an exemplar of godliness, but a perfect type of happiness. It may be foolish of us to insist upon apolaustic happiness, but that is the kind of happiness that we can ourselves, most of us, best understand, and so we offer it to our ideal. In Royalty we find our Bacchus, our Venus.

Certainly George was, in the practical sense of the word, a fine king. His wonderful physique, his wealth, his brilliant talents, he gave them all without stint to Society. From the time when, at Madame Cornelys', he gallivanted with rips and demireps, to the time when he sat, a stout and solitary old king, fishing in the artificial pond at Windsor, his life was beautifully ordered. He indulged to the full in all the delights that England could offer him. That he should have, in his old age, suddenly abandoned his career of vigorous enjoyment is, I confess, rather surprising. The Royal voluptuary generally remains young to the last. No one ever tires of pleasure. It is the pursuit of pleasure, the trouble to grasp it, that makes us old. Only the soldiers who enter Capua with wounded feet leave it demoralized. And yet George, who never had to wait or fight for a pleasure, fell enervate long before his death. I can but attribute this to the constant persecution to which he was subjected by duns and ministers, parents and wives.

Not that I regret the manner in which he spent his last years. On the contrary, I think it was exceedingly cosy. I like to think of the King, at Windsor, lying a-bed all the morning in his darkened room, with all the sporting papers scattered over his quilt and a little decanter of the favourite cherry-brandy within easy reach. I like to think of him sitting by his fire in the afternoon and hearing his ministers ask for him at the door and piling another log upon the fire, as he heard them sent away by his servant. It was not, I acknowledge, a life to kindle popular enthusiasm. But most people knew little of its mode. For all they knew, His Majesty might have been making his soul or writing his memoirs. In reality, George was now 'too fat by far' to brook the observation of casual eyes. Especially he hated to be seen by those whose memories might bear them back to the time when he had yet a waist. Among his elaborate precautions of privacy was a pair of *avant-couriers*, who always preceded his pony-chaise in its daily progress through Windsor Great Park and had strict commands to drive back any intruder. In *The Veiled Majestic Man, Where is the Graceful Despot of England?* and other lampoons not extant, the scribblers mocked his loneliness. At White's one evening, four gentlemen of high fashion vowed, over their wine, they would see the invisible monarch. So they rode down next day to Windsor, and secreted themselves in the branches of a holm-oak. Here they waited *perdus*, beguiling the hours and the frost with their flasks. When dusk was falling, they heard at last the chime of hoofs on the hard road, and saw presently a splash of the Royal livery, as two grooms trotted by, peering warily from side to side, and disappeared in the gloom. The conspirators in the tree held their breath, till they caught the distant sound of wheels. Nearer and louder came the sound, and soon they saw a white, postillioned pony, a chaise and, yes, girth immensurate among the cushions, a weary monarch, whose face, crimson above the dark accumulation of his stock, was like some ominous sunset. . . . He had passed them and they had seen him, monstrous and moribund among the cushions. He had been borne past them like a wounded Bacchanal. The King! The Regent! . . . They shuddered in the frosty branches. The night was gathering and they climbed silently to the ground, with an awful, indispellible image before their eyes.

You see, these gentlemen were not philosophers. Remember, also, that the strangeness of their escapade, the cramped attitude they had been compelled to maintain in the branches of the holm-oak, the intense cold and their frequent resort to the flask must have all conspired to exaggerate their emotions and prevent them from looking at things in a rational way. After all, George had lived his life. He had lived more fully than any other man. And it was better really that his death should be preceded by decline. For every one, obviously, the most *desirable* kind of death is that which strikes men down, suddenly, in their prime. Had they not been so dangerous, railways would never have ousted the old coaches from popular favour. But, however keenly we may court such a death for ourselves or for those who are near and dear to us, we must always be offended whenever it befall one in whom our interest is æsthetic merely. Had his father permitted George to fight at Waterloo, and had some fatal bullet pierced the padding of that splendid breast, I should have been really annoyed, and this essay would never have been written. Sudden death mars the unity of an admirable life. Natural declines, tapering to tranquillity, is its proper end. As a man's life begins, faintly, and gives no token of childhood's intensity and the expansion

37

of youth and the perfection of manhood, so it should also end, faintly. The King died a death that was like the calm conclusion of a great, lurid poem. *Quievit.*

Yes, his life was a poem, a poem in the praise of Pleasure. And it is right that we should think of him always as the great voluptuary. Only let us note that his nature never became, as do the natures of most voluptuaries, corroded by a cruel indifference to the happiness of others. When all the town was agog for the *fête* to be given by the Regent in honour of the French King, Sheridan sent a forged card of invitation to Romeo Coates, the half-witted dandy, who used at this time to walk about in absurd ribbons and buckles, and was the butt of all the streetsters. The poor fellow arrived at the entrance of Carlton House, proud as a peacock, and he was greeted with a tremendous cheer from the by-standing mob, but when he came to the lackeys he was told that his card was a hoax and sent about his business. The tears were rolling down his cheeks as he shambled back into the street. The Regent heard later in the evening of this sorry joke, and next day despatched a kindly-worded message, in which he prayed that Mr. Coates would not refuse to come and 'view the decorations, nevertheless.' Though he does not appear to have treated his inferiors with the extreme servility that is now in vogue, George was beloved by the whole of his household, and many are the little tales that are told to illustrate the kindliness and consideration he showed to his valets and his jockeys and his stable-boys. That from time to time he dropped certain of his favourites is no cause for blaming him. Remember that a Great Personage, like a great genius, is dangerous to his fellow-creatures. The favourites of Royalty live in an intoxicant atmosphere. They become unaccountable for their behaviour. Either they get beyond themselves, and, like Brummell, forget that the King, their friend, is also their master, or they outrun the constable and go bankrupt, or cheat at cards in order to keep up their position, or do some other foolish thing that makes it impossible for the King to favour them more. Old friends are generally the refuge of unsociable persons. Remembering this also, gauge the temptation that besets the very leader of Society to form fresh friendships, when all the cleverest and most charming persons in the land are standing ready, like supers at the wings, to come on and please him! At Carlton House there was a constant succession of wits. Minds were preserved for the Prince of Wales, as coverts are preserved for him to-day. For him Sheridan would flash his best bon-mot, and Theodore Hook play his most practical joke, his swiftest chansonette. And Fox would talk, as only he could, of Liberty and of Patriotism, and Byron would look more than ever like Isidore de Lara as he recited his own bad verses, and Sir Walter Scott would 'pour out with an endless generosity his store of old-world learning, kindness, and humour.' Of such men George was a splendid patron. He did not merely sit in his chair, gaping princely at their wit and their wisdom, but quoted with the scholars and argued with the statesmen and jested with the wits. Doctor Burney, an impartial observer, says that he was amazed by the knowledge of music that the Regent displayed in a half-hour's discussion over the wine. Croker says that 'the Prince and Scott were the two most brilliant story-tellers, in their several ways, he had ever happened to meet. Both exerted themselves, and it was hard to say which shone the most.' Indeed His Royal Highness appears to have been a fine conversationalist, with a wide range of knowledge and great humour. We, who have come at length to look upon stupidity as one of the most sacred prerogatives of Royalty, can scarcely realize that, if George's birth had been never so humble, he would have been known to us as a most admirable scholar and wit, or as a connoisseur of the arts. It is pleasing to think of his love for the Flemish school of painting, for Wilkie and Sir Thomas Lawrence. The splendid portraits of foreign potentates that hang in the Banqueting Room at Windsor bear witness to his sense of the canvas. In his later years he exerted himself strenuously in raising the tone of the drama. His love of the classics never left him. We know he was fond of quoting those incomparable poets, Homer, at great length, and that he was prominent in the 'papyrus-craze.' Indeed, he inspired Society with a love of something more than mere pleasure, a love of the 'humaner delights.' He was a giver of tone. At his coming, the bluff, disgusting ways of the Tom and Jerry period gave way to those florid graces that are still called Georgian.

A pity that George's predecessor was not a man, like the Prince Consort, of strong chastening influence! Then might the bright flamboyance which he gave to Society have made his reign more beautiful than any other—a real renaissance. But he found London a wild city of taverns and cock-pits, and the grace which in the course of years he gave to his subjects never really entered into them. The cock-pits were gilded and the taverns painted with colour, but the heart of the city was vulgar, even as before. The simulation of higher things did indeed give the note of a very interesting period, but how shallow that simulation was and how merely it was due to George's own influence, we may see in the light of what happened after his death. The good that he had done died with him. The refinement he had laid upon vulgarity fell away, like enamel from withered cheeks. It was only George himself who had made the sham endure. The Victorian era came soon, and the angels rushed in and drove the nymphs away and hung the land with reps.

I have often wondered whether it was with a feeling that his influence would be no more than life-long, that George allowed Carlton House, that dear structure, the very work of his life and symbol of his being, to be rased. I wish that Carlton House were still standing. I wish we could still walk through those corridors, whose walls were 'crusted with ormolu,' and parquet-floors were 'so glossy that, were Narcissus to come down from heaven, he would, I maintain, need no other mirror for his *beauté*.' I wish that we could see the pier-glasses and the girandoles and the twisted sofas, the fauns foisted upon the ceiling and the rident goddesses along the wall. These things would make George's memory dearer to us, help us to a fuller knowledge of him. I am glad that the Pavilion still stands here in Brighton. Its trite lawns and wanton cupolæ have taught me much. As I write this essay, I can see them from my window. Last night, in a crowd of trippers and townspeople, I roamed the lawns of that dishonoured palace, whilst a band played us tunes. Once I fancied I saw the shade of a swaying figure and of a wine-red face.

The Pervasion of Rouge

Nay, but it is useless to protest. Artifice must queen it once more in the town, and so, if there be any whose hearts chafe at her return, let them not say, 'We have come into evil times,' and be all for resistance, reformation, or angry cavilling. For did the king's sceptre send the sea retrograde, or the wand of the sorcerer avail to turn the sun from its old course? And what man or what number of men ever stayed that inexorable process by which the cities of this world grow, are very strong, fail, and grow again? Indeed, indeed, there is charm in every period, and only fools and flutterpates do not seek reverently for what is charming in their own day. No martyrdom, however fine, nor satire, however splendidly bitter, has changed by a little tittle the known tendency of things. It is the times that can perfect us, not we the times, and so let all of us wisely acquiesce. Like the little wired marionettes, let us acquiesce in the dance.

For behold! The Victorian era comes to its end and the day of sancta simplicitas is quite ended. The old signs are here and the portents to warn the seer of life that we are ripe for a new epoch of artifice. Are not men rattling the dice-box and ladies dipping their fingers in the rouge-pot? At Rome, in the keenest time of her degringolade, when there was gambling even in the holy temples, great ladies (does not Lucian tell us?) did not scruple to squander all they had upon unguents from Arabia. Nero's mistress and unhappy wife, Poppæa, of shameful memory, had in her travelling retinue fifteen—or, as some say, fifty—she-asses, for the sake of their milk, that was

42

thought an incomparable guard against cosmetics with poison in them. Last century, too, when life was lived by candlelight, and ethics was but etiquette, and even art a question of punctilio, women, we know, gave the best hours of the day to the crafty farding of their faces and the towering of their coiffures. And men, throwing passion into the wine-bowl to sink or swim, turned out thought to browse upon the green cloth. Cannot we even now in our fancy see them, those silent exquisites round the long table at Brooks's, masked, all of them, 'lest the countenance should betray feeling,' in quinze masks, through whose eyelets they sat peeping, peeping, while macao brought them riches or ruin! We can see them, those silent rascals, sitting there with their cards and their rouleaux and their wooden money-bowls, long after the dawn had crept up St. James's and pressed its haggard face against the window of the little club. Yes, we can raise their ghosts—and, more, we can see many where a devotion to hazard fully as meek as theirs. In England there has been a wonderful revival of cards. Baccarat may rival dead faro in the tale of her devotees. We have all seen the sweet English châtelaine at her roulette wheel, and ere long it may be that tender parents will be writing to complain of the compulsory baccarat in our public schools.

In fact, we are all gamblers once more, but our gambling is on a finer scale than ever it was. We fly from the card-room to the heath, and from the heath to the City, and from the City to the coast of the Mediterranean. And just as no one seriously encourages the clergy in its frantic efforts to lay the spirit of chance that has thus resurged among us, so no longer are many faces set against that other great sign of a more complicated life, the love for cosmetics. No longer is a lady of fashion blamed if, to escape the outrageous persecution of time, she fly for sanctuary to the toilet-table; and if a damosel, prying in her mirror, be sure that with brush and pigment she can trick herself into more charm, we are not angry. Indeed, why should we ever have been? Surely it is laudable, this wish to make fair the ugly and overtop fairness, and no wonder that within the last five years the trade of the makers of cosmetics has increased immoderately—twenty-fold, so one of these makers has said to me. We need but walk down any modish street and peer into the little broughams that flit past, or (in Thackeray's phrase) under the bonnet of any woman we meet, to see over how wide a kingdom rouge reigns.

And now the use of pigments is becoming general, and most women are not so young as they are painted, it may be asked curiously how the prejudice ever came into being. Indeed, it is hard to trace folly, for that it is inconsequent, to its start; and perhaps it savours too much of reason to suggest that the prejudice was due to the tristful confusion man has made of soul and surface. Through trusting so keenly to the detection of the one by keeping watch upon the other, and by force of the thousand errors following, he has come to think of surface even as the reverse of soul. He seems to suppose that every clown beneath his paint and lip-salve is moribund and knows it (though in verity, I am told, clowns are as cheerful a class of men as any other), that the fairer the fruit's rind and the more delectable its bloom, the closer are packed the ashes within it. The very jargon of the hunting-field connects cunning with a mask. And so perhaps came man's anger at the embellishment of women—that lovely mask of enamel with its shadows of pink and tiny pencilled veins, what must lurk behind it? Of what treacherous mysteries may it not be the screen? Does not the heathen lacquer her dark face, and the harlot paint her cheeks, because sorrow has made them pale?

After all, the old prejudice is a-dying. We need not pry into the secret of its birth. Rather is this a time of jolliness and glad indulgence. For the era of rouge is upon us, and as only in an elaborate era can man, by the tangled accrescency of his own pleasures and emotions, reach that refinement which is his highest excellence, and by making himself, so to say, independent of Nature, come nearest to God, so only in an elaborate era is woman perfect. Artifice is the strength of the world, and in that same mask of paint and powder, shadowed with vermeil tinct and most trimly pencilled, is woman's strength.

For see! We need not look so far back to see woman under the direct influence of Nature. Early in this century, our grandmothers, sickening of the odour of faded exotics and spilt wine, came out into the daylight once more and let the breezes blow around their faces and enter, sharp and welcome, into their lungs. Artifice they drove forth and they set Martin Tupper upon a throne of mahogany to rule over them. A very reign of terror set in. All things were sacrificed to the fetish Nature. Old ladies may still be heard to tell how, when they were girls, affectation was not; and, if we verify this assertion in the light of such literary authorities as Dickens, we find that it is absolutely true. Women appear to have been in those days utterly natural in their conduct—flighty, fainting, blushing, gushing, giggling, and shaking their curls. They knew no reserve in the first days of the Victorian era. No thought was held too trivial, no emotion too silly, to express. To Nature everything was sacrificed. Great heavens! And in those barren days what influence did women exert! By men they seem not to have been feared nor loved, but regarded rather as 'dear little creatures' or 'wonderful little beings,' and in their relation to life as foolish and ineffectual as the landscapes they did in water-colour. Yet, if the women of those years were of no great account, they had a certain charm, and they at least had not begun to trespass upon men's grounds; if they touched not thought, which is theirs by right, at any rate they refrained from action, which is ours. Far more

serious was it when, in the natural trend of time, they became
enamoured of rinking and archery and galloping along the
Brighton Parade. Swiftly they have sped on since then from
horror to horror. The invasion of the tennis-courts and of the
golf-links, the seizure of the bicycle and of the typewriter, were
but steps preliminary in that campaign which is to end with
the final victorious occupation of St. Stephen's. But stay! The
horrific pioneers of womanhood who gad hither and thither
and, confounding wisdom with the device on her shield, shriek
for the unbecoming, are doomed. Though they spin their
bicycle-treadles so amazingly fast, they are too late. Though
they scream victory, none follow them. Artifice, that fair exile,
has returned.

Yes, though the pioneers know it not, they are doomed
already. For of the curiosities of history not the least strange
is the manner in which two social movements may be seen to
overlap, long after the second has, in truth, given its death-
blow to the first. And, in like manner, as one has seen the
limbs of a murdered thing in lovely movement, so we need
not doubt that, though the voices of those who cry out for
reform be very terribly shrill, they will soon be hushed. Dear
Artifice is with us. It needed but that we should wait.

Surely, without any of my pleading, women will welcome
their great and amiable protectrix, as by instinct. For (have
I not said?) it is upon her that all their strength, their life
almost, depends. Artifice's first command to them is that they
should repose. With bodily activity their powder will fly,
their enamel crack. They are butterflies who must not flit, if
they love their bloom. Now, setting aside the point of view of
passion, from which very many obvious things might be said
(and probably have been by the minor poets), it is, from the
intellectual point of view, quite necessary that a woman should
repose. Hers is the resupinate sex. On her couch she is a
goddess, but so soon as ever she put her foot to the ground—lo,

she is the veriest little sillypop, and quite done for. She cannot rival us in action, but she is our mistress in the things of the mind. Let her not by second-rate athletics, nor indeed by any exercise soever of the limbs, spoil the pretty procedure of her reason. Let her be content to remain the guide, the subtle suggester of what *we* must do, the strategist whose soldiers we are, the little architect whose workmen.

'After all,' as a pretty girl once said to me, 'women are a sex by themselves, so to speak,' and the sharper the line between their worldly functions and ours, the better. This greater swiftness and less erring subtlety of mind, their forte and privilege, justifies the painted mask that Artifice bids them wear. Behind it their minds can play without let. They gain the strength of reserve. They become important, as in the days of the Roman Empire were the Emperor's mistresses, as was the Pompadour at Versailles, as was our Elizabeth. Yet do not their faces become lined with thought; beautiful and without meaning are their faces.

And, truly, of all the good things that will happen with the full revival of cosmetics, one of the best is that surface will finally be severed from soul. That damnable confusion will be solved by the extinguishing of a prejudice which, as I suggest, itself created. Too long has the face been degraded from its rank as a thing of beauty to a mere vulgar index of character or emotion. We had come to troubling ourselves, not with its charm of colour and line, but with such questions as whether the lips were sensuous, the eyes full of sadness, the nose indicative of determination. I have no quarrel with physiognomy. For my own part I believe in it. But it has tended to degrade the face æsthetically, in such wise as the study of cheirosophy has tended to degrade the hand. And the use of cosmetics, the masking of the face, will change this. We shall gaze at a woman merely because she is beautiful, not stare into her face anxiously, as into the face of a barometer.

How fatal it has been, in how many ways, this confusion of soul and surface! Wise were the Greeks in making plain masks for their mummers to play in, and dunces we not to have done the same! Only the other day, an actress was saying that what she was most proud of in her art—next, of course, to having appeared in some provincial pantomime at the age of three—was the deftness with which she contrived, in parts demanding a rapid succession of emotions, to dab her cheeks quite quickly with rouge from the palm of her right hand or powder from the palm of her left. Gracious goodness! why do not we have masks upon the stage? Drama is the presentment of the soul in action. The mirror of the soul is the voice. Let the young critics, who seek a cheap reputation for austerity, by cavilling at 'incidental music,' set their faces rather against the attempt to justify inferior dramatic art by the subvention of a quite alien art like painting, of any art, indeed, whose sphere is only surface. Let those, again, who sneer, so rightly, at the 'painted anecdotes of the Academy,' censure equally the writers who trespass on painters' ground. It is a proclaimed sin that a painter should concern himself with a good little girl's affection for a Scotch greyhound, or the keen enjoyment of their port by elderly gentlemen of the early 'forties. Yet, for a painter to prod the soul with his paint-brush is no worse than for a novelist to refuse to dip under the surface, and the fashion of avoiding a psychological study of grief by stating that the owner's hair turned white in a single night, or of shame by mentioning a sudden rush of scarlet to the cheeks, is as lamentable as may be. But! But with the universal use of cosmetics and the consequent secernment of soul and surface upon which, at the risk of irritating a reader, I must again insist, all those old properties that went to bolster up the ordinary novel—the trembling lips, the flashing eyes, the determined curve of the chin, the nervous trick of biting the moustache, aye, and the hectic spot of red on either cheek—

will be made spiflicate, as the puppets were spiflicated by Don
Quixote. Yes, even now Demos begins to discern. The same
spirit that has revived rouge, smote his mouth as it grinned at
the wondrous painter of mist and river, and now sends him
sprawling for the pearls that Meredith dived for in the deep
waters of romance.

Indeed, the revival of cosmetics must needs be so splendid
an influence, conjuring boons innumerable, that one inclines
almost to mutter against that inexorable law by which Artifice
must perish from time to time. That such branches of painting
as the staining of glass or the illuminating of manuscripts
should fall into disuse seems, in comparison, so likely; these
were esoteric arts; they died with the monastic spirit. But
personal appearance is art's very basis. The painting of the
face is the first kind of painting men can have known. To make
beautiful things—is it not an impulse laid upon few? But to
make oneself beautiful is an universal instinct. Strange that
the resultant art could ever perish! So fascinating an art too!
So various in its materials from stimmis, psimythium, and
fuligo to bismuth and arsenic, so simple in that its ground and
its subject-matter are one, so marvellous in that its very
subject-matter becomes lovely when an artist has selected it!
For surely this is no idle nor fantastic saying. To deny that
'making up' is an art, on the pretext that the finished work
of its exponents depends for beauty and excellence upon the
ground chosen for the work, is absurd. At the touch of a true
artist, the plainest face turns comely. As subject-matter the
face is no more than suggestive, as ground, merely a loom
round which the beatus artifex may spin the threads of any
golden fabric:

The Incomparable Max

'Quae nunc nomen habent operosi signa Maronis
Pondus iners quondam duraque massa fuit.
Multa viros nescire decet; pars maxima rerum
Offendat, si non interiora tegas.'

and, as Ovid would seem to suggest, by pigments any tone
may be set aglow on a woman's cheek, from enamel the features
take any form. Insomuch that surely the advocates of soup-
kitchens and free-libraries and other devices for giving people
what Providence did not mean them to receive should send
out pamphlets in the praise of self-embellishment. For it will
place Beauty within easy reach of many who could not otherwise hope to attain to it.

But of course Artifice is rather exacting. In return for the
repose she forces—so wisely!—upon her followers when the
sun is high or the moon is blown across heaven, she demands
that they should pay her long homage at the sun's rising. The
initiate may not enter lightly upon her mysteries. For, if a
bad complexion be inexcusable, to be ill-painted is unfor-
givable; and, when the toilet is laden once more with the
fulness of its elaboration, we shall hear no more of the proper
occupation for women. And think, how sweet an energy, to
sit at the mirror of coquetry! See the dear merits of the toilet
as shown upon old vases, or upon the walls of Roman ruins,
or, rather still, read Böttiger's alluring, scholarly description
of 'Morgenscenen im Puttzimmer Einer Reichen Römerin.'
Read of Sabina's face as she comes through the curtain of her
bed-chamber to the chamber of her toilet. The slave-girls
have long been chafing their white feet upon the marble floor.
They stand, those timid Greek girls, marshalled in little
battalions. Each has her appointed task, and all kneel in
welcome as Sabina stalks, ugly and frowning, to the toilet
chair. Scaphion steps forth from among them, and, dipping a
tiny sponge in a bowl of hot milk, passes it lightly, ever so

lightly, over her mistress' face. The Poppæan pastes melt beneath it like snow. A cooling lotion is poured over her brow, and is fanned with feathers. Phiale comes after, a clever girl, captured in some sea-skirmish on the Ægean. In her left hand she holds the ivory box wherein are the phucus and that white powder, psimythium; in her right a sheaf of slim brushes. With how sure a touch does she mingle the colours, and in what sweet proportion blushes and blanches her lady's up-turned face. Phiale is the cleverest of all the slaves. Now Calamis dips her quill in a certain powder that floats, liquid and sable, in the hollow of her palm. Standing upon tiptoe and with lips parted, she traces the arch of the eyebrows. The slaves whisper loudly of their lady's beauty, and two of them hold up a mirror to her. Yes, the eyebrows are rightly arched. But why does Psecas abase herself? She is craving leave to powder Sabina's hair with a fine new powder. It is made of the grated rind of the cedar-tree, and a Gallic perfumer, whose stall is near the Circus, gave it to her for a kiss. No lady in Rome knows of it. And so, when four special slaves have piled up the head-dress, out of a perforated box this glistening powder is showered. Into every little brown ringlet it enters, till Sabina's hair seems like a pile of gold coins. Lest the breezes send it flying, the girls lay the powder with sprinkled attar. Soon Sabina will start for the Temple of Cybele.

Ah! Such are the lures of the toilet that none will for long hold aloof from them. Cosmetics are not going to be a mere prosaic remedy for age or plainness, but all ladies and all young girls will come to love them. Does not a certain blithe Marquise, whose *lettres intimes* from the Court of Louis Seize are less read than their wit deserves, tell us how she was scandalized to see '*même les toutes jeunes demoiselles émaillées comme ma tabatière*'? So it shall be with us. Surely the common prejudice against painting the lily can but be based on mere ground of economy. That which is already fair is complete, it may be urged—urged implausibly, for there are not so many lovely things in this world that we can afford not to know each one of them by heart. There is only one white lily, and who that has ever seen—as I have—a lily really well painted could grudge the artist so fair a ground for his skill? Scarcely do you believe through how many nice metaporphoses a lily may be passed by him. In like manner, we all know the young girl, with her simpleness, her goodness, her wayward ignorance. And a very charming ideal for England must she have been, and a very natural one, when a young girl sat even on the throne. But no nation can keep its ideal for ever, and it needed none of Mr. Gilbert's delicate satire in 'Utopia' to remind us that she had passed out of our ken with the rest of the early Victorian era. What writer of plays, as lately asked some pressman, who had been told off to attend many first nights and knew what he was talking about, ever dreams of making the young girl the centre of his theme? Rather he seeks inspiration from the tried and tired woman of the world, in all her intricate maturity, whilst, by way of comic relief, he sends the young girl flitting in and out with a tennis-racket, the poor εἴδωλον ἀμαυρόν of her former self. The season of the unsophisticated is gone by, and the young girl's final extinction beneath the rising tides of cosmetics will leave no gap in life and will rob art of nothing.

'Tush,' I can hear some damned flutterpate exclaim, 'girlishness and innocence are as strong and as permanent as womanhood itself! Why, a few months past, the whole town went mad over Miss Cissie Loftus! Was not hers a success of girlish innocence and the absence of rouge? If such things as these be outmoded, why was she so wildly popular?' Indeed, the triumph of that clever girl, whose *début* made London nice even in August, is but another witness to the truth of my contention. In a very sophisticated time, simplicity has a new dulcedo. Hers was a success of contrast. Accustomed to clever malaperts like Miss Lloyd or Miss Reeve, whose experienced pouts and smiles under the sun-bonnet are a standing burlesque of innocence and girlishness, Demos was really delighted, for once and away, to see the real presentment of these things upon his stage. Coming after all those sly serios, coming so young and mere with her pink frock and straightly combed hair, Miss Cissie Loftus had the charm which things of another period often do possess. Besides, just as we adored her for the abrupt nod with which she was wont at first to acknowledge the applause, so we were glad for her to come upon the stage with nothing to tinge the ivory of her cheeks. It seemed so strange, that neglect of convention. To be behind footlights and not rouged! Yes, hers was a success of contrast. She was like a daisy in the window at Solomons'. She was delightful. And yet, such is the force of convention, that when last I saw her, playing in some burlesque at the Gaiety, her fringe was curled and her pretty face rouged with the best of them. And, if further need be to show the absurdity of having called her performance 'a triumph of naturalness over the jaded spirit of modernity', let us reflect that the little mimic was not a real old-fashioned girl after all. She had none of that restless naturalness that would seem to have characterized the girl of the early Victorian days. She had no pretty ways—no smiles nor blushes nor tremors. Possibly Demos could not have stood a presentment of girlishness unrestrained.

But, with her grave insouciance, Miss Cissie Loftus had much of the reserve that is one of the factors of feminine perfection, and to most comes only, as I have said, with artifice. Her features played very, very slightly. And in truth, this may have been one of the reasons of her great success. For expression is but too often the ruin of a face; and, since we cannot, as yet, so order the circumstances of life that women shall never be betrayed into 'an unbecoming emotion,' when the brunette shall never have cause to blush nor La Gioconda to frown, the safest way by far is to create, by brush and pigments, artificial expression for every face.

And this—say you?—will make monotony? You are mistaken, *toto cœlo* mistaken. When your mistress has wearied you with one expression, then it will need but a few touches of that pencil, a backward sweep of that brush, and lo, you will be revelling in another. For though, of course, the painting of the face is, in manner, most like the painting of canvas, in outcome it is rather akin to the art of music—lasting, like music's echo, not for very long. So that, no doubt, of the many little appurtenances of the Reformed Toilet Table, not the least vital will be a list of the emotions that become its owner, with recipes for simulating them. According to the colour she wills her hair to be for the time—black or yellow or, peradventure, burnished red—she will blush for you, sneer for you, laugh or languish for you. The good combinations of line and colour are nearly numberless, and by their means poor restless woman will be able to realize her moods in all their shades and lights and dappledoms, to live many lives and masquerade through many moments of joy. No monotony will be. And for us men matrimony will have lost its sting.

But that in the world of women they will not neglect this art, so ripping in itself, in its result so wonderfully beneficent, I am sure indeed. Much, I have said, is already done for its full revival. The spirit of the age has made straight the path of its professors. Fashion has made Jezebel surrender her monopoly of the rouge-pot. As yet, the great art of self-embellishment is for us but in its infancy. But if Englishwomen can bring it to the flower of an excellence so supreme as never yet has it known, then, though Old England lose her martial and commercial supremacy, we patriots will have the satisfaction of knowing that she has been advanced at one bound to a place in the councils of æsthetic Europe. And, in sooth, is this hoping too high of my countrywomen? True

that, as the art seems always to have appealed to the ladies of
Athens, and it was not until the waning time of the Republic
that Roman ladies learned to love the practice of it, so Paris,
Athenian in this as in all other things, has been noted hitherto
as a far more vivid centre of the art than London. But it was
in Rome, under the Emperors, that unguentaria reached its
zenith, and shall it not be in London, soon, that unguentaria
shall outstrip its Roman perfection! Surely there must be
among us artists as cunning in the use of brush and puff as any
who lived at Versailles. Surely the splendid, impalpable
advance of good taste, as shown in dress and in the decoration
of houses, may justify my hope of the preëminence of Englishwomen in the cosmetic art. By their innate delicacy of touch
they will accomplish much, and much, of course, by their swift
feminine perception. Yet it were well that they should know
something also of the theoretical side of the craft. Modern
authorities upon the mysteries of the toilet are, it is true, rather
few; but among the ancients many a writer would seem to have
been fascinated by them. Archigenes, a man of science at the
Court of Cleopatra, and Criton at the Court of the Emperor
Trajan, both wrote treatises upon cosmetics—doubtless most
scholarly treatises that would have given many a precious
hint. It is a pity they are not extant. From Lucian or from
Juvenal, with his bitter picture of a Roman *levée*, much may be
learnt; from the staid pages of Xenophon and Aristophanes'
dear farces. But best of all is that fine book of the Ars Amatoria
that Ovid has set aside for the consideration of dyes, perfumes,
and pomades. Written by an artist who knew the allurement
of the toilet and understood its philosophy, it remains without
rival as a treatise upon Artifice. It is more than a poem, it is a
manual; and if there be left in England any lady who cannot
read Latin in the original she will do well to procure a discreet
translation. In the Bodleian Library there is treasured the
only known copy of a very poignant and delightful rendering

of this one book of Ovid's masterpiece. It was made by a certain Wye Waltonstall, who lived in the days of Elizabeth, and, seeing that he dedicated it to 'the Vertuous Ladyes and Gentlewomen of Great Britain,' I am sure that the gallant writer, could he know of our great renaissance of cosmetics, would wish his little work to be placed once more within their reach. 'Inafmuch as to you, ladyes and gentlewomen,' so he writes in his queer little dedication, 'my booke of pigments doth firft addreffe itfelf, that it may kiffe your hands and afterward have the lines thereof in reading fweetened by the odour of your breath, while the dead letters formed into words by your divided lips may receive new life by your paffionate expreffion, and the words marryed in that Ruby coloured temple may thus happily united, multiply your contentment.' It is rather sad to think that, at this crisis in the history of pigments, the Vertuous Ladyes and Gentlewomen cannot read the libellus of Wye Waltonstall, who did so dearly love pigments.

But since the days when these great critics wrote their treatises, with what gifts innumerable has Artifice been loaded by Science! Many little partitions must be added to the narthecium before it can comprehend all the new cosmetics that have been quietly devised since classical days, and will make the modern toilet chalks away more splendid in its possibilities. A pity that no one has devoted himself to the compiling of a new list; but doubtless all the newest devices are known to the admirable unguentarians of Bond Street, who will impart them to their clients. Our thanks, too, should be given to Science for ridding us of the old danger that was latent in the use of cosmetics. Nowadays they cannot, being purged of any poisonous element, do harm to the skin that they make beautiful. There need be no more sowing the seeds of destruction in the furrows of time, no martyrs to the cause like Maria, Countess of Coventry, that fair dame but infelix, who died, so they relate, from the effect of a poisonous rouge upon her lips. No, we need have no fears now. Artifice will claim not another victim from among her worshippers.

Loveliness shall sit at the toilet, watching her oval face in the oval mirror. Her smooth fingers shall flit among the paints and powder, to tip and mingle them, catch up a pencil, clasp a phial, and what not and what *not*, until the mask of vermeil tinct has been laid aptly, the enamel quite hardened. And, heavens, how she will charm us and ensorcel our eyes! Positively rouge will rob us for a time of all our reason; we shall go mad over masks. Was it not at Capua that they had a whole street where nothing was sold but dyes and unguents? We must have such a street, and, to fill our new Seplasia, our Arcade of the Unguents, all herbs and minerals and live creatures shall give of their substance. The white cliffs of Albion shall be ground to powder for Loveliness, and perfumed by the ghost of many a little violet. The fluffy eiderducks, that are swimming round the pond, shall lose their feathers, that the powder-puff may be moonlike as it passes over Loveliness' lovely face. Even the camels shall become ministers of delight, giving many tufts of their hair to be stained in her splendid colour-box, and across her cheek the swift hare's foot shall fly as of old. The sea shall offer her the phucus, its scarlet weed. We shall spill the blood of mulberries at her bidding. And, as in another period of great ecstasy, a dancing wanton, la belle Aubrey, was crowned upon a church's lighted altar, so Arsenic, that 'greentress'd goddess,' ashamed at length of skulking between the soup of the unpopular and the test-tubes of the Queen's analyst, shall be exalted to a place of consummate honour upon the toilet-table of Loveliness.

All these things shall come to pass. Times of jolliness and glad indulgence! For Artifice, whom we drove forth, has returned among us, and, though her eyes are red with crying, she is smiling forgiveness. She is kind. Let us dance and be glad, and trip the cockawhoop! Artifice, sweetest exile is come into her kingdom. Let us dance her a welcome!

Diminuendo

In the year of grace 1890, and in the beautiful autumn of that year, I was a freshman at Oxford. I remember how my tutor asked me what lectures I wished to attend, and how he laughed when I said that I wished to attend the lectures of Mr. Walter Pater. Also I remember how, one morning soon after, I went into Ryman's to order some foolish engraving for my room, and there saw, peering into a portfolio, a small, thick, rock-faced man, whose top-hat and gloves of *bright* dog-skin struck one of the many discords in that little city of learning or laughter. The serried bristles of his moustachio made for him a false-military air. I think I nearly went down when they told me that this was Pater.

Not that even in those more decadent days of my childhood did I admire the man as a stylist. Even then I was angry that he should treat English as a dead language, bored by that sedulous ritual wherewith he laid out every sentence as in a shroud—hanging, like a widower, long over its marmoreal beauty or ever he could lay it at length in his book, its sepulchre. From that laden air, the so cadaverous murmur of that sanctuary, I would hook it at the beck of any jade. The writing of Pater had never, indeed, appealed to me, ἀλλ' αἰεί, having regard to the couth solemnity of his mind, to his philosophy, his rare erudition, τινα φῶτα μέγαν καὶ καλὸν ἐδέγμην.. And I suppose it was when at length I saw him that I first knew him to be fallible.

At school I had read *Marius the Epicurean* in bed and with a dark lantern. Indeed, I regarded it mainly as a tale of adventure, quite as fascinating as *Midshipman Easy*, and far less hard to understand, because there were no nautical terms in it. Marryat, moreover, never made me wish to run away to sea, whilst certainly Pater did make me wish for more 'colour' in the curriculum, for a renaissance of the Farrar period, when there was always 'a sullen spirit of revolt against the authorities'; when lockers were always being broken into and marks falsified, and small boys prevented from saying their prayers, insomuch that they vowed they would no longer buy brandy for their seniors. In some schools, I am told, the pretty old custom of roasting a fourth-form boy, whole, upon Founder's Day still survives. But in my school there was less sentiment. I ended by acquiescing in the slow revolution of its wheel of work and play. I felt that at Oxford, when I should be of age to matriculate, a 'variegated dramatic life' was waiting for me. I was not a little too sanguine, alas!

How sad was my coming to the university! Where were those sweet conditions I had pictured in my boyhood? Those antique contrasts? Did I ride, one sunset, through fens on a palfrey, watching the gold reflections on Magdalen Tower? Did I ride over Magdalen Bridge and hear the consonance of evening-bells and cries from the river below? Did I rein in to wonder at the raised gates of Queen's, the twisted pillars of St. Mary's, the little shops, lighted with tapers? Did bull-pups snarl at me, or dons, with bent backs, acknowledge my salute? Anyone who knows the place as it is, must see that such questions are purely rhetorical. To him I need not explain the disappointment that beset me when, after being whirled in a cab from the station to a big hotel, I wandered out into the streets. *On aurait dit* a bit of Manchester through which Apollo had once passed; for here, among the hideous trams and the brand-new bricks—here, glared at by the electric-lights that hung from poles, screamed at by boys with the *Echo* and the *Star*—here, in a riot of vulgarity, were remnants of beauty, as I discerned. There were only remnants.

Soon also I found that the life of the place, like the place, had lost its charm and its tradition. Gone were the contrasts that made it wonderful. That feud between undergraduates and dons—latent, in the old days, only at times when it behoved the two academic grades to unite against the townspeople—was one of the absurdities of the past. The townspeople now looked just like undergraduates and the dons just like townspeople. So splendid was the train-service between Oxford and London that, with hundreds of passengers daily, the one had become little better than a suburb of the other. What more could extensionists demand? As for me, I was disheartened. Bitter were the comparisons I drew between my coming to Oxford and the coming of Marius to Rome. Could it be that there was at length no beautiful environment wherein a man might sound the harmonies of his soul? Had civilization made beauty, besides adventure, so rare? I wondered what counsel Pater, insistent always upon contact with comely things, would offer to one who could nowhere find them. I had been wondering that very day when I went into Ryman's and saw him there.

When the tumult of my disillusioning was past, my mind grew clearer. I discerned that the scope of my quest for emotion must be narrowed. That abandonment of one's self to life, that merging of one's soul in bright waters, so often suggested in Pater's writing, were a counsel impossible for to-day. The quest of emotions must be no less keen, certainly, but the manner of it must be changed forthwith. To unswitch myself from my surroundings, to guard my soul from contact with the unlovely things that compassed it about, therein lay my hope. I must approach the Benign Mother with great caution. And so, while most of the freshmen were doing her honour with wine and song and wreaths of smoke, I stood aside, pondered. In such seclusion I passed my first term—

ah, how often did I wonder whether I was not wasting my days, and, wondering, abandon my meditations upon the right ordering of the future! Thanks be to Athene, who threw her shadow over me in those moments of weak folly!

At the end of term I came to London. Around me seethed swirls, eddies, torrents, violent cross-currents of human activity. What uproar! Surely I could have no part in modern life. Yet, yet for a while it was fascinating to watch the ways of its children. The prodigious life of the Prince of Wales fascinated me above all; indeed, it still fascinates me. What experience has been withheld from His Royal Highness? Was ever so supernal a type, as he, of mere Pleasure? How often he has watched, at Newmarket, the scud-a-run of quivering homuncules over the vert on horses, or, from some night-boat, the holocaust of great wharves by the side of the Thames; raced through the blue Solent; threaded *les coulisses*! He has danced in every palace of every capital, played in every club. He has hunted elephants through the jungles of India, boar through the forests of Austria, pigs over the plains of Massachusetts. From the Castle of Abergeldie he has led his Princess into the frosty night, Highlanders lighting with torches the path to the deer-larder, where lay the wild things that had fallen to him on the crags. He has marched the Grenadiers to chapel through the white streets of Windsor. He has ridden through Moscow, in strange apparel, to kiss the catafalque of more than one Tzar. For him the Rajahs of India have spoiled their temples, and Blondin has crossed Niagara along the tight-rope, and the Giant Guard done drill beneath the chandeliers of the Neue Schloss. Incline he to scandal, lawyers are proud to whisper their secrets in his ear. Be he gallant, the ladies are at his feet. *Ennuyé*, all the wits from Bernal Osborne to Arthur Roberts have jested for him. He has been 'present always at the focus where the greatest number of forces unite in their purest energy,' for it is his presence that makes those forces unite.

'*Ennuyé?*' I asked. Indeed he never is. How could he be when Pleasure hangs constantly upon his arm! It is those others, overtaking her only after arduous chase, breathless and footsore, who quickly sicken of her company, and fall fainting at her feet. And for me, shod neither with rank nor riches, what folly to join the chase! I began to see how small a thing it were to sacrifice those external 'experiences,' so dear to the heart of Pater, by a rigid, complex civilization made so hard to gain. They gave nothing but lassitude to those who had gained them through suffering. Even to the kings and princes, who so easily gained them, what did they yield besides themselves? I do not suppose that, if we were invited to give authenticated instances of intelligence on the part of our royal pets, we could fill half a column of the *Spectator*. In fact, their lives are so full they have no time for thought, the highest energy of man. Now, it was to thought that *my* life should be dedicated. Action, apart from its absorption of time, would war otherwise against the pleasures of intellect, which, for me, meant mainly the pleasures of imagination. It is only (this is a platitude) the things one has not done, the faces or places one has not seen, or seen but darkly, that have charm. It is only mystery—such mystery as besets the eyes of children—that makes things superb. I thought of the voluptuaries I had known—they seemed so sad, so ascetic almost, like poor pilgrims, raising their eyes never or ever gazing at the moon of tarnished endeavour. I thought of the round, insouciant faces of the monks at whose monastery I once broke bread, and how their eyes sparkled when they asked me of the France that lay around their walls. I thought, *pardie*, of the lurid verses written by young men who, in real life, know no haunt more lurid than a literary public-house. It was, for me, merely a problem how I could best avoid

'sensations,' 'pulsations,' and 'exquisite moments' that were
not purely intellectual. I would not attempt to combine both
kinds, as Pater seemed to fancy a man might. I would make
myself master of some small area of physical life, a life of quiet,
monotonous simplicity, exempt from all outer disturbance. I
would shield my body from the world that my mind might
range over it, not hurt nor fettered. As yet, however, I was
in my first year at Oxford. There were many reasons
that I should stay there and take my degree, reasons that
I did not combat. Indeed, I was content to wait for my
life.

And now that I have made my adieux to the Benign Mother,
I need wait no longer. I have been casting my eye over the
suburbs of London. I have taken a most pleasant little villa
in ——ham, and here I shall make my home. Here there is
no traffic, no harvest. Those of the inhabitants who do anything go away each morning and do it elsewhere. Here no
vital forces unite. Nothing happens here. The days and the
months will pass by me, bringing their sure recurrence of quiet
events. In the spring-time I shall look out from my window
and see the laburnum flowering in the little front garden. In
summer cool syrups will come for me from the grocer's shop.
Autumn will make the boughs of my mountain-ash scarlet,
and, later, the asbestos in my grate will put forth its blossoms
of flame. The infrequent cart of Buszard or Mudie will pass my
window at all seasons. Nor will this be all. I shall have friends.
Next door, there is a retired military man who has offered,
in a most neighbourly way, to lend me his copy of *The Times*.
On the other side of my house lives a charming family, who
perhaps will call on me, now and again. I have seen them sally
forth, at sundown, to catch the theatre-train; among them
walked a young lady, the charm of whose figure was ill con-
cealed by the neat waterproof that overspread her evening-
dress. Some day it may be . . . but I anticipate. These things

will be but the cosy accompaniment of my days. For I shall contemplate the world.

I shall look forth from my window, the laburnum and the mountain-ash becoming mere silhouettes in the foreground of my vision. I shall look forth and, in my remoteness, appreciate the distant pageant of the world. Humanity will range itself in the columns of my morning paper. No pulse of life will escape me. The strife of politics, the intriguing of courts, the wreck of great vessels, wars, dramas, earthquakes, national griefs or joys; the strange sequels to divorces, even, and the mysterious suicides of land-agents at Ipswich—in all such phenomena I shall steep my exhaurient mind. *Delicias quoque bibliothecae experiar.* Tragedy, comedy, chivalry, philosophy will be mine. I shall listen to their music perpetually and their colours will dance before my eyes. I shall soar from terraces of stone upon dragons with shinings wings and make war upon Olympus. From the peaks of hills I shall swoop into recondite valleys and drive the pigmies, shrieking little curses, to their caverns. It may be my whim to wander through infinite parks where the deer lie under the clustering shadow of their antlers and flee lightly over the grass; to whisper with white prophets under the elms or bind a child with a daisy-chain or, with a lady, thread my way through the acacias. I shall swim down rivers into the sea and outstrip all ships. Unhindered I shall penetrate all sanctuaries and snatch the secrets of every dim confessional.

Yes! among books that charm, and give wings to the mind, will my days be spent. I shall be ever absorbing the things great men have written; with such experience I will charge my mind to the full. Nor will I try to give anything in return. Once, in the delusion that Art, loving the recluse, would make his life happy, I wrote a little for a yellow quarterly and had that *succès de fiasco* which is always given to a young writer of talent. But the stress of creation soon overwhelmed me. Only

Art with a capital H gives any consolations to her henchmen. And I, who crave no knighthood, shall write no more. I shall write no more. Already I feel myself to be a trifle outmoded. I belong to the Beardsley period. Younger men, with months of activity before them, with fresher schemes and notions, with newer enthusiasm, have pressed forward since then. *Cedo junioribus*. Indeed, I stand aside with no regret. For to be outmoded is to be a classic, if one has written well. I have acceded to the hierarchy of good scribes and rather like my niche.

Some Words on Royalty

In the memoirs of Count ——, privately printed last year, you will find, if you can gain access to them, many secrets told in a sprightly, yet most authoritative, manner; little that is incredible, little that is not amazing, nothing refutable. The Count has cast upon *la haute politique*, that stage without footlights, many lurid 'limes,' illuminating for us the faces of all the players and even enabling us to understand something of the plot. For years the trusted Minister of the late Emperor —— of ——, the Count has much court-lore to communicate, and is terribly frank about the master whom he served so faithfully until, in 188–, he was ousted from favour by the machinations of a jealous and not too scrupulous cabal. I, who had always been taught to regard this monarch as a wise, gifted, and courageous gentleman, if not actually as a hero, am pleasantly shocked to find him designated with such unkind terms as *'fainéant,'*—the memoirs are written in the Volapuk of diplomacy—and *'roi de paille,'* and *'petit bonhomme à tête montée.'* Indeed, it is undoubtedly when he is describing the life and the character of the Emperor that my author is at his most intimate, his best. Seldom has so realistic a portrait of a modern monarch been painted for our pleasure. Much as we talk and read about royal personages, we know really less about them than about any other kind of human beings. We see the princes of our country caracoling past us in pageants, illustrious monsters whose breasts are all agleam and aglimmer with the symbols of fifty victories at which they were not present, and bunt with enough ribandry to trick forth fifty dairy-maids for a fair. We tell ourselves that beneath all their frippery they are human beings. We have heard that one is industrious, another is genial, another plays the fiddle or collects stamps. And then, maybe, we see them at Newmarket, and we know that, for all the elaborate simplicity of their tweeds and billycocks, they are not as we are, but, rather, creatures of another order, 'specimens of an unrelated species.' We note the curious uniformity of their faces, almost wondering whether they are masked. Those heavy, handsome, amiable, uninteresting and uninterested faces, are they indeed (not masks but) true mirrors of souls which a remote and esoteric life has gradually impoverished? We know that there is a crimson drugget which underlies their every footstep from the cradle to the mausoleum; we know that their progress is beneath an awning, along that level drugget, through an unbroken avenue of bare and bowed heads. They cannot mingle with their fellows. They are kept from all contact with realities. For them there is no reciprocity, no endeavour, no salt of life. 'It is a miserable State of Minde,' wrote a philosopher who was also a courtier, 'to have few Things to desire and many Things to feare. And yet that commonly is the case of Princes.' Fear kept human the Princes of other days. We have taken away their fear now, and we still leave them no loophole for desire. What, we might well wonder, will be the descendants of this race apart, of these men who neither marry nor give in marriage save among their own order? Would anyone choose to be born, in their purple, to their life of morbid and gaudy humdrum? Better, surely, to be thrown, like the ordinary child, into a life of endeavour, with unforeseen chances of success or failure. It is this scroll of chances that makes life tolerable, makes it wonderful. The life of every royal person in England begins and must needs end on the same high, smooth plane. But who shall cast the horoscope of an ordinary child? Who knows the vicissitudes of his journey?

Be he suckled in a pit, or in a castle on a mountain, who shall prophesy the level of his last bed? Cast him up naked to the pit's edge, send him in purple down the wide steps of his father's castle, you know not how long he shall fare in the gloom or light of his origin, nor whither, and by what hostelries, he shall pass. He may come to a dark woodland, where, all night long, the ferns snap under the feet of elusive Dryads, and the moon is privy to the whole grief of Philomel. He may never leave that gentle labyrinth of leaves, or he may tarry there but for one night. Mocked and footsore, he may shuffle along the highways, till he come to that city whose people stone him or make him ruler over them. Exile or empery may be his, flowers or ashes, an aureole or a noose. There are seas for his drowning, and whirlwinds for his overwhelming, and sheer rocks for his ascent. He shall clutch and falter and be afraid. No bloodhounds but shall follow swiftly on his track, nor any nets but shall enmesh him. He shall laugh and conquer. He shall prosper in a great dominion. In strength and scorn there shall not be his equal. But the slaves whom he tortured shall prick him in his exultation. His wine-cup shall be a cup of gall, and a harpy shall lurk in the canopy of his bridal bed. In the blood of his children they shall bathe him. From a clear sky the lightning shall slant down on him. And the ground shall yawn for him in the garden of his design.

That, despite certain faults of exaggeration, is a piece of quite admirable prose; but let it not decoy the reader from consideration of the main theme. Count ——, whose memoirs are my cue, does not seem to have weighed the conditions of royal life. Had he done so, he would have cooled his caustic pen in the lymph of charity, and one would have lost many of his most delightful *mots* and anecdotes. He simply records, out of the fulness and intimacy of his knowledge, many suggestive facts about a monarch in whom a royal environment had not paralysed the ordinary, bright instincts of human nature. In recording with gusto the little strategies used by his master in the pursuit of fun or the flight from duty, the Count moves his reader to tears rather than to laughter.

One of his anecdotes I must really make known, not merely because it is a good sample and deals with a famous incident, but also because it has a suggestive symbolism of its own. Many of my readers can remember the sensation caused in the spring of a late seventy by the attempted assassination of Emperor ——. As his Imperial Majesty was being driven out of the palace gates for his daily progress through the capital, a man in the crowd fired at him with a revolver. The miscreant was immediately seized, and, but for the soldiery, would have been torn limb from limb. 'Luckily,' wrote Reuter's correspondent, 'the Emperor, who was accompanied as usual by Count —— and an aide-de-camp, was untouched. As so often happens in such cases, the assassin, doubtless through excitement, entirely missed his aim. The remarkable thing was the coolness and courage displayed by the Emperor. So far from evincing any alarm, he continued to salute the crowd on either side, smilingly as ever, as though nothing at all had happened; nor was his drive in any way curtailed. As the news spread, a vast crowd of people collected round the palace, and the Emperor, in answer to their continued cheers, at length appeared upon the balcony and bowed repeatedly.'

In the light of the Count's version the Emperor's 'coolness and courage' are somewhat discounted. It seems that, about three years before, the Emperor had declared that he was going to give up the custom of the daily drive: he hated driving, he hated saluting, he hated being stared at. The Count represented to him how unwise it would be to disappoint the people. Finding the Emperor obstinate in his distaste, he conceived the idea of a waxen figure, made in the likeness of his master, with practicable joints worked by interior mechanism. The Emperor promised to endure his drives for the present, and,

70

after secret negotiations with a famous firm in England (conducted by the Count himself, who came over incognito), the
figure was completed and duly delivered at the Imperial
Palace. It was so constructed that, when wound up, it turned
its head slowly from side to side, with a slight bend of the
body, raising its hand in salute. It was considered an admirable likeness, though the Count declares that '*la figure était un
peu trop distinguée.*' At any rate, arrayed as a Colonel of the
—— Dragoons and driven quickly through the capital, it was
good enough to deceive the Emperor's loyal subjects. As I
need hardly say, it was at this automaton that the revolver was
fired. According to the memoirs, the Emperor himself, in a
false beard, was standing near the assassin, and was actually
arrested on suspicion, but managed to escape his captor in the
mêlée and reached the palace in ample time to bow from the
balcony. The Count argues that the only sufferer in the affair
is the poor wretch who was hanged merely for shooting at a
dummy, and who has never even got the credit he deserved
for a very good shot; the bullet pierced right through the
dummy's chest, and, says the Count, had it but lodged one-
eighth of an inch lower down, it must have inevitably stopped
the mechanism.

Even if the whole of this tale be but the naughty figment of
a favourite in disfavour, it is, at any rate, suggestive. A mob
doffing its head-gear, day after day, to a dummy! How easily,
after all, could one get a dummy so constructed as to hold a
levée or sit through an opera, to open a bridge or lay a stone
'well and truly.' There are some persons who would fain
abolish altogether the institution of royalty. I do not go so far
as they. Our royal family is a rather absurd institution, no
doubt. But then, humanity itself is rather absurd. A State can
never be more than a kindergarten, at best, and he who would
fain rule men according to principles of right reason will fare
no better than did poor dear Plato at Syracuse. Put the dream

71

of the *doctrinaire* into practice, and it will soon turn to some
such nightmare as modern France or modern America. Indeed,
fallacies and anomalies are the basis of all good government.
A Crown, like a Garter, implies no 'damned merit'; else were
it void of its impressive magic for most creatures. Strictly,
there is no reason why we should worship the House of
Hanover more than we worship any other family. Strictly,
there was no reason why the Children of Israel should bow
down before brazen images. But man is not rational, and the
spirit of idolatry is strong in him. And, if you take away his
idol, that energy which would otherwise be spent in kotowing
will probably be spent in some less harmless manner. In every
free public there is a fund of patriotic emotion which must,
somehow, be worked off. I may be insular, but I cannot help
thinking it better that this fund should be worked off, as in
England, by cheering the members of the royal family, rather
than by upsetting the current ministry, as in France.

The main good of royalty, then, and the justification of those
fabulous sums of money that we sacrifice annually for its support,
lie in its appeal to that idolatrous instinct which is quite unmoved
by the cheap and nasty inmates of the Elysée or of the White
House. In this century we have greatly restricted the sphere
of royal power, insomuch that royalty cannot, as it once could,
guide directly the trend of politics: politically, it does but 'act
by its presence.' But one should not forget that a Court is for
ornament, as well as for use. A capital without a Court, be
the streets never so beautiful, is even as a garden where the
sun shines not. As a flock of sheep without a shepherd, so is
the Society that has no royal leader to set its fashions, chasten
its follies, or dignify its whims with his approval. Gaiety, wit,
beauty, some measure even of splendour, may be compassed
in the *salons* of a republic; but distinction comes not in save
with one who must be received at the foot of the staircase. In
fact, royalty is indispensable: we cannot spare it. But, you

may well ask, are we justified in preserving an institution which ruins the lives and saps the human nature of a whole family? What of those royal victims whom we sacrifice to our expediency? I have suggested that royal functions could be quite satisfactorily performed by automata made of wax. There, I think, lies the solution of our difficulty. Perhaps, even now, did we but know, it is the triumphs of Tussaud at whose frequent sight our pulses beat with so quick an enthusiasm. If it is so, I do not blame our royal family for its innocent subterfuge. I should welcome any device to lighten the yoke that is on their necks. I should be glad if more people would seriously examine the conditions of royalty, with a view to ameliorating the royal lot. Would that every one could gain access to the memoirs of Count ——! They might serve as an excellent manual, containing, as they do, so much that is well-observed. But they are so frankly written that they cannot, I fear, be made public before many, many years have elapsed. Perhaps the brief trumpet-note which I have sounded will be enough to rouse humanitarianism, in the meantime.

Groups of Myrmidons

It is a custom of the little clubs at Oxford to be photographed in every Summer Term. Some of them are antique enough to have existed before photography, and so the port, lineaments, and costume of their first members have gone unrecorded for their pious successors. But the club which claimed me had been initiated in days not so remote; it dated, indeed, only from a decade which had seen, mourned, and forgotten the demise of the daguerreotype. Our club-room was a gallery of 'groups' that told the full story of the past and illuminated with the pale rays of sentiment every page of our worn minute-book. Often, as I sat there, gazing round at those records of forgotten faces and modes discarded, my heart was softened towards photography. Surely, in some dark corner of every camera, there lurks a good fairy who enchants every plate as it is exposed. The enchantment may not be, is not, obvious at first—it does not make the developed plate less hideous, less harshly mechanical. Yet the enchantment is there, nevertheless, and, after the lapse of years, it fills the photograph with a curious grace. The very coarseness and crudity of the process are turned to good use. In very virtue of its unintelligent realism, an old photograph gains a pathos which is to be found in old pictures. When we look at an old picture, be it bad or good, our minds turn to him by whom, rather than to him of whom, it was painted. But, while the painter always obtrudes himself on us in his work, and there is no escaping him, who in the world ever thinks about a photographer? It is because it was

74

done in an instant, that every 'group' seems so real and, despite
the conventionality and stiffness of its attitudes, so natural.
We know what a Babel of talk and laughter had been suspended only an instant before, and how it burst forth again
with double force an instant later, when the camera had done
its duty. The 'groups' of my old club are things snatched from
the very heart of Oxford. There is symbolism in the fact that
nearly all of them have the same background—the window of
a certain room on the ground floor of the New Buildings. The
men vanish, and their places are filled by others. Whiskers
and velveteens give way gradually to flannels and smooth
faces. But 'wines' are conducted with the same ceremonial as
when *Up in a Balloon, Boys!* and *Have you seen the Shah?* were
the liefest ditties. Bonfires are eternally renewed in the same
grey quadrangles and are danced round in the same old
fashion. Windows are smashed with relentless regularity,
though their frames last for ever. The dawn creeps through
them and still finds young Bacchanals cursing one another,
with the same old freedom, over unlimited loo. Aristotle, with
his Ethics, and Plato, with his Republic, cudgel the brains of
every successive generation. Academic gowns are cut exactly
as they were when men wore them over doublets and trunk-
hose. The youngest freshman will be gathered, hereafter, to
his fathers, and on that night Great Tom will still be droning
the hundred-and-one strokes he droned on the night when the
hoariest of the dons was born into the world. No! Oxford
never changes. It is well that the undergraduates, the bits of
coloured glass in the kaleidoscope, do not realize their
transience. Every wall frowns down on them, but they pay no
heed. They are full of youth and buoyancy and self-importance
—masters of the whole place. Certainly these old photographs
are pregnant with irony and with pathos. They are eloquent
as the walls themselves. See how the President always wears
a very grave aspect, befitting his tremendous office, and sits in

the middle of the group, facing the camera with arms imperially folded!

Where are they, these leaves which the unsparing wind has scattered? Where are they, the outcast citizens of this gay and tiny commonwealth, these old 'Myrmidons'? *O male dilapsos*, how, in what real warfare, are they, who loitered here in Capua, faring now? In the Book of Fate (*q.v. passim*), the name and address, the past and future, of every one of them, I doubt not, are duly entered. But, for me, as for all who have never dipped into that fascinating work of reference, there is a pleasure in studying these old groups, in guessing the character of every member from his port and lineaments, and learning in the light of his peculiar costume the vain whims of Fashion. In my time, it was seldom that any of these old members came among us. The lapse of less than a lustre means a new generation in Oxford, and, after the departure of all his comrades' comrades, Oxford is but a husk of barren and bitter-sweet memories to its revisitor. Now and again, however, some wistful bearded stranger would appear in our midst, revealing himself as one of our own order, and would dine at the house-dinner on Sunday. We respected him as a man of the world; he envied us for what we were. But our jokes were as incomprehensible to him, I fancy, as were his anecdotes tedious to us. We were very polite to him indeed. But 'young barbarians' are far too happy to be sentimental, and their hearts do not go out readily to their forerunners. They know not Joseph, and they don't want to know him. For myself, I rather liked Joseph, and would listen with real pleasure to his reconstruction of the past, and encourage him to tell me of those whose aspects the photographer had handed down to me. Thus, with the help of an occasional Joseph, I came to know a little about some of those old heroes; how they had bearded the bursar, or bonneted the proctor, or slipped the porter; how one had since been killed in Afghanistan, and another had been twice married, and another was sheep-farming in Australia and 'doing very well'; and another had 'gone under,' as Joseph had always foreseen. For the most part, they seemed to have cast behind them for ever their days and nights of gambling and hard drinking, and to have become decent, prosperous gentlemen who lived in various counties and met each other seldom. Those others of whom I heard nothing have probably met a similar fate. I seem to see every one of them as a portly, begaitered man sitting in his study, with the 'groups' of his period hanging upon the wall behind him. Of all the Myrmidons, there is only one who has achieved great fame. The 'group' in which he appeared (prepare, reader, to be disappointed—I could not afford the cheap jest you are expecting) is dated 1870, and the name inscribed under his figure is a name which has passed already, with its dead bearer, into the political history of our time. There he sits, the future leader of the Fourth Party and of the House itself, among his fellow-Myrmidons—a moody boy, dressed, after the fashion of the day, in a suit of very large checks. His hands are resting on a white hat, and, though the photograph is somewhat faded, one can discern on his upper lip the faint presage of that moustache which was to give the cue to in-numerable caricaturists. Except his eyes, there is no feature to distinguish him from any of the young bloods around him. But we, who know now all that Fate was holding for him, cannot but pause, with some stirring of our hearts, under this portrait of him as he was at Merton. How quickly the laurel-branch was to grow for him; how greatly to flourish; to be cut off how untimely, yet not before all the leaves on it were withered! Would one rather be, as, I take it, they who were here portrayed with him still are, sane, healthy, happy, stupid, obscure, or have led, like that young tribune, a short, swift life of triumph and tragedy? Which of these two lots would one rather draw? Which is the luckier? I do not know.

A Cloud of Pinafores

The modish appanage of Beauty in her barouche is not a spaniel, now, but a little child. The wooden wicket which, even in my day, barred the top-most of the stairs, has been taken off its hinges, and the Jewels roll down into Cornelia's drawing-room at will. Cornelia's callers are often privileged to a place at nursery-tea. The bread and butter is not cut thick, as in their day, and that old law, which made it precedent of cake, seems to have been rescinded. Nor is any curb set on little tongues. Cornelia and her callers grow glad in the frolic of artless *aperçus*. They are sick of *sèvres* and scandal. Only the fresh air of the nursery can brace their frail bodies and keep up their weary eyelids.

Yes! A casual optimist might proclaim that the Victorian Era is harking back to its first simplicity. At the risk of saddening him, I must suggest that he examine his opinion. I fear there are flaws in it. Between the Georgian and Victorian Eras came an interval of transition. Society was tired of its old pleasures, but did not quite abandon them. It still masked and gambled, but only a little in a quiet way, as by force of habit. It was really resting. And when William died and was succeeded by a young Queen, herself a symbol of all simplicity, it was ready for renunciation. It had regained its old strength, was strong enough to be simple. In the gradual years, after the Queen-widow had withdrawn herself, ceding the supremacy to her eldest son, Society slipped into its old ways. Surfeit came in due course. Men and women sought refuge in bizarre fashions: æstheticism, slumming, Buddhism.

But now surfeit has come again. They look around. What is
left to them? Simplicity! But they are tired. There is no
interval for rest. Also, they are less strong physically, in-
tellectually stronger, than were their grandparents; not strong
enough, not weak enough, to be simple. But ah! there is one
thing left to them. They can, at least, contemplate simplicity.
There is a nursery somewhere at the top of most houses. 'Let
the children be brought down to lunch! Let us have tea with
the children!'

One may trace, in the evolution of modern literature, a
fairly exact parallel. But the cross-lines which connect the
corresponding points on either side of this parallel are
uniformly oblique. It may be too much to say that Life always
copies Literature, yet certainly Literature is always a little
ahead of Life. Thus we find that Pre-Raphaelite poets were at
work before 1880, that Sir Walter Besant, too, was already
bustling about the slums, and Buddha peeping from many a
first, second, and third volume. Nor did Stevenson write his
Child's Garden, nor Pater his *Child in the House*, to meet a
demand which was as yet uncreated; nor, indeed, did either
work attract any attention. But, now that children are
booming, the publishers and the reviewers are all agog.
Stevenson and Mr. Walter Crane are honoured with reprints.
'Mr. Pater's most exquisite achievement is *The Child in the
House*'—'*Sentimental Tommy* is the supreme outcome of Mr.
Barrie's genius'—'Mr. Kenneth Grahame's *Golden Age* is
indeed a Golden Book.' Yes! Children are in vogue. The
clear carillon of the coral-and-bells has penetrated even to the
back-benches of the Divorce Court, and the assiduous, unimportant authors, who sat scribbling there, have torn up their
flimsies and scuttled forth at the summons. *Faut être dans le
mouvement*, poor creatures! For a while, they will make the
scrap-screen their background. And if their heroine wear a
pinafore, not a strange tea-gown 'of some clinging green

material,' and prefer jam to laudanum and make-believe to introspection, I, for one, shall see nothing lamentable in the difference. Save as a guide to tendencies of the period, such writers do not interest me much.

I find a far subtler and more amusing guide in a little book entitled *The Children*, and written by a lady whose talent is pre-eminently, almost painfully, adult. Here, indeed, is a perfect example of our tecnolatry, our delight in the undirected oddities of children, our wistful effort to understand them as they are. We are told of a boy who, at the seaside, 'assumes a deep, strong, and ultra-masculine note, and a swagger in his walk, and gives himself the name of his father's tallest friend. The tone is not wholly manly; it is a tone of affairs, and withal careless; it is intended to suggest business, and also the possession of a top-hat and a pipe, and is known in the family as his "official voice".' How nicely sympathetic is this analysis of a mood which, in my day, was called 'showing-off,' and was invariably discouraged! ' "Listen to him, mother," ' says a little girl, ' "he's trying to talk like God. He often does." ' In the unkind 'sixties this little girl would have been sent to bed as a blasphemer. In my day, she would have been told that what she said was irreverent, and that irreverence was a very terrible thing. She 'seemed thoroughly to understand the situation' is our author's comment. Indeed the modern feeling is that the child can do no wrong. Its very slips in grammar, its inconsequence, its confusion of names, are all treasured with a loving care and imbued with an exquisite significance. 'A nut-brown child of five was persuading another to play. "Oh come," she said, "and play with me at new maid." ' Formerly, no amount of nut-brownness would have saved her from an explanation that the game was called 'old' maid; as it is, I am quite sure she was kissed for her mistake by whatever grown-up person overheard it.

Certainly, I should be the last to deprecate the vogue of

children, if I were to regard it from a selfish and superficial standpoint. For if there be one thing which people love more than to read about children, now, it is to read what children write. Had I not been *parmi les jeunissimes*, I should not have made the little success I have. The public does not, I suppose, care greatly whether I write well nor whether my premises and conclusions be correct. But it knows me to be a child author, and likes to picture me at my desk, dressed in black velveteen, with legs dangling towards the floor. If I filled this book with the pot-hooks and hangers, which were, till recently, my sole literary output, the public would be just as well pleased. But, though this sparkling tide flows all in my favour, I cannot quite approve of it. To me, there seems some danger in the prevalent desire to observe children in their quiddity, to leave them all to their own devices and let them develop their own natures, swiftly or slowly, at will. Perhaps I am bigoted and old-fashioned, out of touch with the time. But I must confess that, sometimes, my heart does even hark back to those stern old Georgian or Early Victorian days, when nurseries were governed in a spirit of blind despotism. Children were not then recognized as human creatures. They were a race apart; savages that must be driven from the gates; beasts to be kept in cages; devils to whose voices one must not listen. Indeed, the very nature of children was held to be sinful. Lies and sloth, untidiness and irreverence, and a tendency to steal black currant jam, were taken to be its chief constituents. And so all nurseries, as one may learn from old books or from the oral tradition, were the darkened scene of temporal oppression, fitfully lighted with the gaunt reflections of hell-fire. How strange a picture is to be found in those books of 'cautionary verses for children,' irrelevantly entitled *The Daisy* and *The Cowslip*. Anything less flower-like than their tone could not be easily conceived. The good children who move through their pages are the merest puppets, worked by the monstrous autocrat, Mamma, whilst the bad children, placed there as foils, are the most mechanical of drones and dunces. Never once does the authoress betray the briefest wish to treat children objectively. Yet, curious though it seem to modern ideas, she typifies the parents of her period.

Children were not neglected in those days. Their parents' sedulous endeavour was to force them up to a standard of mature conduct. They were taught that only their elders were good, and they were punished always in so far as they behaved childishly. See, even, how they were dressed! Miss Caroline, when she walked out, was framed in a crinoline, and she shaded her ringlets with a minute parasol, whilst Master Richard, her brother, in nankeen trousers, was a small replica of his papa. Later, in the 'seventies and 'eighties, before the Child, as such, was cared for, we see the little girl still tricked out in the latest fashion of maturity, and the little boy masquerading as a highlander or as a sailor. Nowadays, they are both put into the limpest, simplest 'things'. The 'nineties wish children to be children, and nothing more. If—to take but one of the many pregnant comparisons suggested by *The Daisy* or *The Cowslip*—a little girl of this period be suffering toothache, she is coaxed, by all manner of sweet means, to the dentist's chair. Her fears could not anger anyone. She is a child. But read the 'cautionary verses' about two sisters, Miss Clara and Miss Sophie, who 'both had faded teeth.' Miss Clara, like a good grown-up lady, realized that a short wrench were as nothing to such prolonged agony. Miss Sophie held back, trembling. No one reasoned with her. She was suffered to be a foil to the adult fortitude of her sister, whose

> *teeth returned quite fresh and bright,*
> *Whilst Sophie's ached both day and night.*

These are a type of the verses that were written for children of the last generation, as *The Fairchild Family* is a type of the

prose. Even in books like *Struwelpeter* the elements of terror
were lurking everywhere. When children came into the
scheme of a novel, they were, with few exceptions, prigs like
Little Nell and Paul Dombey; dreary abstractions, foredoomed to the earliest of death-beds. In fact, real children
were pariahs. That, you will say, was horrible and inhuman
of their elders. It was. But I am inclined to think that, for the
children themselves, it was a far more wholesome state of
things. For the inherent nature of childhood is far brighter
than the inherent nature of maturity. Childhood has no alien
responsibilities, it is free from all the bitterness of knowledge
and of memory, is careless and hopeful. So that, if the nursery
be turned into a free republic and be rid of its old gloom and
vigilant authority, it must be the scene of absolute happiness,
and its children, when the time comes for them to leave it, will
be appalled by the serious side of life. Finding no pleasure in
a freedom which they have always had, incapable of that self-
control which long discipline produces, they will become
neurotic, ineffectual men and women. In the old days there
could have been no reaction of this kind. The strange sense of
freedom was a recompense for less happiness of heart. Children
were fit for life.

Even from the standpoint of those elders, to whose jaded
longing for simplicity the new form of education must be traced,
there is great reason for misgiving. For it is probable that the
effort to keep children simple by leaving them free, will but
exterminate simplicity, at last. It is only oppression that can
keep human beings as they are. Oppression never crushes
natural instincts. All history proves that it does but intensify
them. Wronged races are always primitive. Left to themselves, they develop. If Home Rule were granted, the Irish
would soon lose their irresponsible gaiety, which centuries of
oppression have preserved for them. Indeed, that is perhaps
the most valid argument against Home Rule. Miss Caroline,

likewise, and Master Richard, driven to bay by their elders, set their back against the nursery wall and were simple to the last. But Jock and Millicent, encouraged in all their childishness, having but their own natures to think of, will very soon become self-conscious. 'Whenever I can't stop laughing I have only to think of home.' These words were written by a little boy from his first boarding-school, and are quoted in *The Children*. So you see that introspection has set in already, and soon every high-chair will hold its lisping Rousseau or Marie Bashkirtseff. And soon there will be no more simplicity to contemplate. And what will a jaded world, straining at its tether, do then? Personally, I should like to think that this passion for simplicity was the sign of a lessening complexity. But wishes beget poor thoughts. I write what I believe to be true about this Victorian era. Good has been followed by evil, evil by the love of mysteries, the love of mysteries by the love of simple things. Observe that I write no fool's prattle about *le fin du siècle*. A phase of social evolution happens to coincide with a certain point in the kalendar. That, of course, is a mere chance. But we may be allowed to laugh, when we see that this century, for which Science promised a mature perfection, is vanishing in a white cloud of pinafores.

Aubrey Beardsley

To all who knew him, and to all who did not know him but are lovers of lineal art, Aubrey Beardsley's death has been the occasion for much sorrow, an irreparable loss. But there is, I think, some consolation in the thought that he did not die suddenly. Though he died, a great artist, in his first youth, and at the very opening of life, as life is usually reckoned, Fate did not deal with him unfairly, did not take him, as she has taken others, with a kind of brutal treachery, before the fulfilment of all the work that was in him. From his quite early boyhood, Aubrey Beardsley had known quite well that his life would inevitably be a short one, and it was to this knowledge, partly, that we owe the great range of his achievement in art. Fate had given him a prematurity of power that was in accurate ratio to the appointed brevity of his life, and, in the exercise and the development of his genius, Aubrey Beardsley never rested. He worked on always, with a kind of desperate courage, and with a degree of force and enthusiasm that is given only to the doomed man. He knew that he had no time to lose. At the age when normal genius is still groping for its method, he was the unerring master of his method. He died, having achieved masterpieces, at an age when normal genius has as yet done little of which it will not be heartily ashamed hereafter. Normal genius is in no hurry. If it be struck down suddenly before its prime, it leaves no great legacy to us: we can only rail against Fate.

But Aubrey Beardsley was bound to die young. All his friends knew that as well as he did. The only wonder was that the fine thread of his life was not severed sooner. I remember that when I first saw him I thought I had never seen so utterly frail a creature—he looked more like a ghost than a living man. He was then, I believe, already in an advanced stage of pulmonary consumption. When I came to know him better, I realized that it was only by sheer force of nerves that he contrived to sustain himself. He was always, whenever one saw him, in the highest spirits, full of fun and of fresh theories about life and art. But one could not help feeling that as soon as he were alone he would sink down, fatigued and listless, with all the spirit gone out of him. One felt that his gaiety resulted from a kind of pride and was only assumed, as who should say, in company. Perhaps one underrated his strength. When he was alone, he must have worked at his drawings almost without intermission. It is a curious thing that none of his visitors ever found him at work, or saw any of his rough sketches, or even so much as his pen, ink, and paper. It was his pose to appear as a man of leisure, living among books. Certainly, he seemed to have read, and to have made his reading into culture, more than any man I have ever met; though how he, whose executive industry was so great, managed to read so much, is a question which I have never quite solved: I can only suppose that he read very rapidly. The literature of the Restoration and of the Eighteenth Century had always especially appealed to him. He delighted (oddly enough) in Voltaire. He was supposed to have read the whole of the *Comédie Humaine*, and he had all the modern schools of France at his finger-tips. He was a good Latin scholar, too, though ill-health had curtailed his schooldays, and he had practically had to teach himself all that he knew. His conversation had always the charm of scholarship. Though not less modest than are most young men, he had strong opinions on most subjects, and he expressed himself with clear precision, and with wit. But he had not the physical strength which is necessary to the really great or inspiring talker. With him, there was always the painful sense of effort. I remember an afternoon I spent with him, at his house in Cambridge Street, soon after *The Yellow Book* was started. He was in great form, and showed even more than his usual wit and animation, as he paced up and down the room, talking, with all his odd, abrupt gestures, about one thing and another, about everything under the sun. I am a very good listener, and I enjoyed myself very much. Next day I heard that his mother and his sister and a doctor had been sitting up with him till daybreak. He had been seized, soon after I had left, with a terribly violent attack of hæmorrhage, and it had been thought, more than once, that he could not live through the night. I remember, also, very clearly, a supper at which Beardsley was present. After the supper we sat up rather late. He was the life and soul of the party, till, quite suddenly, almost in the middle of a sentence, he fell fast asleep in his chair. He had overstrained his vitality, and it had all left him. I can see him now, as he sat there with his head sunk on his breast: the thin face, white as the gardenia in his coat, and the prominent, harshly-cut features; the hair, that always covered his whole forehead in a fringe and was of so curious a colour—a kind of tortoiseshell; the narrow, angular figure, and the long hands that were so full of power.

Last month, when Beardsley's death was announced in the newspapers, the general public must have read the news with some surprise. The 'Beardsley Boom,' as it was called, had begun with *The Yellow Book*, and it had ceased with *The Savoy*, and Beardsley had, to all intents and purposes, been forgotten by the general public. For more than a year, he had been living in this or that quiet place to which invalids are sent. There were no new 'Beardsley posters' on the London hoardings. The paragraphists of the London Press gradually let him be. His book of fifty collected drawings created no outcry, for

even the book-reviewers could no longer assert that he did not
know how to draw, and the tattlers at tea-parties had said all
they had to say about him long ago, and had found other
subjects for their discussion. But, while it lasted, how fierce
the 'Beardsley Boom' had been! The public, as I need hardly
say, never admired Beardsley's drawings. It thought them
hideous. If the 'Beardsley woman' could have been incarnated,
she would have been singularly unattractive. Then how could
anyone admire her on paper? Besides, she was all out of
drawing. Look at her arm! Beardsley didn't know how to
draw. The public itself could draw better than that. Nevertheless, the public took great interest in all Beardsley's work,
as it does in the work of any new artist who either edifies or
shocks it. That Beardsley's really did shock the public, there
can be no doubt. There can be equally little doubt that the
public like being shocked, and sympathy would, therefore, be
superfluous. But, at the same time, there are, of course, people
who do honestly dislike and deplore the morbid spirit that
seemed to inspire Beardsley's work, and at such people I
should not wish to sneer—on the contrary, I respect their
feeling, which I know to be perfectly genuine. Nor would I
seek to deny that in Beardsley's work—more especially in
some of his early work—there is much that is morbid. But it
must be remembered that, when he first began to publish his
drawings, he had hardly emerged from that school-boy age
when the mind is generally apt to brood on unpleasant subjects,
and much of his work, which some people regarded as the sign
of a corrupt nature, was really the outcome of a perfectly
normal phase of mind, finding an abnormal outlet through
premature skill in art. I think, too, that he had a boyish delight
in shocking people, and that it was often in mere mischief that
he chose, as in many of his grotesques for the *Bon-Mots* series,
to present such horribly ugly notions. Many of those who
knew Beardsley only through his general work imagined that

he must be a man of somewhat forbidding character. His powerful, morbid fancy really repelled them, and to them the very beauty of its expression may have seemed a kind of added poison. But I, or anyone else who ever saw him at his home, knew that whatever was morbid in his work reflected only one side of his nature. I knew him to be of a kindly, generous, and affectionate disposition; a devoted son and brother; a very loyal friend.

He lived, when I first saw him and till some two years later, in Cambridge Street, where he shared a house with his mother and sister. Here, every Thursday afternoon, was held a kind of little *salon*, which was always well attended. Aubrey himself was always present, very neatly dressed, handing round cake and bread-and-butter, and talking to each of his mother's guests in turn. There were always three or four new drawings of his passed from hand to hand, and he was always delighted with praise from any of his friends. I think it was at these little half-formal, half-intimate receptions that one saw him at his best. With all his affectations, he had that inborn kindliness which is the basis of all good manners. He was essentially a good host.

I have mentioned his grotesques for the volumes of *Bon-Mots*. These, if I am not mistaken, were among his very earliest published drawings, and simultaneously with them he was working at that great task, the illustration of the *Morte d'Arthur*, on which he spent such a wealth of skilful and appropriate fancy. In the drawings for the *Morte d'Arthur* he was still working, of course, under the influence of Sir Edward Burne-Jones—an influence which was oddly balanced by that of Japanese art in the drawings which he did, at this period, for his own pleasure, and of which *La Femme Incomprise* is a good example. The well-known drawings which, later, he made for *The Yellow Book* were, with their black masses, and very fine lines, arrived at through simplification of the method in *La Femme Incomprise*. These were the drawings that first excited the wrath of the general public and of the book-reviewers. Most of the qualified art-critics, also, were very angry. They did not know what to make of these drawings, which were referable to no established school or known method in art. Beardsley was not at all discouraged by the contempt with which his technique was treated. On the contrary, he revelled in his unfavourable press-cuttings, knowing how little they signified. I think it was in the third number of *The Yellow Book* that two pictures by hitherto-unknown artists were reproduced. One was a large head of Mantegna, by Philip Broughton; the other, a pastel-study of a Frenchwoman, by Albert Foschter. Both the drawings had rather a success with the reviewers, one of whom advised Beardsley 'to study and profit by the sound and scholarly draughtsmanship of which Mr. Philip Broughton furnishes another example in his familiar manner.' Beardsley, who had made both the drawings and invented both the signatures, was greatly amused and delighted.

Meanwhile, Beardsley's acknowledged drawings produced a large crop of imitators, both here and in America. Imitators are the plague to which every original artist is exposed. They inflict the wounds which, in other days, the critics were able to inflict. With the enormous increase of the Press and the wide employment of ignorant and stupid writers, bad criticism has become so general that criticism itself has lost its sting, and the time when an artist could be 'snuffed out by an article' is altogether bygone. Nowadays, it is only through his imitators that an artist can be made to suffer. He sees his power vulgarized and distorted by a hundred apes. Beardsley's *Yellow Book* manner was bound to allure incompetent draughtsmen. It *looked* so simple and so easy—a few blots and random curves, and there you were. Needless to say, the results were appalling. But Beardsley was always, in many ways, developing and modifying his method, and so was always ahead of his apish retinue. His imitators never got so far as to attempt his later manner, the manner of his *Rape of the Lock,* for to do that would have required more patience and more knowledge of sheer drawing than they could possibly afford. Such a design as the 'Coiffing' which came in a late number of *The Savoy,* and which has often seemed to me the most exquisite thing Beardsley ever did, offered them no possible short-cut to talent. To trace the sequence of technical phases through which Beardsley passed, would be outside the scope of this brief essay. But I should like to remind my readers that, as he grew older, he became gradually more 'human,' less curious of horrible things. Of this tendency the best example is perhaps his 'Ave atque Vale,' in *The Savoy.* Nothing could be more dramatic, more moving and simple, than the figure of that Roman who mourns his friend. The drawing was meant to illustrate one of Catullus' Odes, which Beardsley himself has thus rendered:

> By ways remote and distant waters sped,
> Brother, to thy sad grave-side am I come,
> That I may give the last gifts to the dead
> And vainly parley with thine ashes dumb;
> Since she who now bestows and now denies
> Hath ta'en thee, hapless brother, from mine eyes.
>
> But lo! these gifts, the heirlooms of past years,
> Are made sad things to grace thy coffin-shell,
> Take them, all drenchèd with a brother's tears,
> And, brother, for all time, hail and farewell!

These lines, which seem to me no less beautiful than the drawing itself, were written shortly before Beardsley left England for the last time. On the eve of his departure, he was received by Father Sebastian into the Catholic Church, to which he had long inclined. His conversion was no mere passing whim, as some people supposed it to be; it was made from true emotional and intellectual impulse. From that time to his death he was a pious and devout Catholic, whose religion consoled him for all the bodily sufferings he underwent. Almost to the very last he was full of fresh schemes for work. When, at length, he knew that his life could but outlast a few more days, he awaited death with perfect resignation. He died last month, at Mentone, in the presence of his mother and his sister.

Thus ended this brief, tragic, brilliant life. It had been filled with a larger measure of sweet and bitter experience than is given to most men who die in their old age. Aubrey Beardsley was famous in his youth, and to be famous in one's youth has been called the most gracious gift that the gods can bestow. And, unless I am mistaken, he enjoyed his fame, and was proud of it, though, as a great artist who had a sense of humour, he was, perhaps, a little ashamed of it too, now and then. For the rest, was he happy in his life? I do not know. In a fashion, I think he was. He knew that his life must be short, and so he lived and loved every hour of it with a kind of jealous intensity. He had that absolute power of 'living in the moment' which is given only to the doomed man—that kind of self-conscious happiness, the delight in still clinging to the thing whose worth you have only realized through the knowledge that it will soon be taken from you. For him, as for the schoolboy whose holidays are near their close, every hour—every minute, even—had its value. His drawing, his compositions in prose and in verse, his reading—these things were not enough to satisfy his strenuous demands on life. He was himself an accomplished musician, he was a great frequenter of concerts, and seldom, when he was in London, did he miss a 'Wagner night' at Covent Garden. He loved dining out, and, in fact, gaiety of any kind. His restlessness was, I suppose, one of the symptoms of his malady. He was always most content where there was the greatest noise and bustle, the largest number of people, and the most brilliant light. The 'domino room' at the Cafe Royal had always a great fascination for him: he liked the mirrors and the florid gilding, the little parties of foreigners and the smoke and the clatter of the dominoes being shuffled on the marble tables. Yet, though he took such a keen delight in all the manifestations of life, he himself, despite his energy and his high spirits, his frankness and thoughtfulness, seemed always rather remote, rather detached from ordinary conditions, a kind of independent spectator. He enjoyed life, but he was never wholly of it.

This kind of aloofness has been noted in all great artists. Their power isolates them. It is because they stand at a little distance that they can see so much. No man ever *saw* more than Beardsley. He was infinitely sensitive to the aspect of all things around him. And that, I think, was the basis of his genius. All the greatest fantastic art postulates the power to see things, unerringly, as they are.

The Spirit of Caricature

Last night, very vividly, I dreamed a most preposterous dream.

On the pillowed verge of sleep, I had been propounding to myself an old vexatious question: Why is true caricature so rare and so unpopular in England? The delicious art of exaggerating, without fear or favour, the peculiarities of this or that human body, for the mere sake of exaggeration—why can it not be naturalized among us? A certain Italian artist did, indeed, in the late 'sixties, come and try to force it on us. Awhile, from him, we had true caricatures. We did not take kindly to them. We thought them offensive and 'not like.' The pressure of our English atmosphere gradually overbore that temerarious alien. Before the close of the 'seventies he had begun to draw caricatures of a mild and gentlemanly kind, suitable to the susceptibilities of a mild and gentlemanly nation. He was succeeded by one who frankly eschews the art of caricature, to the gratification of every one, and does always a charming portrait, with a playful touch adventured here and there if his sitter be not very eminent, nor very ugly, nor of noble birth. There are others—men of wit, accomplished draughtsmen—who design symbolical cartoons or make rough sketches with the purpose of ridiculing the members of one or other of the two great political parties. In them caricature comes of a moral impulse. It is not the sheer desire and irresponsible lust for bedevilling this or that human body; and it is, accordingly, not successful as caricature; nay! it is not caricature at all. The public believes it to be

caricature, and forgives the perpetrators of it because they are
evidently strenuous partisans—*quia multum amaverunt.* Are
there any other pretenders to the art? Can one point to any
one who dares. . . . Can one find. . . . But the poppies
were nodding to my eyelids. I was asleep. . . .

I knew not how, by whose prayers, the national conversion
had been made. But there was no doubt of the fact that that there
had arisen a sudden and widespread demand for true caricature.
Meetings had been held in all the principal cities. Even the
rural districts were clamorous. The Government, bowing
beneath the storm, had caused to be hewn, and to be imposed
upon the vacant pedestal in Trafalgar Square, a statue of Carlo
Pellegrini, in atonement for England's evil influence on him.
Moreover, in the waste places of South Kensington had been
builded a vast 'School of National Caricature'. The edifice
was complete now. It was a dream (within a dream) of
electric lamps, hot-water-pipes, skylights, cocoanut-matting,
and all else that is supposed to evoke and foster artistic
sensibilities in the young. Royalty had opened it. Archi-
piscopacy had blessed it. Hundreds of the young had enrolled
as students. Still something was lacking. There was no
professor. The country was being scoured, scoured
stringently for a suitable person. They had not yet found
any one possessed of the true spirit of caricature, any one
carrying forward the tradition imported and dropped by
Pellegrini. I began to feel uncomfortable. I knew that I,
as a last resource, should be 'approached,' with a view to my
acceptance of the post. And here, sure enough, was the grey-
bearded deputation approaching me. With the horrible
impotence of the dream-stricken, I was unable to run away.
Vainly I strove to warn them off. Vainly I was arguing with
them. I was pointing out to them that Pellegrini was a great
executant, that my own technique was so vague as to disqualify
me for the honour thrust upon me. They replied that only

the *spirit* of the caricaturist was essential, and that only in my work did it burn. Blushing, I demonstrated that the creative artist was the last person who should be employed as teacher. Able to do the trick himself, he had no pathetic desire to see it done by others. 'That's how it's done!'—the smiling conjuror's formula—was all he could vouchsafe. He had no enthusiasm for teaching. The sterile lovers of an art, they were the proper teachers of it. They wanted to see the trick done, and would see that it was done. 'Besides,' I added, 'they alone know *how* it can be done. The creative artist works by instinct: he knows not how, by what mystic secret of soul and hand, his work evolves itself. He does not care to know. He has no theories. He can formulate no rules. The conjuror could, if he would, lay bare his processes; but the artist, never. The only people who can show how to do things are the people who cannot do them.' 'No doubt,' said the spokesman; 'but it is our national custom to appoint as teachers the artists who have done things. It inspires confidence. False confidence, no doubt; but still confidence.' 'Then,' I cried, 'our system of art schools is a sham; and I, for one, will not fatten on it.' 'It is a wholesome sham,' was the answer. 'The aim of our art schools is not (we admit this in confidence) to produce artists. Artists can be produced only by themselves. Art-training is simply a means of keeping young persons out of mischief. As such, it is necessary to the common-weal. This new craze for the art of caricature is a chance which we could not afford to miss. We are determined to make the best use of it. But we are helpless without a Professor. Young persons must not be fobbed off with a mere dummy. They *must* have an ornament to look up to. Come! We appeal to your civic sense. South Kensington is waiting for you. So is England. The future of the race may depend on your answer. Be a man!' In sheer weariness I consented. The deputation smiled itself out. I was to deliver the inaugural address to the students at nine o'clock next morning. What was I to say? Was there anything to be said? I looked through a portfolio of my own drawings, wondering how they had been done, or what rules could be deduced from them. (It was a painful dream.) Somehow at length, under stress of necessity, with infinite trouble, I hewed out a few first principles, a few hints. . . . The scene dissolved, dissolved into cocoanut-matting and hot-water-pipes. I was about to address the students. Their wide-open eyes and mouths made me horribly nervous. I cleared my throat, loudly, so loudly that I awoke.

My first sensation was one of intense relief. But this presently gave way to resentment that all my labour in the preparation of the address had been so much labour lost. I could recollect more or less exactly the notes I had made. Hating waste, why should I not expand them for a magazine? Here, then, is the gist of what I would have said to those phantom students. I do not suppose it will be illuminative. What I said to that phantom deputation about the futility of tuition by a creative person is really quite true. However, their reply (that the public loved such tuition) was equally true. So I need ask no one's pardon.

As people do sometimes make passionate demands for a thing without knowing at all what it is, I was not going to assume that my pupils knew the nature of true caricature. I was going to start with my definition: the art of exaggerating, without fear or favour, the peculiarities of this or that human body, for the mere sake of exaggeration. I was, then, going to deal with the two reasons for the unpopularity of such portraits—(*a*) the impression that they imply in their maker irreverence and cruelty, (*b*) the impression that they bear little or no resemblance to their originals. The second impression can hardly be cured. It is the result of inherent lack of imagination. Caricature, as I shall demonstrate anon, demands acute imagination from its beholders. The first impression may be gently argued away. A well-known art critic once chid me in print because I 'never hesitated to make a good man ridiculous.' Why should I? Caricature implies no moral judgment on its subject. It eschews any kind of symbolism, tells no story, deals with no matter but the personal appearance of its subject. Therefore, the caricaturist, though he may feel the deepest reverence for the man whom he is drawing, will not make him one jot less ridiculous than he has made another man whom he despises. To make the latter ridiculous gives him no moral pleasure: why should it give him any moral pain to make ridiculous the former? He imports into his vision of the former nothing which is not there: why should he subtract anything from his vision of the latter? He portrays each surface exactly as it appears to his distorted gaze. 'For the mere sake of exaggeration,' I said. But he does not, even, make conscious aim at exaggeration. He does not say, 'I will go for this "point" or that.' If he did, he would be no caricaturist. He exaggerates instinctively, unconsciously. 'But,' you might urge, 'when he finds that the result is pain to his subject's friends and joy to his subject's enemies, he ought to desist from his art.' Maybe, if either the pain or the joy were reasonable, were justified. But they are not. Both are foolish. All that can be expected of the artist is that he should demonstrate their folly from time to time. Even that is rather much to expect of a man passionately absorbed in his own work.

The friends of a man are pained by a caricature of him because they think it will make him despicable to other people; his enemies rejoice for the same reason. They could not harbour a sillier fallacy. Such laughter as may be caused by a caricature is merely æsthetic. It corresponds with such tears as are shed at sight of a very beautiful statue. I do not pity Venus when I see her statue in its chamber at the Louvre; yet

there are tears in my eyes. I do not despise Disraeli when I
look at Pellegrini's picture of him; yet I laugh. It is even so
with any one else who is affected by beauty and by absurdity.
If caricature affected us at all towards its subject, it would
affect us favourably towards it. Tragedy, said Aristotle,
purges us of superfluous awe, by evocation, and comedy likewise purges us of superfluous contempt. Even so might
idealism of a subject purge us of superfluous awe for it, and
caricature purge us of superfluous contempt. If the sight of
Pheidias' masterpiece ministered to our reverence for Venus,
she would pass out of our minds as we passed from the gallery.
If the sight of Pellegrini's Disraeli satisfied our hostility
towards Disraeli himself, we should forgive him all. Indeed,
does nothing of the kind happen? This theory of purgation
has a dangerous charm for me. I have often been tempted to
attribute the Romans' decline in faith to the fair statues of gods
and goddesses imported from Greece by victorious generals.
The extraordinary preponderance of ugly men among those
who have shaped the world's history—may it not be due to the
chance they gave to the contemporary caricaturists? No no;
let me be sensible. Caricature never has had moral influence
of any kind.

The 'chances' given by ugliness! Do not misunderstand
this phrase. Do not mistake me to mean that there is any
such thing as a 'good subject' or a 'bad subject' for caricature.
There are obvious subjects and devious subjects. A short
man is a more obvious subject than a tall man, for shortness is
held to be in itself ridiculous, and thus the uninspired caricaturist will prefer to draw short men. Most caricaturists,
being uninspired, have followed this line of less resistance; and
thus has arisen the foolish convention of a head invariably
bigger than its body. By the man in the street caricature
would probably be defined as the art of putting a big head upon
a little body. Indeed, so strong is the convention that it

affected even Pellegrini, Daumier, and other masters. To you, thoughtful reader, I need hardly point out that in a caricature of a tall man the head ought to be not magnified but diminished. The big-head convention would be all very well if caricature were no more than μίμησις τῶν φαυλοτέρων. But the true art of caricature is much more than that. The master of it never discriminates his subjects, has no preferences. He cares no more whether his subject be tall or short, grotesque or comely, than whether he be a 'good' man or a wicked. He is able to strike as ridiculous effects from the exaggeration of a handsome face and fine figure as from the exaggeration of a street-boy's butt. Hermes or Caliban—it is all one to him. Superficially, indeed, you might guess that Hermes would give him less trouble than Caliban. Sir Willoughby Patterne was said by his creator to be 'so correctly handsome that a slight unfriendly touch precipitated him into caricature.' Truly, the more sublime the subject the more easily may it be burlesqued. But there is a vast difference between burlesque and caricature. Mr. Meredith has confused the two things. Burlesque consists in application of incongruity. Caricature consists merely in exaggeration. The one works from without its subject, the other from within. To burlesque a statue of Hermes, you need but put a top hat on its head. To caricature it, you must exaggerate its every limb and feature. To caricature Sir Willoughby Patterne would have needed the hand of a master. The process of striking a ridiculous effect would have been far more difficult in his case than in the case of an already absurd-looking man. That is what I mean when I speak of 'obvious and devious subjects.' When I object to the notion of 'good and bad subjects,' I mean that handsomeness *can* be made as ridiculous as ugliness. You ask me, 'How about a subject who is neither handsome nor ugly?' In that case, merely, it is the lack of features that must be exaggerated. Through intensification

100

of its nullity, such a subject may be made as ridiculous as any other.

Perfect burlesque may be achieved with a touch. The perfect caricature (be it of a handsome man or a hideous or an insipid) must be an exaggeration of the whole creature, from top to toe. Whatsoever is salient must be magnified, whatsoever is subordinate must be proportionately diminished. The whole man must be melted down, as in a crucible, and then, as from the solution, be fashioned anew. He must emerge with not one particle of himself lost, yet with not a particle of himself as it was before. And not only must every line and curve of him have been tampered with: the fashion of his clothes must have been re-cut to fit them perfectly. His complexion, too, and the colour of his hair must have been changed, scientifically, for the worse. And he will stand there wholly transformed, the joy of his creator, the joy of those who are privy to the art of caricature. By the uninitiated he will not be recognized. Caricature, being so drastic in its methods, demands in its beholders a keen faculty of imagination, as I have said.

The perfect caricature is not a mere snapshot. It is the outcome of study; it is the epitome of its subject's surface, the presentment (once and for all) of his most characteristic pose, gesture, expression. Therefore I should not advise any young caricaturist (however quickly perceptive) to rely on one sight of his subject. On the other hand, let him not make too long a delay, inasmuch as too great familiarity blunts impressions. There is another golden rule, which, if he be worth anything at all, he will know without being told it: he must never draw 'from the model.' While he looks at the model, he is bound by the realities of it. He sees everything as it is. He cannot suborn his pencil to magnify or diminish the proportions, to add or abate one jot. In fact, he cannot begin to caricature. It is only in recollection of his subject

101

that the unconscious process of exaggeration begins to work. Let him allow this process to run its course, leisurely, to his finger-tips. Then, not till then, may he clutch his pencil.

The perfect caricature is bold in its execution, simple and ingenuous to its beholder as a wild flower. Of course, in every work of art elimination and simplification are essential. In a caricature they are doubly so. For a caricature is a form of wit, and nothing so ruthlessly chokes laughter as the suspicion of labour. And, even as brevity is the soul of wit, so is a small scale not less necessary than an air of spontaneity to the perfect caricature. Nor can that spirit abide on a large surface. If you have seen either Pellegrini's big painted caricature of Mr. Whistler, or Mr. Whistler's of a certain art-patron, you will not require me to labour this point. Big canvases and oil paints are fit only for 'seriously serious' art. For a serious art which makes frivolity its aim, a sheet of plain foolscap, a pen or pencil, and a little water-colour are the proper media.

The perfect caricature is in itself a beautiful thing. For caricature, not less than for every other art, beauty is a primal condition. The beauty of a work of art lies not at all in the artist's vision of his subject, but in his presentment of the vision. If the ladies on the chocolate-boxes were exactly incarnate, their beauty would conquer the world. If Daumier's senators and deputies were exactly incarnate, life would be intolerable. Yet no discreet patron of art collects chocolate-boxes; and that series by Daumier is one of the loveliest and most precious things in the whole world.

The most perfect caricature is that which, on a small surface, with the simplest means, most accurately exaggerates, to the highest point, the peculiarities of a human being, at his most characteristic moment, in the most beautiful manner.

Looking back at what I have written, I do really think that my inaugural address to those phantom students might have been illuminative.   I am almost sorry that I have materialized it in this essay.   So much knack of exposition and ratiocination as it betrays inclines me to doubt whether my creative power in caricature can be quite so strong as I had supposed.   However. . . .

'Macbeth'

Shakespeare had his short-comings. Love of him does not blind me to his limitations and his faults of excess. But, after all, the man is dead, and I do not wish to emulate that captious and rancorous spirit—inflamed, as it often seemed to me, by an almost personal animosity—in which my predecessor persecuted him beyond the grave. *Nil de mortuis nisi bonum*, say I: else, what is to become of the classics? In that they were directed against one who could not defend himself, I regarded Mr. Shaw's attacks as cowardly; in that Mr. Shaw was a dramatist himself, I regarded them as suspect. Yet would I have heartily approved of them, had I imagined that they would induce managers not to revive certain of Shakespeare's plays quite so frequently. But I have just said that defamation of the dead will tend to destroy the classics. And so it may, if it be used discreetly. And if it do, so much the better for Shakespeare. When a play has become a classic in drama, it ceases to be a play. It may become a classic in literature without any detriment to itself, but, when it becomes also, like *Hamlet* or *Romeo and Juliet* or *Macbeth*, a classic in drama, all, if I may be allowed to say so, is up with it. One of the reasons for the recent success of *Julius Cæsar* was that so few persons had ever seen *Julius Cæsar* acted. The characters and the situations were moving and impressive, were, in a word, dramatic, because, not having seen them more times than one would care to count, one did not know them all by heart; one saw the play as a play and so derived æsthetic pleasure from it. Now that the dramatic qualities of *Julius*

Cæsar have been demonstrated, it will be revived often in various theatres. Seeing how good are the parts of Antony, Brutus and Cassius, eminent actors will always be seizing an opportunity to play them. The thing will become a classic in drama, and one will be able to regard it only as a vehicle for acting. One will be as deadly familiar with the forum-scene as with the screen-scene in *The School for Scandal,* or the balcony-scene in *Romeo and Juliet.* All its dramatic savour will have been lost. Its interest will be merely histrionic:—'Is Mr. * so powerful as ** ?—you never saw ** ? Ah, what a performance! Not so subtle as ***'s perhaps—but oh! the way he said 'Was this ambition?' He just put his hand in his toga and—why, * holds his hand straight in front of him—misses the whole point of it! For my own part, I always thought that, in some respects, ****'s idea—' . . . Nothing could be drearier than this kind of comparative criticism; yet a classic play makes it quite inevitable. The play is dead. The stage is crowded with ghosts. Every head in the auditorium is a heavy casket of reminiscence. Play they never so wisely, the players cannot lay those circumambient ghosts nor charm those well-packed caskets to emptiness. *Hamlet* and *Romeo* and *Macbeth* can be revived, but not in the literal sense of the word: live again they do not, nor will they ever do so, unless all managers—metropolitan, suburban and provincial—enter into a solemn compact not to revive them for a period of (say) thirty years. Give us but time to forget them and their interpreters, and then they will once more be plays. At present they are but so many parts and so many scenes, so many tests and traps for eminent mimes. For the sake of those mimes no less than for the sake of Shakespeare, let all managers forthwith enter into the compact which I have suggested.

Of all Shakespeare's plays, *Macbeth* is, perhaps, the most often enacted. It is the only one that contains two great parts, each of which, susceptible of many interpretations, can be equally well fitted to the temperaments and methods of various mimes. According to Aubrey the play was first acted in 1606, at Hampton Court, in the presence of King James. It is stated that Hal Berridge, the youth who was to have acted the part of Lady Macbeth, 'fell sudden sicke of a pleurisie, wherefor Master Shakespeare himself did enacte in his stead.' One wishes that Aubrey had given some account of the poet's impersonation. It would be amusing to know Shakespeare's own view of the part—more amusing, however, than valuable, for the actor is the interpreter of the dramatist, and the creative artist is always the least competent interpreter of his own work; besides, as I have said, there can be no final or binding interpretation of so complex a part as Lady Macbeth. Different actresses will always act the part in their different ways, and every way will have its champions among the critics, and every champion will have right on his side. Meanwhile, I find the Macbeth controversy rather tedious. Most critics of the latest production have been talking nonsense about the *Zeitgeist* and about neurotic subtlety and Pre-Raphaelitism and all the rest of it, as though the play had hitherto been acted only in the blood-and-thunder convention of Mrs. Siddons. Mere fallacy! We may be sure that 'the gentle poet-philosopher' himself acted in much the same way as Mrs. Patrick Campbell or, for that matter, Miss Ellen Terry. In Pepys' diary, too, there is certain evidence that Mrs. Knipp's famous impersonation was of much the same kind as that which our critics suppose to be a strange phenomenon of 1898. 'Thence to the Cockpitt Theatre,' writes Pepys in the autumn of 1667, 'to witness my dearest Mrs Knipp in the Tragedie of Macbeth, than which as I did this day say to Mr Killigrew I do know no play more diverting nor more worthie to the eye. Did secure a prime place in the pitt, whereof I was glad, being neare under my Ladie Dorset and her good husband. The latter did twice salute me with effusion, and I was pleased to note that those around me perceived this.   Methought Mrs Knipp did never play so fine, specially in the matter of the two daggers, yet without brawl or overmuch tragick gesture, the which is most wearisome, as though an actress do care more to affright us than to be approved.   She was most comickal and natural when she walks forth sleeping (the which I can testify, for Mrs Pepys also walks sleeping at some times), and did most ingeniously mimick the manner of women who walk thus.' Obviously, then, the critics are wrong in regarding Mrs. Campbell's performance as something peculiar to the spirit of this generation.   In the sleep-walking scene, Mrs. Campbell was not 'comickal', but she was very 'natural,' and throughout the play she made her appeal to the sense of beauty and to the intellect rather than to the sense of terror.   Mr. Forbes Robertson acted in a similar way.   Both took the line laid down for them by their natural method.   I thought that both performances were very beautiful.   It does not matter in what method Macbeth and Lady Macbeth be played, so long as they be both played well in the same method.   A violent Lady Macbeth and a gentle Macbeth, or *vice versâ*, would be a nuisance.   Mrs. Campbell and Mr. Forbes Robertson act in perfect harmony.   Mr. Tabor is most admirable as Macduff. Indeed, the whole production is a great success.   I trust that it will be the latest production of *Macbeth* for many years to come.

Hamlet, Princess of Denmark

I cannot, on my heart, take Sarah's Hamlet seriously. I cannot even imagine any one capable of more than a hollow pretence at taking it seriously. However, the truly great are apt, in matters concerning themselves, to lose that sense of fitness which is usually called sense of humour, and I did not notice that Sarah was once hindered in her performance by any irresistible desire to burst out laughing. Her solemnity was politely fostered by the Adelphi audience. From first to last no one smiled. If any one had so far relaxed himself as to smile, he would have been bound to laugh. One laugh in that dangerous atmosphere, and the whole structure of polite solemnity would have toppled down, burying beneath its ruins the national reputation for good manners. I, therefore, like every one else, kept an iron control upon the corners of my lips. It was not until I was half-way home and well out of earshot of the Adelphi, that I unsealed the accumulations of my merriment.

I had controlled myself merely in deference to Sarah herself, not because I regarded the French prose-version of *Hamlet* as an important tribute to Shakespeare's genius. I take that version to have been intended as a tribute to an actress' genius, rather than a poet's. Frenchmen who know enough of our language to enable them to translate Shakespeare know very well that to translate him at all is a grave disservice. Neither into French poetry nor into French prose can his poetry be translated; and, since every element in his work was the direct, inalienable result of his poetry, it follows that any French translation is ruinous. I do not say that this particular translation is unskilful; on the contrary, it seemed to me very skilful indeed. The authors seemed to have got the nearest equivalents that could be got. But the nearest equivalents were always unsatisfactory and often excruciating. 'Paix, paix, âme troublée!' for 'Rest, rest, perturbed spirit!' is a fair sample of what I mean. Save that it reminds one—an accident which the authors could not foresee—of 'Loo, Loo, I love you!' there is no fault to be found with this rendering. It is, I think, as good as possible. But it carries in it no faintest echo nor most shadowy reflection of the original magic. It is thin, dry, cold—in a word, excruciating. The fact is that the French language, limpid and exquisite though it is, affords no scope for phrases which, like this phrase of Shakespeare's, are charged with a dim significance beyond their meaning and with reverberations beyond their sound. The French language, like the French genius, can give no hint of things beyond those which it definitely expresses. For expression, it is a far finer instrument than our language; but it is not, in the sense that our language is, suggestive. It lacks mystery. It casts none of those purple shadows which do follow and move with the moving phrases of our great poets. In order to be really suggestive, a French poet must, like Mallarmé, deliberately refrain from expressing anything at all. An English poet, on the other hand, may be at once expressive and suggestive. That is a great advantage. It is an advantage which none of our poets has used so superbly as Shakespeare. None of our poets has ever given to his phrases shadows so wonderful as the shadows Shakespeare gave to his. In none of Shakespeare's plays, I think, are these shadows so many and marvellous as in *Hamlet*; and the quality of its theme is such that the shadows are more real to us, and reveal more to us, than the phrases casting them. Cut away those shadows, and you cut away that which makes the play immortal—nay! even that which makes it intelligible. One by one, they were cut away by the two talented Parisians who translated *Hamlet* for Sarah. Reluctantly, no doubt. But I am dealing with the translation as I find it, and (despite my colleagues) I must refuse to regard it as a tribute to Shakespeare. The only tribute a French translator can pay Shakespeare is not to translate him—even to please Sarah.

In England, as I suggested some time ago, *Hamlet* has long ceased to be treated as a play. It has become simply a hoop through which every very eminent actor must, sooner or later, jump. The eminent actor may not have any natural impulse to jump through it, but that does not matter. However unsuited to the part he be in temperament or physique, his position necessitates that he play it. I deplore this custom. I consider that it cheapens both Shakespeare's poetry and the art of acting. However, it is a firmly-established custom, and I must leave it to work itself out. But I do, while there is yet time, earnestly hope that Sarah's example in playing Hamlet will not create a precedent among women. True, Mrs. Bandmann Palmer has already set the example, and it has not been followed; but Mrs. Bandmann Palmer's influence is not so deep and wide as Sarah's, and I have horrible misgivings. No doubt, Hamlet, in the complexity of his nature, had traces of femininity. Gentleness and a lack of executive ability are feminine qualities, and they were both strong in Hamlet. This, I take it, would be Sarah's own excuse for having essayed the part. She would not, of course, attempt to play Othello— at least, I risk the assumption that she would not, dangerous though it is to assume what she might *not* do—any more than her distinguished fellow-countryman, Mounet Sully, would attempt to play Desdemona. But, in point of fact, she is just as well qualified to play Othello as she is to play Hamlet. Hamlet is none the less a man because he is not consistently manly, just as Lady Macbeth is none the less a woman for being a trifle unsexed. Mounet Sully could be no more acceptable as Lady Macbeth than as Desdemona. I hope he is too sensible a person ever to undertake the part. He would be absurd in it, though (this is my point) not one whit more absurd than Sarah is as Hamlet. Sarah ought not to have supposed that Hamlet's weakness set him in any possible relation to her own feminine mind and body. Her friends ought to have restrained her. The native critics ought not to have encouraged her. The custom-house officials at Charing Cross ought to have confiscated her sable doublet and hose. I, lover of her incomparable art, am even more distressed than amused when I think of her aberration at the Adelphi. Had she for one moment betrayed any faintest sense of Hamlet's character, the reminiscence were less painful. Alas! she betrayed nothing but herself, and revealed nothing but the unreasoning vanity which had impelled her to so preposterous an undertaking. For once, even her voice was not beautiful. For once . . . but why should I insist? The best that can be said for her performance is that she acted (as she always does) with that dignity of demeanour which is the result of perfect self-possession. Her perfect self-possession was one of the most delicious elements in the evening's comedy, but one could not help being genuinely impressed by her dignity. One felt that Hamlet, as portrayed by her, was, albeit neither melancholy nor a dreamer, at least a person of consequence and unmistakably 'thoro'bred.' Yes! the only compliment one can conscientiously pay her is that her Hamlet was, from first to last, *très grande dame.*

Duse at the Lyceum

I have often wondered why Sydney Smith said he 'would as soon speak disrespectfully of the Equator.' After all, the Equator is a mere geographical expression. It casts no weird spell of awe over mankind. On the contrary, seafarers, when they come to it, put on false noses and play practical jokes. For 'Equator' read 'Duse,' and then the remark has point. There never was an influence so awe-inspiring as Duse. At her coming, all the voices of the critics are hushed. Or rather, they are uplifted in unisonant dithyrambus. The heaven is rent with superlatives. And these are not the bright little superlatives we flick at Sarah—imagine any one calling Duse 'Eleonora'!—but superlatives of a solemn, almost religious, order. The heaven is rent, and the entrances to the theatre are forthwith besieged by great concourses of people who don't know a word of Italian. Night by night, the English public sits solemnly at the Lyceum (having paid higher prices than it pays for a play in its own language), tremendously bored, tremendously edified. Whatever Duse may be in her own country, here she is a national institution, nay! a supernatural phenomenon, making for righteousness. If a fiery chariot were seen waiting outside the stage-door, no one would be much surprised.

Last week I said that I would write about Duse as soon as I had 'seen her whole repertoire.' That sounded a little pompous, perhaps; as though I were loth to deliver judgment until the whole bulk of the evidence had been adduced. As a matter of fact, it was mere cowardly procrastination. I wished to put off the evil hour of confessing that I could not bow down before the demi-goddess. There are three ways of raving about an actress. One way is to rave about her technique; another, to rave about her conception of the part she is playing; another, to rave about her personality. Well! I am debarred from the first way by the simple fact that I know no more Italian than did poor Mrs. Plornish. This disability is the more humiliating for me, in that I am, evidently, the only critic who labours under it. All the other critics understand the language perfectly; else they would not be able to tell us unanimously that Duse's technique is beyond reproach. The technique of acting lies in the relation of the mime's voice, gesture and facial expression to the words by him or her spoken. Obviously, if those words are for you so much gibberish, you cannot pass any judgment on the mime's technique. You look on, and you see certain movements of the mime's face and hands, and you hear certain inflections of the mime's voice, but I defy you to know whether they are the right movements, the right inflections. You have to take them on trust. I am willing to take Duse's technique on trust, but I cannot rave about it: I can but consume myself with envy of my colleagues, and wish I had made a better use of my opportunities for learning Italian. It is of no use to have seen the play previously in a language which one understands. I have seen *Magda* and *The Second Mrs. Tanqueray*, as played by Mrs. Campbell, and have seen them several times. I have seen *Fedora* in English and in French. I have read that tedious effusion, the *Princesse Georges*. But I do not (nor do you) remember more than a few disjointed fragments of the dialogue in any scene, and I do not (nor do you) often manage to 'spot' one of these fragments when the scene is played in an unknown language. If, by some wild chance, I do 'spot' one of them, I am so surprised and excited that I forget to notice the manner of its delivery. Still less, if possible, am I likely to form any personal opinion of Duse's technique in *La Gioconda*, of which there is nothing for me but a synopsis. Let her play in English or in French, and then, no doubt, I shall have the felicity of raving with the best of them.

I come now to the second way of raving: raving about the mime's conception of the part played. Here, of course, the unknown language is no barrier; it is merely a stumbling-block. If you have seen or read the play in a language which you do understand, you will, by dint of ordinary vigilance, be able to form a sound synthetic idea of what the mimes mean the characters to be. I know Magda, Paula, Fedora and the Princesse Georges well enough to praise or disparage an actress' conception of any one of them. I know them well enough to be convinced that Duse has no conception of any one of them. She treats them as so many large vehicles for expression of absolute self. From first to last, she is the same in Fedora as in Magda, in Magda as in Paula, in Paula as in the Princesse Georges, and in the Princesse Georges as in La Gioconda. 'Io son' Io,' in fact, throughout. Her unpainted face, the unhidden grey of the hair over her brows, are symbolic of her attitude. That Paula is a local English type, and the Princesse Georges a local French type, and that accordingly neither of them can be understood and impersonated by an Italian, matters nothing at all to her. She does not make it part of her business to understand and impersonate. It matters nothing to her that even an Italian equivalent for Paula or the Princesse Georges would be outside her range. 'Io son' Io,' and she cares not under what alias she comport herself. La Gioconda (known to me, as I have said, only through a synopsis) happens to be an Italian part, and it happens to suit Duse. It might be well realized otherwise than by her, but it could not, I imagine, be realized so fully. If I had never seen her in any other part, I should have raved about her conception. 'She *is* La Gioconda,' I should have exclaimed. As it is, I can only remark that La Gioconda is she.

This personal pronoun brings me to the third way of raving. Am I overwhelmed by the personality of Duse? Of course, I ought to be—there can be no question of that. But the wretched fact remains that I am not. True, I see power and nobility in her face; and the little shrill soft voice, which is in such strange contrast with it, has a certain charm for me. I admire, too, her movements, full of grace and strength. But my prevailing emotion is hostile to her. I cannot surrender myself, and see in her the 'incarnate womanhood' and 'the very spirit of the world's tears' and all those other things which other critics see in her. My prevailing impression is of a great egoistic force; of a woman overriding, with an air of sombre unconcern, plays, mimes, critics and public. In a man I should admire this tremendous egoism very much indeed. In a woman it only makes me uncomfortable. I dislike it. I resent it. In the name of art, I protest against it. . . . Thus do I, devil's advocate, resume my seat, trusting to the judge to suppress any disturbance in court.

A Cursory Conspectus of G. B. S.

Assuming that Mr. Shaw will live to the age of ninety (and such is the world's delight in him that even then his death will seem premature), I find that he has already fulfilled one half of his life span. Yet is it only in the past seven years or so that he has gained his vogue. One would suppose that so distinct a creature, so sharply complete in himself, must have been from the outset famous. But the fact remains that every morning for some thirty-seven years Mr. Shaw woke up and found himself obscure. Though, of course, his friends and fellow-workers recognized in him a being apart, for the Anglo-Saxon race he did not exist. I have often wondered what was the reason: was it the world's usual obtuseness, or was it that Mr. Shaw was unusually late in development? I had no means of deciding. I did not possess any of Mr. Shaw's early work. Thus very welcome to me is the reprint of a novel* written by Mr. Shaw in the flush of youth. Of the novel itself Mr. Shaw himself evidently thinks no great shakes. For on this excursion he takes with him even more than his usual armful of light baggage—prefaces, notes, appendices, quotations; he has also a new portable dramatic version of his book. And, as he bustles along the platform with these spick-and-span impedimenta in his grasp, he seems hardly to care whether or not that battered old resuscitated trunk of his be thrown into the van. Yet for me that is the real object of interest. I rush to examine it, and tears of joy well up at the sight of

* *Cashel Byron's Profession.* By Bernard Shaw. London: Grant Richards. 1901. 6s.

116

'G. B. S.' printed on it, as on the new hand-baggage, in letters of flame.

Yes! *Cashel Byron's Profession* is quite mature. Mr. Shaw is fully himself in it, and throughout it. It tallies with all his recent work. Such differences as may be found in it are differences of mere surface, due to the fashions of the decade in which it was written, not essential differences in the writer. Apart from them, it might be his latest book. It has all his well-known merits and faults, and who shall say whether his faults or his merits are the more delicious? His own quick strong brain is behind it all, darting through solid walls of popular fallacy to the truths that lie beyond them, and darting with the impetus of its own velocity far beyond those truths to ram itself against other walls of fallacy not less solid. All through the book we hear the loud, rhythmic machinery of this brain at work. The book vibrates to it as does a steamer to the screw; and we, the passengers, rejoice in the sound of it, for we know that tremendous speed is being made. As a passage by steam is to a voyage by sail, so is Mr. Shaw's fiction to true fiction. A steamboat is nice because it takes us quickly to some destination; a sailing-yacht is nice in itself, nice for its own sake. Mr. Shaw's main wish is to take us somewhere. In other words, he wants to impress certain theories on us, to convert us to this or that view. The true creator wishes mainly to illude us with a sense of actual or imaginative reality. To achieve that aim, he must suppress himself and his theories: they kill illusion. He must accept life as it presents itself to his experience or imagination, not use his brain to twist it into the patterns of a purpose. Such self-sacrifice is beyond Mr. Shaw. He often says (and believes) that he is, despite his propagandism, a true delineator of life. But that is one of his delightful hallucinations, due to the fact that his sight for things as they are is weak in comparison with his insight into himself. In fact, Mr. Shaw is not a creator. He cannot see

117

beyond his own nose. Even the fingers he outstretches from
it to the world are (as I shall suggest) often invisible to him.
Looking into his own heart, he sees clearly the world as it
ought to be, and sees (as I have already suggested) further
still. Of the world as it is he sees a clean-cut phantasmagoria,
in which every phantom is his own unrecognized self. When
he describes what he has seen, himself is the one person illuded.
Some novelists fail through being unable to throw themselves
into the characters they have projected. They remain critically
outside, instead of becoming the characters themselves. This
is not the explanation of Mr. Shaw's failure. He does not
stand outside his characters : a man cannot slip his own skin.
Mr. Shaw fails because the characters are all himself, and all
he can do is to differentiate them by 'quick-changes.' But
these disguises he makes in a very perfunctory way—a few
twists of diaphanous gauze, a new attitude, nothing more.
Thus it is in *Cashel Byron*, as in his plays. Take Cashel
himself. Mr. Shaw means to present him as a very stupid
young man with a genius for pugilism. But soon he turns out
to be a very clever young man, with a genius for introspection
and ratiocinatory exposition. These powers are not incompatible with a genius for prize-fighting. But quite incompatible with it are physical cowardice and lack of any sentiment
for the art practised. Mr. Shaw makes Cashel a coward, and
lets him abandon prize-fighting without a pang at the first
opportunity, in order to prove his thesis that prize-fighting is
a mere mechanical business in which neither sentiment nor
courage is involved. As usual he goes further than the truth.
It is untrue that prize-fighters are heroes and artists and
nothing else, as the public regards them. But it is equally
untrue that you can use your fists (gloved or ungloved) without courage, or that any man with supreme natural ability
can care nothing for the channel in which it exclusively runs.
Thus Cashel does not credibly exist for us : he is the victim of

a thesis. Besides, he is Mr. Shaw. So, of course, is Lydia, the heroine, the imperturbable, strong-minded, blue-stock-inged heroine, who, like the rest of Mr. Shaw's heroines, has nothing to do but set every one right—a sinecure, so easily does she do it. The only characters that really illude us are the subordinate characters, of whom we see merely the surfaces and not the souls. Mr. Shaw has a keen eye for superficial idiosyncrasies, and such figures as Mellish and Mrs. Skene are as possible as they are delicious, though even they are always ready to dart out on us and ratiocinate in Mr. Shaw's manner.

After all, it is Mr. Shaw *qu'il nous faut*. My analogy of the steamship was misleading. Though Mr. Shaw's chief aim, indeed, is to proselytize, we enjoy his preaching for its own sake, without reference to conviction. We enjoy for its own sake the process by which he arrives at his conclusions. At least, we do so if we take him in the right way. We must not take him too seriously. An eminent scholar once said to me that what he disliked in Mr. Shaw was his lack of moral courage. I pricked up my ears, delighted: here was a new idea! Urged by me to explain himself, the eminent scholar said 'Well, whenever he propounds a serious thesis of his own, he does so in a jocular vein, not being sure that he is right, and knowing that if he is wrong he will have saved his face by laughing in his reader's'—or words to that effect. I was disappointed. My interlocutor had betrayed simply his incapacity to understand the rudiments of Shawism. The fact that he is a Scotchman, and that Mr. Shaw is an Irishman, ought to have forewarned me. To take Mr. Shaw thus seriously is as inept as to believe (and many folk do believe) that he is a single-minded buffoon. In him, as in so many Irishmen, seriousness and frivolity are inextricably woven in and out of each other. He is not a serious man trying to be frivolous. He is a serious man who cannot help being

frivolous, and in him height of spirits is combined with depth
of conviction more illustriously than in any of his compatriots.
That is why he amuses me as does no one else. The merely
'comic man' is as intolerable in literature as in social inter-
course. Humour undiluted is the most depressing of all phenomena. Humour must have its background of seriousness.
Without this contrast there comes none of that incongruity
which is the mainspring of laughter. The more sombre the
background the brightlier skips the jest. In most of the serious
writers who are also humorous there is perfect secretion
between the two faculties. Thus in Matthew Arnold's controversial writings the humorous passages are always distinct
interludes or 'asides' consciously made, and distinct from the
scheme of the essay. They are irresistible by reason of the
preceding seriousness. But in Mr. Shaw the contrast is still
sharper and more striking. For there the two moods are, as it
were, arm in arm—inseparable comrades. Mr. Shaw cannot
realize his own pertness, nor can he preserve his own gravity,
for more than a few moments at a time. Even when he sets out
to be funny for fun's sake, he must needs always pretend that
there is a serious reason for the emprise; and he pretends so
strenuously that he ends by convincing us almost as fully as
he convinces himself. Thus the absurdity, whatever it be,
comes off doubly well. Conversely, even when he is really
engrossed in some process of serious argument, or moved to
real eloquence by one of his social ideals, he emits involuntarily
some wild jape which makes the whole thing ridiculous—as
ridiculous to himself as to us; and straightway he proceeds to
caricature his own thesis till everything is topsy-turvy; and
we, rolling with laughter, look up and find him no longer on
his head, but on his heels, talking away quite gravely; and this
sets us off again. For, of course, when seriousness and
frivolity thus co-exist inseparably in a man, the seriousness is
nullified by the frivolity. The latter is fed by the former, but,

graceless and vampire-like, kills it. As a teacher, as a propagandist, Mr. Shaw is no good at all, even in his own generation. But as a personality he is immortal.

Henry Irving

One mourns not merely a great actor, who had been a great manager. Irving was so romantically remarkable a figure in modern life, having such a hold on one's imagination (partly because he left so much to it), that his death is like the loss of a legend. As an actor, and as a manager, he had his faults; and these faults were obvious. But as a personality he was flawless—armed at all points in an impenetrable and darkly-gleaming armour of his own design. 'The Knight from Nowhere' was the title of a little book of pre-Raphaelite poems that I once read. I always thought of Irving as the Knight from Nowhere.

That he, throughout his memorable tenancy of the Lyceum Theatre, did nothing to encourage the better sort of modern playwright, is a fact for which not he himself should be blamed. It was the fault of the Lyceum Theatre. In that vast and yawning gulf the better sort of modern drama would (for that it consists in the realistic handling of a few characters in ordinary modern life) have been drowned and lost utterly. On a huge stage, facing a huge auditorium, there must be plenty of crowds, bustle, uproar. Drama that gives no scope for these things must be performed in reasonably small places. A more plausible grievance against Irving, as manager, is that in quest of bustling romances or melodramas he seemed generally to alight on hack-work. I think there can be no doubt that he was lacking in literary sense, and was content with any play that gave him scope for a great and central display of his genius in acting. He did not, of course, invent the 'star' system. But he carried it as far as it could be carried. And the further he carried it, the greater his success. From an artistic standpoint, I admit that this system is indefensible. But theatres, alas! have box-offices; and the public cares far more, alack! for a favourite actor than for dramatic art. Justice, then, blames rather the public than the favourite actor.

It was as a producer of Shakespeare that Irving was great in management. He was the first man to give Shakespeare a setting contrived with archaic and æsthetic care—a setting that should match the pleasure of the eye with the pleasure of the ear. That was a noble conception. Many people object, quite honestly, that the pleasure of the ear is diminished by that of the eye—that spectacle is a foe to poetry. Of course, spectacle may be overdone. Irving may sometimes have overdone it; but he always overdid it beautifully. And there was this further excuse for him: he could not, even had the stage been as bare as a desert, have given us the true music and magic of Shakespeare's verse. He could not declaim. That was one of the defects in his art. His voice could not be attuned to the glories of rhythmic cadence. It was a strange, suggestive voice that admirably attuned itself to the subtleties of Irving's conception of whatever part he was playing. It was Irving's subtle conception, always, that we went to see. Here, again, Irving was an innovator. I gather that the actors of his day had been simple, rough-and-ready, orotund fellows who plunged into this or that play, very much as the water-horse plunges through the reeds. They were magnificent, but they had no pretensions to intellect. Irving had these pretensions, and he never failed to justify them. One missed the music of the verse, but was always arrested, stimulated, by the meanings that he made the verse yield to him. These subtle and sometimes profound meanings were not always Shakespeare's own. Now and again, the verse seemed to yield them to Irving only after an intense effort, and with a rather bad grace. All the parts that Irving played were exacting parts, but he had his revenge sometimes, exacting even more from them. This was another defect in his art: he could not impersonate. His voice, face, figure, port, were not transformable. But so fine was the personality to which they belonged that none cried shame when this or that part had to submit to be crushed by it. Intransformable, he was—multi-radiant, though, He had, in acting, a keen sense of humour—of sardonic, grotesque, fantastic humour. He had an incomparable power for eeriness—for stirring a dim sense of mystery; and not less masterly was he in evoking a sharp sense of horror. His dignity was magnificent in purely philosophic or priestly gentleness, or in the gaunt aloofness of philosopher or king. He could be benign with a tinge of malevolence, and arrogant with an undercurrent of sweetness. As philosopher or king, poet or prelate, he was matchless. One felt that if Charles the Martyr, Dante, Wolsey, were not precisely as he was, so much the worse for Wolsey, Dante, Charles the Martyr. On the other hand, less august types, such as men of action and men of passion, were outside his range, and suffered badly when he dragged them within it. Macbeth had a philosophic side, which enabled Macbeth to come fairly well out of the ordeal. But Romeo's suicide in the vault of Capulet could only be regarded as a merciful release. Unfortunately, though I saw and can remember Irving as Romeo, I never saw him as Hamlet. This is one of the regrets of my life. I can imagine the gentleness (with a faint strain of cruelty), the aloofness, the grace and force of intellect, in virtue of which that performance must have been a very masterpiece of interpretation. I can imagine, too, the mystery with which Irving must have involved, rightly, the figure of Hamlet, making it loom through the mist mightily, as a world-type, not as a mere individual—making it loom as it loomed in the soul of Shakespeare himself—not merely causing it to strut agreeably, littly, as in the average production. Above all, I can imagine how much of sheer beauty this interpretation must have had. Though, as I have said, Irving could not do justice to the sound of blank-verse, his prime appeal was always to the sense of beauty. It was not, I admit, to a sense of obvious beauty. It was to a sense of strange, delicate, almost mystical and un-earthly beauty. To those who possessed not, nor could acquire, this sense, Irving appeared always in a rather ridiculous light. 'Why does he walk like this? Why does he talk like that?' But, for any one equipped to appreciate him, his gait and his utterance were not less dear than his face—were part of a harmony that was as fine as it was strange. And, though the cruder members of the audience could not fall under the spell of this harmony, they were never irreverent until they reached their homes. Never once at the Lyceum did I hear a titter. Irving's presence dominated even those who could not be en-chanted by it. His magnetism was intense, and unceasing. What exactly magnetism is, I do not know. It may be an exhalation of the soul, or it may be a purely physical thing—an effusion of certain rays which will one day be discovered, and named after their discoverer—Professor Jenkinson, perhaps: the Jenkinson Rays. I only know that Irving possessed this gift of magnetism in a supreme degree. And I conjecture that to it, rather than to the quality of his genius, which was a thing to be really appreciated only by the few, was due the unparalleled sway that he had over the many.

In private life he was not less magnetic than on the stage. The obituarists seem hardly to do justice to the intensely interesting personality of Irving in private life. He has been depicted by them merely as a benevolent gentleman who was always doing this or that obscure person a good turn. Cer-tainly, Irving was benevolent, and all sorts of people profited by his generosity. But these two facts are poor substitutes for the impression that Irving made on those who were brought into contact with him. He was always courteous and gracious, and everybody was fascinated by him; but I think there were few who did not also fear him. Always in the company of his friends and acquaintances—doubtless, not in that of his most intimate friends—there was an air of sardonic reserve behind his cordiality. He seemed always to be watching, and watching from a slight altitude. As when, on the first or last night of a play, he made his speech before the curtain, and concluded by calling himself the public's 'respectful—devoted—loving —servant,' with special emphasis on the word 'servant,' he seemed always so like to some mighty cardinal stooping to wash the feet of pilgrims at the altar-steps, so, when in private life people had the honour of meeting Irving, his exquisite manner of welcome stirred fear as well as love in their hearts. Irving, I think, wished to be feared as well as loved. He was 'a good fellow'; but he was also a man of genius, who had achieved pre-eminence in his art, and, thereby, eminence in the national life; and, naturally, he was not going to let the 'good fellow' in him rob him of the respect that was his due. Also, I think, the process of making himself feared appealed to something elfish in his nature. Remember, he was a comedian, as well as a tragedian. Tragic acting on the stage is, necessarily, an assumption; but comedy comes out of the actor's own soul . Surely, to be ever 'grand seigneur,' to be ever pontifically gracious in what he said and in his manner of saying it, and to watch the effect that he made, was all wine to the comedic soul of Irving. He enjoyed the dignity of his position, but enjoyed even more, I conjecture, the fun of it. I formed the theory, once and for all, one morning in the year 1895— the morning of the day appointed for various gentlemen to be knighted at Windsor Castle. I was crossing the road, opposite the Marble Arch, when a brougham passed me. It contained Irving, evidently on his way to Paddington. Irving, in his most prelatical mood, had always a touch—a trace here and there—of the old Bohemian. But as I caught sight of him on this occasion—a great occasion, naturally, in his career; though to me it had seemed rather a bathos, this superimposition of a smug Hanoverian knighthood on the Knight from Nowhere— he was the old Bohemian, and nothing else. His hat was tilted at more than its usual angle, and his long cigar seemed longer than ever; and on his face was a look of such ruminant, sly fun as I have never seen equalled. I had but a moment's glimpse of him; but that was enough to show me the soul of a comedian revelling in the part he was about to play—of a comedic philosopher revelling in a foolish world. I was sure that when he alighted on the platform of Paddington his bearing would be more than ever grave and stately, with even the usual touch of Bohemianism obliterated now in honour of the honour that was to befall him.

Apart from his genuine kindness, and his grace and mag-netism, it was this sense that he was always playing a part— that he preserved always, for almost every one, a certain barrier of mystery—that made Irving so fascinating a figure. That day, when I saw him on his way to Windsor, and tried to imagine just what impression he would make on Queen Victoria, I found myself thinking of the impression made there by Disraeli; and I fancied that the two impressions might be rather similar. Both men were courtiers, yet incongruous in a court. And both had a certain dandyism—the arrangement of their hair and the fashion of their clothes carefully thought out in reference to their appearance and their temperament. And both, it seemed to me, had something of dandyism in the wider, philosophic sense of the word—were men whose whole life was ordered with a certain ceremonial, as courtly functions are ordered. 'Brodribb,' certainly, was an English name; but surely Irving had some strong strain of foreign blood: neither his appearance nor the quality of his genius was that of an Englishman. Possibly, like Disraeli, he had Spanish blood.

Anyhow, his was an exotic mind, like Disraeli's, dominating its drab environment partly by its strength and partly by its strangeness. Both men were romantic to the core, ever conceiving large and grandiose ideas, which they executed with a fond eye to pageantry. And, above all, both men preserved in the glare of fame that quality of mystery which is not essential to genius, but which is the safest insurance against oblivion. It has been truly said that Irving would have been eminent in any walk of life. Had Disraeli the Younger drifted from literature to the footlights, and had Henry Brodribb strayed from the schoolroom into politics, I daresay that neither our political nor our theatrical history would be very different from what it is—except in the matter of dates.

Coquelin's Death

When a man dies quite suddenly in the fulness of his powers, we are apt to think that Fate has been unkind to him. This is a confusion of ideas. Who would not wish, just for his own sake, to die just such a death? The blow by which Fate strikes down a flourishing ordinary man is cruel only in its effect on those who were his friends. When a great man is stricken down untimely, then there is a vast number of people to be condoled with—people deprived, without warning, of a treasure that they had thought would be theirs to enjoy for many years. The death of Coquelin may without hyperbole be described as a blow to the whole educated world. And the blow falls most heavily on those who knew the man himself, not merely because they lose in him a delightful friend or acquaintance, but because they were of all people the least prepared for his death. His air of soundness and robustness behind the footlights was as nothing to what it was in private life. Sixty-eight years old he was, according to the newspapers. It seems impossible. Time had pushed him into middle age, and then had grown tired of the exertion and left him standing there unmolested, privileged, a brilliant fixture. He had the toughness of the peasant, without the tasks that make the peasant grow old. His stout little legs seemed to be rooted in the soil. It was hard to believe that his father had been a baker. One would have said that a bakery was too artificial a place for the production of so earthy and windy a creature as Coquelin. 'Intellectual' though he was, he had no

'nerves' to trouble him. His brain found all the food it needed
in his blood and muscle.

On the stage it was always with his brain alone that he made
his effects. He had observed, and studied, and thought, and
had thought out the exact means of expression. He never let
emotion come between himself and his part—never trusted to
imagination or inspiration. These, indeed, are qualities which
he did not possess. They are incompatible with absence of
'nerves.' And it was, I suppose, because he could never
surrender himself to a part, was always conscious master of it,
that Sarah Bernhardt wrote of him in her memoirs that he was
'plutôt grand acteur que grand artiste.' Certainly, great
emotional acting does demand the power of self-surrender—
is a passive rather than an active business. Coquelin, in his
writings and in his talk, was a sturdy champion of Diderot's
paradox. And Coquelin, in the last act of *Cyrano de Bergerac*,
was a shining refutation of the truth of that paradox. All the
paraphernalia of emotion were in that memorable passage of
acting—were there most beautifully and authentically; but
emotion itself wasn't there; and many a duffer could have
moved us far more than Coquelin did. If Coquelin had been
capable of the necessary self-surrender, he would not have
been the unapproachable comedian that we loved and revered.
It was because his fine brain was absolutely his master that he
stood absolutely alone in his mastery of comedic art.

That he has died on the brink of what he believed would be
his greatest triumph, and of what probably would have been
his greatest triumph, will have seemed to many people an
especially cruel fate for him to have suffered. There is no
doubt that during the past seven years or so the prospect of
Chantecler was the very pivot of his being. He had always
had, very rightly, and very engagingly, an enormous self-
esteem. But its centre of gravity seemed, in the past few years,
to have shifted away from the past and present into the future

—always the immediate future in which 'cette admirable génie,' Rostand, would complete and let go the MS. of *Chantecler*. Years ago, a Frenchman whom I know, and who has a great talent for mimicry, gave me a general 'sketch' of Coquelin saying stridently, with his sculptured elocution, 'Moi, je ne parle jamais de moi; par-ce-que'—whereon followed a series of the most cogent and lucid reasons for Coquelin's avoidance of the topic. Like all the best satire, this satire was based on a sympathetic understanding of its butt. The mimicry could not have been so perfect if the mimic had not been truly fond of Coquelin. In later years he emended his 'sketch': 'Moi, je ne parle jamais de *Chantecler*; par-ce-que'—. It was always mainly of *Chantecler* that Coquelin would talk to me whenever in recent years, and wherever, I had the honour of meeting him. And always it was in Dieppe (whither he went annually) that he talked with greatest unction and élan. Always an expansive man, he seemed to expand beyond measure in Dieppe. The manager of the Casino, M. Bloch, was an old and devoted admirer of him and his art, and always placed at his disposal a suite of rooms on the Casino's terrace. Year by year, Coquelin's first appearance on this terrace was a great occasion, semi-royal, but wholly human; a sight that did one's heart good. Splendid in a brand-new white yachting-cap and a pair of brand-new white shoes, and swinging in his hand a brand-new white umbrella, he came forth into the sunshine—sunshine than which he was more dazzling to the abonnés. 'That's he!' or 'That's him!' whispered the English ones. 'Voilà la saison qui commence,' murmured the French ones, with a smile that failed to conceal awe. And he, 'la saison,' was a picture of happiness, as he stood inaugurally there, with a plump thumb in the arm-hole of his waistcoat, and with his head thrown back at the well-known angle, snuffing the ozone through those great comedic nostrils. After he had stood awhile, he would make his progress along the terrace, flanked on either side by some friend or henchman for whose benefit he talked and talked, slowly, impressively, delightedly. 'Moi, je ne parle jamais de *Chantecler*; parce-que'. . . Now and again he would pause to salute or accost a passing friend, but always thereafter resumed the thread of his discourse. It was a pleasure to watch the splendid mobile mask that was his face; and the pleasure was greater when you yourself were elected as a companion—as a receiver of laws laid down by him in a voice that was like the twanging of a violoncello, and of theories elaborated in a penetrating whisper and with the cunningest of smiles. His manner alone would have sufficed for edification. But it was a strong and subtle brain, Coquelin's, and what he said was always as good as the way he said it. To converse with him might have been rather up-hill work. I fancy he was not a man to encourage interruptions. But I may be wrong. I was never tempted to interrupt; so well worth while was it to listen.

The last time I saw him, which was five months ago, he was fuller than ever of *Chantecler*—the beauties of it, the inspiring difficulties of it. He spoke especially of the scene in which he, as the cock, would call upon the sun to rise, and would address it, as it rose, in a speech of more than a hundred alexandrines. With tremendous relish he recited two or three score of these, but keeping his face absolutely expressionless, and keeping his hands behind his back. For there was the prime glorious difficulty: to hold the audience solely through the voice, since the face and hands would be hidden by the complete outfit of a cock. Once or twice he scraped the ground with his foot. That was the only gesture a cock would have. . . . His little eyes shone and danced with delight as he dilated on 'le besoin d'achever l'impossible.' He declared that Fate had been very good to him in giving him in his old age an absolutely new task, to make him young again. Rostand had all but finished now, at last—only a few more touches to be added by 'cette admirable génie'! The piece would be produced in the autumn—oh yes, for certain.

I admit I was inwardly sceptical about that date. Coquelin himself, through his bitter experience of the coyness of 'cette admirable génie,' may have had doubts, too; but these he would not have admitted even to himself, dear sanguine soul! When autumn passed into winter, and still there was no imminence of *Chantecler*, I was not surprised. But sooner or later, thought I, in this long-drawn contest between a nervous poet and a sanguine actor-burgess the victory would be to the sanguine actor-burgess. Sooner or later—and it turned out to be sooner. Last week I heard that the nervous poet had come out from the Pyrenees, with his wife, and his sons, and his sons' tutor, and his doctor, and his valet, and his chauffeur, and with *Chantecler* itself, and had made his entry into Paris. My heart was glad for Coquelin. I could imagine his look of triumph. I could imagine him throwing off his 'grippe' in a twinkling. . . . Even now I can hardly imagine him dead— dead by such a master-stroke of irony. It seems impossible that Fate should not have spared him to drink the cup she had at last raised to his lips.

A terrible master-stroke, certainly. But terrible for us, not for the man stricken. He died without warning in the midst of his gladness; a death that is to be envied. And who knows that the cup raised to his lips was not a cup of bitterness? 'Achever l'impossible'! Would even Coquelin have achieved it? He might have failed, even he. And that would have, figuratively, broken his heart. Perhaps it is well for him and us that he died as he did die, literally of heart-failure.

The Fire

If I were 'seeing over' a house, and found in every room an
iron cage let into the wall, and were told by the caretaker that
these cages were for me to keep lions in, I think I should open
my eyes rather wide. Yet nothing seems to me more natural
than a fire in the grate.

Doubtless, when I began to walk, one of my first excursions
was to the fender, that I might gaze more nearly at the live
thing roaring and raging behind it; and I daresay I dimly
wondered by what blessed dispensation this creature was
allowed in a domain so peaceful as my nursery. I do not think
I ever needed to be warned against scaling the fender. I knew
by instinct that the creature within it was dangerous—fiercer
still than the cat which had once strayed into the room and
scratched me for my advances. As I grew older, I ceased to
wonder at the creature's presence and learned to call it 'the
fire,' quite lightly. There are so many queer things in the
world that we have no time to go on wondering at the queer-
ness of the things we see habitually. We are lucky when by
some chance we see again, for a fleeting moment, this thing or
that as we saw it when it first came within our ken. We are
in the habit of saying that 'first impressions are best,' and that
we must approach every question 'with an open mind'; but
we shirk the logical conclusion that we were wiser in our
infancy than we are now. 'Make yourself even as a little child,'
we often say, but recommending the process on moral rather
than on intellectual grounds, and inwardly preening ourselves

all the while on having 'put away childish things,' as though clarity of vision were not one of them.

I look around the room I am writing in—a pleasant room, and my own, yet how irresponsive, how smug and lifeless! The pattern of the wall-paper blamelessly repeats itself from wainscote to cornice; and the pictures are immobile and changeless within their glazed frames—faint, flat mimicries of life. The chairs and tables are just as their carpenter fashioned them, and stand with stiff obedience just where they have been posted. On one side of the room, encased in coverings of cloth and leather, are myriads of words, which to some people, but not to me, are a fair substitute for human company. All around me, in fact, are the products of modern civilization. But in the whole room there are but three things living : myself, my dog, and the fire in my grate. And of these lives the third is very much the most intensely vivid. My dog is descended, doubtless, from prehistoric wolves; but you could hardly decipher his pedigree on his mild, domesticated face. My dog is as tame as his master (in whose veins flows the blood of the old cavemen). But time has not tamed fire. Fire is as wild a thing as when Prometheus snatched it from the empyrean. Fire in my grate is as fierce and terrible a thing as when it was lit by my ancestors, night after night, at the mouths of their caves, to scare away the ancestors of my dog. And my dog regards it with the old wonder and misgiving. Even in his sleep he opens ever and again one eye to see that we are in no danger. And the fire glowers and roars through its bars at him with the scorn that a wild beast must needs have for a tame one. 'You are free,' it rages, 'and yet you do not spring at the man's throat and tear him limb from limb and make a meal of him!' and, gazing at me, it licks its red lips; and I, laughing good-humouredly, rise and give the monster a shovelful of its proper food, which it leaps at and noisily devours.

Fire is the only one of the elements that inspires awe. We

breathe air, tread earth, bathe in water. Fire alone we approach with deference. And it is the only one of the elements that is always alert, always good to watch. We do not see the air we breathe—except sometimes in London, and who shall say that the sight is pleasant? We do not see the earth revolving; and the trees and other vegetables that are put forth by it come up so slowly that there is no fun in watching them. One is apt to lose patience with the good earth, and to hanker for a sight of those multitudinous fires whereover it is, after all, but a thin and comparatively recent crust. Water, when we get it in the form of a river, is pleasant to watch for a minute or so, after which period the regularity of its movement becomes as tedious as stagnation. It is only a whole seaful of water that can rival fire in variety and in loveliness. But even the spectacle of sea at its very best—say in an Atlantic storm—is less thrilling than the spectacle of one building ablaze. And for the rest, the sea has its hours of dullness and monotony, even when it is not wholly calm. Whereas in the grate even a quite little fire never ceases to be amusing and inspiring until you let it out. As much fire as would correspond with a handful of earth or a tumblerful of water is yet a joy to the eyes, and a lively suggestion of grandeur. The other elements, even as presented in huge samples, impress us as less august than fire. Fire alone, according to the legend, was brought down from heaven: the rest were here from the dim outset. When we call a thing earthy we impute cloddishness; by 'watery' we imply insipidness; 'airy' is for something trivial. 'Fiery' has always a noble significance. It denotes such things as faith, courage, genius. Earth lies heavy, and air is void, and water flows down; but flames aspire, flying back towards the heaven they came from. They typify for us the spirit of man, as apart from aught that is gross in him. They are the symbol of purity, of triumph over corruption. Water, air, earth, can all harbour corruption; but where flames are, or have been, there is innocence. Our love of fire comes partly, doubtless, from our natural love of destruction for destruction's sake. Fire is savage, and so, even after all these centuries, are we, at heart. Our civilization is but as the aforesaid crust that encloses the old planetary flames. To destroy is still the strongest instinct of our nature. Nature is still 'red in tooth and claw', though she has begun to make fine flourishes with tooth-brush and nail-scissors. Even the mild dog on my hearth-rug has been known to behave like a wolf to his own species. Scratch his master and you will find the caveman. But the scratch must be a sharp one: I am thickly veneered. Outwardly, I am as gentle as you, gentle reader. And one reason for our delight in fire is that there is no humbug about flames: they are frankly, primævally savage. But this is not, I am glad to say, the sole reason. We have a sense of good and evil. I do not pretend that it carries us very far. It is but the tooth-brush and nail-scissors that we flourish. Our innate instincts, not this acquired sense, are what the world really hinges on. But this acquired sense is an integral part of our minds. And we revere fire because we have come to regard it as especially the foe of evil—as a means for destroying weeds, not flowers; a destroyer of wicked cities, not of good ones.

The idea of hell, as inculcated in the books given to me when I was a child, never really frightened me at all. I conceived the possibility of a hell in which were eternal flames to destroy every one who had not been good. But a hell whose flames were eternally impotent to destroy these people, a hell where evil was to go on writhing yet thriving for ever and ever, seemed to me, even at that age, too patently absurd to be appalling. Nor indeed do I think that to the more credulous children in England can the idea of eternal burning have ever been quite so forbidding as their nurses meant it to be. Credulity is but a form of incaution. I, as I have said, never had any wish to play with fire; but most English children are strongly attracted, and are much less afraid of fire than of the dark. Eternal darkness, with a biting east-wind, were to the English fancy a far more fearful prospect than eternal flames. The notion of these flames arose in Italy, where heat is no luxury, and shadows are lurked in, and breezes prayed for. In England the sun, even at its strongest, is a weak vessel. True we grumble whenever its radiance is a trifle less watery than usual. But that is precisely because we are a people whose nature the sun has not mellowed—a dour people, like all northerners, ever ready to make the worst of things. Inwardly, we love the sun, and long for it to come nearer to us, and to come more often. And it is partly because this craving is unsatisfied that we cower so fondly over our open hearths. Our fires are makeshifts for sunshine. Autumn after autumn, 'we see the swallows gathering in the sky, and in the osier-isle we hear their noise,' and our hearts sink. Happy, selfish little birds, gathering so lightly to fly whither we cannot follow you, will you not, this once, forgo the lands of your desire? 'Shall not the grief of the old time follow?' Do winter with us, this once! We will strew all England, every morning, with breadcrumbs for you, will you but stay and help us to play at summer! But the delicate cruel rogues pay no heed to us, skimming sharplier than ever in pursuit of gnats, as the hour draws near for their long flight over gnatless seas.

Only one swallow have I ever known to relent. It had built its nest under the eaves of a cottage that belonged to a friend of mine, a man who loved birds. He had a power of making birds trust him. They would come at his call, circling round him, perching on his shoulders, eating from his hand. One of the swallows would come too, from his nest under the eaves. As the summer wore on, he grew quite tame. And when summer waned, and the other swallows flew away, this one lingered, day after day, fluttering dubiously over the threshold of the cottage. Presently, as the air grew chilly, he built a new nest for himself, under the mantelpiece in my friend's study. And every morning, so soon as the fire burned brightly, he would flutter down to perch on the fender and bask in the light and warmth of the coals. But after a few weeks he began to ail; possibly because the study was a small one, and he could not get in it the exercise that he needed; more probably because of the draughts. My friend's wife, who was very clever with her needle, made for the swallow a little jacket of red flannel, and sought to divert his mind by teaching him to perform a few simple tricks. For a while he seemed to regain his spirits. But presently he moped more than ever, crouching nearer than ever to the fire, and, sidelong, blinking dim weak reproaches at his disappointed master and mistress. One swallow, as the adage truly says, does not make a summer. So this one's mistress hurriedly made for him a little overcoat of sealskin, wearing which, in a muffled cage, he was personally conducted by his master straight through to Sicily. There he was nursed back to health, and liberated on a sunny plain. He never returned to his English home; but the nest he built under the mantelpiece is still preserved, in case he should come at last.

When the sun's rays slant down upon your grate, then the fire blanches and blenches, cowers, crumbles, and collapses. It cannot compete with its archetype. It cannot suffice a sun-steeped swallow, or ripen a plum, or parch the carpet. Yet, in its modest way, it is to your room what the sun is to the world; and where, during the greater part of the year, would you be without it? I do not wonder that the poor, when they have to choose between fuel and food, choose fuel. Food nourishes the body; but fuel, warming the body, warms the soul too. I do not wonder that the hearth has been regarded from time immemorial as the centre, and used as the symbol, of the home. I like the social tradition that we must not poke a fire in a friend's drawing-room unless our friendship dates back full seven years. It rests evidently, this tradition, on the sentiment that a fire is a thing sacred to the members of the household in which it burns. I daresay the fender has a meaning, as well as a use, and is as the rail round an altar. In 'The New Utopia' these hearths will all have been rased, of course, as demoralizing relics of an age when people went in for privacy and were not always thinking exclusively about the State. Such heat as may be needed to prevent us from catching colds (whereby our vitality would be lowered, and our usefulness to the State impaired) will be supplied through hotwater pipes (white-enamelled), the supply being strictly regulated from the municipal water-works. Or has Mr. Wells arranged that the sun shall always be shining on us? I have mislaid my copy of the book. Anyhow, fires and hearths will have to go. Let us make the most of them while we may.

Personally, though I appreciate the radiance of a family fire, I give preference to a fire that burns for myself alone. And dearest of all to me is a fire that burns thus in the house of another. I find an inalienable magic in my bedroom fire when I am staying with friends; and it is at bed-time that the spell is strongest. '*Good* night,' says my host, shaking my hand warmly on the threshold; 'you've everything you want?' 'Everything,' I assure him; 'good *night*.' 'Good *night*.' '*Good* night,' and I close my door, close my eyes, heave a long sigh, open my eyes, draw the arm-chair close to the fire (*my* fire), sink down, and am at peace, with nothing to mar my happiness except the feeling that it is too good to be true.

At such moments I never see in my fire any likeness to a wild beast. It roars me as gently as a sucking dove, and is as kind and cordial as my host and hostess and the other people in the house. And yet I do not have to say anything to it, I do not have to make myself agreeable to it. It lavishes its warmth on me, asking nothing in return. For fifteen mortal hours or so, with few and brief intervals, I have been making myself agreeable, saying the right thing, asking the apt question, exhibiting the proper shade of mild or acute surprise, smiling the appropriate smile or laughing just so long and just so loud as the occasion seemed to demand. If I were naturally a brilliant and copious talker, I suppose that to stay in another's house would be no strain on me. I should be able to impose myself on my host and hostess and their guests without any effort, and at the end of the day retire quite unfatigued, pleasantly flushed with the effect of my own magnetism. Alas, there is no question of my imposing myself. I can repay hospitality only by strict attention to the humble, arduous process of making myself agreeable. When I go up to dress for dinner, I have always a strong impulse to go to bed and sleep off my fatigue; and it is only by exerting all my will-power that I can array myself for the final labours: to wit, making myself agreeable to some man or woman for a minute or two before dinner, to two women during dinner, to men after dinner, then again to women in the drawing-room, and then once more to men in the smoking-room. It is a dog's life. But one has to have suffered before one gets the full savour out of joy. And I do not grumble at the price I have to pay for the sensation of basking, at length, in solitude and the glow of my own fireside.

Too tired to undress, too tired to think, I am more than content to watch the noble and ever-changing pageant of the fire. The finest part of this spectacle is surely when the flames sink, and gradually the red-gold caverns are revealed, gorgeous, mysterious, with inmost recesses of white heat. It is often thus that my fire welcomes me when the long day's task is done. After I have gazed long into its depths, I close my eyes to rest them, opening them again, with a start, whenever a coal shifts its place, or some belated little tongue of flame spurts forth with a hiss. . . . Vaguely I liken myself to the watchman one sees by night in London, wherever a road is up, huddled half-awake in his tiny cabin of wood, with a cresset of live coal before him. . . . I have come down in the world, and am a night-watchman, and I find the life as pleasant as I had always thought it must be, except when I let the fire out, and awake shivering. . . . Shivering I awake, in the twilight of dawn. Ashes, white and grey, some rusty cinders, a crag or so of coal, are all that is left over from last night's splendour. Grey is the lawn beneath my window, and little ghosts of rabbits are nibbling and hobbling there. But anon the east will be red, and, ere I wake, the sky will be blue, and the grass quite green again, and my fire will have arisen from its ashes, a cackling and comfortable phœnix.

Whistler's Writing

No book-lover, I. Give me an uninterrupted view of my
fellow-creatures. The most tedious of them pleases me better
than the best book. You see, I admit that some of them are
tedious. I do not deem alien from myself nothing that is
human; I discriminate my fellow-creatures according to their
contents. And in that respect I am not more different in my
way from the true humanitarian than from the true bibliophile
in his. To him the content of a book matters not at all. He
loves books because they are books, and discriminates them
only by the irrelevant standard of their rarity. A rare book
is not less dear to him because it is unreadable, even as to the
snob a dull duke is as good as a bright one. Indeed, why
should he bother about readableness? He does not want to
read. 'Unopened edges' for him, when he can get them; and,
even when he can't, the notion of reading a rare edition would
seem to him quite uncouth and preposterous. The aforesaid
snob would as soon question His Grace about the state of His
Grace's soul. I, on the other hand, whenever human company
is denied me, have often a desire to read. Reading, I prefer
cut edges, because a paper-knife is one of the things that have
the gift of invisibility whenever they are wanted; and because
one's thumb, in prising open the pages, so often affects the
text. Many volumes have I thus mutilated, and I hope that in
the sale-rooms of a sentimental posterity they may fetch higher
prices than their duly uncut duplicates. So long as my thumb
tatters merely the margin, I am quite equanimous. If I were
reading a First Folio Shakespeare by my fireside, and if the

matchbox were ever so little beyond my reach, I vow I would light my cigarette with a spill made from the margin of whatever page I were reading. I am neat, scrupulously neat, in regard to the things I care about; but a book, as a book, is not one of these things.

Of course, a book may happen to be in itself a beautiful object. Such a book I treat tenderly, as one would a flower. And such a book is, in its brown-papered boards, whereon gleam little gilt italics and a little gilt butterfly, Whistler's *Gentle Art of Making Enemies.* It happens to be also a book which I have read again and again—a book that has often travelled with me. Yet its cover is as fresh as when first, some twelve years since, it came into my possession. A flower freshly plucked, one would say—a brown-and-yellow flower, with a little gilt butterfly fluttering over it. And its inner petals, its delicately proportioned pages, are as white and undishevelled as though they never had been opened. The book lies open before me, as I write. I must be careful of my pen's transit from inkpot to MS.

Yet, I know, many worthy folk would like the book blotted out of existence. These are they who understand and love the art of painting, but neither love nor understand writing as an art. For them *The Gentle Art of Making Enemies* is but something unworthy of a great man. Certainly, it is a thing incongruous with a great hero. And for most people it is painful not to regard a great man as also a great hero; hence all the efforts to explain away the moral characteristics deducible from *The Gentle Art of Making Enemies,* and to prove that Whistler, beneath a prickly surface, was saturated through and through with the quintessence of the Sermon on the Mount.

Well! hero-worship is a very good thing. It is a wholesome exercise which we ought to all take, now and again. Only, let us not strain ourselves by overdoing it. Let us not indulge in it too constantly. Let hero-worship be reserved for heroes. And there was nothing heroic about Whistler, except his unfaltering devotion to his own ideals in art. No saint was he, and nobody would have been more annoyed than he by canonization; would he were here to play, as he would have played incomparably, the devil's advocate! So far as he possessed the Christian virtues, his faith was in himself, his hope was for the immortality of his own works, and his charity was for the defects in those works. He is known to have been an affectionate son, an affectionate husband; but, for the rest, all the tenderness in him seems to have been absorbed into his love for such things in nature as were expressible through terms of his own art. As a man in relation to his fellow-men, he cannot, from any purely Christian standpoint, be applauded. He was inordinately vain and cantankerous. Enemies, as he has wittily implied, were a necessity to his nature; and he seems to have valued friendship (a thing never really valuable, in itself, to a really vain man) as just the needful foundation for future enmity. Quarrelling and picking quarrels, he went his way through life blithely. Most of these quarrels were quite trivial and tedious. In the ordinary way, they would have been forgotten long ago, as the trivial and tedious details in the lives of other great men are forgotten. But Whistler was great not merely in painting, not merely as a wit and dandy in social life. He had, also, an extraordinary talent for writing. He was a born writer. He wrote, in his way, perfectly; and his way was his own, and the secret of it has died with him. Thus, conducting them through the Post Office, he has conducted his squabbles to immortality.

Immortality is a big word. I do not mean by it that so long as this globe shall endure, the majority of the crawlers round it will spend the greater part of their time in reading *The Gentle Art of Making Enemies*. Even the pre-eminently immortal works of Shakespeare are read very little. The average of time devoted to them by Englishmen cannot (even though one assess Mr. Frank Harris at eight hours per diem, and Mr. Sidney Lee at twenty-four) tot up to more than a small fraction of a second in a lifetime reckoned by the Psalmist's limit. When I dub Whistler an immortal writer, I do but mean that so long as there are a few people interested in the sublter ramifications of English prose as an art-form, so long will there be a few constantly-recurring readers of *The Gentle Art*.

There are in England, at this moment, a few people to whom prose appeals as an art; but none of them, I think, has yet done justice to Whistler's prose. None has taken it with the seriousness it deserves. I am not surprised. When a man can express himself through two media, people tend to take him lightly in his use of the medium to which he devotes the lesser time and energy, even though he use that medium not less admirably than the other, and even though they themselves care about it more than they care about the other. Perhaps this very preference in them creates a prejudice against the man who does not share it, and so makes them sceptical of his power. Anyhow, if Disraeli had been unable to express himself through the medium of political life, Disraeli's novels would long ago have had the due which the expert is just beginning to give them. Had Rossetti not been primarily a poet, the expert in painting would have acquired long ago his present penetration into the peculiar value of Rossetti's painting. Likewise, if Whistler had never painted a picture, and, even so, had written no more than he actually did write, this essay in appreciation would have been forestalled again and again. As it is, I am a sort of herald. And, however loudly I shall blow my trumpet, not many people will believe my message. For many years to come, it will be the fashion among literary critics to pooh-pooh Whistler, the writer, as an amateur. For Whistler was primarily a painter—not less than was Rossetti primarily a poet, and Disraeli a statesman. And he will not live down quicklier than they the taunt of amateurishness in his secondary art. Nevertheless, I will, for my own pleasure, blow the trumpet.

I grant you, Whistler was an amateur. But you do not dispose of a man by proving him to be an amateur. On the contrary, an amateur with real innate talent may do, must do, more exquisite work than he could if he were a professional. His very ignorance and tentativeness may be, must be, a means of especial grace. Not knowing 'how to do things,' having no ready-made and ready-working apparatus, and being in constant fear of failure, he has to grope always in the recesses of his own soul for the best way to express his soul's meaning. He has to shift for himself, and to do his very best. Consequently, his work has a more personal and fresher quality, and a more exquisite 'finish,' than that of a professional, howsoever finely endowed. All of the much that we admire in Walter Pater's prose comes of the lucky chance that he was an amateur, and never knew his business. Had Fate thrown him out of Oxford upon the world, the world would have been the richer for the prose of another John Addington Symonds, and would have forfeited Walter Pater's prose. In other words, we should have lost a half-crown and found a shilling. Had Fate withdrawn from Whistler his vision for form and colour, leaving him only his taste for words and phrases and cadences, Whistler would have settled solidly down to the art of writing, and would have mastered it and, mastering it, have lost that especial quality which the Muse grants only to them who approach her timidly, bashfully, as suitors.

Perhaps I am wrong. Perhaps Whistler would never, in any case, have acquired the professional touch in writing. For we know that he never acquired it in the art to which he dedicated all but the surplus of his energy. Compare him with other great modern painters. He was a child beside them.

They, with sure science, solved roughly and readily problems of modelling and drawing and what not that he never dared to meddle with. It has often been said that his art was an art of evasion. But the reason of the evasion was reverence. He kept himself reverently at a distance. He knew how much he could not do, nor was he ever confident even of the things that he could do; and these things, therefore, he did superlatively well, having to grope for the means in the recesses of his soul. The particular quality of exquisiteness and freshness that gives to all his work, whether on canvas or on stone or on copper, a distinction from and above any contemporary work, and makes it dearer to our eyes and hearts, is a quality that came to him because he was an amateur, and stayed with him because he never ceased to be an amateur. He was a master through his lack of mastery. In the art of writing, too, he was a master through his lack of mastery. There is an almost exact parallel between the two sides of his genius. Nothing could be more absurd than the general view of him as a masterly professional on the one side and a trifling amateur on the other. He was, certainly, a painter who wrote; but, by the slightest movement of Fate's little finger, he might have been a writer who painted, and this essay have been written not by me from my standpoint, but by some painter, eager to suggest that Whistler's painting was a quite serious thing.

Yes, that painting and that writing are marvellously akin; and such differences as you will see in them are superficial merely. I spoke of Whistler's vanity in life, and I spoke of his timidity and reverence in art. That contradiction is itself merely superficial. Bob Acres was timid, but he was also vain. His swagger was not an empty assumption to cloak his fears; he really did regard himself as a masteful and dare-devil fellow, except when he was actually fighting. Similarly, except when he was at his work, Whistler, doubtless, really did think of himself as a brilliant effortless butterfly. The pose

148

was, doubtless, a quite sincere one, a necessary reaction of feeling. Well, in his writing he displays to us his vanity; whilst in his painting we discern only his reverence. In his writing, too, he displays his harshness—swoops hither and thither, a butterfly equipped with sharp little beak and talons; whereas in his painting we are conscious only of his caressing sense of beauty. But look from the writer, as shown by himself, to the means by which himself is shown. You will find that for words as for colour-tones he has the same reverent care, and for phrases as for forms the same caressing sense of beauty. Fastidiousness—'daintiness,' as he would have said —dandyishness, as we might well say: by just that which marks him a painter is he marked as a writer, too. His meaning was ever ferocious; but his method, how delicate and tender! The portrait of his mother, whom he loved, was not wrought with a more loving hand than were his portraits of Mr. Harry Quilter for *The World*.

His style never falters. The silhouette of no sentence is ever blurred. Every sentence is ringing with a clear vocal cadence. There, after all, in that vocal quality, is the chief test of good writing. Writing, as a means of expression, has to compete with talking. The talker need not rely wholly on what he says. He has the help of his mobile face and hands, and of his voice, with its various inflexions and its variable pace, whereby he may insinuate fine shades of meaning, qualifying or strengthening at will, and clothing naked words with colour, and making dead words live. But the writer? He can express a certain amount through his handwriting, if he write in a properly elastic way. But his writing is not printed in facsimile. It is printed in cold, mechanical, monotonous type. For his every effect he must rely wholly on the words that he chooses, and on the order in which he ranges them, and on his choice among the few hard-and-fast symbols of punctuation. He must so use these slender means that they shall express all that he himself can express through his voice and face and hands, or all that he *would* thus express if he were a good talker. Usually, the good talker is a dead failure when he tries to express himself in writing. For that matter, so is the bad talker. But the bad talker has the better chance of success, inasmuch as the inexpressiveness of his voice and face and hands will have sharpened his scent for words and phrases that shall in themselves convey such meanings as he has to express. Whistler was that rare phenomenon, the good talker who could write as well as he talked. Read any page of *The Gentle Art of Making Enemies*, and you will hear a voice in it, and see a face in it, and see gestures in it. And none of these is quite like any other known to you. It matters not that you never knew Whistler, never even set eyes on him. You see him and know him here. The voice drawls slowly, quickening to a kind of snap at the end of every sentence, and sometimes rising to a sudden screech of laughter; and, all the while, the fine fierce eyes of the talker are flashing out at you and his long nervous fingers are tracing extravagant arabesques in the air. No! you need never have seen Whistler to know what he was like. He projected through printed words the clean-cut image and clear-ringing echo of himself. He was a born writer, achieving perfection through pains which must have been infinite for that we see at first no trace of them at all.

Like himself, necessarily, his style was cosmopolitan and eccentric. It comprised Americanisms and Cockneyisms and Parisian *argot*, with constant reminiscences of the authorized version of the Old Testament, and with chips off Molière, and with shreds and tags of what-not snatched from a hundred-and-one queer corners. It was, in fact, an Autolycine style. It was a style of the maddest motley, but of motley so deftly cut and fitted to the figure, and worn with such an air, as to become a very gracious harmony.

After all, what matters is not so much the vocabulary as the manner in which the vocabulary is used. Whistler never failed to find right words, and the right cadence for a dignified meaning, when dignity was his aim. 'And when the evening mist clothes the riverside with poetry, as with a veil, and the poor buildings lose themselves in the dim sky, and the tall chimneys become campanili, and the warehouses are palaces in the night, and the whole city hangs in the heavens, and fairyland is before us . . .' That is as perfect, in its dim and delicate beauty, as any of his painted 'nocturnes'. But his aim was more often to pour ridicule and contempt. And herein the weirdness of his natural vocabulary and the patchiness of his reading were of very real value to him. Take the opening words of his letter to Tom Taylor: 'Dead for a ducat, dead! my dear Tom: and the rattle has reached me by post. *Sans rancune*, say you? Bah! you scream unkind threats and die badly . . .' And another letter to the same unfortunate man: 'Why, my dear old Tom, I never *was* serious with you, even when you were among us. Indeed, I killed you quite, as who should say, without seriousness, "A rat! A rat!" you know, rather cursorily . . .' There the very lack of coherence in the style, as of a man gasping and choking with laughter, drives the insults home with a horrible precision. Notice the technical skill in the placing of 'you know, rather cursorily' at the end of the sentence. Whistler was full of such tricks—tricks that could never have been played by him, could never have occurred to him, had he acquired the professional touch. And not a letter in the book but has some such little sharp felicity of cadence or construction.

The letters, of course, are the best thing in the book, and the best of the letters are the briefest. An exquisite talent like Whistler's, whether in painting or in writing, is always at its best on a small scale. On a large scale it strays and is distressed. Thus the 'Ten O'Clock', from which I took that passage about the evening mist and the riverside, does not leave me with a sense of artistic satisfaction. It lacks structure. It is not a roundly conceived whole : it is but a row of fragments. Were it otherwise, Whistler could never have written so perfectly the little letters. For no man who can finely grasp a big theme can play exquisitely round a little one.

Nor can any man who excels in scoffing at his fellows excel also in taking abstract subjects seriously. Certainly, the little letters are Whistler's passport among the elect of literature. Luckily, I can judge them without prejudice. Whether in this or that case Whistler was in the right or in the wrong is not a question which troubles me at all. Enough time has elapsed for me to read the letters simply from a literary standpoint. As controversial essays, certainly, they were often in very bad taste. An urchin scribbling insults upon somebody's garden wall would not go further than Whistler often went. Whistler's mode of controversy reminds me, in another sense, of the writing on the wall. They who were so foolish as to oppose him really did have their souls required of them. After an encounter with him they never again were quite the same men in the eyes of their fellows. Whistler's insults always stuck—stuck and spread round the insulted, who found themselves at length encased in them, like flies in amber.

You may shed a tear over the flies, if you will. For myself, I am content to laud the amber.

The Mote in the Middle Distance

By H*NRY J*M*S

It was with the sense of a, for him, very memorable something
that he peered now into the immediate future, and tried, not
without compunction, to take that period up where he had,
prospectively, left it. But just where the deuce *had* he left it?
The consciousness of dubiety was, for our friend, not, this
morning, quite yet clean-cut enough to outline the figures on
what she had called his 'horizon,' between which and himself
the twilight was indeed of a quality somewhat intimidating.
He had run up, in the course of time, against a good number of
'teasers'; and the function of teasing them back—of, as it were,
giving them, every now and then, 'what for'—was in him so
much a habit that he would have been at a loss had there been,
on the face of it, nothing to lose. Oh, he always had offered
rewards, of course—had ever so liberally pasted the windows
of his soul with staring appeals, minute descriptions, promises
that knew no bounds. But the actual recovery of the article—
the business of drawing and crossing the cheque, blotched
though this were with tears of joy—had blankly appeared to
him rather in the light of a sacrilege, casting, he sometimes
felt, a palpable chill on the fervour of the next quest. It was
just this fervour that was threatened as, raising himself on his
elbow, he stared at the foot of his bed. That his eyes refused to
rest there for more than the fraction of an instant, may be
taken—*was*, even then, taken by Keith Tantalus—as a hint of
his recollection that after all the phenomenon wasn't to be
singular. Thus the exact repetition, at the foot of Eva's bed,
of the shape pendulous at the foot of *his* was hardly enough to

account for the fixity with which he envisaged it, and for which he was to find, some years later, a motive in the (as it turned out) hardly generous fear that Eva had already made the great investigation 'on her own.' Her very regular breathing presently reassured him that, if she *had* peeped into 'her' stocking, she must have done so in sleep. Whether he should wake her now, or wait for their nurse to wake them both in due course, was a problem presently solved by a new development. It was plain that his sister was now watching him between her eyelashes. He had half expected that. She really was—he had often told her that she really was—magnificent; and her magnificence was never more obvious than in the pause that elapsed before she all of a sudden remarked, 'They so very indubitably *are*, you know!'

It occurred to him as befitting Eva's remoteness, which was a part of Eva's magnificence, that her voice emerged some-what muffled by the bed-clothes. She was ever, indeed, the most telephonic of her sex. In talking to Eva you always had, as it were, your lips to the receiver. If you didn't try to meet her fine eyes, it was that you simply couldn't hope to: there were too many dark, too many buzzing and bewildering and all frankly not negotiable leagues in between. Snatches of other voices seemed often to intertrude themselves in the parley; and your loyal effort not to overhear these was com-plicated by your fear of missing what Eva might be twittering. 'Oh, you certainly haven't, my dear, the trick of propinquity!' was a thrust she had once parried by saying that, in that case, *he* hadn't—to which his unspoken rejoinder that she had caught her tone from the peevish young women at the Central seemed to him (if not perhaps in the last, certainly in the last but one, analysis) to lack finality. With Eva, he had found, it was always safest to 'ring off.' It was with a certain sense of his rashness in the matter, therefore, that he now, with an air of feverishly 'holding the line,' said, 'Oh, as to that!'

Had *she*, he presently asked himself, 'rung off'? It was characteristic of our friend—was indeed 'him all over'—that his fear of what she was going to say was as nothing to his fear of what she might be going to leave unsaid. He had, in his converse with her, been never so conscious as now of the intervening leagues; they had never so insistently beaten the drum of his ear; and he caught himself in the act of awfully computing, with a certain statistical passion, the distance between Rome and Boston. He has never been able to decide which of these points he was psychically the nearer to at the moment when Eva, replying, 'Well, one does, anyhow, leave a margin for the pretext, you know!' made him, for the first time in his life, wonder whether she were not more magnificent than even he had ever given her credit for being. Perhaps it was to test this theory, or perhaps merely to gain time, that he now raised himself to his knees, and, leaning with outstretched arm towards the foot of his bed, made as though to touch the stocking which Santa Claus had, overnight, left dangling there. His posture, as he stared obliquely at Eva, with a sort of beaming defiance, recalled to him something seen in an 'illustration.' This reminiscence, however—if such it was, save in the scarred, the poor dear old woebegone and so very beguilingly *not* refractive mirror of the moment—took a peculiar twist from Eva's behaviour. She had, with startling suddenness, sat bolt upright, and looked to him as if she were overhearing some tragedy at the other end of the wire, where, in the nature of things, she was unable to arrest it. The gaze she fixed on her extravagant kinsman was of a kind to make him wonder how he contrived to remain, as he beautifully did, rigid. His prop was possibly the reflection that flashed on him that, if *she* abounded in attenuations, well, hang it all, so did *he*! It was simply a difference of plane. Readjust the 'values,' as painters say, and there you were! He was to feel that he was only too crudely 'there' when, leaning further forward, he laid a chubby forefinger on the stocking, causing that receptacle to rock ponderously to and fro. This effect was more expected than the tears which started to Eva's eyes and the intensity with which 'Don't you,' she exclaimed, 'see?'

'The mote in the middle distance?' he asked. 'Did you ever, my dear, know me to see anything else? I tell you it blocks out everything. It's a cathedral, it's a herd of elephants, it's the habitable globe. Oh, it's, believe me, of an obsessiveness!' But his sense of the one thing it *didn't* block out from his purview enabled him to launch at Eva a speculation as to just how far Santa Claus had, for the particular occasion, gone. The gauge, for both of them, of this seasonable distance seemed almost blatantly suspended in the silhouettes of the two stockings. Over and above the basis of (presumably) sweetmeats in the toes and heels, certain extrusions stood for a very plenary fulfilment of desire. And since Eva *had* set her heart on a doll of ample proportions and practicable eyelids— *had* asked that most admirable of her sex, their mother, for it with not less directness than he himself had put into his demand for a sword and helmet—her coyness now struck Keith as lying near to, at indeed a hardly measurable distance from, the border line of his patience. If she didn't *want* the doll, why the deuce had she made such a point of getting it? He was perhaps on the verge of putting this question to her, when, waving her hand to include both stockings, she said, 'Of course, my dear, you *do* see. There they are, and you know I know you know we wouldn't, either of us, dip a finger into them.' With a vibrancy of tone that seemed to bring her voice quite close to him, 'One doesn't,' she added, 'violate the shrine —pick the pearl from the shell!'

Even had the answering question 'Doesn't one just?' which for an instant hovered on the tip of his tongue, been uttered, it could not have obscured for Keith the change which her magnificence had wrought in him. Something, perhaps, of the bigotry of the convert was already discernible in the way that, averting his eyes, he said: 'One doesn't even peer.' As to whether, in the years that have elapsed since he said this, either of our friends (now adult) has, in fact, 'peered,' is a question which, whenever I call at the house, I am tempted to put to one or other of them. But any regret I may feel in my invariable failure to 'come up to the scratch' of yielding to this temptation is balanced, for me, by my impression—my sometimes all but throned and anointed certainty—that the answer, if vouchsafed, would be in the negative.

Euphemia Clashthought[*]

AN IMITATION OF MEREDITH

In the heart of insular Cosmos, remote by some scores of
leagues of Hodge-trod arable or pastoral, not more than a
snuff-pinch for gaping tourist nostrils accustomed to in-
halation of prairie winds, but enough for perspective, from
those marginal sands, trident-scraped, we are to fancy, by a
helmeted Dame Abstract familiarly profiled on discs of current
bronze—price of a loaf for humbler maws disdainful of Gallic
side-dishes for the tittilation of choicer palates—stands
Clashthought Park, a house of some pretension, mentioned at
Runnymede, with the spreading exception of wings given to it
in later times by Daedalean masters not to be baulked of
billiards or traps for Terpsichore, and owned for unbroken
generations by a healthy line of procreant Clashthoughts, to
the undoing of collateral branches eager for the birth of a
female. Passengers through cushioned space, flying top-speed
or dallying with obscure stations not alighted at apparently,
have had it pointed out to them as beheld dimly for a privileged
instant before they sink back behind crackling barrier of in-
structive paper with a 'Thank you, Sir,' or 'Madam,' as the
case may be. Guidebooks praise it. I conceive they shall be
studied for a cock-shy of rainbow epithets slashed in at the

[*] It were not, as a general rule, well to republish after a man's
death the skit you made of his work while he lived. Meredith, however, was so transcendent that such skits must ever be harmless, and
so lasting will his fame be that they can never lose what freshness
they may have had at first. So I have put this thing in with the others,
making improvements that were needed—M.B. (1912)

target of Landed Gentry, premonitorily. The tintinna-
bulation's enough. Periodical footings of Clashthoughts into
Mayfair or the Tyrol, signalled by the slide from its mast of a
crested index of Aeolian caprice, blazon of their presence, give
the curious a right to spin through the halls and galleries under
a cackle of housekeeper guideship—scramble for a chuck of the
dainties, dog fashion. There is something to be said for the
rope's twist. Wisdom skips.

It is recorded that the goblins of this same Lady Wisdom
were all agog one Christmas morning between the doors of the
house and the village church, which crouches on the outskirt of
the park, with something of a lodge in its look, you might say
more than of celestial twinkles, even with Christmas hoar-
frost bleaching the grey of it in sunlight, as one sees imaged on
seasonable missives for amity in the trays marked 'sixpence and
upwards,' here and there, on the counters of barter.

Be sure these goblins made obeisance to Sir Peter Clashthought, as he passed by, starched beacon of squirearchy, wife
on arm, sons to heel. After him, certain members of the household—rose-chapped males and females, bearing books of
worship. The pack of goblins glance up the drive with
nudging elbows and whisperings of 'Where is daughter
Euphemia? Where Sir Rebus, her affianced?'

Off they scamper for a peep through the windows of the
house. They throng the sill of the library, ears acock and eyelids twittering admiration of a prospect. Euphemia was in
view of them—essence of her. Sir Rebus was at her side.
Nothing slips the goblins.

'Nymph in the Heavy Dragoons' was Mrs. Cryptic-
Sparkler's famous definition of her. The County took it for
final—an uncut gem with a fleck in the heart of it. Euphemia
condoned the imagery. She had breadth. Heels that spread
ample curves over the ground she stood on, and hands that
might floor you with a clench of them, were hers. Grey eyes

looked out lucid and fearless under swelling temples that were
lost in a ruffling copse of hair. Her nose was virginal, with
hints of the Iron Duke at most angles. Square chin, cleft
centrally, gave her throat the look of a tower with a gun
protrudent at top. She was dressed for church evidently, but
seemed no slave to Time. Her bonnet was pushed well back
from her head, and she was fingering the ribbons. One saw she
was a woman. She inspired deference.

'Forefinger for Shepherd's Crook' was what Mrs. Cryptic-
Sparkler had said of Sir Rebus. It shall stand at that.

'You have Prayer Book?' he queried.

She nodded. Juno catches the connubial trick.

'Hymns?'

'Ancient and Modern.'

'I may share with you?'

'I know by heart. Parrots sing.'

'Philomel carols,' he bent to her.

'Complaints spoil a festival.'

He waved hand to the door. 'Lady, your father has started.'

'He knows the adage. Copy-books instil it.'

'Inexorable truth in it.'

'We may dodge the scythe.'

'To be choked with the sands?'

She flashed a smile. 'I would not,' he said, 'that my
Euphemia were late for the Absolution.'

She cast eyes to the carpet. He caught them at the rebound.

'It snows,' she murmured, swimming to the window.

'A flake, no more. The season claims it.'

'I have thin boots.'

'Another pair?'

'My maid buttons. She is at church.'

'My fingers?'

'Ten on each.'

'Five,' he corrected.

'Buttons.'

'I beg your pardon.'

She saw opportunity. She swam to the bell-rope and grasped it for a tinkle. The action spread feminine curves to her lover's eyes. He was a man.

Obsequiousness loomed in the doorway. Its mistress flashed an order for port—two glasses. Sir Rebus sprang a pair of eyebrows on her. Suspicion slid down the banisters of his mind, trailing a blue ribbon. Inebriates were one of his hobbies. For an instant she was sunset.

'Medicinal,' she murmured.

'Forgive me, Madam. A glass, certainly. 'Twill warm us for worshipping.'

The wine appeared, seemed to blink owlishly through the facets of its decanter, like some hoary captive dragged forth into light after years of subterraneous darkness—something querulous in the sudden liberation of it. Or say that it gleamed benignant from its tray, steady-borne by the hands of reverence, as one has seen Infallibility pass with uplifting of jewelled fingers through genuflexions to the Balcony. Port has this in it: that it compels obeisance, master of us; as opposed to brother and sister wines wooing us with a coy flush in the gold of them to a cursory tope or harlequin leap shimmering up the veins with a sly wink at us through eyelets. Hussy vintages swim to a cosset. We go to Port, mark you!

Sir Rebus sipped with an affectionate twirl of thumb at the glass's stem. He said: 'One scents the cobwebs.'

'Catches in them,' Euphemia flung at him.

'I take you. Bacchus laughs in the web.'

'Unspun but for Pallas.'

'A lady's jealousy.'

'Forethought, rather.'

'Brewed in the paternal pate. Grant it!'

'For a spring in accoutrements.'

161

Sir Rebus inclined gravely. Port precludes prolongment of the riposte.

She replenished glasses. Deprecation yielded. 'A step,' she said, 'and we are in time for the First Lesson.'

'This,' he agreed, 'is a wine.'

'There are blasphemies in posture. One should sit to it.'

'Perhaps.' He sank to commodious throne of leather indicated by her finger.

Again she filled for him. 'This time, no heel-taps,' she was imperative. 'The Litany demands basis.'

'True.' He drained, not repelling the decanter placed at his elbow.

'It is a wine,' he presently repeated with a rolling tongue over it.

'Laid down by my great-grandfather. Cloistral.'

'Strange,' he said, examining the stopper, 'no date. Antediluvian. Sound, though.'

He drew out his note-book. '*The senses,*' he wrote, '*are internecine. They shall have learned esprit de corps before they enslave us.*' This was one of his happiest flings to general from particular. '*Visual distraction cries havoc to ultimate delicacy of palate*' would but have pinned us a butterfly best a-hover; nor even so should we have had truth of why the aphorist, closing note-book and nestling back of head against that of chair, closed eyes also.

As by some such law as lurks in meteorological toy for our guidance in climes close-knit with Irony for bewilderment, making egress of old woman synchronize inevitably with old man's ingress, or the other way about, the force that closed the aphorist's eye-lids parted his lips in degree according. Thus had Euphemia, erect on hearth-rug, a cavern to gaze down into. Outworks of fortifying ivory cast but denser shadows into the inexplorable. The solitudes here grew murmurous. To and fro through secret passages in the recesses leading up deviously to lesser twin caverns of nose above, the gnomes Morphean went about their business, whispering at first, but presently bold to wind horns in unison—Rolandwise, not less.

Euphemia had an ear for it; whim also to construe lord and master relaxed but reboant and soaring above the verbal to harmonic truths of abstract or transcendental, to be hummed subsequently by privileged female audience of one bent on a hook-or-crook plucking out of pith for salvation.

She caught tablets pendent at her girdle. *'How long,'* queried her stilus, *'has our sex had humour? Jael hammered.'*

She might have hitched speculation further. But Mother Earth, white-mantled, called to her.

Casting eye of caution at recumbence, she paddled across the carpet and anon swam out over the snow.

Pagan young womanhood, six foot of it, spanned eight miles before luncheon.

Enoch Soames

When a book about the literature of the eighteen-nineties was given by Mr. Holbrook Jackson to the world, I looked eagerly in the index for SOAMES, ENOCH. I had feared he would not be there. He was not there. But everybody else was. Many writers whom I had quite forgotten, or remembered but faintly, lived again for me, they and their work, in Mr. Holbrook Jackson's pages. The book was as thorough as it was brilliantly written. And thus the omission found by me was an all the deadlier record of poor Soames' failure to impress himself on his decade.

I daresay I am the only person who noticed the omission. Soames had failed so piteously as all that! Nor is there a counterpoise in the thought that if he had had some measure of success he might have passed, like those others, out of my mind, to return only at the historian's beck. It is true that had his gifts, such as they were, been acknowledged in his life-time, he would never have made the bargain I saw him make— that strange bargain whose results have kept him always in the foreground of my memory. But it is from those very results that the full piteousness of him glares out.

Not my compassion, however, impels me to write of him. For his sake, poor fellow, I should be inclined to keep my pen out of the ink. It is ill to deride the dead. And how can I write about Enoch Soames without making him ridiculous? Or rather, how am I to hush up the horrid fact that he *was* ridiculous? I shall not be able to do that. Yet, sooner or later, write about him I must. You will see, in due course, that I have no option. And I may as well get the thing done now.

In the Summer Term of '93 a bolt from the blue flashed down on Oxford. It drove deep, it hurtlingly embedded itself in the soil. Dons and undergraduates stood around, rather pale, discussing nothing but it. Whence came it, this meteorite? From Paris. Its name? Will Rothenstein. Its aim? To do a series of twenty-four portraits in lithograph. These were to be published from the Bodley Head, London. The matter was urgent. Already the Warden of A, and the Master of B, and the Regius Professor of C, had meekly 'sat.' Dignified and doddering old men, who had never consented to sit to any one, could not withstand this dynamic little stranger. He did not sue: he invited; he did not invite: he commanded. He was twenty-one years old. He wore spectacles that flashed more than any other pair ever seen. He was a wit. He was brimful of ideas. He knew Whistler. He knew Edmond de Goncourt. He knew every one in Paris. He knew them all by heart. He was Paris in Oxford. It was whispered that, so soon as he had polished off his selection of dons, he was going to include a few undergraduates. It was a proud day for me when I—I—was included. I liked Rothenstein not less than I feared him; and there arose between us a friendship that has grown ever warmer, and been more and more valued by me, with every passing year.

At the end of Term he settled in—or rather, meteoritically into—London. It was to him I owed my first knowledge of that forever enchanting little world-in-itself, Chelsea, and my first acquaintance with Walter Sickert and other august elders who dwelt there. It was Rothenstein that took me to see, in Cambridge Street, Pimlico, a young man whose drawings were already famous among the few—Aubrey Beardsley, by name. With Rothenstein I paid my first visit to the Bodley Head.

By him I was inducted into another haunt of intellect and daring, the domino room of the Café Royal.

There, on that October evening—there, in that exuberant vista of gilding and crimson velvet set amidst all those opposing mirrors and upholding caryatids, with fumes of tobacco ever rising to the painted and pagan ceiling, and with the hum of presumably cynical conversation broken into so sharply now and again by the clatter of dominoes shuffled on marble tables, I drew a deep breath, and 'This indeed,' said I to myself, 'is life!'

It was the hour before dinner. We drank vermouth. Those who knew Rothenstein were pointing him out to those who knew him only by name. Men were constantly coming in through the swing-doors and wandering slowly up and down in search of vacant tables, or of tables occupied by friends. One of these rovers interested me because I was sure he wanted to catch Rothenstein's eye. He had twice passed our table, with a hesitating look; but Rothenstein, in the thick of a disquisition on Puvis de Chavannes, had not seem him. He was a stooping, shambling person, rather tall, very pale, with longish and brownish hair. He had a thin vague beard—or rather, he had a chin on which a large number of hairs weakly curled and clustered to cover its retreat. He was an odd-looking person; but in the 'nineties odd apparitions were more frequent, I think, than they are now. The young writers of that era—and I was sure this man was a writer—strove earnestly to be distinct in aspect. This man had striven unsuccessfully. He wore a soft black hat of clerical kind but of Bohemian intention, and a grey waterproof cape which, perhaps because it was waterproof, failed to be romantic. I decided that 'dim' was the *mot juste* for him. I had already essayed to write, and was immensely keen on the *mot juste*, that Holy Grail of the period.

The dim man was now again approaching our table, and this

time he made up his mind to pause in front of it. 'You don't remember me,' he said in a toneless voice.

Rothenstein brightly focussed him. 'Yes, I do,' he replied after a moment, with pride rather than effusion—pride in a retentive memory. 'Edwin Soames.'

'Enoch Soames,' said Enoch.

'Enoch Soames,' repeated Rothenstein in a tone implying that it was enough to have hit on the surname. 'We met in Paris two or three times when you were living there. We met at the Café Groche.'

'And I came to your studio once.'

'Oh yes; I was sorry I was out.'

'But you were in. You showed me some of your paintings, you know. . . . I hear you're in Chelsea now.'

'Yes.'

I almost wondered that Mr. Soames did not, after this monosyllable, pass along. He stood patiently there, rather like a dumb animal, rather like a donkey looking over a gate. A sad figure, his. It occurred to me that 'hungry' was perhaps the *mot juste* for him; but—hungry for what? He looked as if he had little appetite for anything. I was sorry for him; and Rothenstein, though he had not invited him to Chelsea, did ask him to sit down and have something to drink.

Seated, he was more self-assertive. He flung back the wings of his cape with a gesture which—had not those wings been waterproof—might have seemed to hurl defiance at things in general. And he ordered an absinthe. '*Je me tiens toujours fidèle,*' he told Rothenstein, '*à la sorcière glauque.*'

'It is bad for you,' said Rothenstein drily.

'Nothing is bad for one,' answered Soames. '*Dans ce monde il n'y a ni de bien ni de mal.*'

'Nothing good and nothing bad? How do you mean?'

'I explained it all in the preface to *Negations.*'

'*Negations*?'

167

'Yes; I gave you a copy of it.'

'Oh yes, of course. But did you explain—for instance—that there was no such thing as bad or good grammar?'

'N-no,' said Soames. 'Of course in Art there is the good and the evil. But in Life—no.' He was rolling a cigarette. He had weak white hands, not well washed, and with finger-tips much stained by nicotine. 'In Life there are illusions of good and evil, but'—his voice trailed away to a murmur in which the words 'vieux jeu' and 'rococo' were faintly audible. I think he felt he was not doing himself justice, and feared that Rothenstein was going to point out fallacies. Anyway, he cleared his throat and said *'Parlons d'autre chose.'*

It occurs to you that he was a fool? It didn't to me. I was young, and had not the clarity of judgment that Rothenstein already had. Soames was quite five or six years older than either of us. Also, he had written a book.

It was wonderful to have written a book.

If Rothenstein had not been there, I should have revered Soames. Even as it was, I respected him. And I was very near indeed to reverence when he said he had another book coming out soon. I asked if I might ask what kind of book it was to be.

'My poems,' he answered. Rothenstein asked if this was to be the title of the book. The poet meditated on this suggestion, but said he rather thought of giving the book no title at all. 'If a book is good in itself——' he murmured, waving his cigarette.

Rothenstein objected that absence of title might be bad for the sale of a book. 'If,' he urged, 'I went into a bookseller's and said simply "Have you got?" or "Have you a copy of?" how would they know what I wanted?'

'Oh, of course I should have my name on the cover,' Soames answered earnestly. 'And I rather want,' he added, looking hard at Rothenstein, 'to have a drawing of myself as frontispiece.' Rothenstein admitted that this was a capital idea, and mentioned that he was going into the country and would be there for some time. He then looked at his watch, exclaimed at the hour, paid the waiter, and went away with me to dinner. Soames remained at his post of fidelity to the glaucous witch.

'Why were you so determined not to draw him?' I asked.

'Draw him? Him? How can one draw a man who doesn't exist?'

'He is dim,' I admitted. But my *mot juste* fell flat. Rothenstein repeated that Soames was non-existent.

Still, Soames had written a book. I asked if Rothenstein had read *Negations*. He said he had looked into it, 'but,' he added crisply, 'I don't profess to know anything about writing.' A reservation very characteristic of the period! Painters would not then allow that any one outside their own order had a right to any opinion about painting. This law (graven on the tablets brought down by Whistler from the summit of Fujiyama) imposed certain limitations. If other arts than painting were not utterly unintelligible to all but the men who practised them, the law tottered—the Monroe Doctrine, as it were, did not hold good. Therefore no painter would offer an opinion of a book without warning you at any rate that his opinion was worthless. No one is a better judge of literature than Rothenstein; but it wouldn't have done to tell him so in those days; and I knew that I must form an unaided judgment on *Negations*.'

Not to buy a book of which I had met the author face to face would have been for me in those days an impossible act of self-denial. When I returned to Oxford for the Christmas Term I had duly secured *Negations*. I used to keep it lying carelessly on the table in my room, and whenever a friend took it up and asked what it was about I would say 'Oh, it's rather a remarkable book. It's by a man whom I know.' Just 'what it was about' I never was able to say. Head or tail was just what I hadn't made of that slim green volume. I found in the preface no clue to the exiguous labyrinth of contents, and in that labyrinth nothing to explain the preface.

Lean near to life. Lean very near—nearer.
Life is web, and therein nor warp nor woof is, but web only.
It is for this I am Catholick in church and in thought, yet do let
swift Mood weave there what the shuttle of Mood wills.

These were the opening phrases of the preface, but those which followed were less easy to understand. Then came 'Stark: A *Conte*', about a midinette who, so far as I could gather, murdered, or was about to murder, a mannequin. It seemed to me like a story by Catulle Mendès in which the translator had either skipped or cut out every alternate sentence. Next, a dialogue between Pan and St. Ursula—lacking, I rather felt, in 'snap'. Next, some aphorisms (entitled ἀφορίσματα). Throughout, in fact, there was a great variety of form; and the forms had evidently been wrought with much care. It was rather the substance that eluded me. Was there, I wondered, any substance at all? It did now occur to me: suppose Enoch Soames was a fool! Up cropped a rival hypothesis: suppose *I* was! I inclined to give Soames the benefit of the doubt. I had read *L'Après-midi d'un Faune* without extracting a glimmer of meaning. Yet Mallarmé—of course—was a Master. How was I to know that Soames wasn't another? There was a sort of music in his prose, not indeed arresting, but perhaps, I thought, haunting, and laden perhaps with meanings as deep as Mallarmé's own. I awaited his poems with an open mind.

And I looked forward to them with positive impatience after I had had a second meeting with him. This was on an evening in January. Going into the aforesaid domino room, I passed a table at which sat a pale man with an open book before him. He looked from his book to me, and I looked back over my shoulder with a vague sense that I ought to have recognized him. I returned to pay my respects. After exchanging a few words, I said with a glance to the open book, 'I see I am interrupting you,' and was about to pass on, but 'I prefer,' Soames replied in his toneless voice, 'to be interrupted,' and I obeyed his gesture that I should sit down.

I ask him if he often read here. 'Yes; things of this kind I read here,' he answered, indicating the title of his book— *The Poems of Shelley*.

'Anything that you really'—and I was going to say 'admire?' But I cautiously left my sentence unfinished, and was glad that I had done so, for he said, with unwonted emphasis, 'Anything second-rate.'

I had read little of Shelley, but 'Of course,' I murmured, 'he's very uneven.'

'I should have thought evenness was just what was wrong with him. A deadly evenness. That's why I read him here. The noise of this place breaks the rhythm. He's tolerable here.' Soames took up the book and glanced through the pages. He laughed. Soames' laugh was a short, single and mirthless sound from the throat, unaccompanied by any movement of the face or brightening of the eyes. 'What a period!' he uttered, laying the book down. And 'What a country!' he added.

I asked rather nervously if he didn't think Keats had more or less held his own against the drawbacks of time and place. He admitted that there were 'passages in Keats,' but did not specify them. Of 'the older men,' as he called them, he seemed to like only Milton. 'Milton,' he said, 'wasn't sentimental.' Also, 'Milton had a dark insight.' And again, 'I can always read Milton in the reading-room.'

'The reading-room?'

'Of the British Museum. I go there every day.'

'You do? I've only been there once. I'm afraid I found it rather a depressing place. It—it seemed to sap one's vitality.'

'It does. That's why I go there. The lower one's vitality, the more sensitive one is to great art. I live near the Museum. I have rooms in Dyott Street.'

'And you go round to the reading-room to read Milton?'

'Usually Milton.' He looked at me. 'It was Milton,' he certificatively added, 'who converted me to Diabolism.'

'Diabolism? Oh yes? Really?' said I, with that vague discomfort and that intense desire to be polite which one feels when a man speaks of his own religion. 'You—worship the Devil?'

Soames shook his head. 'It's not exactly worship,' he qualified, sipping his absinthe. 'It's more a matter of trusting and encouraging.'

'Ah, yes. . . . But I had rather gathered from the preface to *Negations* that you were a—a Catholic.'

'*Je l'étais à cette époque.* Perhaps I still am. Yes, I'm a Catholic Diabolist.'

This profession he made in an almost cursory tone. I could see that what was upmost in his mind was the fact that I had read *Negations*. His pale eyes had for the first time gleamed. I felt as one who is about to be examined, *viva voce*, on the very subject in which he is shakiest. I hastily asked him how soon his poems were to be published. 'Next week,' he told me.

'And are they to be published without a title?'

'No. I found a title, at last. But I shan't tell you what it is,' as though I had been so impertinent as to inquire. 'I am not sure that it wholly satisfies me. But it is the best I can find. It does suggest something of the quality of the poems. . . . Strange growths, natural and wild; yet exquisite,' he added, 'and many-hued, and full of poisons.'

I asked him what he thought of Baudelaire. He uttered the snort that was his laugh, and 'Baudelaire,' he said, 'was a *bourgeois malgré lui.*' France had had only one poet: Villon; 'and two-thirds of Villon were sheer journalism.' Verlaine was 'an *épicier malgré lui.*' Altogether, rather to my surprise, he rated French literature lower than English. There were 'passages' in Villiers de l'Isle-Adam. But, 'I,' he summed up, 'owe nothing to France.' He nodded at me. 'You'll see,' he predicted.

I did not, when the time came, quite see that. I thought the author of *Fungoids* did—unconsciously, no doubt—owe something to the young Parisian décadents, or to the young English ones who owed something to *them*. I still think so. The little book—bought by me in Oxford—lies before me as I write. Its pale grey buckram cover and silver lettering have not worn well. Nor have its contents. Through these, with a melancholy interest, I have again been looking. They are not much. But at the time of their publication I had a vague suspicion that they *might* be. I suppose it is my capacity for faith, not poor Soames' work, that is weaker than it once was. . . .

To a Young Woman

Thou art, who hast not been!
  Pale tunes irresolute
  And traceries of old sounds
  Blown from a rotted flute
Mingle with noise of cymbals rouged with rust,
Nor not strange forms and epicene
  Lie bleeding in the dust,
    Being wounded with wounds.

    For this it is
  That is thy counterpart
  Of age-long mockeries
  Thou hast not been nor art!

There seemed to me a certain inconsistency as between the

first and last lines of this. I tried, with bent brows, to resolve
the discord. But I did not take my failure as wholly incompatible with a meaning in Soames' mind. Might it not rather
indicate the depth of his meaning? As for the craftsmanship,
'rouged with rust' seemed to me a fine stroke, and 'nor not'
instead of 'and' had a curious felicity. I wondered who the
Young Woman was, and what she had made of it all. I sadly
suspect that Soames could not have made more of it than she.
Yet, even now, if one doesn't try to make any sense at all of the
poem, and reads it just for the sound, there is a certain grace of
cadence. Soames was an artist—in so far as he was anything,
poor fellow!

It seemed to me, when first I read *Fungoids*, that, oddly
enough, the Diabolistic side of him was the best. Diabolism
seemed to be a cheerful, even a wholesome, influence in his life.

NOCTURNE

Round and round the shutter'd Square
I stroll'd with the Devil's arm in mine.
No sound but the scrape of his hoofs was there
And the ring of his laughter and mine.
    We had drunk black wine.

I scream'd 'I will race you, Master!'
'What matter,' he shriek'd, 'to-night
Which of us runs the faster?
There is nothing to fear to-night
    In the foul moon's light!'

Then I look'd him in the eyes,
And I laugh'd full shrill at the lie he told
And the gnawing fear he would fain disguise.
It was true, what I'd time and again been told:
    He was old—old.

There was, I felt, quite a swing about that first stanza—a joyous and rollicking note of comradeship. The second was slightly hysterical perhaps. But I liked the third: it was so bracingly unorthodox, even according to the tenets of Soames' peculiar sect in the faith. Not much 'trusting and encouraging' here! Soames triumphantly exposing the Devil as a liar, and laughing 'full shrill,' cut a quite heartening figure, I thought—then! Now, in the light of what befell, none of his poems depresses me so much as 'Nocturne'.

I looked out for what the metropolitan reviewers would have to say. They seemed to fall into two classes: those who had little to say and those who had nothing. The second class was the larger, and the words of the first were cold; insomuch that

Strikes a note of modernity throughout. . . . These tripping numbers.—*Preston Telegraph*.

was the sole lure offered in advertisements by Soames' publisher. I had hoped that when next I met the poet I could congratulate him on having made a stir; for I fancied he was not so sure of his intrinsic greatness as he seemed. I was but able to say, rather coarsely, when next I did see him, that I hoped *Fungoids* was 'selling splendidly.' He looked at me across his glass of absinthe and asked if I had bought a copy. His publisher had told him that three had been sold. I laughed, as at a jest.

'You don't suppose I *care*, do you?' he said, with something like a snarl. I disclaimed the notion. He added that he was not a tradesman. I said mildly that I wasn't, either, and murmured that an artist who gave truly new and great things to the world had always to wait long for recognition. He said he cared not a sou for recognition. I agreed that the act of creation was its own reward.

His moroseness might have alienated me if I had regarded

175

myself as a nobody. But ah! hadn't both John Lane and Aubrey Beardsley suggested that I should write an essay for the great new venture that was afoot—*The Yellow Book*? And hadn't Henry Harland, as editor, accepted my essay? And wasn't it to be in the very first number? At Oxford I was still *in statu pupillari*. In London I regarded myself as very much indeed a graduate now—one whom no Soames could ruffle. Partly to show off, partly in sheer good-will, I told Soames he ought to contribute to *The Yellow Book*. He uttered from the throat a sound of scorn for that publication.

Nevertheless, I did, a day or two later, tentatively ask Harland if he knew anything of the work of a man called Enoch Soames. Harland paused in the midst of his characteristic stride around the room, threw up his hands towards the ceiling, and groaned aloud: he had often met 'that absurd creature' in Paris, and this very morning had received some poems in manuscript from him.

'Has he *no* talent?' I asked.

'He has an income. He's all right.' Harland was the most joyous of men and most generous of critics, and he hated to talk of anything about which he couldn't be enthusiastic. So I dropped the subject of Soames. The news that Soames had an income did take the edge off solicitude. I learned afterwards that he was the son of an unsuccessful and deceased bookseller in Preston, but had inherited an annuity of £300 from a married aunt, and had no surviving relatives of any kind. Materially, then, he was 'all right.' But there was still a spiritual pathos about him, sharpened for me now by the possibility that even the praises of the *Preston Telegraph* might not have been forthcoming had he not been the son of a Preston man. He had a sort of weak doggedness which I could not but admire. Neither he nor his work received the slightest encouragement; but he persisted in behaving as a personage: always he kept his dingy little flag flying. Wherever con-

gregated the *jeunes féroces* of the arts, in whatever Soho
restaurant they had just discovered, in whatever music-hall
they were most frequenting, there was Soames in the midst of
them, or rather on the fringe of them, a dim but inevitable
figure. He never sought to propitiate his fellow-writers, never
bated a jot of his arrogance about his own work or of his
contempt for theirs. To the painters he was respectful, even
humble; but for the poets and prosaists of *The Yellow Book*,
and later of *The Savoy*, he had never a word but of scorn. He
wasn't resented. It didn't occur to anybody that he or his
Catholic Diabolism mattered. When, in the autumn of '96, he
brought out (at his own expense, this time) a third book, his
last book, nobody said a word for or against it. I meant, but
forgot, to buy it. I never saw it, and am ashamed to say I don't
even remember what it was called. But I did, at the time of its
publication, say to Rothenstein that I thought poor old Soames
was really a rather tragic figure, and that I believed he would
literally die for want of recognition. Rothenstein scoffed. He
said I was trying to get credit for a kind heart which I didn't
possess; and perhaps this was so. But at the private view of
the New English Art Club, a few weeks later, I beheld a pastel
portrait of 'Enoch Soames, Esq.' It was very like him, and very
like Rothenstein to have done it. Soames was standing near it,
in his soft hat and his waterproof cape, all through the afternoon. Anybody who knew him would have recognized the
portrait at a glance, but nobody who didn't know him would
have recognized the portrait from its bystander: it 'existed' so
much more than he; it was bound to. Also, it had not that
expression of faint happiness which on this day was discernible,
yes, in Soames' countenance. Fame had breathed on him.
Twice again in the course of the month I went to the New
English, and on both occasions Soames himself was on view
there. Looking back, I regard the close of that exhibition as
having been virtually the close of his career. He had felt the

breath of Fame against his cheek—so late, for such a little
while; and at its withdrawal he gave in, gave up, gave out.
He, who had never looked strong or well, looked ghastly now
—a shadow of the shade he had once been. He still frequented
the domino room, but, having lost all wish to excite curiosity,
he no longer read books there. 'You read only at the Museum
now?' asked I, with attempted cheerfulness. He said he never
went there now. 'No absinthe there,' he muttered. It was the
sort of thing that in the old days he would have said for effect;
but it carried conviction now. Absinthe, erst but a point in the
'personality' he had striven so hard to build up, was solace and
necessity now. He no longer called it 'la sorcière glauque.'
He had shed away all his French phrases. He had become a
plain, unvarnished, Preston man.

Failure, if it be a plain, unvarnished, complete failure, and
even though it be a squalid failure, has always a certain dignity.
I avoided Soames because he made me feel rather vulgar. John
Lane had published, by this time, two little books of mine, and
they had had a pleasant little success of esteem. I was a—
slight but definite—'personality.' Frank Harris had engaged
me to kick up my heels in *The Saturday Review*, Alfred Harms-
worth was letting me do likewise in the *Daily Mail*. I was
just what Soames wasn't. And he shamed my gloss. Had I
known that he really and firmly believed in the greatness of
what he as an artist had achieved, I might not have shunned
him. No man who hasn't lost his vanity can be held to have
altogether failed. Soames' dignity was an illusion of mine.
One day in the first week of June, 1897, that illusion went.
But on the evening of that day Soames went too.

I had been out most of the morning, and, as it was too late to
reach home in time for luncheon, I sought 'the Vingtième.'
This little place—Restaurant du Vingtième Siècle, to give it its
full title—had been discovered in '96 by the poets and prosaists,
but had now been more or less abandoned in favour of some

later find. I don't think it lived long enough to justify its name; but at that time there it still was, in Greek Street, a few doors from Soho Square, and almost opposite to that house where, in the first years of the century, a little girl, and with her a boy named De Quincey, made nightly encampment in darkness and hunger among dust and rats and old legal parchments. The Vingtième was but a small whitewashed room, leading out into the street at one end and into a kitchen at the other. The proprietor and cook was a Frenchman, known to us as Monsieur Vingtième; the waiters were his two daughters, Rose and Berthe; and the food, according to faith, was good. The tables were so narrow, and were set so close together, that there was space for twelve of them, six jutting from either wall.

Only the two nearest to the door, as I went in, were occupied. On one side sat a tall, flashy, rather Mephistophelian man whom I had seen from time to time in the domino room and elsewhere. On the other side sat Soames. They made a queer contrast in that sunlit room—Soames sitting haggard in that hat and cape which nowhere at any season had I seen him doff, and this other, this keenly vital man, at sight of whom I more than ever wondered whether he were a diamond merchant, a conjurer, or the head of a private detective agency. I was sure Soames didn't want my company; but I asked, as it would have seemed brutal not to, whether I might join him, and took the chair opposite to his. He was smoking a cigarette, with an untasted salmi of something on his plate and a half-empty bottle of Sauterne before him; and he was quite silent. I said that the preparations for the Jubilee made London impossible. (I rather liked them, really.) I professed a wish to go right away till the whole thing was over. In vain did I attune myself to his gloom. He seemed not to hear me nor even to see me. I felt that his behaviour made me ridiculous in the eyes of the other man. The gangway between the two rows of tables at the Vingtième was hardly more than two feet

wide (Rose and Berthe, in their ministrations, had always to
edge past each other, quarrelling in whispers as they did so),
and any one at the table abreast of yours was practically at
yours. I thought our neighbour was amused at my failure to
interest Soames, and so, as I could not explain to him that my
insistence was merely charitable, I became silent. Without
turning my head, I had him well within my range of vision. I
hoped I looked less vulgar than he in contrast with Soames. I
was sure he was not an Englishman, but what *was* his
nationality? Though his jet-black hair was *en brosse*, I did
not think he was French. To Berthe, who waited on him, he
spoke French fluently, but with a hardly native idiom and
accent. I gathered that this was his first visit to the Vingtième;
but Berthe was off-hand in her manner to him: he had not
made a good impression. His eyes were handsome, but—like
the Vingtième's tables—too narrow and set too close together.
His nose was predatory, and the points of his moustache,
waxed up beyond his nostrils, gave a fixity to his smile.
Decidedly, he was sinister. And my sense of discomfort in his
presence was intensified by the scarlet waistcoat which tightly,
and so unseasonably in June, sheathed his ample chest. This
waistcoat wasn't wrong merely because of the heat, either. It
was somehow all wrong in itself. It wouldn't have done on
Christmas morning. It would have struck a jarring note at the
first night of *Hernani*. I was trying to account for its wrongness when Soames suddenly and strangely broke silence. 'A
hundred years hence!' he murmured, as in a trance.

'We shall not be here!' I briskly but fatuously added.

'We shall not be here. No,' he droned, 'but the Museum
will still be just where it is. And the reading-room, just where
it is. And people will be able to go and read there.' He
inhaled sharply, and a spasm as of actual pain contorted his
features.

I wondered what train of thought poor Soames had been

following. He did not enlighten me when he said, after a long pause, 'You think I haven't minded.'

'Minded what, Soames?'

'Neglect. Failure.'

'*Failure?*' I said heartily. 'Failure?' I repeated vaguely. 'Neglect—yes, perhaps; but that's quite another matter. Of course you haven't been—appreciated. But what then? Any artist who—who gives——' What I wanted to say was, 'Any artist who gives truly new and great things to the world has always to wait long for recognition'; but the flattery would not out: in the face of his misery, a misery so genuine and so unmasked, my lips would not say the words.

And then—he said them for me. I flushed. 'That's what you were going to say, isn't it?' he asked.

'How did you know?'

'It's what you said to me three years ago, when *Fungoids* was published.' I flushed the more. I need not have done so at all, for 'It's the only important thing I ever heard you say,' he continued. 'And I've never forgotten it. It's a true thing. It's a horrible truth. But—d'you remember what I answered? I said "I don't care a sou for recognition." And you believed me. You've gone on believing I'm above that sort of thing. You're shallow. What should *you* know of the feelings of a man like me? You imagine that a great artist's faith in himself and in the verdict of posterity is enough to keep him happy. . . . You've never guessed at the bitterness and loneliness, the'—his voice broke; but presently he resumed, speaking with a force that I had never known in him. 'Posterity! What use is it to *me*? A dead man doesn't know that people are visiting his grave—visiting his birthplace—putting up tablets to him—unveiling statues of him. A dead man can't read the books that are written about him. A hundred years hence! Think of it! If I could come back to life *then*—just for a few hours—and go to the reading-room, and *read*! Or better still:

181

if I could be projected, now, at this moment, into the future, into that reading-room, just for this one afternoon! I'd sell myself body and soul to the devil, for that! Think of the pages and pages in the catalogue: "SOAMES, ENOCH" endlessly— endless editions, commentaries, prolegomena, biographies'— but here he was interrupted by a sudden loud creak of the chair at the next table. Our neighbour had half risen from his place. He was leaning towards us, apologetically intrusive.

'Excuse—permit me,' he said softly. 'I have been unable not to hear. Might I take a liberty? In this little restaurant-sans-façon'—he spread wide his hands—'might I, as the phrase is, "cut in"?'

I could but signify our acquiescence. Berthe had appeared at the kitchen door, thinking the stranger wanted his bill. He waved her away with his cigar, and in another moment had seated himself beside me, commanding a full view of Soames.

'Though not an Englishman,' he explained, 'I know my London well, Mr. Soames. Your name and fame—Mr. Beerbohm's too—very known to me. Your point is: who am *I*?' He glanced quickly over his shoulder, and in a lowered voice said 'I am the Devil.'

I couldn't help it: I laughed. I tried not to, I knew there was nothing to laugh at, my rudeness shamed me, but—I laughed with increasing volume. The Devil's quiet dignity, the surprise and disgust of his raised eyebrows, did but the more dissolve me. I rocked to and fro, I lay back aching. I behaved deplorably.

'I am a gentleman, and,' he said with intense emphasis, 'I thought I was in the company of *gentlemen*.'

'Don't!' I gasped faintly. 'Oh, don't!'

'Curious, *nicht wahr*?' I heard him say to Soames. 'There is a type of person to whom the very mention of my name is— oh-so-awfully-funny! In your theatres the dullest comédien needs only to say "The Devil!" and right away they give him "the loud laugh that speaks the vacant mind." Is it not so?'

I had now just breath enough to offer my apologies. He accepted them, but coldly, and re-addressed himself to Soames.

'I am a man of business,' he said, 'and always I would put things through "right now," as they say in the States. You are a poet. *Les affaires*—you detest them. So be it. But with me you will deal, eh? What you have said just now gives me furiously to hope.'

Soames had not moved, except to light a fresh cigarette. He sat crouched forward, with his elbows squared on the table, and his head just above the level of his hands, staring up at the Devil. 'Go on,' he nodded. I had no remnant of laughter in me now.

'It will be the more pleasant, our little deal,' the Devil went on, 'because you are—I mistake not?—a Diabolist.'

'A Catholic Diabolist,' said Soames.

The Devil accepted the reservation genially. 'You wish,' he resumed, 'to visit now—this afternoon as-ever-is—the reading-room of the British Museum, yes? but of a hundred years hence, yes? *Parfaitement*. Time—an illusion. Past and future—they are as ever-present as the present, or at any rate only what you call "just-round-the-corner." I switch you on to any date. I project you—pouf! You wish to be in the reading-room just as it will be on the afternoon of June 3rd, 1997? You wish to find yourself standing in that room, just past the swing-doors, this very minute, yes? and to stay there till closing time? Am I right?'

Soames nodded.

The Devil looked at his watch. 'Ten past two,' he said. 'Closing time in summer same then as now: seven o'clock. That will give you almost five hours. At seven o'clock— pouf!—you find yourself again here, sitting at this table. I am dining to-night *dans le monde—dans le higlif*. That concludes my present visit to your great city. I come and fetch you here, Mr. Soames, on my way home.'

'Home?' I echoed.

'Be it never so humble!' said the Devil lightly.

'All right,' said Soames.

'Soames!' I entreated. But my friend moved not a muscle.

The Devil had made as though to stretch forth his hand across the table and touch Soames' forearm; but he paused in his gesture.

'A hundred years hence, as now,' he smiled, 'no smoking allowed in the reading-room. You would better there-fore——'

Soames removed the cigarette from his mouth and dropped it into his glass of Sauterne.

'Soames!' again I cried. 'Can't you'—but the Devil had now stretched forth his hand across the table. He brought it slowly down on—the table-cloth. Soames' chair was empty. His cigarette floated sodden in his wine-glass. There was no other trace of him.

For a few moments the Devil let his hand rest where it lay, gazing at me out of the corners of his eyes, vulgarly triumphant.

A shudder shook me. With an effort I controlled myself and rose from my chair. 'Very clever,' I said condescendingly. 'But—*The Time Machine* is a delightful book, don't you think? So entirely original!'

'You are pleased to sneer,' said the Devil, who had also risen, 'but it is one thing to write about a not possible machine; it is a quite other thing to be a Supernatural Power.' All the same, I had scored.

Berthe had come forth at the sound of our rising. I explained to her that Mr. Soames had been called away, and that both he and I would be dining here. It was not until I was out in the open air that I began to feel giddy. I have but the haziest recollection of what I did, where I wandered, in the glaring sunshine of that endless afternoon. I remember the sound of carpenters' hammers all along Piccadilly, and the bare chaotic look of the half-erected 'stands.' Was it in the Green Park, or in Kensington Gardens, or *where* was it that I sat on a chair beneath a tree, trying to read an evening paper? There was a phrase in the leading article that went on repeating itself in my fagged mind—'Little is hidden from this august Lady full of the garnered wisdom of sixty years of Sovereignty.' I remember wildly conceiving a letter (to reach Windsor by express messenger told to await answer):

'MADAM,—Well knowing that your Majesty is full of the garnered wisdom of sixty years of Sovereignty, I venture to ask your advice in the following delicate matter. Mr. Enoch Soames, whose poems you may or may not know,' . . .

Was there *no* way of helping him—saving him? A bargain was a bargain, and I was the last man to aid or abet any one in wriggling out of a reasonable obligation. I wouldn't have lifted a little finger to save Faust. But poor Soames!—doomed to pay without respite an eternal price for nothing but a fruitless search and a bitter disillusioning. . .

Odd and uncanny it seemed to me that he, Soames, in the flesh, in the waterproof cape, was at this moment living in the last decade of the next century, poring over books not yet written, and seeing and seen by men not yet born. Uncannier and odder still, that to-night and evermore he would be in Hell. Assuredly, truth was stranger than fiction.

Endless that afternoon was. Almost I wished I had gone with Soames—not indeed to stay in the reading-room, but to sally forth for a brisk sight-seeing walk around a new London. I wandered restlessly out of the Park I had sat in. Vainly I tried to imagine myself an ardent tourist from the eighteenth century. Intolerable was the strain of the slow-passing and empty minutes. Long before seven o'clock I was back at the Vingtième.

I sat there just where I had sat for luncheon. Air came in listlessly through the open door behind me. Now and again Rose or Berthe appeared for a moment. I had told them I would not order any dinner till Mr. Soames came. A hurdy-gurdy began to play, abruptly drowning the noise of a quarrel between some Frenchmen further up the street. Whenever the tune was changed I heard the quarrel still raging. I had bought another evening paper on my way. I unfolded it. My eyes gazed ever away from it to the clock over the kitchen door. . .

Five minutes, now, to the hour! I remembered that clocks in restaurants are kept five minutes fast. I concentrated my eyes on the paper. I vowed I would not look away from it again. I held it upright, at its full width, close to my face, so that I had no view of anything but it. . . . Rather a tremulous sheet? Only because of the draught, I told myself.

My arms gradually became stiff; they ached; but I could not drop them—now. I had a suspicion, I had a certainty. Well, what then? . . . What else had I come for? Yet I held tight that barrier of newspaper. Only the sound of Berthe's brisk footstep from the kitchen enabled me, forced me, to drop it, and to utter:

'What shall we have to eat, Soames?'

'*Il est souffrant, ce pauvre Monsieur Soames?*' asked Berthe.

'He's only—tired.' I asked her to get some wine—Burgundy—and whatever food might be ready. Soames sat crouched forward against the table, exactly as when last I had seen him. It was as though he had never moved—he who had moved so unimaginably far. Once or twice in the afternoon it had for an instant occurred to me that perhaps his journey was not to be fruitless—that perhaps we had all been wrong in our estimate of the works of Enoch Soames. That we had been horribly right was horribly clear from the look of him. But

'Don't be discouraged,' I falteringly said. 'Perhaps it's only that you—didn't leave enough time. Two, three centuries hence, perhaps——'

'Yes,' his voice came. 'I've thought of that.'

'And now—now for the more immediate future! Where are you going to hide? How would it be if you caught the Paris express from Charing Cross? Almost an hour to spare. Don't go on to Paris. Stop at Calais. Live in Calais. He'd never think of looking for you in Calais.'

'It's like my luck,' he said, 'to spend my last hours on earth with an ass.' But I was not offended. 'And a treacherous ass,' he strangely added, tossing across to me a crumpled bit of paper which he had been holding in his hand. I glanced at the writing on it—some sort of gibberish, apparently. I laid it impatiently aside.

'Come, Soames! pull yourself together! This isn't a mere matter of life and death. It's a question of eternal torment, mind you! You don't mean to say you're going to wait limply here till the Devil comes to fetch you?'

'I can't do anything else. I've no choice.'

'Come! This is "trusting and encouraging" with a vengeance! This is Diabolism run mad!' I filled his glass with wine. 'Surely, now that you've *seen* the brute——'

'It's no good abusing him.'

'You must admit there's nothing Miltonic about him, Soames.'

'I don't say he's not rather different from what I expected.'

'He's a vulgarian, he's a swell-mobsman, he's the sort of man who hangs about the corridors of trains going to the Riviera and steals ladies' jewel-cases. Imagine eternal torment presided over by *him*!'

'You don't suppose I look forward to it, do you?'

'Then why not slip quietly out of the way?'

Again and again I filled his glass, and always, mechanically,

he emptied it; but the wine kindled no spark of enterprise in
him. He did not eat, and I myself ate hardly at all. I did not in
my heart believe that any dash for freedom could save him.
The chase would be swift, the capture certain. But better
anything than this passive, meek, miserable waiting. I told
Soames that for the honour of the human race he ought to make
some show of resistance. He asked what the human race had
ever done for him. 'Besides,' he said, 'can't you understand
that I'm in his power? You saw him touch me, didn't you?
There's an end of it. I've no will. I'm sealed.'

I made a gesture of despair. He went on repeating the word
'sealed'. I began to realize that the wine had clouded his brain.
No wonder! Foodless he had gone into futurity, foodless he
still was. I urged him to eat at any rate some bread. It was
maddening to think that he, who had so much to tell, might tell
nothing. 'How was it all,' I asked, 'yonder? Come! Tell me
your adventures.'

'They'd make first-rate "copy," wouldn't they?'

'I'm awfully sorry for you, Soames, and I make all possible
allowances; but what earthly right have you to insinuate that I
should make "copy," as you call it, out of you?'

The poor fellow pressed his hands to his forehead. 'I don't
know,' he said. 'I had some reason, I'm sure. . . I'll try to
remember.'

'That's right. Try to remember everything. Eat a little
more bread. What did the reading-room look like?'

'Much as usual,' he at length muttered.

'Many people there?'

'Usual sort of number.'

'What did they look like?'

Soames tried to visualize them. 'They all,' he presently
remembered, 'looked very like one another.'

My mind took a fearsome leap. 'All dressed in Jaeger?'

'Yes. I think so. Greyish-yellowish stuff.'

'A sort of uniform?' He nodded. 'With a number on it, perhaps?—a number on a large disc of metal sewn on to the left sleeve? DKF 78,910—that sort of thing?' It was even so. 'And all of them—men and women alike—looking very well-cared-for? very Utopian? and smelling rather strongly of carbolic? and all of them quite hairless?' I was right every time. Soames was only not sure whether the men and women were hairless or shorn. 'I hadn't time to look at them very closely,' he explained.

'No, of course not. But——'

'They stared at *me*, I can tell you. I attracted a great deal of attention.' At last he had done that! 'I think I rather scared them. They moved away whenever I came near. They followed me about at a distance, wherever I went. The men at the round desk in the middle seemed to have a sort of panic whenever I went to make inquiries.'

'What did you do when you arrived?'

Well, he had gone straight to the catalogue, of course—to the S volumes, and had stood long before SN-SOF, unable to take this volume out of the shelf, because his heart was beating so. . . At first, he said, he wasn't disappointed—he only thought there was some new arrangement. He went to the middle desk and asked where the catalogue of *twentieth*-century books was kept. He gathered that there was still only one catalogue. Again he looked up his name, stared at the three little pasted slips he had known so well. Then he went and sat down for a long time. . . .

'And then,' he droned, 'I looked up the *Dictionary of National Biography* and some encyclopædias. . . . I went back to the middle desk and asked what was the best modern book on late nineteenth-century literature. They told me Mr. T. K. Nupton's book was considered the best. I looked it up in the catalogue and filled in a form for it. It was brought to me. My name wasn't in the index, but—— Yes!' he said with a sudden change of tone. 'That's what I'd forgotten. Where's that bit of paper? Give it me back.'

I, too, had forgotten that cryptic screed. I found it fallen on the floor, and handed it to him.

He smoothed it out, nodding and smiling at me disagreeably. 'I found myself glancing through Nupton's book,' he resumed. 'Not very easy reading. Some sort of phonetic spelling. . . . All the modern books I saw were phonetic.'

'Then I don't want to hear any more, Soames, please.'

'The proper names seemed all to be spelt in the old way. But for that, I mightn't have noticed my own name.'

'Your own name? Really? Soames, I'm *very* glad.'

'And yours.'

'No!'

'I thought I should find you waiting here to-night. So I took the trouble to copy out the passage. Read it.'

I snatched the paper. Soames' handwriting was characteristically dim. It, and the noisome spelling, and my excitement, made me all the slower to grasp what T. K. Nupton was driving at.

The document lies before me at this moment. Strange that the words I here copy out for you were copied out for me by poor Soames just seventy-eight years hence. . . .

From p. 234 of 'Inglish Littracher 1890–1900,' bi T. K. Nupton, published bi th Stait, 1992 :

'Fr. egzarmpl, a riter ov th time, naimd Max Beerbohm, hoo woz stil alive in th twentieth senchri, rote a stauri in wich e pautraid an immajnari karrakter kauld "Enoch Soames"—a thurdrait poit hoo beleevz imself a grate jeneus an maix a bargin with th Devvl in auder ter no wot posterriti thinx ov im! It iz a sumwot labud sattire but not without vallu az showing hou seriusli the yung men ov th aiteen-ninetiz took themselvz. Nou that the littreri profeshn haz bin auganized az a department of publik servis, our riters hav found their levvl an hav lernt ter doo their duti without thort ov th morro. "Th laibrer iz werthi ov hiz hire," an that iz aul. Thank hevvn we hav no Enoch Soameses amung us to-dai!'

I found that by murmuring the words aloud (a device which I commend to my reader) I was able to master them, little by little. The clearer they became, the greater was my bewilderment, my distress and horror. The whole thing was a nightmare. Afar, the great grisly background of what was in store for the poor dear art of letters; here, at the table, fixing on me a gaze that made me hot all over, the poor fellow whom —whom evidently . . . but no: whatever down-grade my character might take in coming years, I should never be such a brute as to——

Again I examined the screed. 'Immajnari"—but here Soames was, no more imaginary, alas! than I. And 'labud'— what on earth was that? (To this day, I have never made out that word.) 'It's all very—baffling,' I at length stammered.

Soames said nothing, but cruelly did not cease to look at me.

'Are you sure,' I temporized, 'quite sure you copied the thing out correctly?'

'Quite.'

'Well, then it's this wretched Nupton who must have made —must be going to make—some idiotic mistake. . . . Look here, Soames! you know me better than to suppose that I . . . After all, the name "Max Beerbohm" is not at all an uncommon one, and there must be several Enoch Soameses running around—or rather, "Enoch Soames" is a name that might occur to any one writing a story. And I don't write stories: I'm an essayist, an observer, a recorder. . . . I admit that it's an extraordinary coincidence. But you must see——'

'I see the whole thing,' said Soames quietly. And he added,

with a touch of his old manner, but with more dignity than I had ever known in him, '*Parlons d'autre chose.*'

I accepted that suggestion very promptly. I returned straight to the more immediate future. I spent most of the long evening in renewed appeals to Soames to slip away and seek refuge somewhere. I remember saying at last that if indeed I was destined to write about him, the supposed 'stauri' had better have at least a happy ending. Soames repeated those last three words in a tone of intense scorn. 'In Life and in Art,' he said, 'all that matters is an *inevitable* ending.'

'But,' I urged, more hopefully than I felt, 'an ending that can be avoided *isn't* inevitable.'

'You aren't an artist,' he rasped. 'And you're so hopelessly not an artist that, so far from being able to imagine a thing and make it seem true, you're going to make even a true thing seem as if you'd made it up. You're a miserable bungler. And it's like my luck.'

I protested that the miserable bungler was not I—was not going to be I—but T. K. Nupton; and we had a rather heated argument, in the thick of which it suddenly seemed to me that Soames saw he was in the wrong: he had quite physically cowered. But I wondered why—and now I guessed with a cold throb just why—he stared so, past me. The bringer of that 'inevitable ending' filled the doorway.

I managed to turn in my chair and to say, not without a semblance of lightness, 'Aha, come in!' Dread was indeed rather blunted in me by his looking so absurdly like a villain in a melodrama. The sheen of his tilted hat and of his shirt-front, the repeated twists he was giving to his moustache, and most of all the magnificence of his sneer, gave token that he was there only to be foiled.

He was at our table in a stride. 'I am sorry,' he sneered witheringly, 'to break up your pleasant party, but——'

'You don't: you complete it,' I assured him. 'Mr. Soames

192

and I want to have a little talk with you. Won't you sit? Mr. Soames got nothing—frankly nothing—by his journey this afternoon. We don't wish to say that the whole thing was a swindle—a common swindle. On the contrary, we believe you meant well. But of course the bargain, such as it was, is off.'

The Devil gave no verbal answer. He merely looked at Soames and pointed with rigid forefinger to the door. Soames was wretchedly rising from his chair when, with a desperate quick gesture, I swept together two dinner-knives that were on the table, and laid their blades across each other. The Devil stepped sharp back against the table behind him, averting his face and shuddering.

'You are not superstitious!' he hissed.

'Not at all,' I smiled.

'Soames!' he said as to an underling, but without turning his face, 'put those knives straight!'

With an inhibitive gesture to my friend, 'Mr. Soames,' I said emphatically to the Devil, 'is a *Catholic* Diabolist'; but my poor friend did the Devil's bidding, not mine; and now, with his master's eyes again fixed on him, he arose, he shuffled past me. I tried to speak. It was he that spoke. 'Try,' was the prayer he threw back at me as the Devil pushed him roughly out through the door, '*try* to make them know that I did exist!'

In another instant I too was through that door. I stood staring all ways—up the street, across it, down it. There was moonlight and lamplight, but there was not Soames nor that other.

Dazed, I stood there. Dazed, I turned back, at length, into the little room; and I suppose I paid Berthe or Rose for my dinner and luncheon, and for Soames': I hope so, for I never went to the Vingtième again. Ever since that night I have avoided Greek Street altogether. And for years I did not set foot even in Soho Square, because on that same night it was there that I paced and loitered, long and long, with some such dull sense of hope as a man has in not straying far from the place where he has lost something. . . . 'Round and round the shutter'd Square'—that line came back to me on my lonely beat, and with it the whole stanza, ringing in my brain and bearing in on me how tragically different from the happy scene imagined by him was the poet's actual experience of that prince in whom of all princes we should put not our trust.

But—strange how the mind of an essayist, be it never so stricken, roves and ranges!—I remember pausing before a wide doorstep and wondering if perchance it was on this very one that the young De Quincey lay ill and faint while poor Ann flew as fast as her feet would carry her to Oxford Street, the 'stony-hearted stepmother' of them both, and came back bearing that 'glass of port wine and spices' but for which he might, so he thought, actually have died. Was this the very doorstep that the old De Quincey used to revisit in homage? I pondered Ann's fate, the cause of her sudden vanishing from the ken of her boy-friend; and presently I blamed myself for letting the past over-ride the present. Poor vanished Soames!

And for myself, too, I began to be troubled. What had I better do? Would there be a hue and cry—Mysterious Disappearance of an Author, and all that? He had last been seen lunching and dining in my company. Hadn't I better get a hansom and drive straight to Scotland Yard? . . . They would think I was a lunatic. After all, I reassured myself, London was a very large place, and one very dim figure might easily drop out of it unobserved—now especially, in the blinding glare of the near Jubilee. Better say nothing at all, I thought.

And I was right. Soames' disappearance made no stir at all. He was utterly forgotten before any one, so far as I am aware, noticed that he was no longer hanging around. Now and again some poet or prosaist may have said to another, 'What has become of that man Soames?' but I never heard any such question asked. The solicitor through whom he was paid his annuity may be presumed to have made inquiries, but no echo of these resounded. There was something rather ghastly to me in the general unconsciousness that Soames had existed, and more than once I caught myself wondering whether Nupton, that babe unborn, were going to be right in thinking him a figment of my brain.

In the extract from Nupton's repulsive book there is one point which perhaps puzzles you. How is it that the author, though I have here mentioned him by name and have quoted the exact words he is going to write, is not going to grasp the obvious corollary that I have invented nothing? The answer can but be this: Nupton will not have read the later passages of this memoir. Such lack of thoroughness is a serious fault in any one who undertakes to do scholar's work. And I hope these words will meet the eye of some contemporary rival to Nupton and be the undoing of Nupton.

I like to think that some time between 1992 and 1997 somebody will have looked up this memoir, and will have forced on the world his inevitable and startling conclusions. And I have reasons for believing that this will be so. You realize that the reading-room into which Soames was projected by the Devil was in all respects precisely as it will be on the afternoon of June 3rd, 1997. You realize, therefore, that on that afternoon, when it comes round, there the self-same crowd will be, and there Soames too will be, punctually, he and they doing precisely what they did before. Recall now Soames' account of the sensation he made. You may say that the mere difference of his costume was enough to make him sensational in that uniformed crowd. You wouldn't say so if you had ever seen him. I assure you that in no period could Soames be anything but dim. The fact that people are going to stare at him, and follow him around, and seem afraid of him, can be explained only on the hypothesis that they will somehow have been prepared for his ghostly visitation. They will have been awfully waiting to see whether he really would come. And when he does come the effect will of course be—awful.

An authentic, guaranteed, proven ghost, but—only a ghost, alas! Only that. In his first visit, Soames was a creature of flesh and blood, whereas the creatures into whose midst he was projected were but ghosts, I take it—solid, palpable, vocal, but unconscious and automatic ghosts, in a building that was itself an illusion. Next time, that building and those creatures will be real. It is of Soames that there will be but the semblance. I wish I could think him destined to revisit the world actually, physically, consciously. I wish he had this one brief escape, this one small treat, to look forward to. I never forget him for long. He is where he is, and forever. The more rigid moralists among you may say he has only himself to blame. For my part, I think he has been very hardly used. It is well that vanity should be chastened; and Enoch Soames' vanity was, I admit, above the average, and called for special treatment. But there was no need for vindictiveness. You say he contracted to pay the price he is paying; yes; but I maintain that he was induced to do so by fraud. Well-informed in all things, the Devil must have known that my friend would gain nothing by his visit to futurity. The whole thing was a very shabby trick. The more I think of it, the more detestable the Devil seems to me.

Of him I have caught sight several times, here and there, since that day at the Vingtième. Only once, however, have I seen him at close quarters. This was in Paris. I was walking, one afternoon, along the Rue d'Antin, when I saw him advancing from the opposite direction—over-dressed as ever, and swinging an ebony cane, and altogether behaving as though the whole pavement belonged to him. At thought of Enoch Soames and the myriads of other sufferers eternally in this brute's dominion, a great cold wrath filled me, and I drew myself up to my full height. But—well, one is so used to nodding and smiling in the street to anybody whom one knows, that the action becomes almost independent of oneself: to prevent it requires a very sharp effort and great presence of mind. I was miserably aware, as I passed the Devil, that I nodded and smiled to him. And my shame was the deeper and hotter because he, if you please, stared straight at me with the utmost haughtiness.

To be cut—deliberately cut—by *him*! I was, I still am, furious at having had that happen to me.

A. V. Laider

I unpacked my things and went down to await luncheon.

It was good to be here again in this little old sleepy hostel by the sea. Hostel I say, though it spelt itself without an s and even placed a circumflex above the o. It made no other pretension. It was very cosy indeed.

I had been here just a year before, in mid-February, after an attack of influenza. And now I had returned, after an attack of influenza. Nothing was changed. It had been raining when I left, and the waiter—there was but a single, a very old waiter—had told me it was only a shower. That waiter was still here, not a day older. And the shower had not ceased.

Steadfastly it fell on to the sands, steadfastly into the iron-grey sea. I stood looking out at it from the windows of the hall, admiring it very much. There seemed to be little else to do. What little there was I did. I mastered the contents of a blue hand-bill which, pinned to the wall just beneath the framed engraving of Queen Victoria's Coronation, gave token of a concert that was to be held—or rather, was to have been held some weeks ago—in the Town Hall, for the benefit of the Life-Boat Fund. I looked at the barometer, tapped it, was not the wiser. I glanced at a pamphlet about Our Dying Industries (a theme on which Mr. Joseph Chamberlain was at that time trying to alarm us). I wandered to the letter-board.

These letter-boards always fascinate me. Usually some two or three of the envelopes stuck into the cross-garterings have a certain newness and freshness. They seem sure they will yet be claimed. Why not? Why *shouldn't* John Doe, Esq., or Mrs

198

Richard Roe, turn up at any moment? I do not know. I can only say that nothing in the world seems to me more unlikely. Thus it is that these young bright envelopes touch my heart even more than do their dusty and sallow seniors. Sour resignation is less touching than impatience for what will not be, than the eagerness that has to wane and wither. Soured beyond measure these old envelopes are. They are not nearly so nice as they should be to the young ones. They lose no chance of sneering and discouraging. Such dialogues as this are only too frequent:

A VERY YOUNG ENVELOPE. Something in me whispers that he will come to-day!

A VERY OLD ENVELOPE. He? Well, that's good! Ha, ha, ha! Why didn't he come last week, when *you* came? What reason have you for supposing he'll ever come *now*? It isn't as if he were a frequenter of the place. He's never been here. His name is utterly unknown here. You don't suppose he's coming on the chance of finding *you*?

A. V. Y. E. It may seem silly, but—something in me whispers——

A. V. O. E. Something in *you*? One has only to look at you to see there's nothing in you but a note scribbled to him by a cousin. Look at *me*! There are three sheets, closely written, in *me*. The lady to whom I am addressed——

A. V. Y. E. Yes, sir, yes; you told me all about her yesterday.

A. V. O. E. And I shall do so to-day and to-morrow and every day and all day long. That young lady was a widow. She stayed here many times. She was delicate, and the air suited her. She was poor, and the tariff was just within her means. She was lonely, and had need of love. I have in me for her a passionate avowal and strictly honourable proposal, written to her, after many rough copies, by a gentleman who had made her acquaintance under this very roof. He was rich, he was charming, he was in the prime of life. He had asked if he might write to her. She had flutteringly granted his request. He posted me to her the day after his return to London. I looked forward to being torn open by her. I was very sure she would wear me and my contents next to her bosom. She was gone. She had left no address. She never returned. . . . This I tell you, and shall continue to tell you, not because I want any of your callow sympathy,—no, *thank* you!—but that you may judge how much less than slight are the chances that you yourself ——

But my reader has overheard these dialogues as often as I. He wants to know what was odd about this particular letter-board before which I was standing. At first glance I saw nothing odd about it. But presently I distinguished a hand-writing that was vaguely familiar. It was mine. I stared, I wondered. There is always a slight shock in seeing an envelope of one's own after it has gone through the post. It looks as if it had gone through so much. But this was the first time I had ever seen an envelope of mine eating its heart out in bondage on a letter-board. This was outrageous. This was hardly to be believed. Sheer kindness had impelled me to write to 'A. V. Laider, Esq.', and this was the result! I hadn't minded receiving no answer. Only now, indeed, did I remember that I hadn't received one. In multitudinous London the memory of A. V. Laider and his trouble had soon passed from my mind. But—well, what a lesson not to go out of one's way to write to casual acquaintances!

My envelope seemed not to recognize me as its writer. Its gaze was the more piteous for being blank. Even so had I once been gazed at by a dog that I had lost and, after many days, found in the Battersea Home. 'I don't know who you are, but, whoever you are, claim me, take me out of this!' That was my dog's appeal. This was the appeal of my envelope.

I raised my hand to the letter-board, meaning to effect a

swift and lawless rescue, but paused at sound of a footstep behind me. The old waiter had come to tell me that my luncheon was ready. I followed him out of the hall, not, however, without a bright glance across my shoulder to reassure the little captive that I should come back.

I had the sharp appetite of the convalescent, and this the sea-air had whetted already to a finer edge. In touch with a dozen oysters, and with stout, I soon shed away the unreasoning anger I had felt against A. V. Laider. I became merely sorry for him that he had not received a letter which might perhaps have comforted him. In touch with cutlets, I felt how sorely he had needed comfort. And anon, by the big bright fireside of that small dark smoking-room where, a year ago, on the last evening of my stay here, he and I had at length spoken to each other, I reviewed in detail the tragic experience he had told me: and I fairly revelled in reminiscent sympathy with him. . . .

A. V. Laider—I had looked him up in the visitor's book on the night of his arrival. I myself had arrived the day before, and had been rather sorry there was no one else staying here. A convalescent by the sea likes to have some one to observe, to wonder about, at meal-time. I was glad when, on my second evening, I found seated at the table opposite to mine another guest. I was the gladder because he was just the right kind of guest. He was enigmatic. By this I mean that he did not look soldierly nor financial nor artistic nor anything definite at all. He offered a clean slate for speculation. And thank heaven! he evidently wasn't going to spoil the fun by engaging me in conversation later on. A decently unsociable man, anxious to be left alone.

The heartiness of his appetite, in contrast with his extreme fragility of aspect and limpness of demeanour, assured me that he, too, had just had influenza. I liked him for that. Now and again our eyes met and were instantly parted. We managed, as a rule, to observe each other indirectly. I was sure it was not merely because he had been ill that he looked interesting. Nor did it seem to me that a spiritual melancholy, though I imagined him sad at the best of times, was his sole asset. I conjectured that he was clever. I thought he might also be imaginative. At first glance I had mistrusted him. A shock of white hair, combined with a young face and dark eyebrows, does somehow make a man look like a charlatan. But it is foolish to be guided by an accident of colour. I had soon rejected my first impression of my fellow-diner. I found him very sympathetic.

Anywhere but in England it would be impossible for two solitary men, howsoever much reduced by influenza, to spend five or six days in the same hostel and not exchange a single word. That is one of the charms of England. Had Laider and I been born and bred in any other land we should have become acquainted before the end of our first evening in the small smoking-room, and have found ourselves irrevocably committed to go on talking to each other throughout the rest of our visit. We might, it is true, have happened to like each other more than any one we had ever met. This off-chance may have occurred to us both. But it counted for nothing as against the certain surrender of quietude and liberty. We slightly bowed to each other as we entered or left the dining-room or smoking-room, and as we met on the widespread sands or in the shop that had a small and faded circulating library. That was all. Our mutual aloofness was a positive bond between us.

Had he been much older than I, the responsibility for our silence would of course have been his alone. But he was not, I judged, more than five or six years ahead of me, and thus I might without impropriety have taken it on myself to perform that hard and perilous feat which English people call, with a shiver, 'breaking the ice.' He had reason, therefore, to be as grateful to me as I to him. Each of us, not the less frankly because silently, recognized his obligation to the other. And when, on the last evening of my stay, the ice actually was broken no ill-will rose between us: neither of us was to blame.

It was a Sunday evening. I had been out for a long last walk and had come in very late to dinner. Laider left his table almost immediately after I sat down to mine. When I entered the smoking-room I found him reading a weekly review which I had bought the day before. It was a crisis. He could not silently offer, nor could I have silently accepted, sixpence. It was a crisis. We faced it like men. He made, by word of mouth, a graceful apology. Verbally, not by signs, I besought him to go on reading. But this, of course, was a vain counsel of perfection. The social code forced us to talk now. We obeyed it like men. To reassure him that our position was not so desperate as it might seem, I took the earliest opportunity to mention that I was going away early next morning. In the tone of his 'Oh, are you?' he tried bravely to imply that he was sorry, even now, to hear that. In a way, perhaps, he really was sorry. We had got on so well together, he and I. Nothing could efface the memory of that. Nay, we seemed to be hitting it off even now. Influenza was not our sole theme. We passed from that to the aforesaid weekly review, and to a correspondence that was raging therein on Faith and Reason.

This correspondence had now reached its fourth and penultimate stage—its Australian stage. It is hard to see why these correspondences spring up; one only knows that they do spring up, suddenly, like street crowds. There comes, it would seem, a moment when the whole English-speaking race is unconsciously bursting to have its say about some one thing —the split infinitive, or the habits of migratory birds, or faith and reason, or what-not. Whatever weekly review happens at such a moment to contain a reference, however remote, to

the theme in question reaps the storm. Gusts of letters blow
in from all corners of the British Isles. These are presently
reinforced by Canada in full blast. A few weeks later the
Anglo-Indians weigh in. In due course we have the help of
our Australian cousins. By that time, however, we of the
Mother Country have got our second wind, and so determined
are we to make the most of it that at last even the Editor
suddenly loses patience and says 'This correspondence must
now cease.—Ed.' and wonders why on earth he ever allowed
anything so tedious and idiotic to begin.

I pointed out to Laider one of the Australian letters that had
especially pleased me in the current issue. It was from 'A
Melbourne Man,' and was of the abrupt kind which declares
that 'all your correspondents have been groping in the dark'
and then settles the whole matter in one short sharp flash. The
flash in this instance was 'Reason is faith, faith reason—that is
all we know on earth and all we need to know.' The writer
then enclosed his card and was, etc., 'A Melbourne Man.' I
said to Laider how very restful it was, after influenza, to read
anything that meant nothing whatsoever. Laider was inclined
to take the letter more seriously than I, and to be mildly meta-
physical. I said that for me faith and reason were two separate
things, and (as I am no good at metaphysics, however mild) I
offered a definite example, to coax the talk on to ground where
I should be safe. 'Palmistry, for example,' I said. 'Deep down
in my heart I believe in palmistry.'

Laider turned in his chair. 'You believe in palmistry?'

I hesitated. 'Yes, somehow I do. Why? I haven't the
slightest notion. I can give myself all sorts of reasons for
laughing it to scorn. My common sense utterly rejects it. Of
course the shape of the hand means something—is more or
less an index of character. But the idea that my past and future
are neatly mapped out on my palms——' I shrugged my
shoulders.

'You don't like that idea?' asked Laider in his gentle, rather academic voice.

'I only say it's a grotesque idea.'

'Yet you do believe in it?'

'I've a grotesque belief in it, yes.'

'Are you sure your reason for calling this idea "grotesque" isn't merely that you dislike it?'

'Well,' I said, with the hope that he was a companion in absurdity, 'doesn't it seem grotesque to *you*?'

'It seems strange.'

'You believe in it?'

'Oh, absolutely.'

'Hurrah!'

He smiled at my pleasure, and I, at the risk of re-entanglement in metaphysics, claimed him as standing shoulder to shoulder with me against 'A Melbourne Man.' This claim he gently disputed. 'You may think me very prosaic,' he said, 'but I can't believe without evidence.'

'Well, I'm equally prosaic and equally at a disadvantage: I can't take my own belief as evidence, and I've no other evidence to go on.'

He asked me if I had ever made a study of palmistry. I said I had read one of Desbarolles' books years ago, and one of Heron-Allen's. But, he asked, had I tried to test them by the lines on my own hands or on the hands of my friends? I confessed that my actual practice in palmistry had been of a merely passive kind – the prompt extension of my palm to anyone who would be so good as to 'read' it and truckle for a few minutes to my egoism. (I hoped Laider might do this.)

'Then, I almost wonder,' he said, with his sad smile, 'that you haven't lost your belief, after all the nonsense you must have heard. There are so many young girls who go in for palmistry. I am sure all the five foolish virgins were "awfully keen on it" and used to say "You can be led, but not driven," and "You are likely to have a serious illness between the ages of forty and forty-five," and "You are by nature rather lazy, but can be very energetic by fits and starts." And most of the professionals, I'm told, are as silly as the young girls.'

For the honour of the profession, I named three practitioners whom I had found really good at reading character. He asked whether any of them had been right about past events. I confessed that, as a matter of fact, all three of them had been right in the main. This seemed to amuse him. He asked whether any of them had predicted anything which had since come true. I confessed that all three had predicted that I should do several things which I had since done rather unexpectedly. He asked if I didn't accept this as at any rate a scrap of evidence. I said I could only regard it as a fluke—a rather remarkable fluke.

The superiority of his sad smile was beginning to get on my nerves. I wanted him to see that he was as absurd as I. 'Suppose,' I said, 'suppose for sake of argument that you and I are nothing but helpless automata created to do just this and that, and to have just that and this done to us. Suppose in fact, we *haven't* any free will whatsoever. Is it likely or conceivable that the Power that fashioned us would take the trouble to jot down in cipher on our hands just what was in store for us?'

Laider did not answer this question, he did but annoyingly ask me another. 'You believe in free will?'

'Yes, of course. I'll be hanged if I'm an automaton.'

'And you believe in free will just as in palmistry—without any reason?'

'Oh no. Everything points to our having free will.'

'Everything? What, for instance?'

This rather cornered me. I dodged out, as lightly as I could, by saying 'I suppose *you* would say it was written in my hand that I should be a believer in free will.'

'Ah, I've no doubt it is.'

I held out my palms. But, to my great disappointment, he

206

looked quickly away from them. He had ceased to smile.
There was agitation in his voice as he explained that he never
looked at people's hands now. 'Never now—never again.'
He shook his head as though to beat off some memory.

I was much embarrassed by my indiscretion. I hastened to
tide over the awkward moment by saying that if I could read
hands I wouldn't, for fear of the awful things I might see there.

'Awful things, yes,' he whispered, nodding at the fire.

'Not,' I said in self-defence, 'that there's anything very
awful, so far as I know, to be read in *my* hands.'

He turned his gaze from the fire to me. 'You aren't a
murderer, for example?'

'Oh, no,' I replied, with a nervous laugh.

'*I* am.'

This was a more than awkward, it was a painful, moment
for me; and I am afraid I must have started or winced, for he
instantly begged my pardon. 'I don't know,' he exclaimed,
'why I said it. I'm usually a very reticent man. But sometimes——' He pressed his brow. 'What you must think of
me!'

I begged him to dismiss the matter from his mind.

'It's very good of you to say that; but—I've placed myself
as well as you in a false position. I ask you to believe that I'm
not the sort of man who is "wanted" or ever was "wanted"
by the police. I should be bowed out of any police-station at
which I gave myself up. I'm not a murderer in any bald sense
of the word. No.'

My face must have perceptibly brightened, for 'Ah,' he said,
'don't imagine I'm not a murderer at all. Morally, I am. ' He
looked at the clock. I pointed out that the night was young.
He assured me that his story was not a long one. I assured
him that I hoped it was. He said I was very kind. I denied
this. He warned me that what he had to tell might rather tend
to stiffen my unwilling faith in palmistry, and to shake my

opposite and cherished faith in free will. I said 'Never mind.' He stretched his hands pensively toward the fire. I settled myself back in my chair.

'My hands,' he said, staring at the backs of them, 'are the hands of a very weak man. I daresay you know enough of palmistry to see that for yourself. You notice the slightness of the thumbs and of the two "little" fingers. They are the hands of a weak and over-sensitive man—a man without confidence, a man who would certainly waver in an emergency. Rather Hamlet-ish hands,' he mused. 'And I'm like Hamlet in other respects, too : I'm no fool, and I've rather a noble disposition, and I'm unlucky. But Hamlet was luckier than I in one thing : he was a murderer by accident, whereas the murders that I committed one day fourteen years ago—for I must tell you it wasn't one murder, but many murders that I committed—were all of them due to the wretched inherent weakness of my own wretched self.

'I was twenty-six—no, twenty-seven years old, and rather a nondescript person, as I am now. I was supposed to have been called to the Bar. In fact, I believe I *had* been called to the Bar. I hadn't listened to the call. I never intended to practise, and I never did practise. I only wanted an excuse in the eyes of the world for existing. I suppose the nearest I have ever come to practising is now at this moment : I am defending a murderer. My father had left me well enough provided with money. I was able to go my own desultory way, riding my hobbies where I would. I had a good stableful of hobbies. Palmistry was one of them. I was rather ashamed of this one. It seemed to me absurd, as it seems to you. Like you, though, I believed in it. Unlike you, I had done more than merely read a book or so about it. I had read innumerable books about it. I had taken casts of all my friends' hands. I had tested and tested again the points at which Desbarolles dissented from the gipsies, and—well, enough that I had gone into it all rather thoroughly, and was as sound a palmist as a man may be without giving his whole life to palmistry.

'One of the first things I had seen in my own hand, as soon as I had learned to read it, was that at about the age of twenty-six I should have a narrow escape from death—from a violent death. There was a clean break in the life-line, and a square joining it—the protective square, you know. The markings were precisely the same in both hands. It was to be the narrowest escape possible. And I wasn't going to escape without injury, either. That is what bothered me. There was a faint line connecting the break in the life-line with a star on the line of health. Against that star was another square. I was to recover from the injury, whatever it might be. Still, I didn't exactly look forward to it. Soon after I had reached the age of twenty-five, I began to feel uncomfortable. The thing might be going to happen at any moment. In palmistry, you know, it is impossible to pin an event down hard and fast to one year. This particular event was to be when I was *about* twenty-six; it mightn't be till I was twenty-seven; it might be while I was only twenty-five.

'And I used to tell myself that it mightn't be at all. My reason rebelled against the whole notion of palmistry, just as yours does. I despised my faith in the thing, just as you despise yours. I used to try not to be so ridiculously careful as I was whenever I crossed a street. I lived in London at that time. Motor-cars had not yet come in, but—what hours, all told, I must have spent standing on curbs, very circumspect, very lamentable! It was a pity, I suppose, that I had no definite occupation—something to take me out of myself. I was one of the victims of private means. There came a time when I drove in four-wheelers rather than in hansoms, and was doubtful of four-wheelers. Oh, I assure you, I was very lamentable indeed.

'If a railway-journey could be avoided, I avoided it. My uncle had a place in Hampshire. I was very fond of him and of his wife. Theirs was the only house I ever went to stay in now. I was there for a week in November, not long after my twenty-seventh birthday. There were other people staying there, and at the end of the week we all travelled back to London together. There were six of us in the carriage: Colonel Elbourn and his wife, and their daughter, a girl of seventeen; and another married couple, the Blakes. I had been at Winchester with Blake, but had hardly seen him since that time. He was in the Indian Civil, and was home on leave. He was sailing for India next week. His wife was to remain in England for some months, and then join him out there. They had been married five years. She was now just twenty-four years old. He told me that this was her age.

'The Elbourns I had never met before. They were charming people. We had all been very happy together. The only trouble had been that on the last night, at dinner, my uncle asked me if I still went in for "the gipsy business," as he always called it; and of course the three ladies were immensely excited, and implored me to "do" their hands. I told them it was all nonsense, I said I had forgotten all I once knew, I made various excuses; and the matter dropped. It was quite true that I had given up reading hands. I avoided anything that might remind me of what was in my own hands. And so, next morning, it was a great bore to me when, soon after the train started, Mrs. Elbourn said it would be "too cruel" of me if I refused to do their hands now. Her daughter and Mrs. Blake also said it would be "brutal"; and they were all taking off their gloves, and—well, of course I had to give in.

'I went to work methodically on Mrs. Elbourn's hands, in the usual way, you know, first sketching the character from the backs of them; and there was the usual hush, broken by the usual little noises—grunts of assent from the husband, cooings of recognition from the daughter. Presently I asked to see the palms, and from them I filled in the details of Mrs. Elbourn's character before going on to the events in her life. But while I talked I was calculating how old Mrs. Elbourn might be. In my first glance at her palms I had seen that she could not have been less than twenty-five when she married. The daughter was seventeen. Suppose the daughter had been born a year later—how old would the mother be? Forty-three, yes. Not less than that, poor woman!'

Laider looked at me. 'Why "poor woman," you wonder? Well, in that first glance I had seen other things than her marriage-line. I had seen a very complete break in the lines of life and of fate. I had seen violent death there. At what age? Not later, not possibly *later*, than forty-three. While I talked to her about the things that had happened in her girlhood, the back of my brain was hard at work on those marks of catastrophe. I was horribly wondering that she was still alive. It was impossible that between her and that catastrophe there could be more than a few short months. And all the time I was talking; and I suppose I acquitted myself well, for I remember that when I ceased I had a sort of ovation from the Elbourns.

'It was a relief to turn to another pair of hands. Mrs. Blake was an amusing young creature, and her hands were very characteristic, and prettily odd in form. I allowed myself to be rather whimsical about her nature, and, having begun in that vein, I went on in it—somehow—even after she had turned her palms. In those palms were re-duplicated the signs I had seen in Mrs. Elbourn's. It was as though they had been copied neatly out. The only difference was in the placing of them; and it was this difference that was the most horrible point. The fatal age in Mrs. Blake's hands was—not past, no, for here *she* was. But she might have died when she was twenty-one. Twenty-three seemed to be the utmost span. She was twenty-four, you know.

'I have said that I am a weak man. And you will have good proof of that directly. Yet I showed a certain amount of strength that day—yes, even on that day which has humiliated and saddened the rest of my life. Neither my face nor my voice betrayed me when in the palms of Dorothy Elbourn I was again confronted with those same signs. She was all for knowing the future, poor child! I believe I told her all manner of things that were to be. And she had no future—none, none in *this* world—except——

'And then, while I talked, there came to me suddenly a suspicion. I wondered it hadn't come before. You guess what it was? It made me feel very cold and strange. I went on talking. But, also, I went on—quite separately—thinking. The suspicion wasn't a certainty. This mother and daughter were always together. What was to befall the one might anywhere—anywhere—befall the other. But a like fate, in an equally near future, was in store for that other lady. The coincidence was curious, very. Here we all were together— here; they and I—I who was narrowly to escape, so soon now, what they, so soon now, were to suffer. Oh, there was an inference to be drawn. Not a *sure* inference, I told myself. And always I was talking, talking, and the train was swinging and swaying noisily along—to what? It was a fast train. Our carriage was near the engine. I was talking loudly. Full well I had known what I should see in the Colonel's hands. I told myself I had not known. I told myself that even now the thing I dreaded was not sure to be. Don't think I was dreading it for myself. I wasn't so "lamentable" as all that—now. It was only of them that I thought—only for them. I hurried over the Colonel's character and career; I was perfunctory. It was Blake's hands that I wanted. *They* were the hands that mattered. If *they* had the marks—— Remember, Blake was to start for India in the coming week, his wife was to remain in England. They would be apart. Therefore——

'And the marks were there. And I did nothing—nothing but hold forth on the subtleties of Blake's character. There was a thing for me to do. I wanted to do it. I wanted to spring to the window and pull the communication-cord. Quite a simple thing to do. Nothing easier than to stop a train. You just give a sharp pull, and the train slows down, comes to a standstill. And the Guard appears at your window. You explain to the Guard.

'Nothing easier than to tell him there is going to be a collision. Nothing easier than to insist that you and your friends and every other passenger in the train must get out at once. . . . There *are* easier things than this ? Things that need less courage than this ? Some of *them* I could have done, I dare-say. This thing I was going to do. Oh, I was determined that I would do it—directly.

'I had said all I had to say about Blake's hands. I had brought my entertainment to an end. I had been thanked and complimented all round. I was quite at liberty. I was going to do what I had to do. I was determined, yes.

'We were near the outskirts of London. The air was grey, thickening; and Dorothy Elbourn had said, "Oh, this horrible old London! I suppose there's the same old fog!" And presently I heard her father saying something about "pre-vention" and "a short act of Parliament" and "anthracite." And I sat and listened and agreed and——'

Laider closed his eyes. He passed his hand slowly through the air.

'I had a racking headache. And when I said so, I was told not to talk. I was in bed, and the nurses were always telling me not to talk. I was in a hospital. I knew that. But I didn't know why I was there. One day I thought I should like to know why, and so I asked. I was feeling much better now. They told me, by degrees, that I had had concussion of the brain. I had been brought there unconscious, and had re-mained unconscious for forty-eight hours. I had been in an accident—a railway accident. This seemed to me odd. I had

arrived quite safely at my uncle's place, and I had no memory
of any journey since that. In cases of concussion, you know,
it's not uncommon for the patient to forget all that happened
just before the accident; there may be a blank of several hours.
So it was in my case. One day my uncle was allowed to come
and see me. And somehow, suddenly, at sight of him, the
blank was filled in. I remembered, in a flash, everything. I
was quite calm, though. Or I made myself seem so, for I
wanted to know how the collision had happened. My uncle
told me that the engine-driver had failed to see a signal because
of the fog, and our train had crashed into a goods-train. I
didn't ask him about the people who were with me. You see,
there was no need to ask. Very gently my uncle began to tell
me, but—I had begun to talk strangely, I suppose. I remember
the frightened look of my uncle's face, and the nurse scolding
him in whispers.

'After that, all a blur. It seems that I became very ill indeed,
wasn't expected to live.

'However, I live.'

There was a long silence. Laider did not look at me, nor I
at him. The fire was burning low, and he watched it.

At length he spoke. 'You despise me. Naturally. I despise
myself.'

'No, I don't despise you; but——'

'You blame me.' I did not meet his gaze. 'You blame me,'
he repeated.

'Yes.'

'And there, if I may say so, you are a little unjust. It isn't
my fault that I was born weak.'

'But a man may conquer weakness.'

'Yes, if he is endowed with the strength for that.'

His fatalism drew from me a gesture of disgust. 'Do you
really mean,' I asked, 'that because you didn't pull that cord,
you *couldn't* have pulled it?'

'Yes.'

'And it's written in your hands that you couldn't?'

He looked at the palms of his hands. 'They are the hands of a very weak man,' he said.

'A man so weak that he cannot believe in the possibility of free will for himself or for any one?'

'They are the hands of an intelligent man, who can weigh evidence and see things as they are.'

'But answer me: Was it fore-ordained that you should not pull that cord?'

'It was fore-ordained.'

'And was it actually marked in your hands that you were not going to pull it?'

'Ah, well, you see, it's rather the things one *is* going to do that are actually marked. The things one *isn't* going to do,—the innumerable negative things,—how could one expect *them* to be marked?'

'But the consequences of what one leaves undone may be positive?'

'Horribly positive,' he winced. 'My hand is the hand of a man who has suffered a great deal in later life.'

'And was it the hand of a man *destined* to suffer?'

'Oh, yes. I thought I told you that.'

There was a pause.

'Well,' I said, with awkward sympathy, 'I suppose all hands are the hands of people destined to suffer.'

'Not of people destined to suffer so much as *I* have suffered —as I still suffer.'

The insistence of his self-pity chilled me, and I harked back to a question he had not straightly answered. 'Tell me: Was it marked in your hands that you were not going to pull that cord?'

Again he looked at his hands, and then, having pressed them for a moment to his face, 'It was marked very clearly,'

215

he answered, 'in *their* hands.'

Two or three days after this colloquy there had occurred to me in London an idea—an ingenious and comfortable doubt. How was Laider to be sure that his brain, recovering from concussion, had *remembered* what happened in the course of that railway-journey? How was he to know that his brain hadn't simply, in its abeyance, *invented* all this for him? It might be that he had never seen those signs in those hands. Assuredly, here was a bright loop-hole. I had forthwith written to Laider, pointing it out.

This was the letter which now, at my second visit, I had found miserably pent on the letter-board. I remembered my promise to rescue it. I arose from the retaining fireside, stretched my arms, yawned, and went forth to fulfil my Christian purpose. There was no one in the hall. The 'shower' had at length ceased. The sun had positively come out, and the front door had been thrown open in its honour. Everything along the sea-front was beautifully gleaming, drying, shimmering. But I was not to be diverted from my errand. I went to the letter-board. And—my letter was not there! Resourceful and plucky little thing—it had escaped! I did hope it would not be captured and brought back. Perhaps the alarm had already been raised by the tolling of that great bell which warns the inhabitants for miles around that a letter has broken loose from the letter-board. I had a vision of my envelope skimming wildly along the coast-line, pursued by the old but active waiter and a breathless pack of local worthies. I saw it out-distancing them all, dodging past coast-guards, doubling on its tracks, leaping breakwaters, unluckily injuring itself, losing speed, and at last, in a splendour of desperation, taking to the open sea. But suddenly I had another idea. Perhaps Laider had returned?

He had. I espied afar on the sands a form that was recognizably, by the listless droop of it, his. I was glad and sorry—rather glad, because he completed the scene of last year; and very sorry because this time we should be at each other's mercy: no restful silence and liberty, for either of us, this time. Perhaps he had been told I was here, and had gone out to avoid me while he yet could. Oh weak, weak! Why palter? I put on my hat and coat, and marched out to meet him.

'Influenza, of course?' we asked simultaneously.

There is a limit to the time which one may may spend in talking to another about his own influenza; and presently, as we paced the sands, I felt that Laider had passed this limit. I wondered that he didn't break off and thank me now for my letter. He must have read it. He ought to have thanked me for it at once. It was a very good letter, a remarkable letter. But surely he wasn't waiting to answer it by post? His silence about it gave me the absurd sense of having taken a liberty, confound him! He was evidently ill at ease while he talked. But it wasn't for me to help him out of his difficulty, whatever that might be. It was for him to remove the strain imposed on myself.

Abruptly, after a long pause, he did now manage to say, 'It was—very good of you to—to write me that letter.' He told me he had only just got it, and he drifted away into otiose explanations of this fact. I thought he might at least say it was a remarkable letter; and you can imagine my annoyance when he said, after another interval, 'I was very much touched indeed.' I had wished to be convincing, not touching. I can't bear to be called touching.

'Don't you,' I asked, 'think it *is* quite possible that your brain invented all those memories of what—what happened before that accident?'

He drew a sharp sigh. 'You make me feel very guilty.'

'That's exactly what I tried to make you *not* feel!'

'I know, yes. That's why I feel so guilty.'

217

We had paused in our walk. He stood nervously prodding the hard wet sand with his walking-stick. 'In a way,' he said, 'your theory was quite right. But—it didn't go far enough. It's not only possible, it's a fact, that I didn't see those signs in those hands. I never examined those hands. They weren't there. *I* wasn't there. I haven't an uncle in Hampshire, even. I never had.'

I, too, prodded the sand. 'Well,' I said at length, 'I do feel rather a fool.'

'I've no right even to beg your pardon, but——'

'Oh, I'm not vexed. Only—I rather wish you hadn't told me this.'

'I wish I hadn't had to. It was your kindness, you see, that forced me. By trying to take an imaginary load off my conscience, you laid a very real one on it.'

'I'm sorry. But you, of your own free will, you know, exposed your conscience to me last year. I don't yet quite understand why you did that.'

'No, of course not. I don't deserve that you should. But I think you will. May I explain? I'm afraid I've talked a great deal already about my influenza, and I shan't be able to keep it out of my explanation. Well, my weakest point—I told you this last year, but it happens to be perfectly true that my weakest point—is my will. Influenza, as you know, fastens unerringly on one's weakest point. It doesn't attempt to undermine my imagination. That would be a forlorn hope. I have, alas! a very strong imagination. At ordinary times my imagination allows itself to be governed by my will. My will keeps it in check by constant nagging. But when my will isn't strong enough even to nag, then my imagination stampedes. I become even as a little child. I tell myself the most preposterous fables, and—the trouble is—I can't help telling them to my friends. Until I've thoroughly shaken off influenza, I'm not fit company for any one. I perfectly realize

this, and I have the good sense to go right away till I'm quite
well again. I come here usually. It seems absurd, but I must
confess I was sorry last year when we fell into conversation. I
knew I should very soon be letting myself go, or rather, very
soon be swept away. Perhaps I ought to have warned you;
but—I'm a rather shy man. And then you mentioned the
subject of palmistry. You said you believed in it. I wondered
at that. I had once read Desbarolles' book about it, but I am
bound to say I thought the whole thing very great nonsense
indeed.'

'Then,' I gasped, 'it isn't even true that you believe in
palmistry?'

'Oh, no. But I wasn't able to tell you that. You had begun
by saying that you believed in palmistry, and then you proceeded to scoff at it. While you scoffed I saw myself as a man
with a terribly good reason for *not* scoffing; and in a flash I
saw the terribly good reason; I had the whole story—at least
I had the broad outlines of it—clear before me.'

'You hadn't ever thought of it before?' He shook his head.
My eyes beamed. 'The whole thing was a sheer improvisation?'

'Yes,' said Laider, humbly, 'I am as bad as all that. I don't
say that all the details of the story I told you that evening were
filled in at the very instant of its conception. I was filling them
in while we talked about palmistry in general, and while I was
waiting for the moment when my story would come in most
effectively. And I've no doubt I added some extra touches in
the course of the actual telling. Don't imagine that I took the
slightest pleasure in deceiving you. It's only my will, not my
conscience, that is weakened after influenza. I simply can't
help telling what I've made up, and telling it to the best of my
ability. But I'm thoroughly ashamed all the time.'

'Not of your ability, surely?'

'Yes, of that, too,' he said with his sad smile. 'I always feel that I'm not doing justice to my idea.'

'You are too stern a critic, believe me.'

'It is very kind of you to say that. You are very kind altogether. Had I known that you were so essentially a man of the world—in the best sense of that term—I shouldn't have so much dreaded seeing you just now and having to confess to you. But I'm not going to take advantage of your urbanity and your easy-going ways. I hope that some day we may meet somewhere when I haven't had influenza and am a not wholly undesirable acquaintance. As it is, I refuse to let you associate with me. I am an older man than you, and so I may without impertinence warn you against having anything to do with me.'

I deprecated this advice, of course; but for a man of weakened will, he showed great firmness. 'You,' he said, 'in your heart of hearts, don't want to have to walk and talk continually with a person who might at any moment try to bamboozle you with some ridiculous tale. And I, for my part, don't want to degrade myself by trying to bamboozle any one—especially one whom I have taught to see through me. Let the two talks we have had be as though they had not been. Let us bow to each other, as last year, but let that be all. Let us follow in all things the precedent of last year.'

With a smile that was almost gay he turned on his heel, and moved away with a step that was almost brisk. I was a little disconcerted. But I was also more than a little glad. The restfulness of silence, the charm of liberty—these things were not, after all, forfeit. My heart thanked Laider for that; and throughout the week I loyally seconded him in the system he had laid down for us. All was as it had been last year. We did not smile to each other, we merely bowed, when we entered or left the dining-room or smoking-room, and when we met on the widespread sands or in that shop which had a small and faded, but circulating, library.

Once or twice in the course of the week it did occur to me

that perhaps Laider had told the simple truth at our first interview and an ingenious lie at our second. I frowned at this possibility. The idea of any one wishing to be quit of *me* was most distasteful. However, I was to find reassurance. On the last evening of my stay, I suggested, in the small smoking-room, that he and I should, as sticklers for precedent, converse. We did so, very pleasantly. And after a while I happened to say that I had seen this afternoon a great number of sea-gulls flying close to the shore.

'Sea-gulls?' said Laider, turning in his chair.

'Yes. And I don't think I had ever realized how extraordinarily beautiful they are when their wings catch the light.'

'Beautiful?' Laider threw a quick glance at me and away from me. 'You think them beautiful?'

'Surely.'

'Well, perhaps they are, yes; I suppose they are. But—I don't like seeing them. They always remind me of something —rather an awful thing—that once happened to me.' . . .

It was a very awful thing indeed.

No. 2. The Pines

[*Early in the year 1914 Mr. Edmund Gosse told me he was asking certain of his friends to write for him a few words apiece in description of Swinburne as they had known or seen him at one time or another; and he was so good as to wish to include in this gathering a few words by myself. I found it hard to be brief without seeming irreverent. I failed in the attempt to make of my subject a snapshot that was not a grotesque. So I took refuge in an ampler scope. I wrote a reminiscential essay. From that essay I made an extract, which I gave to Mr. Gosse. From that extract he made a quotation in his enchanting biography. The words quoted by him reappear here in the midst of the whole essay as I wrote it. I dare not hope they are unashamed of their humble surroundings.—M. B.*]

In my youth the suburbs were rather looked down on—I never quite knew why. It was held anomalous, and a matter for merriment, that Swinburne lived in one of them. For my part, had I known as a fact that Catullus was still alive, I should have been as ready to imagine him living in Putney as elsewhere. The marvel would have been merely that he lived. And Swinburne's survival struck as surely as could his have struck in me the chord of wonder.

Not, of course, that he had achieved a feat of longevity. He was far from the Psalmist's limit. Nor was he one of those men whom one associates with the era in which they happened to be young. Indeed, if there was one man belonging less than any other to Mid-Victorian days, Swinburne was that man.

But by the calendar it was in those days that he had blazed—
blazed forth with so unexampled a suddenness of splendour;
and in the light of that conflagration all that he had since done,
much and magnificent though this was, paled. The essential
Swinburne was still the earliest. He was and would always be
the flammiferous boy of the dim past—a legendary creature,
sole kin to the phœnix. It had been impossible that he should
ever surpass himself in the artistry that was from the outset
his; impossible that he should bring forth rhythms lovelier and
greater than those early rhythms, or exercise over them a
mastery more than—absolute. Also, it had been impossible
that the first wild ardour of spirit should abide unsinkingly in
him. Youth goes. And there was not in Swinburne that basis
on which a man may in his maturity so build as to make good,
in some degree, the loss of what is gone. He was not a thinker:
his mind rose ever away from reason to rhapsody; neither was
he human. He was a king crowned but not throned. He was a
singing bird that could build no nest. He was a youth who
could not afford to age. Had he died young, literature would
have lost many glories; but none so great as the glories he had
already given, nor any such as we should fondly imagine
ourselves bereft of by his early death. A great part of Keats'
fame rests on our assumption of what he *would* have done.
But—even granting that Keats may have had in him more than
had Swinburne of stuff for development—I believe that had he
lived on we should think of him as author of the poems that in
fact we know. Not philosophy, after all, not humanity, just
sheer joyous power of song, is the primal thing in poetry.
Ideas, and flesh and blood, are but reserves to be brought up
when the poet's youth is going. When the bird can no longer
sing in flight, let the nest be ready. After the king has dazzled
us with his crown, let him have something to sit down on. But
the session on throne or in nest is not the divine period. Had
Swinburne's genius been of the kind that solidifies, he would

yet at the close of the nineteenth century have been for us young men virtually—though not so definitely as in fact he was—the writer of *Atalanta in Calydon* and of *Poems and Ballads.*

Tennyson's death in '98 had not taken us at all by surprise. We had been fully aware that he was alive. He had always been careful to keep himself abreast of the times. Anything that came along—the Nebular Hypothesis at one moment, the Imperial Institute at another—won mention from his Muse. He had husbanded for his old age that which he had long ago inherited: middle age. If in our mourning for him there really was any tincture of surprise, this was due to merely the vague sense that he had in the fullness of time died rather prematurely: his middle age might have been expected to go on flourishing for ever. But assuredly Tennyson dead laid no such strain on our fancy as Swinburne living.

It is true that Swinburne did, from time to time, take public notice of current affairs; but what notice he took did but seem to mark his remoteness from them, from us. The Boers, I remember, were the theme of a sonnet which embarrassed even their angriest enemies in our midst. He likened them, if I remember rightly, to 'hell-hounds foaming at the jaws.' This was by some people taken as a sign that he had fallen away from that high generosity of spirit which had once been his. To me it meant merely that he thought of poor little England writhing under the heel of an alien despotism, just as, in the days when he really was interested in such matters, poor little Italy had writhen. I suspect, too, that the first impulse to write about the Boers came not from the Muse within, but from Theodore Watts-Dunton without. . . . 'Now, Algernon, we're at war, you know—at war with the Boers. I don't want to bother you at all, but I do think, my dear old friend, you oughtn't to let slip this opportunity of,' etc., etc.

No. 2. The Pines

Some such hortation is easily imaginable by any one who saw the two old friends together. The first time I had this honour, this sight for lasting and affectionate memory, must have been in the Spring of '99. In those days Theodore Watts (he had but recently taken on the -Dunton) was still something of a gad-about. I had met him here and there, he had said in his stentorian tones pleasant things to me about my writing, I sent him a new little book of mine, and in acknowledging this he asked me to come down to Putney and 'have luncheon and meet Swinburne.' Meet Catullus!

On the day appointed 'I came as one whose feet half linger.' It is but a few steps from the railway-station in Putney High Street to No. 2. The Pines. I had expected a greater distance to the sanctuary—a walk in which to compose my mind and prepare myself for initiation. I laid my hand irresolutely against the gate of the bleak trim front-garden, I withdrew my hand, I went away. Out here were all the aspects of common modern life. In there was Swinburne. A butcher-boy went by, whistling. He was not going to see Swinburne. He could afford to whistle. I pursued my dilatory course up the slope of Putney, but at length it occurred to me that un-punctuality would after all be an imperfect expression of reverence, and I retraced my footsteps.

No. 2—prosaic inscription! But as that front-door closed behind me I had the instant sense of having slipped away from the harsh light of the ordinary and contemporary into the dimness of an odd, august past. Here, in this dark hall, the past was the present. Here loomed vivid and vital on the walls those women of Rossetti whom I had known but as shades. Familiar to me in small reproductions by photogravure, here they *themselves* were, life-sized, 'with curled-up lips and amorous hair' done in the original warm crayon, all of them intently looking down on me while I took off my overcoat—all wondering who was this intruder from posterity. That they hung in the hall, evidently no more than an overflow, was an earnest of packed plenitude within. The room I was ushered into was a back-room, a dining-room, looking on to a good garden. It was, in form and 'fixtures,' an inalienably Mid-Victorian room, and held its stolid own in the riot of Rossettis. Its proportions, its window-sash bisecting the view of garden, its folding-doors (through which I heard the voice of Watts-Dunton booming mysteriously in the front room), its mantel-piece, its gas-brackets, all proclaimed that nothing ever would seduce them from their allegiance to Martin Tupper. 'Nor me from mine,' said the sturdy cruet-stand on the long expanse of table-cloth. The voice of Watts-Dunton ceased suddenly, and a few moments later its owner appeared. He had been dictating, he explained. 'A great deal of work on hand just now—a great deal of work.' . . . I remember that on my subsequent visits he was always, at the moment of my arrival, dictating, and always greeted me with that phrase, 'A great deal of work on hand just now.' I used to wonder what work it was, for he published little enough. But I never ventured to inquire, and indeed rather cherished the mystery: it was a part of the dear little old man; it went with the something gnome-like about his swarthiness and chubbiness—went with the shaggy hair that fell over the collar of his eternally crumpled frock-coat, the shaggy eyebrows that overhung his bright little brown eyes, the shaggy moustache that hid his small round chin. It was a mystery inherent in the richly-laden atmosphere of The Pines. . . .

While I stood talking to Watts-Dunton—talking as loudly as he, for he was very deaf—I enjoyed the thrill of suspense in watching the door through which would appear—Swinburne. I asked after Mr. Swinburne's health. Watts-Dunton said it was very good: 'He always goes out for his long walk in the morning—wonderfully active. Active in mind, too. But I'm afraid you won't be able to get into touch with him. He's

almost stone-deaf, poor fellow—almost stone-deaf now.' He
changed the subject, and I felt I must be careful not to seem
interested in Swinburne exclusively. I spoke of *Aylwin*. The
parlourmaid brought in the hot dishes. The great moment
was at hand.

Nor was I disappointed. Swinburne's entry was for me a
great moment. Here, suddenly visible in the flesh, was the
legendary being and divine singer. Here he was, shutting the
door behind him as might anybody else, and advancing—a
strange small figure in grey, having an air at once noble and
roguish, proud and skittish. My name was roared to him. In
shaking his hand, I bowed low, of course—a bow *de cœur*; and
he, in the old aristocratic manner, bowed equally low, but with
such swiftness that we narrowly escaped concussion. You do
not usually associate a man of genius, when you see one, with
any social class; and, Swinburne being of an aspect so unrelated as it was to any species of human kind, I wondered the
more that almost the first impression he made on me, or would
make on any one, was that of a very great gentleman indeed.
Not of an *old* gentleman, either. Sparse and straggling though
the grey hair was that fringed the immense pale dome of his
head, and venerably haloed though he was for me by his greatness, there was yet about him something—boyish? girlish?
childish, rather; something of a beautifully well-bred child.
But he had the eyes of a god, and the smile of an elf. In figure,
at first glance, he seemed almost fat; but this was merely
because of the way he carried himself, with his long neck
strained so tightly back that he all receded from the waist
upwards. I noticed afterwards that this deportment made the
back of his jacket hang quite far away from his legs; and so
small and sloping were his shoulders that the jacket seemed
ever so likely to slip right off. I became aware, too, that when
he bowed he did not unbend his back, but only his neck—the
length of the neck accounting for the depth of the bow. His

hands were tiny, even for his size, and they fluttered helplessly, touchingly, unceasingly.

Directly after my introduction, we sat down to the meal. Of course I had never hoped to 'get into touch with him' reciprocally. Quite apart from his deafness, I was too modest to suppose he could be interested in anything I might say. But —for I knew he had once been as high and copious a singer in talk as in verse—I had hoped to hear utterances from him. And it did not seem that my hope was to be fulfilled. Watts-Dunton sat at the head of the table, with a huge and very Tupperesque joint of roast mutton in front of him, Swinburne and myself close up to him on either side. He talked only to me. This was the more tantalizing because Swinburne seemed as though he were bubbling over with all sorts of notions. Not that he looked at either of us. He smiled only to himself, and to his plateful of meat, and to the small bottle of Bass's pale ale that stood before him—ultimate allowance of one who had erst clashed cymbals in Naxos. This small bottle he eyed often and with enthusiasm, seeming to waver between the rapture of broaching it now and the grandeur of having it to look forward to. It made me unhappy to see what trouble he had in managing his knife and fork. Watts-Dunton told me on another occasion that this infirmity of the hands had been lifelong— had begun before Eton days. The Swinburne family had been alarmed by it and had consulted a specialist, who said that it resulted from 'an excess of electric vitality,' and that any attempt to stop it would be harmful. So they had let it be. I have known no man of genius who had not to pay, in some affliction or defect either physical or spiritual, for what the gods had given him. Here, in this fluttering of his tiny hands, was a part of the price that Swinburne had to pay. No doubt he had grown accustomed to it many lustres before I met him, and I need not have felt at all unhappy at what I tried not to see. He, evidently, was quite gay, in his silence—and in the world that was for him silent. I had, however, the maddening suspicion that he would have liked to talk. Why wouldn't Watts-Dunton roar him an opportunity? I felt I had been right perhaps in feeling that the lesser man was—no, not jealous of the greater whom he had guarded so long and with such love, but anxious that he himself should be as fully impressive to visitors as his fine gifts warranted. Not, indeed, that he monopolized the talk. He seemed to regard me as a source of information about all the latest 'movements,' and I had to shout banalities while he munched his mutton— banalities whose one saving grace for me was that they were inaudible to Swinburne. Had I met Swinburne's gaze, I should have faltered. Now and again his shining light-grey eyes roved from the table, darting this way and that—across the room, up at the ceiling, out of the window; only never at us. Somehow this aloofness gave no hint of indifference. It seemed to be, rather, a point in good manners—the good manners of a child 'sitting up to table,' not 'staring,' not 'asking questions,' and reflecting great credit on its invaluable old nurse. The child sat happy in the wealth of its inner life; the child was content not to speak until it were spoken to; but, but, I felt it did want to be spoken to. And, at length, it *was*.

So soon as the mutton had been replaced by the apple-pie, Watts-Dunton leaned forward and 'Well, Algernon,' he roared, 'how was it on the Heath to-day?' Swinburne, who had meekly inclined his ear to the question, now threw back his head, uttering a sound that was like the cooing of a dove, and forthwith, rapidly, ever so musically, he spoke to us of his walk; spoke not in the strain of a man who had been taking his daily exercise on Putney Heath, but rather in that of a Peri who had at long last been suffered to pass through Paradise. And rather than that he spoke would I say that he cooingly and flutingly *sang* of his experience. The wonders of this morning's wind and sun and clouds were expressed in a flow of words so

229

right and sentences so perfectly balanced that they would have seemed pedantic had they not been clearly as spontaneous as the wordless notes of a bird in song. The frail, sweet voice rose and fell, lingered, quickened, in all manner of trills and roulades. That he himself could not hear it, seemed to me the greatest loss his deafness inflicted on him. One would have expected this disability to mar the music; but it didn't; save that now and again a note would come out metallic and over-shrill, the tones were under good control. The whole manner and method had certainly a strong element of oddness; but no one incapable of condemning as unmanly the song of a lark would have called it affected. I had met young men of whose enunciation Swinburne's now reminded me. In them the thing had always irritated me very much; and I now became sure that it had been derived from people who had derived it in old Balliol days from Swinburne himself. One of the points familiar to me in such enunciation was the habit of stressing extremely, and lackadaisically dwelling on, some particular syllable. In Swinburne this trick was delightful—because it wasn't a trick, but a need of his heart. Well do I remember his ecstasy of emphasis and immensity of pause when he described how he had seen in a perambulator on the Heath to-day 'the most BEAUT——iful babbie ever beheld by mortal eyes.' For babies, as some of his later volumes testify, he had a sort of idolatry. After Mazzini had followed Landor to Elysium, and Victor Hugo had followed Mazzini, babies were what among live creatures most evoked Swinburne's genius for self-abasement. His rapture about this especial 'babbie' was such as to shake within me my hitherto firm conviction that, whereas the young of the brute creation are already beautiful at the age of five minutes, the human young never begin to be so before the age of three years. I suspect Watts-Dunton of having shared my lack of innate enthusiasm. But it was one of Swinburne's charms, as I was to find, that he took for granted every one's delight in what he himself so fervidly delighted in. He could as soon have imagined a man not loving the very sea as not doting on the aspect of babies and not reading at least one play by an Elizabethan or Jacobean dramatist every day.

I forget whether it was at this my first meal or at another that he described a storm in which, one night years ago, with Watts-Dunton, he had crossed the Channel. The rhythm of his great phrases was as the rhythm of those waves, and his head swayed in accordance to it like the wave-rocked boat itself. He hymned in memory the surge and darkness, the thunder and foam and phosphorescence—'You remember, Theodore? You remember the PHOS——phorescence?'—all so beautifully and vividly that I almost felt storm-bound and in peril of my life. To disentangle one from another of the several occasions on which I heard him talk is difficult because the procedure was so invariable: Watts-Dunton always dictating when I arrived, Swinburne always appearing at the moment of the meal, always the same simple and substantial fare, Swinburne never allowed to talk before the meal was half over. As to this last point, I soon realized that I had been quite unjust in suspecting Watts-Dunton of selfishness. It was simply a sign of the care with which he watched over his friend's welfare. Had Swinburne been admitted earlier to the talk, he would not have taken his proper quantity of roast mutton. So soon, always, as he had taken that, the embargo was removed, the chance was given him. And, swiftly though he embraced the chance, and much though he made of it in the courses of apple-pie and of cheese, he seemed touchingly ashamed of 'holding forth.' Often, before he had said his really full say on the theme suggested by Watts-Dunton's loud interrogation, he would curb his speech and try to eliminate himself, bowing his head over his plate; and then, when he had promptly been brought in again, he would always try to atone for his inhibiting deafness by much reference and deference to all that we might otherwise have to say. 'I hope,' he would coo to me, 'my friend Watts-Dunton, who'—and here he would turn and make a little bow to Watts-Dunton—'is himself a scholar, will bear me out when I say'—or 'I hardly know,' he would flute to his old friend, 'whether Mr. Beerbohm'—here a bow to me—'will agree with me in my opinion of' some delicate point in Greek prosody or some incident in an old French romance I had never head of.

On one occasion, just before the removal of the mutton, Watts-Dunton had been asking me about an English translation that had been made of M. Rostand's *Cyrano de Bergerac*. He then took my information as the match to ignite the Swinburnian tinder. 'Well, Algernon, it seems that *Cyrano de Bergerac*'—but this first spark was enough: instantly Swinburne was praising the works of Cyrano de Bergerac. Of M. Rostand he may have heard, but him he forgot. Indeed I never heard Swinburne mention a single contemporary writer. His mind ranged and revelled always in the illustrious or obscure past. To him the writings of Cyrano de Bergerac were as fresh as paint—as fresh as to me, alas, was the news of their survival. 'Of course, of course, you have real *L'Histoire Comique des États et des Empires de la Lune?*' I admitted, by gesture and facial expression, that I had not. Whereupon he reeled out curious extracts from that allegory—'almost as good as *Gulliver*'—with a memorable instance of the way in which the traveller to the moon was shocked by the conversation of the natives, and the natives' sense of propriety was outraged by the conversation of the traveller.

In life, as in (that for him more truly actual thing) literature, it was always the preterit that enthralled him. Of any passing events, of anything the newspapers were full of, never a word from him; and I should have been sorry if there had been. But I did, through the medium of Watts-Dunton, sometimes start him on topics that might have led him to talk of Rossetti and other old comrades. For me the names of those men breathed the magic of the past, just as it was breathed for me by Swinburne's presence. For him, I suppose, they were but a bit of the present, and the mere fact that they had dropped out of it was not enough to hallow them. He never mentioned them. But I was glad to see that he revelled as wistfully in the days just before his own as I in the days just before mine. He recounted to us things he had been told in his boyhood by an aged aunt, or great-aunt—'one of the Ashburnhams'; how, for example, she had been taken by her mother to a county ball, a distance of many miles, and, on the way home through the frosty and snowy night, the family-coach had suddenly stopped: there was a crowd of dark figures in the way . . . at which point Swinburne stopped too, before saying, with an ineffable smile and in a voice faint with appreciation, 'They were burying a suicide at the cross-roads.'

Vivid as this Hogarthian night-scene was to me, I saw beside it another scene: a great panelled room, a grim old woman in a high-backed chair, and, restless on a stool at her feet, an extraordinary little nephew with masses of auburn hair and with tiny hands clasped in supplication—'Tell me more, Aunt Ashburnham, tell me more!'

And now, clearlier still, as I write in these after-years, do I see that dining-room of The Pines; the long white stretch of table-cloth, with Swinburne and Watts-Dunton and another at the extreme end of it; Watts-Dunton between us, very low down over his plate, very cosy and hirsute, and rather like the dormouse at that long tea-table which Alice found in Wonderland. I see myself sitting there wide-eyed, as Alice sat. And, had the hare been a great poet, and the hatter a great gentleman, and neither of them mad but each only very odd and vivacious, I might see Swinburne as a glorified blend of those two.

When the meal ended—for, alas! it was not, like that meal

in Wonderland, unending—Swinburne would dart round the table, proffer his hand to me, bow deeply, bow to Watts-Dunton also, and disappear. 'He always walks in the morning, writes in the afternoon, and reads in the evening,' Watts-Dunton would say with a touch of tutorial pride in this regimen.

That parting bow of Swinburne to his old friend was characteristic of his whole relation to him. Cronies though they were, these two, knit together with bonds innumerable, the greater man was always *aux petits soins* for the lesser, treating him as a newly-arrived young guest might treat an elderly host. Some twenty years had passed since that night when, ailing and broken—thought to be nearly dying, Watts-Dunton told me—Swinburne was brought in a four-wheeler to The Pines. Regular private nursing-homes either did not exist in those days or were less in vogue than they are now. The Pines was to be a sort of private nursing-home for Swinburne. It was a good one. He recovered. He was most grateful to his friend and saviour. He made as though to depart, was persuaded to stay a little longer, and then a little longer than that. But I rather fancy that, to the last, he never did, in the fullness of his modesty and good manners, consent to regard his presence as a matter of course, or as anything but a terminable intrusion and obligation. His bow seemed always to convey that.

Swinburne having gone from the room, in would come the parlourmaid. The table was cleared, the fire was stirred, two leather arm-chairs were pushed up to the hearth. Watts-Dunton wanted gossip of the present. I wanted gossip of the great past. We settled down for a long, comfortable afternoon together.

Only once was the ritual varied. Swinburne (I was told before luncheon) had expressed a wish to show me his library. So after the meal he did not bid us his usual adieu, but with

much courtesy invited us and led the way. Up the staircase he
then literally bounded—three, literally three, stairs at a time.
I began to follow at the same rate, but immediately slackened
speed for fear that Watts-Dunton behind us might be em-
bittered at sight of so much youth and legerity. Swinburne
waited on the threshold to receive us, as it were, and pass us in.
Watts-Dunton went and ensconced himself snugly in a corner.
The sun had appeared after a grey morning, and it pleasantly
flooded this big living-room whose walls were entirely lined
with the mellow backs of books. Here, as host, among his
treasures, Swinburne was more than ever attractive. He was
as happy as was any mote in the sunshine about him; and the
fluttering of his little hands, and feet too, was but as a token
of so much felicity. He looked older, it is true, in the strong
light. But these added years made only more notable his
youngness of heart. An illustrious bibliophile among his
books? A birthday child, rather, among his toys.

Proudly he explained to me the general system under
which the volumes were ranged in this or that division of
shelves. Then he conducted me to a chair near the window,
left me there, flew away, flew up the rungs of a mahogany
ladder, plucked a small volume, and in a twinkling was at my
side: 'This, I *think*, will please you!' It did. It had a beautifully engraved title-page and a pleasing scent of old, old
leather. It was *editio princeps* of a play by some lesser Elizabethan or Jacobean. 'Of course you know it?' my host fluted.
How I wished I could say that I knew it and loved it well!
I revealed to him (for by speaking very loudly towards his
inclined head I was able to make him hear) that I had not read
it. He envied any one who had such pleasure in store. He
darted to the ladder, and came back thrusting gently into my
hands another volume of like date: 'Of course you know *this*?'
Again I had to confess that I did not, and to shout my
appreciation of the fount of type, the margins, the binding.

He beamed agreement, and fetched another volume. Archly he indicated the title, cooing. 'You are a lover of *this*, I hope?' And again I was shamed by my inexperience.

I did not pretend to know this particular play, but my tone implied that I had always been *meaning* to read it and had always by some mischance been prevented. For his sake as well as my own I did want to acquit myself passably. I wanted for him the pleasure of seeing his joys shared by a representative, however humble, of the common world. I turned the leaves caressingly, looking from them to him, while he dilated on the beauty of this and that scene in the play. Anon he fetched another volume, and another, always with the same faith that *this* was a favourite of mine. I quibbled, I evaded, I was very enthusiastic and uncomfortable. It was with intense relief that I beheld the title-page of yet another volume which (silently, this time) he laid before me—*The Country Wench.* '*This* of *course* I have read,' I heartily shouted.

Swinburne stepped back. 'You have? You have read it? Where?' he cried, in evident dismay.

Something was wrong. Had I *not*, I quickly wondered, read this play? 'Oh yes,' I shouted, 'I have read it.'

'But when? Where?' entreated Swinburne, adding that he had supposed it to be the sole copy extant.

I floundered. I wildly said I thought I must have read it years ago in the Bodleian.

'Theodore! Do you hear this? It seems that they have now a copy of *The Country Wench* in the Bodleian! Mr. Beerbohm found one there—oh when? in what year?' he appealed to me.

I said it might have been six, seven, eight years ago. Swinburne knew for certain that no copy had been there *twelve* years ago, and was surprised that he had not heard of the acquisition. 'They might have told me,' he wailed.

I sacrificed myself on the altar of sympathy. I admitted that I might have been mistaken—must have been—must have confused this play with some other. I dipped into the pages and 'No,' I shouted, 'this I have *never* read.'

His equanimity was restored. He was up the ladder and down again, showing me further treasures with all pride and ardour. At length, Watts-Dunton, afraid that his old friend would tire himself, arose from his corner, and presently he and I went downstairs to the dining-room. It was in the course of our session together that there suddenly flashed across my mind the existence of a play called *The Country Wife*, by—wasn't it Wycherley? I had once read it—or read something about it. . . . But this matter I kept to myself. I thought I had appeared fool enough already.

I loved those sessions in that Tupperossettine dining-room, lair of solid old comfort and fervid old romanticism. Its odd duality befitted well its owner. The distinguished critic and poet, Rossetti's closest friend and Swinburne's, had been, for a while, in the dark ages, a solicitor; and one felt he had been a good one. His frock-coat, though the Muses had crumpled it, inspired confidence in his judgment of other things than verse. But let there be no mistake. He was no mere *bourgeois parnassien*, as his enemies insinuated. No doubt he had been very useful to men of genius, in virtue of qualities they lacked, but the secret of his hold on them was in his own rich nature. He was not only a born man of letters, he was a deeply emotional human being whose appeal was as much to the heart as to the head. The romantic Celtic mysticism of *Aylwin*, with its lack of fashionable Celtic nebulosity, lends itself, if you will, to laughter, though personally I saw nothing funny in it: it seemed to me, before I was in touch with the author, a work of genuine expression from within; and that it truly was so I presently knew. The mysticism of Watts-Dunton (who, once comfortably settled at the fireside, knew no reserve) was in contrast with the frock-coat and the practical abilities; but it was essential, and they were of the surface. For humorous

Rossetti, I daresay, the very contrast made Theodore's company the more precious. He himself had assuredly been, and the memory of him still was, the master-fact in Watts-Dunton's life. 'Algernon' was as an adopted child, 'Gabriel' as a long-lost only brother. As he was to the outer world of his own day, so too to posterity Rossetti, the man, is conjectural and mysterious. We know that he was in his prime the most inspiring and splendid of companions. But we know this only by faith. The evidence is as vague as it is emphatic. Of the style and substance of not a few great talkers in the past we can piece together some more or less vivid and probably erroneous notion. But about Rossetti nothing has been recorded in such a way as to make him even faintly emerge. I suppose he had in him what reviewers seem to find so often in books: a quality that defies analysis. Listening to Watts-Dunton, I was always in hope that when next the long-lost turned up—for he was continually doing so—in the talk, I should *see* him, *hear* him, and share the rapture. But the revelation was not to be. You might think that to hear him called 'Gabriel' would have given me a sense of propinquity. But I felt no nearer to him than you feel to the Archangel who bears that name and no surname.

It was always when Watts-Dunton spoke carelessly, casually, of some to me illustrious figure in the past, that I had the sense of being wafted right into that past and plumped down in the very midst of it. When he spoke with reverence of this and that great man whom he had known, he did not thus waft and plump me; for I, too, revered those names. But I had the magical transition whenever one of the immortals was mentioned in the tone of those who knew him before he had put on immortality. Browning, for example, was a name deeply honoured by me. 'Browning, yes,' said Watts-Dunton, in the course of an afternoon, 'Browning,' and he took a sip of the steaming whisky-toddy that was a point in our day's ritual.

'I was a great diner-out in the old times. I used to dine out every night in the week. Browning was a great diner-out, too. We were always meeting. What a pity he went on writing all those plays! He hadn't any gift for drama—none. I never could understand why he took to play-writing.' He wagged his head, gazing regretfully into the fire, and added, 'Such a *clever* fellow, too!'

Whistler, though alive and about, was already looked to as a hierarch by the young. Not so had he been looked to by Rossetti. The thrill of the past was always strong in me when Watts-Dunton mentioned—seldom without a guffaw did he mention—'Jimmy Whistler.' I think he put in the surname because 'that fellow' had not behaved well to Swinburne. But he could not omit the nickname, because it was impossible for him to feel the right measure of resentment against 'such a funny fellow.' As heart-full of old hates as of old loves was Watts-Dunton, and I take it as high testimony to the charm of Whistler's quaintness that Watts-Dunton did not hate *him*. You may be aware that Swinburne, in '88, wrote for one of the monthly reviews a criticism of the 'Ten O'Clock' lecture. He paid courtly compliments to Whistler as a painter, but joined issue with his theories. Straightway there appeared in the *World* a little letter from Whistler, deriding 'one Algernon Swinburne—outsider—Putney.' It was not in itself a very pretty or amusing letter; and still less so did it seem in the light of the facts which Watts-Dunton told me in some such words as these: 'After he'd published that lecture of his, Jimmy Whistler had me to dine with him at Kettner's or somewhere. He said "Now, Theodore, I want you to do me a favour." He wanted to get me to get Swinburne to write an article about his lecture. I said "No, Jimmy Whistler, I can't ask Algernon to do that. He's got a great deal of work on hand just now—a great deal of work. And besides, this sort of thing wouldn't be at all in his line." But Jimmy Whistler went on

appealing to me. He said it would do him no end of good if
Swinburne wrote about him. And—well, I half gave in: I said
perhaps I *would* mention the matter to Algernon. And next
day I did. I could see Algernon didn't want to do it at all. But
—well, there, he said he'd do it to please *me*. And he did it.
And then Jimmy Whistler published that letter. A very
shabby trick—very shabby indeed.' Of course I do not vouch
for the exact words in which Watts-Dunton told me this tale;
but this was exactly the tale he told me. I expressed my
astonishment. He added that of course he 'never wanted to see
the fellow again after that, and never did.' But presently, after
a long gaze into the coals, he emitted a chuckle, as for earlier
memories of 'such a funny fellow.' One quite recent memory
he had, too. 'When I took on the name of Dunton, I had a note
from him. Just this, with his butterfly signature: *Theodore!
What's Dunton?* That was very good—very good. . . . But,
of course,' he added gravely, 'I took no notice.' And no doubt,
quite apart from the difficulty of finding an answer in the same
vein, he did well in not replying. Loyalty to Swinburne
forbade. But I see a certain pathos in the unanswered message.
It was a message from the hand of an old jester, but also, I
think, from the heart of an old man—a signal waved jauntily,
but in truth wistfully, across the gulf of years and estrangement; and one could wish it had not been ignored.

Some time after Whistler died I wrote for one of the
magazines an appreciation of his curious skill in the art of
writing. Watts-Dunton told me he had heard of this from
Swinburne. 'I myself,' he said, 'very seldom read the
magazines. But Algernon always has a look at them.' There
was something to me very droll, and cheery too, in this picture
of the illustrious recluse snatching at the current issues of our
twaddle. And I was immensely pleased at hearing that my
article had 'interested him very much.' I inwardly promised
myself that as soon as I reached home I would read the article,

to see just how it might have struck Swinburne. When in due course I did this, I regretted the tone of the opening sentences, in which I declared myself 'no book-lover' and avowed a preference for 'an uninterrupted view of my fellow-creatures.' I felt that had I known my article would meet the eye of Swinburne I should have cut out that overture. I dimly remembered a fine passage in one of his books of criticism—something (I preferred not to verify it) about 'the dotage of duncedom which cannot perceive, or the impudence of insignificance so presumptuous as to doubt, that the elements of life and literature are indivisibly mingled one in another, and that he to whom books are less real than life will assuredly find in men and women as little reality as in his accursed crassness he deserves to discover.' I quailed, I quailed. But mine is a resilient nature, and I promptly reminded myself that Swinburne's was a very impersonal one: he would not think the less highly of me, for he never had thought about me in any way whatsoever. All was well. I knew I could revisit The Pines, when next Watts-Dunton should invite me, without misgiving. And to this day I am rather proud of having been mentioned, though not by name, and not consciously, and unfavourably, by Swinburne.

I wonder that I cannot recall more than I do recall of those hours at The Pines. It is odd how little remains to a man of his own past—how few minutes of even his memorable hours are not clean forgotten, and how few seconds in any one of those minutes can be recaptured. . . . I am middle-aged, and have lived a vast number of seconds. Subtract $\frac{1}{3}$ of these, for one mustn't count sleep as life. The residual number is still enormous. Not a single one of those seconds was unimportant to me in its passage. Many of them bored me, of course; but even boredom is a positive state: one chafes at it and hates it; strange that one should afterwards forget it! And stranger still that of one's actual happinesses and unhappinesses so tiny and tattered a remnant clings about one! Of those hours at The Pines, of that past within a past, there was not a minute nor a second that I did not spend with pleasure. Memory is a great artist, we are told; she selects and rejects and shapes and so on. No doubt. Elderly persons would be utterly intolerable if they remembered *everything*. *Everything*, nevertheless, is just what they themselves would like to remember, and just what they would like to tell to *everybody*. Be sure that the Ancient Mariner, though he remembered quite as much as his audience wanted to hear, and rather more, about the albatross and the ghastly crew, was inwardly raging at the sketchiness of his own mind; and believe me that his stopping only one of three was the merest oversight. I should like to impose on the world many tomes about The Pines.

But, scant though my memories are of the moments there, very full and warm in me is the whole fused memory of the two dear old men that lived there. I wish I had Watts-Dunton's sure faith in meetings beyond the grave. I am glad I do not disbelieve that people may so meet. I like to think that some day in Elysium I shall—not without diffidence—approach those two and reintroduce myself. I can see just how courteously Swinburne will bow over my hand, not at all remembering who I am. Watts-Dunton will remember me after a moment: 'Oh, to be sure, yes indeed! I've a great deal of work on hand just now—a great deal of work, but' we shall sit down together on the asphodel, and I cannot but think we shall have whisky-toddy even there. He will not have changed. He will still be shaggy and old and chubby, and will wear the same frock-coat, with the same creases in it. Swinburne, on the other hand, will be quite, quite young, with a full mane of flaming auburn locks, and no clothes to hinder him from plunging back at any moment into the shining Elysian waters from which he will have just emerged. I see him skim lightly away into that element. On the strand is sitting a man of noble and furrowed brow. It is Mazzini, still thinking of Liberty. And anon the tiny young English amphibian comes ashore to fling himself dripping at the feet of the patriot and to carol the Republican ode he has composed in the course of his swim. 'He's wonderfully active—active in mind and body,' Watts-Dunton says to me. 'I come to the shore now and then, just to see how he's getting on. But I spend most of my time inland. I find I've so much to talk over with Gabriel. Not that he's quite the fellow he was. He always had rather a cult for Dante, you know, and now he's more than ever under the Florentine influence. He lives in a sort of monastery that Dante has here; and there he sits painting imaginary portraits of Beatrice, and giving them all to Dante. But he still has his great moments, and there's no one quite like him—no one. Algernon won't ever come and see him, because that fellow Mazzini's as Anti-Clerical as ever and makes a principle of having nothing to do with Dante. Look!—there's Algernon going into the water again! He'll tire himself out, he'll catch cold, he'll——' and here the old man rises and hurries down to the sea's edge. 'Now, Algernon,' he roars, 'I don't want to interfere with you, but I do think, my dear old friend,'—and then, with a guffaw, he breaks off, remembering that his friend is not deaf now nor old, and that here in Elysium, where no ills are, good advice is not needed.

Hosts and Guests

Beautifully vague though the English language is, with its meanings merging into one another as softly as the facts of landscape in the moist English climate, and much addicted though we always have been to ways of compromise, and averse from sharp hard logical outlines, we do not call a host a guest, nor a guest a host. The ancient Romans did so. They, with a language that was as lucid as their climate and was a perfect expression of the sharp hard logical outlook fostered by that climate, had but one word for those two things. Nor have their equally acute descendants done what might have been expected of them in this matter. *Hôte* and *ospite* and *héspide* are as mysteriously equivocal as *hospes*. By weight of all this authority I find myself being dragged to the conclusion that a host and a guest must be the same thing, after all. Yet in a dim and muzzy way, deep down in my breast, I feel sure that they are different. Compromise, you see, as usual. I take it that strictly the two things *are* one, but that our division of them is yet another instance of that sterling common-sense by which, etc., etc.

I would go even so far as to say that the difference is more than merely circumstantial and particular. I seem to discern also a temperamental and general difference. You ask me to dine with you in a restaurant, I say I shall be delighted, you order the meal, I praise it, you pay for it, I have the pleasant sensation of not paying for it; and it is well that each of us should have a label according to the part he plays in this transaction. But the two labels are applicable in a larger and more philosophic way. In every human being one or the other of these two instincts is predominant: the active or positive instinct to offer hospitality, the negative or passive instinct to accept it. And either of these instincts is so significant of character that one might well say that mankind is divisible into two great classes: hosts and guests.

I have already (see third sentence of foregoing paragraph) somewhat prepared you for the shock of a confession which candour now forces from me. I am one of the guests. You are, however, so shocked that you will read no more of me? Bravo! Your refusal indicates that you have not a guestish soul. Here am I trying to entertain you, and you will not be entertained. You stand shouting that it is more blessed to give than to receive. Very well. For my part, I would rather read than write, any day. You shall write this essay for me. Be it never so humble, I shall give it my best attention and manage to say something nice about it. I am sorry to see you calming suddenly down. Nothing but a sense of duty to myself, and to guests in general, makes me resume my pen. I believe guests to be as numerous, really, as hosts. It may be that even you, if you examine yourself dispassionately, will find that you are one of them. In which case, you may yet thank me for some comfort. I think there are good qualities to be found in guests, and some bad ones in even the best hosts.

Our deepest instincts, bad or good, are those which we share with the rest of the animal creation. To offer hospitality, or to accept it, is but an instinct which man has acquired in the long course of his self-development. Lions do not ask one another to their lairs, nor do birds keep open nest. Certain wolves and tigers, it is true, have been so seduced by man from their natural state that they will deign to accept man's hospitality. But when you give a bone to your dog, does he run out and invite another dog to share it with him?—and does your cat insist on having a circle of other cats around her saucer of milk? Quite the contrary. A deep sense of personal property is common to all these creatures. Thousands of years hence they may have acquired some willingness to share things with their friends. Or rather, dogs may; cats, I think, not. Meanwhile, let us not be censorious. Though certain monkeys assuredly were of finer and more malleable stuff than any wolves or tigers, it was a very long time indeed before even we began to be hospitable. The cavemen did not entertain. It may be that now and again—say, towards the end of the Stone Age—one or another among the more enlightened of them said to his wife, while she plucked an eagle that he had snared the day before, 'That red-haired man who lives in the next valley seems to be a decent, harmless sort of person. And sometimes I fancy he is rather lonely. I think I will ask him to dine with us to-night,' and, presently going out, met the red-haired man and said to him, 'Are you doing anything tonight? If not, won't you dine with us? It would be a great pleasure to my wife. Only ourselves. Come just as you are.' 'That is most good of you, but,' stammered the red-haired man, 'as ill-luck will have it, I *am* engaged to-night. A long-standing, formal invitation. I wish I could get out of it, but I simply can't. I have a morbid conscientiousness about such things.' Thus we see that the will to offer hospitality was an earlier growth than the will to accept it. But we must beware of thinking these two things identical with the mere will to give and the mere will to receive. It is unlikely that the red-haired man would have refused a slice of eagle if it had been offered to him where he stood. And it is still more unlikely that his friend would have handed it to him. Such is not the way of hosts. The hospitable instinct is not wholly altruistic. There is pride and egoism mixed up with it, as I shall show.

Meanwhile, why did the red-haired man babble those excuses? It was because he scented danger. He was not by nature suspicious, but—what possible motive, except murder,

could this man have for enticing him to that cave? Acquaintance in the open valley was all very well and pleasant, but a
strange den after dark—no, no! You despise him for his fears?
Yet these were not really so absurd as they may seem. As man
progressed in civilization, and grew to be definitely gre-
garious, hospitality became more a matter of course. But even
than it was not above suspicion. It was not hedged around with
those unwritten laws which make it the safe and eligible thing
we know to-day. In the annals of hospitality there are many
pages that make painful reading; many a great dark blot is
there which the Recording Angel may wish, but will not be
able, to wipe out with a tear.

If I were a host, I should ignore those tomes. Being a guest,
I sometimes glance into them, but with more of horror, I assure
you, than of malicious amusement. I carefully avoid those
which treat of hospitality among barbarous races. Things
done in the best periods of the most enlightened peoples are
quite bad enough. The Israelites were the salt of the earth.
But can you imagine a deed of colder-blooded treachery than
Jael's? You would think it must have been held accursed by
even the basest minds. Yet thus sang Deborah and Barak,
'Blessed above women shall Jael the wife of Heber the Kenite
be, blessed shall she be among women in the tent.' And
Barak, remember, was a gallant soldier, and Deborah was a
prophetess who 'judged Israel at that time.' So much for the
ideals of hospitality among the children of Israel.

Of the Homeric Greeks it may be said that they too were the
salt of the earth; and it may be added that in their pungent and
antiseptic quality there was mingled a measure of sweetness,
not to be found in the children of Israel. I do not say outright
that Odysseus ought not to have slain the suitors. That is a
debatable point. It is true that they were guests under his
roof. But he had not invited them. Let us give him the benefit
of the doubt. I am thinking of another episode in his life. By

what Circe did, and by his disregard of what she had done, a
searching light is cast on the laxity of Homeric Greek notions
as to what was due to guests. Odysseus was a clever, but not a
bad man, and his standard of general conduct was high enough.
Yet, having foiled Circe in her purpose to turn him into a
swine, and having forced her to restore his comrades to
human shape, he did not let pass the barrier of his teeth any
such winged words as 'Now will I bide no more under thy
roof, Circe, but fare across the sea with my dear comrades,
even unto mine own home, for that which thou didst was an
evil thing, and one not meet to be done unto strangers by the
daughter of a god.' He seems to have said nothing in particular, to have accepted with alacrity the invitation that he and
his dear comrades should prolong their visit, and to have
prolonged it with them for a whole year, in the course of which
Circe bore him a son, named Telegonus. As Matthew Arnold
would have said, 'What a set!'

My eye roves, for relief, to those shelves where the later
annals are. I take down a tome at random. Rome in the
fifteenth century: civilization never was more brilliant than
there and then, I imagine; and yet—no, I replace that tome. I
saw enough in it to remind me that the Borgias selected and
laid down rare poisons in their cellars with as much thought as
they gave to their vintage wines. Extraordinary!—but the
Romans do not seem to have thought so. An invitation to dine
at the Palazzo Borghese was accounted the highest social
honour. I am aware that in recent books of Italian history
there has been a tendency to whiten the Borgias' characters.
But I myself hold to the old romantic black way of looking at
the Borgias. I maintain that though you would often in the
fifteenth century have heard the snobbish Roman say, in a
would-be off-hand tone, 'I am dining with the Borgias to-
night,' no Roman ever was able to say 'I dined last night with
the Borgias.'

Hosts and Guests

To mankind in general Macbeth and Lady Macbeth stand out as the supreme type of all that a host and hostess should not be. Hence the marked coolness of Scotsmen towards Shakespeare, hence the untiring efforts of that proud and sensitive race to set up Burns in his stead. It is a risky thing to offer sympathy to the proud and sensitive, yet I must say that I think the Scots have a real grievance. The two actual, historic Macbeths were no worse than innumerable other couples in other lands that had not yet fully struggled out of barbarism. It is hard that Shakespeare happened on the story of that particular pair, and so made it immortal. But he meant no harm, and, let Scotsmen believe me, did positive good. Scotch hospitality is proverbial. As much in Scotland as in America does the English visitor blush when he thinks how perfunctory and niggard, in comparison, English hospitality is. It was Scotland that first formalized hospitality, made of it an exacting code of honour, with the basic principle that the guest must in all circumstances be respected and at all costs protected. Jacobite history bristles with examples of the heroic sacrifices made by hosts for their guests, sacrifices of their own safety and even of their own political convictions, for fear of infringing, however slightly, that sacred code of theirs. And what was the origin of all this noble pedantry? Shakespeare's *Macbeth*.

Perhaps if England were a bleak and rugged country, like Scotland, or a new country, like America, the foreign visitor would be more overwhelmed with kindness here than he is. The landscapes of our country-side are so charming, London abounds in public monuments so redolent of history, so romantic and engrossing, that we are perhaps too apt to think the foreign visitor would have neither time nor inclination to sit dawdling in private dining-rooms. Assuredly there is no lack of hospitable impulse among the English. In what may be called mutual hospitality they touch a high level. The

249

French, also the Italians, entertain one another far less frequently. In England the native guest has a very good time indeed—though of course he pays for it, in some measure, by acting as host too, from time to time.

In practice, no, there cannot be any absolute division of mankind into my two categories, hosts and guests. But psychologically a guest does not cease to be a guest when he gives a dinner, nor is a host not a host when he accepts one. The amount of entertaining that a guest need do is a matter wholly for his own conscience. He will soon find that he does not receive less hospitality for offering little; and he would not receive less if he offered none. The amount received by him depends wholly on the degree of his agreeableness. Pride makes an occasional host of him; but he does not shine in that capacity. Nor do hosts want him to assay it. If they accept an invitation from him, they do so only because they wish not to hurt his feelings. As guests they are fish out of water.

Circumstances do, of course, react on character. It is conventional for the rich to give, and for the poor to receive. Riches do tend to foster in you the instincts of a host, and poverty does create an atmosphere favourable to the growth of guestish instincts. But strong bents make their own way. Not all guests are to be found among the needy, nor all hosts among the affluent. For sixteen years after my education was, by courtesy, finished—from the age, that is, of twenty-two to the age of thirty-eight—I lived in London, seeing all sorts of people all the while; and I came across many a rich man who, like the master of the shepherd Corin, was 'of churlish disposition' and little recked 'to find the way to heaven by doing deeds of hospitality.' On the other hand, I knew quite poor men who were incorrigibly hospitable.

To such men, all honour. The most I dare claim for myself is that if I had been rich I should have been better than Corin's master. Even as it was, I did my best. But I had no authentic joy in doing it. Without the spur of pride I might conceivably have not done it at all. There recurs to me from among memories of my boyhood an episide that is rather significant. In my school, as in most others, we received now and again 'hampers' from home. At the mid-day dinner, in every house, we all ate together; but at breakfast and supper we ate in four or five separate 'messes.' It was customary for the receiver of a hamper to share the contents with his mess-mates. On one occasion I received, instead of the usual variegated hamper, a box containing twelve sausage-rolls. It happened that when this box arrived and was opened by me there was no one around. Of sausage-rolls I was particularly fond. I am sorry to say that I carried the box up to my cubicle, and, having eaten two of the sausage-rolls, said nothing to my friends, that day, about the other ten, nor anything about them when, three days later, I had eaten them all—all, up there, alone.

Thirty years have elapsed, my school-fellows are scattered far and wide, the chance that this page may meet the eyes of some of them does not much dismay me; but I am glad there was no collective and contemporary judgment by them on my strange exploit. What defence could I have offered? Suppose I had said 'You see, I am so essentially a guest,' the plea would have carried little weight. And yet it would not have been a worthless plea. On receipt of a hamper, a boy did rise, always, in the esteem of his mess-mates. His sardines, his marmalade, his potted meat, at any rate while they lasted, did make us think that his parents 'must be awfully decent' and that he was a not unworthy son. He had become our central figure, we expected him to lead the conversation, we liked listening to him, his jokes were good. With those twelve sausage-rolls I could have dominated my fellows for a while. But I had not a dominant nature. I never trusted myself as a leader. Leading abashed me. I was happiest in the comity of the crowd. Having received a hamper, I was always glad when it was finished, glad to fall back into the ranks. Humility is a virtue, and it is a virtue innate in guests.

Boys (as will have been surmised from my record of the effect of hampers) are all of them potential guests. It is only as they grow up that some of them harden into hosts. It is likely enough that if I, when I grew up, had been rich, my natural bent to guestship would have been diverted, and I too have become a (sort of) host. And perhaps I should have passed muster. I suppose I did pass muster whenever, in the course of my long residence in London, I did entertain friends. But the memory of those occasions is not dear to me—especially not the memory of those that were in the more distinguished restaurants. Somewhere in the back of my brain, while I tried to lead the conversation brightly, was always the haunting fear that I had not brought enough money in my pocket. I never let this fear master me. I never said to any one 'Will you have a liqueur?'—always 'What liqueur will you have?' But I postponed as far as possible the evil moment of asking for the bill. When I had, in the proper casual tone (I hope and believe), at length asked for it, I wished always it were not brought to me *folded* on a plate, as though the amount were so hideously high that I alone must be privy to it. So soon as it was laid beside me, I wanted to know the worst at once. But I pretended to be so occupied in talk that I was unaware of the bill's presence; and I was careful to be always in the middle of a sentence when I raised the upper fold and took my not (I hope) frozen glance. In point of fact, the amount was always much less than I had feared. Pessimism does win us great happy moments.

Meals in the restaurants of Soho tested less severely the pauper guest masquerading as host. But to them one could not ask rich persons—not even poor persons unless one knew them very well. Soho is so uncertain that the fare is often not good enough to be palmed off on even one's poorest and oldest friends. A very magnetic host, with a great gift for bluffing, might, no doubt, even in Soho's worst moments, diffuse among his guests a conviction that all was of the best. But I never was good at bluffing. I had always to let food speak for itself. 'It's cheap' was the only pæan that in Soho's bad moments ever occurred to me, and this of course I did not utter. And *was* it so cheap, after all? Soho induces a certain optimism. A bill there was always larger than I had thought it would be.

Every one, even the richest and most munificent of men, pays much by cheque more light-heartedly than he pays little in specie. In restaurants I should have liked always to give cheques. But in any restaurant I was so much more often seen as guest than as host that I never felt sure the proprietor would trust me. Only in my club did I know the luxury, or rather the painlessness, of entertaining by cheque. A cheque—especially if it is a club cheque, as supplied for the use of members, not a leaf torn out of his own book—makes so little mark on any man's imagination. He dashes off some words and figures, he signs his name (with that vague momentary pleasure which the sight of his own signature anywhere gives him), he walks away and forgets. Offering hospitality in my club, I was inwardly calm. But even there I did not glow (though my face and manner, I hoped, glowed). If my guest was by nature a guest, I managed to forget somewhat that I myself was a guest by nature. But if, as now and then happened, my guest was a true and habitual host, I did feel that we were in an absurdly false relation; and it was not without difficulty that I could restrain myself from saying to him, 'This is all very well, you know, but—frankly: your place is at the head of your own table.'

The host as guest is far, far worse than the guest as host. He never even passes muster. The guest, in virtue of a certain hability that is part of his natural equipment, can more or less ape the ways of a host. But the host, with his more positive

253

temperament, does not even attempt the graces of a guest. By 'graces' I do not mean to imply anything artificial. The guest's manners are, rather, as wild flowers springing from good rich soil—the soil of genuine modesty and gratitude. He honourably wishes to please in return for the pleasure he is receiving. He wonders that people should be so kind to him, and, without knowing it, is very kind to *them*. But the host, as I said earlier in this essay, is a guest against his own will. That is the root of the mischief. He feels that it is more blessed, etc., and that he is conferring rather than accepting a favour. He does not adjust himself. He forgets his place. He leads the conversation. He tries genially to draw you out. He never comments on the goodness of the food or wine. He looks at his watch abruptly and says he must be off. He doesn't say he has had a delightful time. In fact, his place is at the head of his own table.

His own table, over his own cellar, under his own roof—it is only there that you see him at his best. To a club or restaurant he may sometimes invite you, but not there, not there, my child, do you get the full savour of his quality. In life or literature there has been no better host than Old Wardle, Appalling though he would have been as a guest in club or restaurant, it is hardly less painful to think of him as a host there. At Dingley Dell, with an ample gesture, he made you free of all that was his. He could not have given you a club or a restaurant. Nor, when you come to think of it, did he give you Dingley Dell. The place remained his. None knew better than Old Wardle that this was so. Hospitality, as we have agreed, is not one of the most deep-rooted instincts in man, whereas the sense of possession certainly is. Not even Old Wardle was a communist. 'This,' you may be sure he said to himself, 'is *my* roof, these are *my* horses, that's a picture of *my* dear old grandfather.' And 'This,' he would say to us, 'is *my* roof: sleep soundly under it. These are *my* horses: ride them.

That's a portrait of *my* dear old grandfather: have a good look
at it.' But he did not ask us to walk off with any of these things.
Not even what he actually did give us would he regard as
having passed out of his possession. 'That,' he would muse if
we were torpid after dinner, 'is *my* roast beef,' and 'That,' if we
staggered on the way to bed, 'is *my* cold milk punch.' 'But
surely,' you interrupt me, 'to give and then not feel that one
has given is the very best of all ways of giving.' I agree. I
hope you didn't think I was trying to disparage Old Wardle. I
was merely keeping my promise to point out that from among
the motives of even the best hosts pride and egoism are not
absent.

Every virtue, as we were taught in youth, is a mean between
two extremes; and I think any virtue is the better understood
by us if we glance at the vice on either side of it. I take it that
the virtue of hospitality stands midway between churlishness
and mere ostentation. Far to the left of the good host stands
he who doesn't want to see anything of any one; far to the
right, he who wants a horde of people to be always seeing
something of *him*. I conjecture that the figure on the left, just
discernible through my field-glasses, is that of old Corin's
master. His name was never revealed to us, but Corin's brief
account of his character suffices. 'Deeds of hospitality' is a
dismal phrase that could have occurred only to the servant of a
very dismal master. Not less tell-tale is Corin's idea that men
who do these 'deeds' do them only to save their souls in the
next world. It is a pity Shakespeare did not actually bring
Corin's master on to the stage. One would have liked to see
the old man genuinely touched by the charming eloquence of
Rosalind's appeal for a crust of bread, and conscious that he
would probably go to heaven if he granted it, and yet not quite
able to grant it. Far away though he stands to the left of the
good host, he has yet something in common with that third
person discernible on the right—that speck yonder, which I

believe to be Lucullus. Nothing that we know of Lucullus suggests that he was less inhuman than the churl of Arden. It does not appear that he had a single friend, nor that he wished for one. His lavishness was indiscriminate except in that he entertained only the rich. One would have liked to dine with him, but not even in the act of digestion could one have felt that he had a heart. One would have acknowledged that in all the material resources of his art he was a master, and also that he practised his art for sheer love of it, wishing to be admired for nothing but his mastery, and cocking no eye on any of those ulterior objects but for which some of the most prominent hosts would not entertain at all. But the very fact that he was an artist is repulsive. When hospitality becomes an art it loses its very soul. With this reflection I look away from Lucullus and, fixing my gaze on the middle ground, am the better able to appreciate the excellence of the figure that stands before me— the figure of Old Wardle. Some pride and egoism in that capacious breast, yes, but a great heart full of kindness, and ever a warm spontaneous welcome to the stranger in need, and to all old friends and young. Hark! he is shouting something. He is asking us both down to Dingley Dell. And you have shouted back that you will be delighted. Ah, did I not suspect from the first that you too were perhaps a guest?

But—I constrain you in the act of rushing off to pack your things—one moment: this essay has yet to be finished. We have yet to glance at those two extremes between which the mean is good guestship. Far to the right of the good guest, we descry the parasite; far to the left, the churl again. Not the same churl, perhaps. We do not know that Corin's master was ever sampled as a guest. I am inclined to call yonder speck Dante—Dante Alighieri, of whom we do know that he received during his exile much hospitality from many hosts and repaid them by writing how bitter was the bread in their houses, and how steep the stairs were. To think of dour Dante as a guest is less dispiriting only than to think what he would have been as a host had it ever occurred to him to entertain any one or anything except a deep regard for Beatrice; and one turns with positive relief to have a glimpse of the parasite —Mr. Smurge, I presume, 'whose gratitude was as boundless as his appetite, and his presence as unsought as it appeared to be inevitable.' But now, how gracious and admirable is the central figure—radiating gratitude, but not too much of it; never intrusive, ever within call; full of dignity, yet all amenable; quiet, yet lively; never echoing, ever amplifying; never contradicting, but often lighting the way to truth; an ornament, an inspiration, anywhere.

Such is he. But *who* is he? It is easier to confess a defect than to claim a quality. I have told you that when I lived in London I was nothing as a host; but I will not claim to have been a perfect guest. Nor indeed was I. I was a good one, but, looking back, I see myself not quite in the centre—slightly to the left, slightly to the churlish side. I was rather *too* quiet, and I did sometimes contradict. And, though I always liked to be invited anywhere, I very often preferred to stay at home. If any one hereafter shall form a collection of the notes written by me in reply to invitations, I am afraid he will gradually suppose me to have been more in request than ever I really was, and to have been also a great invalid, and a great traveller.

Quia Imperfectum

I have often wondered that no one has set himself to collect unfinished works of art. There is a peculiar charm for all of us in that which was still in the making when its maker died, or in that which he laid aside because he was tired of it, or didn't see his way to the end of it, or wanted to go on to something else. Mr. Pickwick and the Ancient Mariner are valued friends of ours, but they do not preoccupy us like Edwin Drood or Kubla Khan. Had that revolving chair at Gad's Hill become empty but a few weeks later than it actually did, or had Samuel Taylor Coleridge in the act of setting down his dream about the Eastern potentate *not* been interrupted by 'a person on business from Porlock' and so lost the thread of the thing for ever, from two what delightful glades for roaming in would our fancy be excluded! The very globe we live on is a far more fascinating sphere than it can have been when men supposed that men like themselves would be on it to the end of time. It is only since we heard what Darwin had to say, only since we have had to accept as improvisible what lies far ahead, that the Book of Life has taken so strong a hold on us and 'once taken up, cannot,' as the reviewers say, 'readily be laid down.' The work doesn't strike us as a masterpiece yet, certainly; but who knows that it isn't—that it won't be, judged as a whole?

For sheer creativeness, no human artist, I take it, has a higher repute than Michael Angelo; none perhaps has a repute so high. But what if Michael Angelo had been a little more persevering? All those years he spent in the process of just a-going to begin Pope Julius' tomb, and again, all those blank spaces for his pictures and bare pedestals for his statues in the Baptistery of San Lorenzo—ought we to regret them quite so passionately as we do? His patrons were apt to think him an impossible person to deal with. But I suspect that there may have been a certain high cunning in what appeared to be a mere lovable fault of temperament. When Michael Angelo actually did bring a thing off, the result was not always more than magnificent. His David is magnificent, but it isn't David. One is duly awed, but, to see the master at his best, back one goes from the Accademia to that marvellous bleak Baptistery which he left that we should see, in the mind's eye, just that very best.

It was there, some years ago, as I stood before the half-done marvel of the Night and Morning, that I first conceived the idea of a museum of incomplete masterpieces. And now I mean to organize the thing on my own account. The Baptistery itself, so full of unfulfilment, and with such a wealth, at present, of spare space, will be the ideal setting for my treasures. There be it that the public shall throng to steep itself in the splendour of possibilities, beholding, under glass, and perhaps in excellent preservation, Penelope's web and the original designs for the Tower of Babel, the draft made by Mr. Asquith for a reformed House of Lords and the notes jotted down by the sometime German Emperor for a proclamation from Versailles to the citizens of Paris. There too shall be the MS. of that fragmentary *Iphigénie* which Racine laid aside so meekly at the behest of Mlle. de Trèves—'*quoique cela fût de mon mieux*'; and there an early score of that one unfinished Symphony of Beethoven's—I forget the number of it, but anyhow it is my favourite. Among the pictures, Rossetti's oil-painting of 'Found' must be ruled out, because we know by more than one drawing just what it would have been, and how much less good than those drawings. But Leonardo's St. Sebastian (even if it isn't Leonardo's) shall be there, and

Whistler's Miss Connie Gilchrist, and numerous other pictures that I would mention if my mind were not so full of one picture to which, if I can find it and acquire it, a special place of honour shall be given: a certain huge picture in which a life-sized gentleman, draped in a white mantle, sits on a fallen obelisk and surveys the ruined temples of the Campagna Romana.

The reader knits his brow? Evidently he has not just been reading Goethe's *Travels in Italy*. I have. Or rather, I have just been reading a translation of it, published in 1885 by George Bell & Sons. I daresay it isn't a very good translation (for one has always understood that Goethe, despite a re-sistant medium, wrote well—an accomplishment which this translator hardly wins one to suspect). And I daresay the painting I so want to see and have isn't a very good painting. Wilhelm Tischbein is hardly a name to conjure with, though in his day, as a practitioner in the 'historical' style, and as a rapturous resident in Rome, Tischbein did great things; big things, at any rate. He did crowds of heroes in helmets looked down at by gods on clouds; he did centaurs leaping ravines; Sabine women; sieges of Troy. And he did this portrait of Goethe. At least he began it. Why didn't he finish it? That is a problem as to which one can but hazard guesses, reading between the lines of Goethe's letters. The great point is that it never was finished. By that point, as you read between those lines, you will be amused if you are unkind, and worried if you are humane.

Worried, yet also pleased. Goethe has more than once been described as 'the perfect man.' He was assuredly a personage on the great scale, in the grand manner, gloriously balanced, rounded. And it is a fact that he was not made of marble. He started with all the disadvantages of flesh and blood, and retained them to the last. Yet from no angle, as he went his long way, could it be plausibly hinted that he wasn't sublime. Endearing though failure always is, we grudge no man a moderately successful career, and glory itself we will wink at if it befall some thoroughly good fellow. But a man whose career was glorious without intermission, decade after decade, does sorely try our patience. He, we know, cannot have been a thoroughly good fellow. Of Goethe we are shy for such reasons as that he was never injudicious, never lazy, always in his best form—and always in love with some lady or another just so much as was good for the development of his soul and his art, but never more than that by a tittle. Fate decreed that Sir Willoughby Patterne should cut a ridiculous figure and so earn our forgiveness. Fate may have had a similar plan for Goethe; if so, it went all agley. Yet, in the course of that pageant, his career, there did happen just one humiliation—one thing that needed to be hushed up. There Tischbein's defalcation was; a chip in the marble, a flaw in the crystal, just one thread loose in the great grand tapestry.

Men of genius are not quick judges of character. Deep thinking and high imagining blunt that trivial instinct by which you and I size people up. Had you and I been at Goethe's elbow when, in the October of 1786, he entered Rome and was received by the excited Tischbein, no doubt we should have whispered in his ear, 'Beware of that man! He will one day fail you.' Unassisted Goethe had no misgivings. For some years he had been receiving letters from this Herr Tischbein. They were the letters of a man steeped in the Sorrows of Werther and in all else that Goethe had written. This was a matter of course. But also they were the letters of a man familiar with all the treasures of Rome. All Italy was desirable; but it was especially towards great Rome that the soul of the illustrious poet, the confined State Councillor of Weimar, had been ever yearning. So that when came the longed-for day, and the Duke gave leave of absence, and

Goethe, closing his official portfolio with a snap and im-
printing a fervent but hasty kiss on the hand of Frau von Stein,
fared forth on his pilgrimage, Tischbein was a prospect
inseparably bound up for him with that of the Seven Hills.
Baedeker had not been born. Tischbein would be a great
saviour of time and trouble. Nor was this hope unfulfilled.
Tischbein was assiduous, enthusiastic, indefatigable. In the
early letters to Frau von Stein, to Herder and others, his name
is always cropping up for commendation. 'Of Tischbein I have
much to say and much to boast'—'A thorough and original
German'—'He has always been thinking of me, ever providing
for my wants'—'In his society all my enjoyments are more
than doubled.' He was thirty-five years old (two years
younger than Goethe), and one guesses him to have been a
stocky little man, with those short thick legs which denote
indefatigability. One guesses him blond and rosy, very
voluble, very guttural, with a wealth of forceful but not
graceful gesture.

One is on safer ground in guessing him vastly proud of
trotting Goethe round. Such fame throughout Europe had
Goethe won by his works that it was necessary for him to
travel incognito. Not that his identity wasn't an open secret,
nor that he himself would have wished it hid. Great artists are
always vain. To say that a man is vain means merely that he is
pleased with the effect he produces on other people. A con-
ceited man is satisfied with the effect he produces on himself.
Any great artist is far too perceptive and too exigent to be
satisfied with that effect, and hence in vanity he seeks solace.
Goethe, you may be sure, enjoyed the hero-worshipful gaze
focussed on him from all the tables of the Caffè Greco. But
not for adulation had he come to Rome. Rome was what he
had come for; and the fussers of the coteries must not pester
him in his golden preoccupation with the antique world.
Tischbein was very useful in warding off the profane throng—

fanning away the flies. Let us hope he was actuated solely by zeal in Goethe's interest, not by the desire to swagger as a monopolist.

Clear it is, though, that he scented fine opportunities in Goethe's relation to him. Suppose he could rope his illustrious friend in as a collaborator! He had begun a series of paintings on the theme of primaeval man. Goethe was much impressed by these. Tischbein suggested a great poem on the theme of primaeval man—a volume of engravings after Tischbein, with running poetic commentary by Goethe. 'Indeed, the frontispiece for such a joint work,' writes Goethe in one of his letters, 'is already designed.' Pushful Tischbein! But Goethe, though he was the most courteous of men, was not of the stuff of which collaborators are made. 'During our walks together' —and can you not see those two together, pacing up and down the groves of the Villa Pamphili, or around the ruins of the Temple of Jupiter?—little Tischbein gesticulating and peering up into Goethe's face, and Goethe with his hands clasped behind him, ever nodding in a non-committal manner—'he has talked with me in the hope of gaining me over to his views, and getting me to enter upon the plan.' Goethe admits in another letter that 'the idea is beautiful; only,' he adds, 'the artist and the poet must be many years together, in order to carry out and execute such a work'; and one conceives that he felt a certain lack of beauty in the idea of being with Tischbein for many years. 'Did I not fear to enter upon any new tasks at present, I might perhaps be tempted.' This I take to be but the repetition of a formula often used in the course of those walks. In no letter later than November is the scheme mentioned. Tischbein had evidently ceased to press it. Anon he fell back on a scheme less glorious but likelier to bear fruit.

'Latterly,' writes Goethe, 'I have observed Tischbein regarding me; and now'—note the demure pride!—'it appears that he has long cherished the idea of painting my

portrait.' Earnest sight-seer though he was, and hard at work
on various MSS. in the intervals of sight-seeing, it is evident
that to sit for his portrait was a new task which he did *not* 'fear
to enter upon at present.' Nor need we be surprised. It seems
to be a law of nature that no man, unless he has some obvious
physical deformity, ever *is* loth to sit for his portrait. A man
may be old, he may be ugly, he may be burdened with grave
responsibilities to the nation, and that nation be at a crisis of its
history; but none of these considerations, nor all of them
together, will deter him from sitting for his portrait. Depend
on him to arrive at the studio punctually, to surrender himself
and sit as still as a mouse, trying to look his best in whatever
posture the painter shall have selected as characteristic, and
talking (if he have leave to talk) with a touching humility and
with a keen sense of his privilege in being allowed to pick up a
few ideas about art. To a dentist or a hairdresser he surrenders
himself without enthusiasm, even with resentment. But in the
atmosphere of a studio there is something that entrances him.
Perhaps it is the smell of turpentine that goes to his head. Or
more likely it is the idea of immortality. Goethe was one of the
handsomest men of his day, and (remember) vain, and now in
the prime of life; so that he was specially susceptible to the
notion of being immortalized. 'The design is already settled,
and the canvas stretched'; and I have no doubt that in the
original German these words ring like the opening of a ballad.
'The anchor's up and the sail is spread,' as I (and you, belike)
recited in childhood. The ship in that poem foundered, if I
remember rightly; so that the analogy to Goethe's words is
all the more striking.

It is in this same letter that the poet mentions those three
great points which I have already laid before you: the fallen
obelisk for him to sit on, the white mantle to drape him, and
the ruined temples for him to look at. 'It will form a beautiful
piece, but,' he sadly calculates, 'it will be rather too big for our

northern habitations.' Courage! There will be plenty of room
for it in the Baptistery of San Lorenzo.

Meanwhile, the work progressed. A brief visit to Naples
and Sicily was part of Goethe's well-pondered campaign, and
he was to set forth from Rome (taking Tischbein with him)
immediately after the close of the Carnival—but not a moment
before. Needless to say, he had no idea of flinging himself
himself into the Carnival, after the fashion of lesser and
lighter tourists. But the Carnival was a great phenomenon to
be studied. All-embracing Goethe, remember, was nearly as
keen on science as on art. He had ever been patient in poring
over plants botanically, and fishes ichthyologically, and
minerals mineralogically. And now, day by day, he studied
the Carnival from a strictly carnivalogical standpoint,
taking notes on which he founded later a classic treatise. His
presence was not needed in the studio during these days, for
the life-sized portrait 'begins already to stand out from the
canvas,' and Tischbein was now painting the folds of the mantle,
which were swathed around a clay figure. 'He is working
away diligently, for the work must, he says, be brought to a
certain point before we start for Naples.' Besides the mantle,
Tischbein was doing the Campagna. I remember that some
years ago an acquaintance of mine, a painter who was neither
successful nor talented, but always buoyant, told me he was
starting for Italy next day. 'I am going,' he said, 'to paint the
Campagna. The Campagna WANTS painting.' Tischbein was
evidently giving it a good dose of what it wanted. 'It takes no
little time,' writes Goethe to Frau von Stein, 'merely to
cover so large a field of canvas with colours.'

Ash Wednesday ushered itself in, and ushered the Carnival
out. The curtain falls, rising a few days later on the Bay of
Naples. Re-enter Goethe and Tischbein. Bright blue back-
cloth. Incidental music of barcaroles, ets. For a while, all
goes splendidly well. Sane Quixote and aesthetic Sancho

visit the churches, the museums; visit Pompeii; visit our Ambassador, Sir William Hamilton, that accomplished man. Vesuvius is visited too; thrice by Goethe, but (here, for the first time, we feel a vague uneasiness) only once by Tischbein. To Goethe, as you may well imagine, Vesuvius was strongly attractive. At his every ascent he was very brave, going as near as possible to the crater, which he approached very much as he had approached the Carnival, not with any wish to fling himself into it, but as a resolute scientific inquirer. Tischbein, on the other hand, merely disliked and feared Vesuvius. He said it had no æsthetic value, and at his one ascent did not accompany Goethe to the crater's edge. He seems to have regarded Goethe's bravery as rashness. Here, you see, is a rift, ever so slight, but of evil omen; what seismologists call 'a fault.'

Goethe was unconscious of its warning. Throughout his his sojourn in Naples he seems to have thought that Tischbein in Naples was the same as Tischbein in Rome. Of some persons it is true that change of sky works no change of soul. Oddly enough, Goethe reckoned himself among the changeable. In one of his letters he calls himself 'quite an altered man,' and asserts that he is given over to 'a sort of intoxicated self-forgetfulness'—a condition to which his letters testify not at all. In a last bulletin he is nearer the mark: 'Were I not impelled by the German spirit, and desire to learn and do rather than to enjoy, I should tarry a little longer in this school of a light-hearted and happy life, and try to profit by it still more.' A truly priceless passage, this, with a solemnity transcending logic—as who should say, 'Were I not so thoroughly German, I should be thoroughly German.' Tischbein was of less stern stuff, and it is clear that Naples fostered in him a lightness which Rome had repressed. Goethe says that he himself puzzled the people in Neapolitan society: 'Tischbein pleases them far better. This evening he hastily painted some heads of the size of life, and about these they disported themselves as strangely as the New Zealanders at the sight of a ship of war.' One feels that but for Goethe's presence Tischbein would have cut New Zealand capers too. A week later he did an utterly astounding thing. He told Goethe that he would not be accompanying him to Sicily.

He did not, of course, say 'The novelty of your greatness has worn off. Your solemnity oppresses me. Be off, and leave me to enjoy myself in Naples-on-Sea—Naples, the Queen of Watering Places!' He spoke of work which he had undertaken, and recommended as travelling companion for Goethe a young man of the name of Kniep.

Goethe, we may be sure, was restrained by pride from any show of wrath. Pride compelled him to make light of the matter in his epistles to the Weimarians. Even Kniep he accepted with a good grace, though not without misgivings. He needed a man who would execute for him sketches and paintings of all that in the districts passed through was worthy of record. He had already 'heard Kniep highly spoken of as a clever draughtsman—only his industry was not much commended.' Our hearts sink. 'I have tolerably studied his character, and think the ground of this censure arises rather from a want of decision, which may certainly be overcome, if we are long together.' Our hearts sink lower. Kniep will never do. Kniep will play the deuce, we are sure of it. And yet (such is life) Kniep turns out very well. Throughout the Sicilian tour Goethe gives the rosiest reports of the young man's cheerful ways and strict attention to the business of sketching. It may be that these reports were coloured partly by a desire to set Tischbein down. But there seems to be no doubt that Goethe liked Kniep greatly and rejoiced in the quantity and quality of his work. At Palermo, one evening, Goethe sat reading Homer and 'making an impromptu translation for the benefit of Kniep, who had well deserved by his diligent exertions this day some agreeable refreshment over a glass of wine.'

This is a pleasing little scene, and is typical of the whole tour.

In the middle of May, Goethe returned to Naples. And lo! —Tischbein was not there to receive him. Tischbein, if you please, had skipped back to Rome, bidding his Neapolitan friends look to his great compatriot. Pride again forbade Goethe to show displeasure, and again our reading has to be done between the lines. In the first week of June he was once more in Rome. I can imagine with what high courtesy, as though there were nothing to rebuke, he treated Tischbein. But it is possible that his manner would have been less perfect had the portrait not been unfinished.

His sittings were resumed. It seems that Signora Zucchi, better known to the world as Angelica Kauffmann, had also begun to paint him. But, great as was Goethe's esteem for the mind of that nice woman, he set no store on this fluttering attempt of hers: 'her picture is a pretty fellow, to be sure, but not a trace of me.' It was by the large and firm 'historic' mode of Tischbein that he, not exactly in his habit as he lived, but in the white mantle that so well became him, and on the worthy throne of that fallen obelisk, was to be handed down to the gaze of future ages. Was to be, yes. On June 27th he reports that Tischbein's work 'is succeeding happily; the likeness is striking, and the conception pleases everybody.' Three days later: 'Tischbein goes to Naples.'

Incredible! We stare aghast, as in the presence of some great dignitary from behind whom, by a ribald hand, a chair is withdrawn when he is in the act of sitting down. Tischbein had, as it were, withdrawn the obelisk. What was Goethe to do? What *can* a dignitary, in such case, do? He cannot turn and recriminate. That would but lower him the more. Can he behave as though nothing has happened? Johann Wolfgang von Goethe tried to do so. And it must have been in support of this attempt that he consented to leave his own quarters and reside awhile in the studio of the outgoing Tischbein. That slippery man does, it is true, seem to have given out that he would not be away very long; and the prospect of his return may well have been reckoned in mitigation of his going. Goethe had leave from the Duke of Weimar to prolong his Italian holiday till the spring of next year. It is possible that Tischbein really did mean to come back and finish the picture. Goethe had, at any rate, no reason for not hoping.

'When you think of me, think of me as happy,' he directs. And had he not indeed reasons for happiness? He had the most perfect health, he was writing masterpieces, he was in Rome— Rome which no pilgrim had loved with a rapture deeper than his; the wonderful old Rome that lingered on almost to our own day, under the conserving shadow of the Temporal Power; a Rome in which the Emperors kept unquestionably their fallen day about them. No pilgrim had wandered with a richer enthusiasm along those highways and those great storied spaces. It is pleasing to watch in what deep draughts Goethe drank Rome in. But—but—I fancy that now in his second year of sojourn he tended to remain within the city walls, caring less than of yore for the Campagna; and I suspect that if ever he did stray out there he averted his eyes from anything in the nature of a ruined temple. Of one thing I am sure. The huge canvas in the studio had its face to the wall. There is never a reference to it by Goethe in any letter after that of June 27th. But I surmise that its nearness continually worked on him, and that sometimes, when no one was by, he all unwillingly approached it, he moved it out into a good light and, stepping back, gazed at it for a long time. And I wonder that Tischbein was not shamed, telepathically, to return.

What was it that had made Tischbein—not once, but thrice —abandon Goethe? We have no right to suppose he had plotted to avenge himself for the poet's refusal to collaborate with him on the theme of primaeval man. A likelier explanation is merely that Goethe, as I have suggested, irked him. Forty years elapsed before Goethe collected his letters from Italy and made a book of them; and in this book he included—how magnanimous old men are!—several letters written to him from Naples by his deserter. These are shallow but vivid documents—the effusions of one for whom the visible world suffices. I take it that Tischbein was an 'historic' painter because no ambitious painter in those days wasn't. In Goethe the historic sense was as innate as the aesthetic; so was the ethical sense; so was the scientific sense; and the three of them, forever cropping up in his discourse, may well be understood to have been too much for the simple Tischbein. But, you ask, can mere boredom make a man act so cruelly as this man acted? Well, there may have been another cause, and a more interesting one. I have mentioned that Goethe and Tischbein visited our Ambassador in Naples. His Excellency was at that time a widower, but his establishment was already graced by his future wife, Miss Emma Harte, whose beauty is so well known to us all. 'Tischbein,' wrote Goethe a few days afterwards, 'is engaged in painting her.' Later in the year, Tischibein, soon after his return to Naples, sent to Goethe a sketch for a painting he had now done of Miss Harte as Iphigenia at the Sacrificial Altar. Perhaps he had wondered that she should sacrifice herself to Sir William Hamilton. . . . 'I like Hamilton uncommonly' is a phrase culled from one of his letters; and when a man is very hearty about the protector of a very beautiful woman one begins to be suspicious. I do not mean to suggest that Miss Harte—though it is true she had not met Nelson—was fascinated by Tischbein. But we have no reason to suppose that Tischbein was less susceptible than Romney.

Altogether, it seems likely enough that the future Lady Hamilton's fine eyes were Tischbein's main reason for not going to Sicily, and afterwards for his sudden exodus from Rome. But why, in this case, did he leave Naples, why go back to Rome, when Goethe was in Sicily? I hope he went for the purpose of shaking off his infatuation for Miss Harte. I am loth to think he went merely to wind up his affairs in Rome. I will assume that only after a sharp conflict, in which he fought hard on the side of duty against love, did he relapse to Naples. But I won't pretend to wish he had finished that portrait.

If you know where that portrait is, tell me. I want it. I have tried to trace it—vainly. What became of it? I thought I might find this out in George Henry Lewes' *Life of Goethe.* But Lewes had a hero-worship for Goethe: he thought him greater than George Eliot, and in the whole book there is but one cold mention of Tischbein's name. Mr. Oscar Browning, in the *Encyclopaedia Britannica*, names Tischbein as Goethe's 'constant companion' in the early days at Rome—and says nothing else about him! In fact, the hero-worshippers have evidently conspired to hush up the affront to their hero. Even the *Penny Cyclopaedia* (1842), which devotes a column to little Tischbein himself, and goes into various details of his career, is silent about the portrait of Goethe. I learn from that column that Tischbein became director of the Neapolitan Academy, at a salary of 600 ducats, and resided in Naples until the Revolution of '99, when he returned in haste to Germany. Suppose he passed through Rome on his way. A homing fugitive would not pause to burden himself with a vast unfinished canvas. We may be sure the canvas remained in that Roman studio—an object of mild interest to successive occupants. Is it there still? Does the studio itself still exist? Belike it has been demolished, with so much else. What became of the expropriated canvas? It wouldn't have been buried in the new foundations. Some one must have staggered away with it. Whither? Somewhere, I am sure, in some dark vault or cellar, it languishes.

Seek it, fetch it out, bring it to me in triumph. You will always find me in the Baptistery of San Lorenzo. But I have formed so clear and sharp a preconception of the portrait that I am likely to be disappointed at sight of what you bring me. I see in my mind's eye every falling fold of the white mantle; the nobly-rounded calf of the leg on which rests the forearm; the high-light on the black silk stocking. The shoes, the hands, are rather sketchy, the sky is a mere slab; the ruined temples are no more than adumbrated. But the expression of the face is perfectly, epitomically, that of a great man surveying a great alien scene and gauging its import not without a keen sense of its dramatic conjunction with himself—Marius in Carthage and Napoleon before the Sphinx, Wordsworth on London Bridge and Cortes on the peak in Darien, but most of all, certainly, Goethe in the Campagna. So, you see, I cannot promise not to be horribly let down by Tischbein's actual handiwork. I may even have to take back my promise that it shall have a place of honour. But I shall not utterly reject it—unless on the plea that a collection of unfinished works should itself have some great touch of incompletion.

'A Clergyman'

Fragmentary, pale, momentary; almost nothing; glimpsed and gone; as it were, a faint human hand thrust up, never to re-appear, from beneath the rolling waters of Time, he forever haunts my memory and solicits my weak imagination. Nothing is told of him but that once, abruptly, he asked a question, and received an answer.

This was on the afternoon of April 7th, 1778, at Streatham, in the well-appointed house of Mr. Thrale. Johnson, on the morning of that day, had entertained Boswell at breakfast in Bolt Court, and invited him to dine at Thrale Hall. The two took coach and arrived early. It seems that Sir John Pringle had asked Boswell to ask Johnson 'what were the best English sermons for style.' In the interval before dinner, accordingly, Boswell reeled off the names of several divines whose prose might or night not win commendation. 'Atterbury?' he suggested. 'JOHNSON: Yes, Sir, one of the best. BOSWELL: Tillotson? JOHNSON: Why, not now. I should not advise any one to imitate Tillotson's style; though I don't know; I should be cautious of censuring anything that has been applauded by so many suffrages.—South is one of the best, if you except his peculiarities, and his violence, and sometimes coarseness of language.—Seed has a very fine style; but he is not very theological. Jortin's sermons are very elegant. Sherlock's style, too, is very elegant, though he has not made it his principal study.—And you may add Smalridge. BOSWELL: I like Ogden's Sermons on Prayer very much, both for neatness of style and subtility of reasoning. JOHNSON: I should like to read all that Ogden has written. BOSWELL: What I want to know is, what sermons afford the best specimen of English pulpit eloquence. JOHNSON: We have no sermons addressed to the passions, that are good for anything; if you mean that kind of eloquence. A CLERGYMAN, whose name I do not recollect: Were not Dodd's sermons' addressed to the passions? JOHNSON: They were nothing, Sir, be they addressed to what they may.'

The suddenness of it! Bang!—and the rabbit that had popped from its burrow was no more.

I know not which is the more startling—the début of the unfortunate clergyman, or the instantaneousness of his end. Why hadn't Boswell told us there was a clergyman present? Well, we may be sure that so careful and acute an artist had some good reason. And I suppose the clergyman was left to take us unawares because just so did he take the company. Had we been told he was there, we might have expected that sooner or later he would join in the conversation. He would have had a place in our minds. We may assume that in the minds of the company around Johnson he had no place. He sat forgotten, overlooked; so that his self-assertion startled every one just as on Boswell's page it startles us. In Johnson's massive and magnetic presence only some very remarkable man, such as Mr. Burke, was sharply distinguishable from the rest. Others might, if they had something in them, stand out slightly. This unfortunate clergyman may have had something in him, but I judge that he lacked the gift of seeming as if he had. That deficiency, however, does not account for the horrid fate that befell him. One of Johnson's strongest and most inveterate feelings was his veneration for the Cloth. To any one in Holy Orders he habitually listened with a grave and charming deference. To-day moreover, he was in excellent good humour. He was at the Thrales', where he so loved to be; the day was fine; a fine dinner was in close prospect; and he had had what he always declared to be the sum of human felicity—a ride in a coach. Nor was there in the question put by the clergyman anything likely to enrage him. Dodd was one whom Johnson had befriended in adversity; and it had always been agreed that Dodd in his pulpit was very emotional. What drew the blasting flash must have been not the question itself, but the manner in which it was asked. And I think we can guess what that manner was.

Say the words aloud: 'Were not Dodd's sermons addressed to the passions?' They are words which, if you have any dramatic and histrionic sense, *cannot* be said except in a high, thin voice.

You may, from sheer perversity, utter them in a rich and sonorous baritone or bass. But if you do so, they sound utterly unnatural. To make them carry the conviction of human utterance, you have no choice: you must pipe them.

Remember, now, Johnson was very deaf. Even the people whom he knew well, the people to whose voices he was accustomed, had to address him very loudly. It is probable that this unregarded, young, shy clergyman, when at length he suddenly mustered courage to 'cut in,' let his high, thin voice soar *too* high, insomuch that it was a kind of scream. On no other hypothesis can we account for the ferocity with which Johnson turned and rended him. Johnson didn't, we may be sure, mean to be cruel. The old lion, startled, just struck out blindly. But the force of paw and claws was not the less lethal. We have endless testimony to the strength of Johnson's voice; and the very cadence of those words, 'They were nothing, Sir, be they addressed to what they may,' convinces me that the old lion's jaws never gave forth a louder roar. Boswell does not record that there was any further conversation before the announcement of dinner. Perhaps the whole company had been temporarily deafened. But I am not bothering about *them*. My heart goes out to the poor dear clergyman exclusively.

I said a moment ago that he was young and shy; and I admit that I slipped those epithets in without having justified them to you by due process of induction. Your quick mind will have already supplied what I omitted. A man with a high, thin voice, and without power to impress any one with a sense of his importance, a man so null in effect that even the retentive mind of Boswell did not retain his very name, would assuredly not be a self-confident man. Even if he were not naturally shy, social courage would soon have been sapped in him, and would in time have been destroyed, by experience. That he had not yet given himself up as a bad job, that he still had faint wild hopes, is proved by the fact that he did snatch the opportunity for asking that question. He must, accordingly, have been young. Was he the curate of the neighbouring church? I think so. It would account for his having been invited. I see him as he sits there listening to the great Doctor's pronouncement on Atterbury and those others. He sits on the edge of a chair in the background. He has colourless eyes, fixed earnestly, and a face almost as pale as the clerical bands beneath his somewhat receding chin. His forehead is high and narrow, his hair mouse-coloured. His hands are clasped tight before him, the knuckles standing out sharply. This constriction does not mean that he is steeling himself to speak. He has no positive intention of speaking. Very much, nevertheless, is he wishing in the back of his mind that he *could* say something—something whereat the great Doctor would turn on him and say, after a pause for thought, 'Why yes, Sir. That is most justly observed' or 'Sir, this has never occurred to me. I thank you—' thereby fixing the observer for ever high in the esteem of all. And now in a flash the chance presents itself. 'We have,' shouts Johnson, 'no sermons addressed to the passions, that are good for anything.' I see the curate's frame quiver with

sudden impulse, and his mouth fly open, and—no, I can't bear
it, I shut my eyes and ears. But audible, even so, is something
shrill, followed by something thunderous.

Presently I re-open my eyes. The crimson has not yet
faded from that young face yonder, and slowly down either
cheek falls a glistening tear. Shades of Atterbury and Tillotson! Such weakness shames the Established Church. What
would Jortin and Smalridge have said?—what Seed and South?
And, by the way, who *were* they, these worthies? It is a solemn
thought that so little is conveyed to us by names which to the
palaeo-Georgians conveyed so much. We discern a dim,
composite picture of a big man in a big wig and a billowing
black gown, with a big congregation beneath him. But we are
not anxious to hear what he is saying. We know it is all very
elegant. We know it will be printed and be bound in finely-
tooled full calf, and no palaeo-Georgian gentleman's library
will be complete without it. Literate people in those days were
comparatively few; but, bating that, one may say that sermons
were as much in request as novels are to-day. I wonder, will
mankind continue to be capricious? It is a very solemn thought
indeed that no more than a hundred-and-fifty years hence the
novelists of our time, with all their moral and political and
sociological outlook and influence, will perhaps shine as in-
distinctly as do those old preachers, with all their elegance,
now. 'Yes, Sir,' some great pundit may be telling a disciple at
this moment, 'Wells is one of the best. Galsworthy is one of
the best, if you except his concern for delicacy of style. Mrs.
Ward has a very firm grasp of problems, but is not very
creational.—Caine's book are very edifying. I should like to
read all that Caine has written. Miss Corelli, too, is very
edifying.—And you may add Upton Sinclair.' 'What I want
to know,' says the disciple, 'is, what English novels may be
selected as specially enthralling.' The pundit answers: 'We
have no novels addressed to the passions that are good for

anything, if you mean that kind of enthralment.' And here some poor wretch (whose name the disciple will not remember) inquires: 'Are not Mrs. Glyn's novels addressed to the passions?' and is in due form annihilated. Can it be that a time will come when readers of this passage in our pundit's Life will take more interest in the poor nameless wretch than in all the bearers of those great names put together, being no more able or anxious to discriminate between (say) Mrs. Ward and Mr. Sinclair than we are to set Ogden above Sherlock, or Sherlock above Ogden? It seems impossible. But we must remember that things are not always what they seem.

Every man illustrious in his day, however much he may be gratified by his fame, looks with an eager eye to posterity for a continuance of past favours, and would even live the remainder of his life in obscurity if by so doing he could insure that future generations would preserve a correct attitude towards him forever. This is very natural and human, but, like so many very natural and human things, very silly. Tillotson and the rest need not, after all, be pitied for our neglect of them. They either know nothing about it, or are above such terrene trifles. Let us keep our pity for the seething mass of divines who were *not* elegantly verbose, and had no fun or glory while they lasted. And let us keep a specially large portion for one whose lot was so much worse than merely undistinguished. If that nameless curate had not been at the Thrales' that day, or, being there, had kept the silence that so well became him, his life would have been drab enough, in all conscience. But at any rate an unpromising career would not have been nipped in the bud. And that is what in fact happened, I'm sure of it. A robust man might have rallied under the blow. Not so our friend. Those who knew him in infancy had not expected that he would be reared. Better for him had they been right. It is well to grow up and be ordained, but not if you are delicate and very sensitive, and shall happen to annoy the greatest, the most stentorian and roughest of contemporary personages. 'A Clergyman' never held up his head or smiled again after the brief encounter recorded for us by Boswell. He sank into a rapid decline. Before the next blossoming of Thrale Hall's almond trees he was no more. I like to think that he died forgiving Dr. Johnson.

William and Mary

Memories, like olives, are an acquired taste. William and Mary (I give them the Christian names that were indeed theirs—the joint title by which their friends always referred to them) were for some years an interest in my life, and had a hold on my affection. But a time came when, though I had known and liked them too well ever to forget them, I gave them but a few thoughts now and then. How, being dead, could they keep their place in the mind of a young man surrounded with large and constantly renewed consignments of the living? As one grows older, the charm of novelty wears off. One finds that there is no such thing as novelty—or, at any rate, that one has lost the faculty for perceiving it. One sees every newcomer not as something strange and special, but as a ticketed specimen of this or that very familiar genus. The world has ceased to be remarkable; and one tends to think more and more often of the days when it was so very remarkable indeed.

I suppose that had I been thirty years older when first I knew him, William would have seemed to me little worthier of attention than a twopenny postage-stamp seems to-day. Yet, no: William really had some oddities that would have caught even an oldster's eye. In himself he was commonplace enough (as I, coeval though I was with him, soon saw). But in details of surface he was unusual. In them he happened to be rather ahead of his time. He was a socialist, for example. In 1890 there was only one other socialist in Oxford, and he not at all an undergraduate, but a retired chimney-sweep, named

Hines, who made speeches, to which nobody, except perhaps William, listened, near the Martyrs' Memorial. And William wore a flannel shirt, and rode a bicycle—very strange habits in those days, and very horrible. He was said to be (though he was short-sighted and wore glasses) a first-rate 'back' at football; but, as football was a thing frowned on by the rowing men, and coldly ignored by the bloods, his talent for it did not help him: he was one of the principal pariahs of our College; and it was rather in a spirit of bravado, and to show how sure of myself I was, that I began, in my second year, to cultivate his acquaintance.

We had little in common. I could not think Political Economy 'the most exciting thing in the world,' as he used to call it. Nor could I without yawning listen to more than a few lines of Mr. William Morris' interminable smooth Icelandic Sagas, which my friend, pious young socialist that he was, thought 'glorious'. He had begun to write an Icelandic Saga himself, and had already achieved some hundreds of verses. None of these pleased him, though to me they seemed very like his master's. I can see him now, standing on his hearth-rug, holding his MS. close to his short-sighted eyes, declaiming the verses and trying, with many angular gestures of his left hand, to animate them—a tall, broad, raw-boned fellow, with long brown hair flung back from his forehead, and a very shabby suit of clothes. Because of his clothes and his socialism, and his habit of offering beer to a guest, I had at first supposed him quite poor; and I was surprised when he told me that he had from his guardian (his parents being dead) an allowance of £350, and that when he came of age he would have an income of £400. 'All out of dividends,' he would groan. I would hint that Mr. Hines and similar zealots might disembarrass him of this load, if he asked them nicely. 'No,' he would say quite seriously, 'I can't do that,' and would read out passages from *Fabian Essays* to show that in the present anarchical

conditions only mischief could result from sporadic dispersal of
rent. 'Ten, twelve years hence——' he would muse more
hopefully. 'But by that time,' I would say, 'you'll probably be
married, and your wife mightn't quite——', whereat he would
hotly repeat what he had said many times: that he would never
marry. Marriage was an anti-social anachronism. I think its
survival was in some part due to the machinations of Capital.
Anyway, it was doomed. Temporary civil contracts between
men and women would be the rule 'ten, twelve years hence';
pending which time the lot of any man who had civic sense
must be celibacy, tempered perhaps with free love.

Long before that time was up, nevertheless, William
married. One afternoon in the spring of '95 I happened to meet
him at a corner of Cockspur Street. I wondered at the immense
cordiality of his greeting; for our friendship, such as it was, had
waned in our two final years at Oxford. 'You look very
flourishing, and,' I said, 'you're wearing a new suit!' 'I'm
married,' he replied, obviously without a twinge of conscience.
He told me he had been married just a month. He declared that
to be married was the most splendid thing in all the world; but
he weakened the force of this generalization by adding that
there never was any one like his wife. 'You must see her,' he
said; and his impatience to show her proudly off to some one
was so evident, and so touching, that I could but accept his
invitation to go and stay with them for two or three days—
'why not next week?' They had taken and furnished 'a sort of
cottage' in ——shire, and this was their home. He had 'run up
for the day, on business—journalism' and was now on his way
to Charing Cross. 'I know you'll like my wife,' he said at
parting. 'She's—well, she's glorious.'

As this was the epithet he had erst applied to *Beowulf* and
to *Sigurd the Volsung* it raised no high hopes. And indeed, as
I was soon to find, he had again misused it. There was nothing
glorious about his bride. Some people might even have not

thought her pretty. I myself did not, in the flash of first sight. Neat, insignificant, pleasing, was what she appeared to me, rather than pretty, and far rather than glorious. In an age of fringes, her brow was severely bare. She looked 'practical.' But an instant later, when she smiled, I saw that she was pretty, too. And presently I thought her delightful. William had met me in a 'governess cart,' and we went to see him unharness the pony. He did this in a fumbling, experimental way, confusing the reins with the traces, and profiting so little by his wife's directions that she began to laugh. And her laugh was a lovely thing; quite a small sound, but exquisitely clear and gay, coming in a sequence of notes that neither rose nor fell, that were quite even; a trill of notes, and then another, and another, as though she were pulling repeatedly a little silver bell . . . As I describe it, perhaps the sound may be imagined irritating. I can only say it was enchanting.

I wished she would go on laughing; but she ceased, she darted forward and (William standing obediently aside, and I helping unhelpfully) unharnessed the pony herself, and led it into its small stable. Decidedly, she was 'practical,' but—I was prepared now to be lenient to any quality she might have.

Had she been feckless, no doubt I should have forgiven her that, too; but I might have enjoyed my visit less than I did, and might have been less pleased to go often again. I had expected to 'rough it' under William's roof. But everything thereunder, within the limits of a strict Arcadian simplicity, was well-ordered. I was touched, when I went to my bedroom, by the precision with which the very small maid had unpacked and disposed my things. And I wondered where my hostess had got the lore she had so evidently imparted. Certainly not from William. Perhaps (it only now strikes me) from a handbook. For Mary was great at handbooks. She had handbooks about gardening, and others about poultry, and one about 'the stable', and others on cognate themes. From these she had filled up

the gaps left in her education by her father, who was a widower
and either a doctor or a solicitor—I forget which—in one of
the smallest towns of an adjoining county. And I daresay she
may have had, somewhere hidden away, a manual for young
hostesses. If so, it must have been a good one. But to say this
is to belittle Mary's powers of intuition. It was they, sharpened by her adoration of William, and by her intensity for
everything around him, that made her so efficient a housewife.

If she possessed a manual for young house-hunters it was
assuredly not by the light of this that she had chosen the home
they were installed in. The 'sort of cottage' had been vacant
for many years—an unpromising and ineligible object, a mile
away from a village, and three miles away from a railway
station. The main part of it was an actual cottage, of seven-
teenth-century workmanship; but a little stuccoed wing had
been added to each side of it, in 1850 or thereabouts, by an
eccentric old gentleman who at that time chose to make it his
home. He had added also the small stable, a dairy and other
appanages. For these, and for garden, there was plenty of
room, as he had purchased and enclosed half an acre of the
surrounding land. Those two stuccoed, very Victorian wings
of his, each with a sash-window above and a French window
below, consorted queerly with the old red brick and the
latticed panes. And the long wooden veranda that he had
invoked did not unify the trinity. But one didn't want it to. The
wrongness had a character all its own. The wrongness was
right—at any rate after Mary had hit on it for William. As a
spinster, she would, I think, have been happiest in a trim
modern villa. But it was a belief of hers that she had married a
man of strange genius. She had married him for himself, not
for his genius; but this added grace in him was a thing to be
reckoned with, ever so much; a thing she must coddle to the
utmost in a proper setting. She was a year older than he
(though, being so small and slight, she looked several years

younger), and in her devotion the maternal instinct played a great part. William, as I have already conveyed to you, was not greatly gifted. Mary's instinct, in this one matter, was at fault. But endearingly, rightly at fault. And, as William *was* outwardly odd, wasn't it well that his home should be so, too? On the inside, comfort was what Mary always aimed at for him, and achieved.

The ground floor had all been made one room, into which you stepped straight from the open air. Quite a long big room (or so it seemed, from the lowness of the ceiling), and well-freshened in its antiquity, with rush-mats here and there on the irregular red tiles, and very white whitewash on the plaster between the rafters. This was the dining-room, drawing-room, and general focus throughout the day, and was called simply the Room. William had a 'den' on the ground floor of the left wing; and there, in the mornings, he used to write a great deal. Mary had no special place of her own: her place was wherever her duties needed her. William wrote reviews of books for the *Daily* ——. He did also creative work. The vein of poetry in him had worked itself out—or rather, it expressed itself for him in Mary. For technical purposes, the influence of Ibsen had superseded that of Morris. At the time of my first visit, he was writing an extraordinarily gloomy play about an extraordinarily unhappy marriage. In subsequent seasons (Ibsen's disc having been somehow eclipsed for him by George Gissing's) he was usually writing novels in which every one—or do I exaggerate?—had made a disastrous match. I think Mary's belief in his genius had made him less diffident than he was at Oxford. He was always emerging from his den, with fresh pages of MS., into the Room. 'You don't mind?' he would say, waving his pages, and then would shout 'Mary!' She was always promptly forth-coming—sometimes from the direction of the kitchen, in a white apron, sometimes from the garden, in a blue one. She never looked at him while he read. To do so would have been lacking in respect for his work. It was on this that she must concentrate her whole mind, privileged auditor that she was. She sat looking straight before her, with her lips slightly compressed, and her hands folded on her lap. I used to wonder that there had been that first moment when I did not think her pretty. Her eyes were of a very light hazel, seeming all the lighter because her hair was of so dark a brown; and they were beautifully set in a face of that 'pinched oval' kind which is rather rare in England. Mary as listener would have atoned to me for any defects there may have been in dear old William's work. Nevertheless, I sometimes wished this work had some comic relief in it. Publishers, I believe, shared this wish; hence the eternal absence of William's name from among their announcements. For Mary's sake, and his, I should have liked him to be 'successful'. But at any rate he didn't need money. He didn't need, in addition to what he had, what he made by his journalism. And as for success—well, didn't Mary think him a genius? And wasn't he Mary's husband? The main reason why I wished for light passages in what he read to us was that they would have been cues for Mary's laugh. This was a thing always new to me. I never tired of that little bell-like euphony; those funny little lucid and level trills.

There was no stint of that charm when William was not reading to us. Mary was in no awe of him, apart from his work, and in no awe at all of me: she used to laugh at us both, for one thing and another—just the same laugh as I had first heard when William tried to unharness the pony. I cultivated in myself whatever amused her in me; I drew out whatever amused her in William; I never let slip any of the things that amused her in herself. 'Chaff' is a great bond; and I should have enjoyed our bouts of it even without Mary's own special *obbligato*. She used to call me (for I was very urban in those days) the Gentleman from London. I used to call her the

Brave Little Woman. Whatever either of us said or did could be twisted easily into relation to those two titles; and our bouts, to which William listened with a puzzled, benevolent smile, used to cease only because Mary regarded me as a possible purveyor of what William, she was sure, wanted and needed, down there in the country, alone with her: intellectual conversation, after his work. She often, I think, invented duties in garden or kitchen so that he should have this stimulus, or luxury, without hindrance. But when William was alone with me it was about her that he liked to talk, and that I myself liked to talk too. He was very sound on the subject of Mary; and so was I. And if, when I was alone with Mary, I seemed to be sounder than I was on the subject of William's wonderfulness, who shall blame me?

Had Mary been a mother, William's wonderfulness would have been less greatly important. But he was her child as well as her lover. And I think, though I do not know, she believed herself content that this should always be, if so it were destined. It was not destined so. On the first night of a visit I paid them in April, 1899, William, when we were alone, told me news. I had been vaguely conscious, throughout the evening, of some change; conscious that Mary had grown gayer, and less gay—somehow different, somehow remote. William said that her child would be born in September, if all went well. 'She's immensely happy,' he told me. I realized that she was indeed happier than ever . . . 'And of course it would be a wonderful thing, for both of us,' he said presently, 'to have a son—or a daughter.' I asked him which he would rather it were, a son or a daughter. 'Oh, either,' he answered wearily. It was evident that he had misgivings and fears. I tried to reason him out of them. He did not, I am thankful to say, ever let Mary suspect them. *She* had no misgivings. But it was destined that her child should live only for an hour, and that she should die in bearing it.

I had stayed again at the cottage in July, for some days. At the end of that month I had gone to France, as was my custom, and a week later had written to Mary. It was William that answered this letter, telling me of Mary's death and burial. I returned to England next day. William and I wrote to each other several times. He had not left his home. He stayed there, 'trying,' as he said in a grotesque and heart-rending phrase, 'to finish a novel.' I saw him in the following January. He wrote to me from the Charing Cross Hotel, asking me to lunch with him there. After our first greetings, there was a silence. He wanted to talk of—what he could not talk of. We stared helplessly at each other, and then, in the English way, talked of things at large. England was engaged in the Boer War. William was the sort of man whom one would have expected to be violently Pro-Boer. I was surprised at his fervour for the stronger side. He told me he had tried to enlist, but had been rejected on account of his eyesight. But there was, he said, a good chance of his being sent out, almost immediately, as one of the *Daily* ——'s special correspondents. 'And then,' he exclaimed, 'I shall see something of it.' I had a presentiment that he would not return, and a belief that he did not want to return. He did not return. Special correspondents were not so carefully shepherded in that war as they have since been. They were more at liberty to take risks, on behalf of the journals to which they were accredited. William was killed a few weeks after he had landed at Cape Town.

And there came, as I have said, a time when I did not think of William and Mary often; and then a time when I did more often think of them. And especially much did my mind hark back to them in the late autumn of last year; for on the way to the place I was staying at I had passed the little railway station whose name had always linked itself for me with the names of those two friends. There were but four intervening stations.

It was not a difficult pilgrimage that I made some days later—back towards the past, for that past's sake and honour. I had thought I should not remember the way, the three miles of way, from the station to the cottage; but I found myself remembering it perfectly, without a glance at the finger-posts. Rain had been falling heavily, driving the late leaves off the trees; and everything looked rather sodden and misty, though the sun was now shining. I had known this landscape only in spring, summer, early autumn. Mary had held to a theory that at other seasons I could not be acclimatized. But there were groups of trees that I knew, even without their leaves; and farm-houses and small stone bridges that had not at all changed. Only what mattered was changed. Only what mattered was gone. Would what I had come to see be there still? In comparison with what it had held, it was not much. But I wished to see it, melancholy spectacle though it must be for me if it were extant, and worse than melancholy if it held something new. I began to be sure it had been demolished, built over. At the corner of the lane that had led to it, I was almost minded to explore no further, to turn back. But I went on, and suddenly I was at the four-barred iron gate, that I remembered, between the laurels. It was rusty, and was fastened with a rusty padlock, and beyond it there was grass where a winding 'drive' had been. From the lane the cottage never had been visible, even when these laurels were lower and sparser than they were now. Was the cottage still standing? Presently, I climbed over the gate, and walked through the long grass, and—yes, there was Mary's cottage; still there; William's and Mary's cottage. Trite enough, I have no doubt, were the thoughts that possessed me as I stood gazing. There is nothing new to be thought about the evanescence of human things; but there is always much to be felt about it by one who encounters in his maturity some such intimate instance and reminder as confronted me, in that cold sunshine, across that small wilderness of long rank wet grass and weeds.

Incredibly woebegone and lonesome the house would have looked even to one for whom it contained no memories; all the more because in its utter dereliction it looked so durable. Some of the stucco had fallen off the walls of the two wings; thick flakes of it lay on the discoloured roof of the veranda, and thick flakes of it could be seen lying in the grass below. Otherwise, there were few signs of actual decay. The sash-window and the French window of each wing were shuttered, and, from where I was standing, the cream-coloured paint of those shutters behind the glass looked almost fresh. The latticed windows between had all been boarded up from within. The house was not to be let perish soon.

I did not want to go nearer to it; yet I did go nearer, step by step, across the wilderness, right up to the edge of the veranda itself, and within a yard of the front-door.

I stood looking at that door. I had never noticed it in the old days, for then it had always stood open. But it asserted itself now, master of the threshold.

It was a narrow door—narrow even for its height, which did not exceed mine by more than two inches or so; a door that even when it was freshly painted must have looked mean. How much meaner now, with its paint all faded and mottled, cracked and blistered! It had no knocker, not even a slit for letters. All that it had was a large-ish key-hole. On this my eyes rested; and presently I moved to it, stooped down to it, peered through it. I had a glimpse of—darkness impenetrable.

Strange it seemed to me, as I stood back, that there the Room was, the remembered Room itself, separated from me by nothing but this unremembered door . . . and a quarter of a century, yes. I saw it all, in my mind's eye, just as it had been: the way the sunlight came into it through this same door-way and through the lattices of these same four windows; the way the little bit of a staircase came down into it, so crookedly yet so confidently; and how uneven the tiled floor was, and how low the rafters were, and how littered the whole place was with books brought in from his den by William, and how bright with flowers brought in by Mary from her garden. The rafters, the stairs, the tiles, were still existing, changeless in despite of cobwebs and dust and darkness, all quite changeless on the other side of the door, so near to me. I wondered how I should feel if by some enchantment the door slowly turned on its hinges, letting in light. I should not enter, I felt, not even look, so much must I hate to see those inner things lasting when all that had given to them a meaning was gone from them, taken away from them, finally. And yet, why blame them for their survival? And how know that *nothing* of the past ever came to them, revisiting, hovering? Something—sometimes—perhaps? One knew so little. How not be tender to what, as it seemed to me, perhaps the dead loved?

So strong in me now was the wish to see again all those things, to touch them and, as it were, commune with them, and so queerly may the mind be wrought upon in a solitude among memories, that there were moments when I almost expected that the door would obey my will. I was recalled to a clearer sense of reality by something which I had not before noticed. In the door-post to the right was a small knob of rusty iron—mocking reminder that to gain admission to a house one does not 'will' the door: one rings the bell—unless it is rusty and had quite obviously no one to answer it; in which case one goes away. Yet I did not go away. The movement that I made, in despite of myself, was towards the knob itself. But, I hesitated, suppose I did what I half meant to do, and there were no sound. That would be ghastly. And surely there *would* be no sound. And if sound there were, wouldn't that be worse still? My hand drew back, wavered, suddenly closed on the knob. I heard the scrape of the wire—and then, from somewhere within the heart of the shut house, a tinkle.

It had been the weakest, the puniest of noises. It had been no more than is a fledgling's first attempt at a twitter. But I was not judging it by its volume. Deafening peals from steeples had meant less to me than that one single note breaking the silence—in there. In there, in the dark, the bell that had answered me was still quivering, I supposed, on its wire. But there was no one to answer *it*, no footstep to come hither from those recesses, making prints in the dust. Well, *I* could answer it; and again my hand closed on the knob, unhesitatingly this time, pulling further. That was my answer; and the rejoinder to it was more than I had thought to hear—a whole quick sequence of notes, faint but clear, playful, yet poignantly sad, like a trill of laughter echoing out of the past, or even merely out of this neighbouring darkness. It was so like something I had known, so recognizable and, oh, recognizing, that I was lost in wonder. And long must I have remained standing at that door, for I heard the sound often, often. I must have rung again and again, tenaciously, vehemently, in my folly.

From a Brother's Standpoint

On a wintry and damp afternoon, in the year 1908, I was standing on the doorstep of my mother's house in Upper Berkeley Street, seeing off a man who had been lunching with us. A taxi stopped at the curb, and my brother Herbert stepped out of it in the dreamy yet ample and energetic way that he had of stepping out of taxis. 'Oh, how are you, Mr. Tree?' my friend greeted him. 'I?' said Herbert, shaking the proffered hand and gazing around him. 'I? Oh, I'm radiant!'

My friend, when I went to see him a few days later, said to me that this epithet, if any ordinary man applied it to himself, would doubtless seem rather absurd, but that Herbert's use of it was perfectly right and proper: he looked radiant, it was obvious that he felt radiant, and he told the simple truth in saying that he *was* radiant. My friend, having spoken thus, looked in the glass and, I remember, sighed.

Herbert was for many reasons an enviable man, but I think that what most of us most envied him was that incessant zest of his. Nothing ever seemed to derange for one moment that large, wholesome appetite for life and art. Difficulties that would have crushed any man of no more than ordinary power to cope with them were for Herbert a mere pleasant incentive —or rather, as he was the last man to need any incentive, a mere pleasant challenge to be lightly accepted and quickly dealt with on the way to something else. The gigantic risks of His Majesty's Theatre never, so far as I could see, caused him to turn a hair. He was glad if things were going well; if they weren't, he had a plan for making them do so within a few weeks. He could look Ruin in the face and say, 'Oh, I'm radiant'; whereat Ruin always slunk away, drawing her hood over her face—foiled again.

First impressions are sharpest, and in describing anybody it is always from them that one would wish to start. But when first I saw Herbert I was too young to be impressed by him in any way. I was but a few hours old; and when those few hours had become a few years, Herbert was already one of the accepted figures on my horizon. He was nineteen years older than I, and, as I have no memory of anything that was going on before my fourth year, he must have been quite twenty-two at the time of which I have faint glimpses. My parents, and my sisters and I, lived in Clanricarde Gardens, a cul-de-sac off the Bayswater Road—a double row of houses that seemed to me far taller than the modern skyscrapers seem. Herbert seemed very tall, too, and his hair was of a very bright red, at which I used to look up, with interest. It would seem that his hair had touched the imagination of other children before me. In the early 'seventies young laymen were apt to be less wholly lay than they are now; and Herbert, at the age of eighteen, had felt it his duty to preach in the Sunday-school of a neighbouring church, and had ceased to do so only when the children, presuming on his lack of sternness, began to call him 'Ha'porth o' Carrots.' It was not until many years later that the tuitional instinct revived in him and led him to found the Academy of Dramatic Art.

Besides teaching on Sundays, Herbert was also learning on week-days. My father was in the City. He was for many years a corn merchant, and subsequently started a journal, *The Evening Corn Trade List* (which was carried on after his death in 1892 and only recently ceased to exist). His three eldest sons, Ernest, Herbert and Julius, all graduated as clerks in his office. I doubt whether any one of them learnt much there, or was solemnly expected to learn much there. My father, though devoted to his own work, had the most liberal of minds, and was, I imagine, very well content that his sons should do as they willed. It was not their will to stay for ever at their desks. Ernest had a desire for sheep-farming in the wilds. He went out to Cape Colony, married, and made his home there. Julius went to explore Patagonia, explored it quite thoroughly, and wrote a delightful book about it. Herbert wanted to go on the stage. That, in those days, was a wild, an awful inclination, and somewhat horrified even my father; insomuch that Herbert confined himself to a whirl of amateur theatricals. In this whirl he had so much success that by the time he made his first appearance in public all fatherly misgivings had vanished, giving place to fatherly pride.

The Globe Theatre was, I believe, the scene of that first appearance. And, as the year of it was certainly 1878, I can claim to remember Herbert as he was before the seal of his profession was set on him. But, as what I remember is scanty —just that memory of a bright redness high up—my boast had better be that I remember him in days long before he had set his seal upon his profession. In 1879, or thereabouts, I had acquired a habit of drawing pictures; and what I liked about Herbert, whenever he came to see us, was that *he* could draw pictures, too. I think I liked him all the better for that our styles did not clash. I drew *and* painted—especially painted. Herbert used pencil only. The subjects I chose were soldiers, policemen, cottages, and knights in armour. These subjects he would sometimes essay, but only to please *me*: they did not really interest him, and his handling of them was (I still think) inferior to mine. What he excelled me in was Mr. Gladstone and Lord Beaconsfield. He could draw either of them equally well in profile or in full-face, and as the features of both of them were very familiar to me in *Punch*, whose cartoons I was fond of colouring week by week, I was in a position to appreciate his skill. I was a Conservative, and Herbert (to my wonder and grief) a Liberal. Yet his Lord Beaconsfield amused me not less than his Mr. Gladstone. My mother, too, was very fond of watching him draw, and for her he used to draw all sorts of people—people whom he had recently met. 'This is Whistler, the painter,' he would say, 'This is E. W. Godwin,' or 'Here's Oscar Wilde, the poet.' Henry Irving, however, was his favourite theme. And I remember him saying, one day, with some importance: 'The Routledges have asked me to dine on Sunday night, and Irving is to be there.' Whereat I communed with myself: 'Dinner? On *Sunday* night?' Mr. Edmund Routledge had the house opposite to my father's, and on the following Sunday, at my bed-time, I looked out at those lit windows, looked long at them. I was fascinated, in spite of myself, and, much as I pitied Herbert for being so unlikely now to go to Heaven, I was also envying him not a little, too.

I wanted to grow up quickly and belong (on week-days) to the great world in which Herbert was moving. And of that world I was soon to have a closer, more inspiring glimpse than had been vouchsafed by the Routledges' lit windows. I think the date of this glimpse was in March, 1882. I was now nine years old, and went to a day-school that was graced with a whole-holiday every Saturday. Herbert nobly invited me to spend a Saturday morning with him. He had rooms in Maddox Street, sharing them with his friend A. K. Moore. I remember a room that seemed to me rather shabby (I had expected marble columns), and I remember the smell of the smoke puffed continually from A. K. Moore's pipe. I did not like this smoke, and did not form a high opinion of A. K. Moore. I did not know that he had greatly distinguished himself at Oxford, and that he was destined to write very brilliant leading articles for *The Morning Post*. And even had I known these things I should still have regarded him as the man who smoked that pipe and stared at me and laughed again and again at the notion that Herbert had so small a brother. Herbert himself went on writing at a table by the window; but this pre-occupation I excused, for he told me he was writing something for—*Punch*! And he told me that in a few minutes he was going to take his manuscript—and me!—round to Bouverie Street and show us both to Mr. Burnand. At about this time Herbert wrote several skits for *Punch*. One of them, I know, was on the 'interviews' given to reporters by Oscar Wilde during his American tour, and another was on the press-notices of Mrs. Langtry's impersonation of Lady Macbeth. Excellent fun they were—and are, in the bound volume. It may have been one of these two skits that Herbert was writing on that marvellous morning in my life. I remember A. K. Moore looking through the manuscript and laughing, but doubting (which seemed to me just like him) whether Mr. Burnand would put it in.

There were no marble columns even in the office of *Punch* itself; but there was, and I saw him with my own eyes, Mr. Burnand; and he seemed to me the more greatly a prince of men because he was not smoking, and because he sat in a chair that swung round towards us in a most fascinating manner, and because he did not laugh at me. I liked also Mrs. Bernard Beere, the famous actress, to whom, after another drive in a hansom, I was presented as she lay, in the middle of a large room somewhere, on a sofa of crimson velvet, with a great deal of lace around her head, and an enormous bunch of hothouse grapes on a small table beside her, and a company of important-looking men standing and sitting around her. I liked her for giving me so many of her grapes; but my enjoyment of these was somewhat marred by the more-than-A.-.K.-Moorish mirth of one gentleman at the smallness of 'Beerbohm Tree's brother.' This gentleman was of immense height and girth; and I was just old enough to think of saying, and just too well-brought-up to say, that *I* might as well laugh at the bigness of

'Beerbohm Tree's friend.' I did but look fixedly at the striped shirt-collar that he wore; and later, when, in another hansom, Herbert told me that the gentleman was Mr. Edmund Yates, I merely said that I did not like his striped collar.

The greatest event of that great day was yet to come: we were to lunch at Herbert's club. Was it the 'Arundel,' perhaps? The 'Savage'? I know not. I cared not. It was Herbert's club, and I lunched in it, and was presented to the great Mr. Godwin in it. At first I thought he must be a 'conspirator,' for he wore a large black cloak and a large soft black hat. But he had the most charming manners, and treated me as an equal, and I quite agreed with the opinion, so often expressed by Herbert in those days, that Godwin was a Master. I left the club in company with these two, and Herbert, after hailing a hansom for me and paying the driver, gave me a ten-shilling piece. To have gold seemed to me at that time hardly less wonderful than it would seem in this age of paper. That gold piece soon became some mere silver; that silver, vanishing copper; but the memory of those hours with Herbert was a treasure to be jealously hoarded.

Herbert was (then and always) a hero to me. But, let me add, Julius was a god. And he was not so because he had explored Patagonia (remote and savage things had no magic for me), nor because he had written a much-praised book about Patagonia (I was not literary), but because he was so cool and calm and elegant. Herbert seemed always to be in a hurry, Julius never. Herbert would overpay and dismiss his hansom whenever he came to see us, and at his departure would whistle frantically and piercingly for another. Julius always kept *his* hansom waiting, hour after hour. And *his* hansom was always one of that new and lordly kind, padded throughout with black leather, and fitted with two little looking-glasses, and drawn by a spirited horse, and driven by a not tipsy driver. Herbert talked excitedly, and used to pass his hands through his hair, and leave it all standing up on end. Julius never raised his deep voice, and never put any expression into it, and his straw-coloured hair lay around his head as smoothly as satin. Herbert's necktie was often on one side, and his top hat always lustreless, and he never had a flower in his buttonhole. Julius had always a gardenia or Parma violets, and his hat was dazzling, and his linen was washed in Paris. Also, he had a moustache. Not to have that when one was grown up seemed to me to argue a deficiency in sense of fitness. I knew that Herbert, being an actor, had to be clean-shaven. But I felt that I myself, if hereafter I had to choose between being an actor and having a moustache, should not hesitate. Not in virtue of his acting, but rather in virtue of himself, was Herbert a hero to me. More than once, schoolfellows of mine had said to me: 'Your brother's an actor, isn't he?' They had not said this in a tone implying actual condemnation. But—

In some early month of '84 my classification of the two brothers underwent a sudden change. Herbert became a god, Julius sank to the level of a hero. For Herbert was engaged to be married; and being married had always seemed to me an even finer thing, a thing even more essential to the full glory of the adult state, than having a moustache. My father and mother, my sisters and I, were all of us equally enthusiastic about Miss Maud Holt. She and Herbert used to come and lunch in Clanricarde Gardens every Sunday, and these Sundays were great days. Miss Holt was so charming and amusing. Also, she used to play and sing to us; and I can see Herbert now, hanging over the piano, rapt, in devotion. A goddess, decidedly.

But the greatest Sunday of all was yet to come. In September Miss Holt came to stay with us in Kent, in the house where we were spending the summer holidays. Herbert was in London, acting. He was due to arrive only on the bridal Sunday. Of the preparations for that day, I recall especially the two triumphal arches of flowers and branches, one at the gate of the garden, the other at the gate of the little church hard by. These were conceived and erected by the gardener and his brother; and I remember the surprise I felt when the gardener's brother said to me: 'They're not what you might call awful grand, but they're what you might call rustic.' To me they appeared awful grand. Under the garden-gate's arch, on the Sunday morning, I posted myself a full hour before Herbert was expected to arrive. I was to be his 'best man,' and so delicious was the foretaste of that duty that it could not be too long for me. When at last he appeared, I was glad to see that his hat was of almost Julian splendour; but he looked so pale and excited that I gasped out instinctively: 'Have you lost the ring?' I felt, god though he was, that it would be rather like him to have lost the ring. However, all was well. The wedding was conducted as smoothly as the most exacting 'best man' could wish. And at the wedding-breakfast there were sillabubs, my favourite dish. I remember Herbert saying that they sounded Biblical—'And Sillabub, the son of Sillabub, reigned in his stead,' a remark which shocked but amused me.

The reason for my being best man was that Julius was away in Spain. A few weeks later, we heard that Julius, too, had married. It seemed to me, when presently I saw her, that his bride was as delightful and wonderful as Herbert's. Julius rose from his brief abeyance among heroes. Julius was once more a god.

In the years that followed, as I grew in understanding, and was somewhat able to understand what a play was about, I acquired a greater respect than I had had for the art of acting. And particularly did I admire and applaud Herbert's exploits in that art. Such a preference was natural? I think it was not due wholly to my affection. I was just old enough to appreciate something of that elastic subtlety, that unflagging imagination, which Herbert brought to the task of his every embodiment. I could see the enormous difference between him and the ordinary 'sound' actor, and why it was that his fame was so great now, and always becoming greater. No boy now ever asked me if I had a brother who was an actor. It was known that I was a brother of Beerbohm Tree, and the knowledge was fraught with awe—awe that perceptibly deepened when, in the year of the first Jubilee, Herbert became a Manager.

Ripened judgment has not inclined me to think *The Red Lamp* the greatest play ever written. But I thought it so on its first night—the first night of Herbert's management. And I saw it seventeen times, without changing my opinion. Herbert always let me sit in his dressing-room during the entr'actes, and there I met many of the most interesting men of the period —none of whom, however, interested me so much as Herbert. *Partners* and *The Pompadour* pleased me almost as much as *The Red Lamp*, and so did the plays that came after; and it seems to me, as I look back, that even during term-time, when my body was at Charterhouse, my soul was in the Haymarket Theatre.

I think the magic of the Haymarket lost something of its power for me when I left school. Oxford was so wondrous in itself. My soul was undoubtedly there during term-time. But in the vacations I was constantly at the theatre, and I stayed often, with an unfailing sense of romance, at the house that Herbert now had in Hampstead. A very lovely old house it was, with low-ceiled rooms and plenty of chintz; and with plenty of garden; and with Bully Boy, the celebrated bulldog of *The Dancing Girl*, ugliest and most beauteous of beasts; and with Viola, not the least charming of children. And supper was so very late up there, after the theatre down yonder; and breakfast so very late, too, and dinner so very early. Early though dinner was, there was never a day when I didn't feel sure that Herbert would be late for the theatre. It had always been an odd thing about him that his restless energy seemed to be coupled with a perfect vagueness as to time and place and distance. He did, it is true, carry a watch, and often looked at it; but one never could believe he had drawn any deduction from it. And yet he was never late for anything that mattered. His punctuality was a great mystery. It would seem that he had some kind of queer instinct that saved him the trouble of taking thought.

And it would seem that he had this in regard to other things than time. I never saw him read a newspaper; yet he appeared always to know just what was going on all the world round. He had read fewer books than any man I have ever known; yet I have known few men of letters who had a keener discernment of good writing, or a keener delight in it. He had no standards of comparison to guide him. He had merely an innate sense of literary form.

He was, also, an acute judge of human character. Almost everybody prides himself on being that. Herbert had the rather rare distinction of being it. I think that the correctness of his judgment of the people he met may have been due partly to the unperceiving manner he had—that 'radiant' but abstracted and roving regard of his. It was apt to put people off their guard. Nor was this the only way in which Herbert's famous 'vagueness' was useful to him. Especially after he became a manager, and was accordingly beset by all manner of people with axes to grind, it was immensely useful to him in saving him from committing himself. It was an escape from the necessity of using the dangerous word *yes* or the unpleasant word *no*. And when his vagueness became a by-word and a legend, he humorously cultivated it for its own sake— cultivated it partly, too, perhaps, because it seemed to fit in so well with the unworldliness on which he prided himself.

Unworldly he was, in so far as he had, like all artists, an imaginary world of his own. And he was unworldly also in the sense that he cared little or not at all for money. He was, however, amongst other things, a very capable man of the world.

Of his shrewdness wrapped in vagueness I can give an example that befell me one day while I was staying with him in Hampstead. He asked meditatively what I intended to *be*. I reminded him that I was going to the Bar. 'Ah . . . The Bar. . . . You at the Bar . . . I should have thought you'd better be a—a sort of writer, and then, perhaps,' he added, 'drift into Diplomacy.' This was merely his way of saying what the average man would have said thus: 'You haven't a single one of the qualities that make for success at the Bar. But I fancy you might do well in journalism.' Or more likely the average man would but have advised me to cultivate the acquaintance of solicitors, and would *not* (as I hadn't ever attempted to write anything) have guessed that I had a bent for writing. The delightful touch about 'drifting' into the Diplomatic Service was added merely to please himself and me.

He liked the company of very young men. For them his manner was apt to shed much of its indirectness. With them, being himself so young at heart, he was always, I think, more at his ease than he was with men not very young. He liked their ingenuousness and their pomposity. He revelled in drawing them out. Whenever I took this or that fellow under-graduate to a play at the Haymarket, Herbert always invited us both to sup at the Garrick. We used to wonder at his power of sitting up into the small hours, and the not so small, without a trace of fatigue. We didn't know how much we amused him.

Until I was twenty-two I had never seen Herbert for more than a few hours or days at a time. During the first three months of 1895 I saw him continuously. For he took me with him on his first tour to America. My sister-in-law has said, in speaking of the voyage out, that Mr. Lionel Brough and I went below after the first day and were not seen again. This is an unintentional injustice to the memory of Lionel Brough. I only wish he had not been so perfectly, so exuberantly good a sailor as he was. He and I shared a cabin. The sea was very stormy indeed. For three days and nights I remained in my berth. I preferred the nights to the days, for then Brough was sound asleep in the berth beneath me, and even the sight of Brough's saucy little yachting-cap, swaying to and fro on its peg whenever I opened my eyes to the dim lamp-light, was preferable to the knowledge that Brough himself might at any moment come breezily in at the door with that same cap surmounting his fresh pink face and his crisp silver hair. He was the kindest of men, and was always coming down from the smoking-room, laden with the scent of that meeting-place, to cheer me up for a few minutes. He was the bluffest of York-shiremen, and the best of professional *raconteurs*, and he was always asking me : 'Have yer heard the one about the parson's bull finch ?' or 'Have yer heard the one about the coal-heaver's ticket to Blackpool ?' or 'Have yer heard the one about the old lady who didn't like shrimps ?' Also, he wore in his scarf a large and unusual pin which I think he thought might act as a talisman for me against sea-sickness. He had recently appeared in some 'command' performance at Windsor, and 'This,' he would tell me, 'is the pin Her Gracious Majesty gave me'; but somehow it always made me feel worse.

On the last three days I was well enough to be on deck, nevertheless, and to share something of Herbert's delight in the look of the Atlantic, and something of his immense excitement as to what America would be like, and something of the incidental pleasure he took in the intentness with which crew and passengers gazed on the actor-pilgrim. I remember that on the day before landing he went to have his hair cut by the ship's barber, and how amused and pleased he was that the man said : 'This is a bit of a responsibility for *me*, sir!' To the last day of his life, he never was habituated to fame. The stares of passers-by, eulogistic letters from strangers, invitations to preside over meetings and things, snapshots in the illustrated press—it was a sign of his abiding youngness that such things, though they befell him so abundantly, never lost for him the savour of freshness. They seemed always to take him by surprise and make him the more 'radiant'. And it was characteristic of his complexity that he was greatly amused at his own naïveté. He once handed me a letter from a stranger who had seen him act on the previous night. 'That's very nice,' I said after reading it. 'Very,' said he. 'I can stand any amount of flattery so long as it's fulsome enough.'

To the magic of New York, on our arrival, he was instantly responsive. He was not the sort of tourist who takes a home-made tuning-fork about with him and condemns the discords. He regarded himself not as a responsible judge, but as a quite irresponsible flitter-through. He liked the over-heated rooms and the over-iced streets, liked not only the slow, low voices of the New York men, but also the piercing voices of the New York ladies, and also the fabulous expensiveness of cabs, and the manners of street-car conductors, and being expected to make a speech after the play's last act but one. Nor was Chicago too grim for him, nor Boston too prim. Almost every member of his company had brought over a tuning-fork. There was a great deal of grumbling and growling, especially during railway journeys. Herbert was a shining example of adaptability, and I had never admired him more. What an appalling amount of work and play he had to go through! Yet from early morning to late night, or rather to early morning again, he was never out of temper. In some of his work it was my mission to help him. I had been given the post of private secretary (with salary). But my mission was rather a failure. The letters that I wrote in his stead were so carefully thought out and worded that many of the letters sent to him could get no answers at all. After two or three weeks (Herbert insisting, however, on my retention of full salary) one of the regular managerial staff, a less scrupulous writer, took over the main part of my duties.

People often said of Herbert that he lived nineteen to the dozen. Twenty-nine is the number I would use in speaking of his life in America. And that number was too high for even him to touch with impunity. At the end of the three months, after the series of farewell performances, farewell speeches, farewell banquets and what-not, Herbert did, soon after the boat weighed anchor, say he thought he would go to bed rather early to-night; and for two or three days, as my sister-in-law has related, he *stayed* in bed—he! After which he arose, and was the life and soul of the liner. The concert to be given on the last evening of the voyage was organized by him as eagerly as though his whole future career depended on its success. But from this task, as from all his tasks, he derived plenty of light amusement by the way. I shall never forget the conversation between him and a very earnest, a very 'ahr-nesst,' actor who had volunteered to recite Mark Antony's funeral speech. On the afternoon of the day before the concert this actor invited Herbert, and Herbert invited me, to a rehearsal of the speech, down in the dining-saloon where the concert was to be held. He posted himself at the end of the saloon, in front of the organ-screen, folded his arms, and for a while regarded Herbert and me, very sombre and beetle-browed. 'Friends,' he suddenly began in a voice of thunder. It would have been fatal for me to catch Herbert's eye. 'Romans,' he resumed. 'Countrymen'—'One instant, Mr.—!' cried Herbert's voice.— 'Well, Mr. Tree?'—'An idea has just struck me. Didn't Antony address the crowd from *above*?'—'From the rostrum, Mr. Tree.'—'Rostrum, yes—rostrum. My idea is this: How would it be if'—Herbert pointed to the organist's gallery— 'you spoke your speech from that little place up there?' Mr.—

looked up, considered, nodded his head gravely, and was about to disappear up the winding staircase. 'One instant, Mr. —! Another idea! What did Antony *wear*?'—'A toga, Mr. Tree.' —'Toga, yes—toga.' Herbert had already snatched a table-cloth off one of the tables; and I know not which face was the more solemn—the face of that actor while Herbert draped him, or Herbert's face. For some reason or another, Mr. — decided that on 'the night,' as he called it, he would not wear costume. But he did actually, when the time came, deliver his speech from the organ-loft, with terrific effect. There was, however, a rather awkward moment when he reappeared at the foot of the winding staircase. Major-General Sir Some-body Something, who was acting as chairman and sitting in the middle of the front row, sprang up and went to shake him warmly by the hand. The Major-General was warded off with a fierce gesture. The end was not yet. Antony had but, as in the play, come down among us to read Cæsar's will. 'If you have tee-arrs, prepare to shed them now,' and so forth.

Such expressions as 'the night,' just quoted by me, never were used by Herbert. He disliked slang. And especially did he dislike theatrical slang. To him the theatre was always a thing romantic and marvellous. 'Knowingness' about it jarred his sensibility. But he did, as it were, study theatrical slang, feeling a horrid fascination in the subject. 'Do you know,' he once asked me, 'what they call the curtain? They call it "the rag".' And he began to improvise various phrases around this expression; one of which was: 'My boy, the rag came down on mud,' meaning 'The play failed on the first night.'

Herbert, when he was in the vein, was a fine improviser. His wit was a thing carefully thought out, and if he were going to say something witty he would keep you waiting a moment or so. But his humour was all spontaneous, and came, unlike that of many humorists, not in spurts, but in a stream. I have said that he was self-conscious, though 'radiant,' in general company; and so he was. But his self-consciousness quickly melted away when he was alone with friends at a dinner-table or supper-table. He was, for all his shyness, an essentially sociable man, not merely in the sense that he liked to be often with many people, but in the further and rarer sense that he liked to be with anybody rather than be alone. If he were alone in a hansom or a taxi, and saw on the pavement *any* man he knew, he would stop the vehicle and offer that man a lift. Whenever he came to our house, he would always, as I saw him off, say that he was going to such-and-such a place and ask me to go there with him. I do not, in telling this, mean that I was no fitter company than *any* man. But I am afraid that as the years went by, and the gap between our ages was accordingly contracted, each of us found himself even more shy in presence of the other than he was wont to be with people at large. An old friend of Herbert's once said to him and me, in the course of a dinner in the 'Dome' of His Majesty's: 'You two, when you're together, always seem to be in an attitude of armed neutrality.' I suggested to Herbert that 'terrified love' would be a truer description.

It was a great thing to me, the love that I knew in my heart he had for me in his. I do believe he took as much pride in my little career as I took in his big one. 'Big' is a word that attaches itself in my mind to so much concerning Herbert. His body was big, and his nature big, and he did so love big things! Mountains, cathedrals, frescoes, Shakespeare, summer skies, Wagnerian opera—his spacious temperament welcomed everything of that sort. Things on a small scale, however exquisite, did not satisfy him. I doubt whether even His Majesty's Theatre was quite big enough according to his standard.

A curious and little-known fact about that theatre is that by reason of me it had a narrow escape from never existing at all.

When Herbert was in Philadelphia, Paul Potter's dramatic version of Du Maurier's *Trilby* was being acted at one of the theatres there. The book had had a tremendous 'boom' in America. The play was a great success. I went one evening as emissary of Herbert, to see it and report on it. My report across the supper-table was a very brief one, to the effect that the play in itself was utter nonsense and could only be a dismal failure in London. Thus I, in my wisdom; whereby impressed, Herbert put *Trilby* from his mind. Six weeks later, in New York, two nights before we embarked for England, he gave his final performance at Abbey's Theatre, and on the next night accordingly was free to visit one of the other theatres. He thought he might as well go and see *Trilby* . . . and it was on the proceeds of his production of *Trilby* in England that His Majesty's presently began to rise.

For twenty years after its completion it was a source of immense happiness to him; it enabled him to realize his dreams; it fulfilled him. He achieved there things that he could not have attempted elsewhere; and these were the things nearest his heart and most agreeable to his ambition. I shall always be thankful for His Majesty's. For my own pleasure in play-going, let me admit, I prefer small theatres. And for my own delight in the genius of Herbert as actor I liked His Majesty's less than the Haymarket. Robust though he was in mind and body, it was not in sweeping effects that his acting was pre-eminent. The full strength of his art was in its amazing delicacy. His humour and imagination, and his beautiful power for pathos, found their best expression in ways that were subtlest. Subtleties have a hard time on a large stage, in front of a large auditorium. Herbert had to adapt his method to his surroundings. He did this with great skill and success; but I often wished he had not to do it at all. Apart from his acting—and his acting was but one of the many parts of him— I am entirely glad for him that he had His Majesty's.

I think that in the last years of his life he grew to care less for acting. His versatility had ranged over so vast a number of diverse interpretations. What new thing was there for him to do?—for him, to whom the notion of marking time was so utterly repugnant? Especially after the outbreak of the War did I notice in him an impatience of his work. The last time we met was at my mother's house, just after his return from America. He was looking, as usual, splendidly well, and was full of animation. But in all his talk there was not a word about acting.

I shall always miss him. He was a great feature in my life, and I am always wishing him back again. But I am grateful, for his sake, that he died in the fullness of health and vigour. I am glad that but two moments before his death he was talking and laughing, paring a peach for his dessert. When I saw him early next morning, he lay surrounded already with the flowers he had been fondest of. His face was both familiar and strange. Death, that preserves only what is essential, had taken away whatever it is that is peculiar to the face of an actor. Extreme strength of character and purpose was all that remained and outstood now. But at the corners of the lips there was the hint of an almost whimsical, an entirely happy smile. And I felt that Herbert, though he was no longer breathing, was somehow still 'radiant.'

A Note on the Einstein Theory

It is said that there are, besides Dr. Einstein himself, only two men who can claim to have grasped the Theory in full. I cannot claim to be either of these. But I do know a good thing when I see it; and here is a thing that is excellent in its kind—romantically excellent in a kind that is itself high. When I think of rays being deflected by gravity, and of parallel lines at long last converging so that there isn't perhaps, after all, any such thing as Infinity, I draw a very deep breath indeed. The attempt to conceive Infinity had always been quite arduous enough for me. But to imagine the absence of it; to feel that perhaps we and all the stars beyond our ken are somehow cosily (though awfully) closed in by curtain curves beyond which is nothing; and to convince myself, by the way, that this exterior is not (in virtue of *being* nothing) something, and therefore . . . but I lose the thread.

Enough that I never lose the thrill. It excites, it charms me to think of elderly great mathematicians of this and that nation packing their portmanteaus whenever there is to be a solar eclipse, and travelling over land and sea to the Lick Observatory, or to some hardly accessible mountain-top in Kamchatka, and there testing, to the best of their power, the soundness, or unsoundness of the tremendous Theory. So far, the weather has not been very favourable to these undertakings. Nature, who is proud and secretive, has opposed many clouds to the batteries of telescopes. But she has had only a partial success, it seems. Some observations have been more or less clearly made, some conclusions more or less clearly drawn. And these more or less clearly point to the likelihood that what Dr. Einstein in his humdrum home evolved from his inner consciousness is all delightfully correct.

But is the British public delighted? It gives no sign of being so. Its newspapers did at the first news of Einstein's existence try, very honourably, to excite it about Einstein and even about his work. It would *not* be excited. Strange! The tamest batting of Hertfordshire *v.* Australia, the feeblest goal-keeping of Wormwood Scrubbs *v.* Hornsey Rise, the lightest word that falls from the lips of the least accomplished negro boxer, are better 'copy' than any challenge to our notion of the Cosmos. This is all the stranger because the public is not careless of other things than Sport. Its passionate interest in archæology, for instance, rose to boiling-point, only the other day: it could *not* hear too much about the tomb of Tutankhamen, nor tire of debating whether or not the bones of that king might rightly be disturbed. Why never a word as to the disturbance of our belief that parallel lines can nowhere converge? I haven't grudged Tutankhamen the renewal and immense enlargement of the fame he once had. I have but deplored the huge cold shoulder turned on the living Einstein.

Newton, no greater an innovator than he, is popular enough. Everybody knows something about Gravitation—and all about the apple. Perhaps if Newton had not mentioned that apple, he too would be generally ignored. It is a great advantage for a discoverer to have been inspired by some homely little incident. Newton and the apple, Copernicus and the whipping-top, James Watt and the kettle. But Einstein and——? Poor Einstein!

Men of his magnitude are not avid of popularity? True; but this does not mean that popularity would be disagreeable to them. When the newspapers were trying to make Relativity a household word, I read an account of Einstein, written by one who knew him, and enhanced by a photograph of him. A very human person, I gathered; far from stand-offish; a player of the fiddle; the constant smoker of a large pipe; a genial, though thoughtful, critic of current things. I liked his views on education. Why all this forcing of a child's memory? Memory —a matter of little moment. Let the child be taught to see, and to think, for itself. And let every child be taught a trade. And 'after all,' said Einstein, dismissing tuition, 'the best thing in the world is a happy face.' It was clear from the photograph that his own face was a happy one. But I discerned in it a certain wistfulness, too—the wistfulness of a thorough good fellow whose work somehow repels the attention of that good fellow, the average man. My heart went out to him. I wished I could help him. And now, I think, I can. Hark!

Yesterday afternoon I was walking on the coast-road from Rapallo to Zoagli when I saw approaching in the distance a man of strenuous gait, and of aspect neither Italian nor English. His brow was bare to the breeze; and as he drew near I perceived the brow to be a fine one; and as he drew nearer still I perceived the face to be a very happy one—with just a hint in it of wistfulness, which, however, vanished at my words, 'Dr. Einstein, I presume?' He clapped a cordial hand on my shoulder; he treated me as an old friend, as a brother, and insisted that we should sit together on the low wall that divides the road from the cliff. Presently—after he had praised the sun and the sea, and had expressed an ardent sympathy with Fascismo, and with Socialismo, no less—I said to him, 'Master (if one who is not a disciple may so address you), tell me: What was it that first put you on the track of the tremendous Theory?' He knitted his fine brow, saying that his memory was not a very good one; but after a while he remembered, and spoke to me as follows:

'One winter's evening, after a hard day's work, I was sitting by my fireside—for I have an open fire in the English fashion, not a stove: I like to sit watching the happy faces in the coals—

when my eye lighted on the tongs in the fender. Of course it had often lighted on them before; but this time it carried to my brain a message which my brain could not understand. "Here," I mused, "are two perfectly parallel lines. And yet, and yet, they meet at the extreme ends. How is that?" My friend Professor Schultz had promised to drop in and smoke a pipe with me that evening, and when he came I drew his attention to the phenomenon. He knelt down by the fender, pushed his spectacles up on to his forehead, gazed closely, and muttered, "Gott im Himmel—ja!" I asked him—for he is a very ready man—if he had any explanation to offer. He rose from his knees and sat down on a chair heavily, burying his head in his hands. Suddenly he sprang to his feet. "Einstein," he said, "I believe I have it! I believe that the ironworker who made those bars must have heated them red-hot and then bent the ends towards each other." Dear old Schulz! Always so ready!—so shallow! I suppose I ought not to have laughed; but I did; and Schultz went out in some anger. It was dawn when I rose from the fireside. The fire had long ago burnt itself out, and I was stiff with cold. But my mind was all aglow with the basic principles of Relativismus.'

'The world,' I said quietly, 'shall hear of this, Dr. Einstein.'

London Revisited

One of the greatest of Englishmen said that the man who is tired of London is tired of life.

Well, Dr. Johnson had a way of being right. But he had a way of being wrong too—otherwise we shouldn't love him so much. And I think that a man who is tired of London may merely be tired of life *in London*. He won't, certainly, feel any such fatigue if he was born and bred in a distant county, and came to London and beheld London only when he had reached maturity. Almost all the impassioned lovers of London have spent, like Dr. Johnson, their childhood and adolescence in the country. Such was not my own fate. I was born within sound of Bow Bells. I am, in fact, a genuine Cockney (as you will already have guessed from my accent). Before I was able to speak or think my eyes must have been familiar with endless vistas of streets; countless people passing by without a glance at the dear little fellow in the perambulator; any number of cart-horses drawing carts, cab-horses drawing cabs, carriage-horses drawing carriages, through the more or less smoke-laden atmosphere. I was smoke-dried before I could reason and prattle. For me there was never the great apocalyptic moment of initiation into the fabulous metropolis. I never said, 'So this—is London!'

Years passed: I became a small boy. And I daresay I used to exclaim, 'So these are Kensington Gardens!' I liked the grass and the trees. But there were the railings that bounded them, and the pavements and thoroughfares beyond the railings. These had no magic for me. It was the country—

the *real* country—the not imitation country—that I loved.

I became a young man. London was the obvious place for me to earn a living in. In my native city I abode until the year 1910, at which time I was thirty-seven years old. Then I escaped. I had known some parts of the vast affair pretty well. I wish I had appreciated their beauty more vividly while it lasted: a beauty that is gone—or all but gone. I am going to be depressing. Perhaps you had better switch me off.

London is a Cathedral town. And in my day—in the 'eighties of my boyhood and the 'nineties of my youth—London, with all her faults, seemed not wholly unlike a Cathedral town, I do assure you. There was a demure poetry about her: one could think of her as 'her': nowadays she cannot be called 'she': she is essentially 'it'. Down by the docks, along the Mile End Road, throughout the arid reaches of South Kensington, and so on, I daresay she was 'it' already; full of later-nineteenth-century utilitarianism and efficiency, throwing out harsh hints of what the twentieth century had up its horrid sleeve. But in such districts as I liked and, whenever I could, frequented, she kept the eighteenth century about her. Hampstead, upon its hill, was a little old remote village; and so was Chelsea, down yonder by the river. Mayfair and Westminster and St. James's were grand, of course, very urban, in a proudly unostentatious way. There were Victorian intrusions here and there in their architecture. But the eighteenth century still beautifully reigned over them. They were places of leisure—of *leesure*, one might almost have said in the old-fashioned way. And, very urban though they were, they were not incongruous with rusticity. St. James's Park seemed a natural appanage to St. James's Street; and the two milkmaids who milked two cows there, and sold the milk, did not seem strangely romantic. The Green Park seemed not out of keeping with the houses of Piccadilly. Nor did the Piccadilly goat strike one as more than a little odd in Piccadilly.

I don't know much about him, though I so often saw him and liked him so much. He lived in a large mews in a side-street, opposite to Gloucester House, the home of the venerable Duke of Cambridge. At about ten o'clock in the morning he would come treading forth with a delicately clumsy gait down the side-street—come very slowly, as though not quite sure there mightn't be some grass for him to nibble at between the paving-stones. Then he would pause at the corner of Piccadilly and flop down against the railings of the nearest house. He would remain there till luncheon-time and return in the early afternoon. He was a large, handsome creature, with great intelligence in his amber eyes. He never slept. He was always interested in the passing scene. I think nothing escaped him. I wish he could have written his memoirs when he finally retired. He had seen, day by day, much that was worth seeing.

He had seen a constant procession of the best-built vehicles in the world, drawn by very beautifully-bred and beautifully-groomed and beautifully-harnessed horses, and containing very ornate people. Vehicles of the most diverse kinds. High-swung barouches, with immense armorial bearings on their panels, driven by fat, white-wigged coachmen, and having powdered footmen up behind them; signorial phætons; daring tandems; discreet little broughams, brown or yellow; flippant high dog-carts; low but flippant Ralli-carts; very frivolous private hansoms shaming the more serious public ones. And all these vehicles went by with a cheerful briskness; there was hardly ever a block for them in the traffic. And their occupants were very visible and were looking their best. The occupants of those low-roofed machines which are so pitifully blocked nowadays all along Piccadilly may, for aught one knows, be looking their best. But they aren't on view. The student of humanity must be content to observe the pedestrians.

These, I fear, would pain my old friend the goat. He was accustomed to what was called the man-about-town—a now extinct species, a lost relic of the eighteenth century and of the days before the great Reform Bill of 1831; a leisurely personage, attired with great elaboration, on his way to one of his many clubs; not necessarily interesting in himself; but fraught with external character and point: very satisfactory to those for whom the visible world exists. From a sociological standpoint perhaps he was all wrong, and perhaps his successor—the earnest fellow in a 'trilby' and a 'burberry' and a pair of horn-rimmed spectacles, hurrying along to his job—or in quest of some job—is all right. But one does rather wish the successor looked as if he felt himself to be all right. Let him look serious by all means. But need he look so nervous? He needs must. He doesn't want to be killed, he doesn't even want to be maimed, at the next crossing. He must keep his wits about him. I advise him to dash down with me into one of the Tubes. He will be safer there, as were the early Christians in the catacombs.

They are not beautiful, these Tubes; nor are they even interesting in character, except to engineers. But are the streets above them beautiful—or interesting in character—nowadays, to anybody of my own kind and age? London never had any formal or obvious beauty, such as you find in Paris; or any great, overwhelming grandeur, such as Rome has. But the districts for which I loved her, and several other districts too, had a queer beauty of their own, and were intensely characteristic—inalienably Londonish. To an intelligent foreigner, visiting London for the first time, what would you hasten to show? Except some remnants here and there, and some devious little nooks, there is nothing that would excite or impress him. The general effect of the buildings that have sprung up everywhere in recent years is not such an effect as the intelligent foreigner may not have seen in divers other places—Chicago, for example, or Berlin, or Pittsburg. London has been cosmopolitanized, democratized, commercialized, mechanized, standardized, vulgarized, so extensively that one's pride in showing it to a foreigner is changed to a wholesome humility. One feels rather as Virgil may have felt in showing Hell to Dante.

It is a bright, cheerful, salubrious Hell, certainly. But still— to *my* mind—Hell. In some ways a better place, I readily concede, than it was in my day, and in days before mine. Heinrich Heine was horrified by the poverty—the squalor and starvation—that abounded in the midst of the immense wealth and splendour. Some years later Gavarni's soul was shocked by it; and then Dostoievsky's; and presently Monsieur Ludovic Halévy's; and in due course Mr. Henry James's. I too am human. I am therefore glad that Seven Dials—and similar places which I used to skirt with romantic horror—are gone. Had I been acting as guide to those distinguished visitors, I should have tried to convince them that no such places existed, save in the creative alien fancy. But I ask myself: Suppose those illustrious visitors rose from their graves to-day and asked me to show them round the sights that would best please their æsthetic sensibilities in the London of this year of grace, what should I say, what do, in my patriotic embarrassment? I suppose I would, with vague waves of the hand, stammeringly redirect them to their graves.

I could not ask them to accompany me along Piccadilly or up Park Lane, to admire the vast excesses of contemporary architecture. I could not say to them, 'Never mind the rasure of certain unassuming houses that were called "great houses" in your day—and in mine. Cast up your eyes—up, up, up!— at the houses that have displaced them. Try to count the little uniform slits that serve as windows in the splendid ferro-concrete surface. Admire the austerity of the infinite *ensemble*. Think how inspiring to the historic imagination it will all be, a century or so hence!' I couldn't speak thus, for I cannot imagine any history being made in these appallingly bleak yet

garish tenements. Or, at any rate, I refuse to suppose that they
or any of the similar monstrosities that have been springing up
in all the more eligible districts could ever take on an historic
tone. They will continue to look like—what shall I say?—
what *do* they look like?—improper workhouses.

Odious though they are in themselves, one might not hate
them much if one found them on some barren plain in (say)
the middle-west of America—some plain as barren and as
meaningless as they. But when one thinks of the significant
houses, the old habitable homes, that were demolished to make
way for them, and when one sees how what remains of decent
human architecture is reduced by them to the scale of hardly
noticeable hovels, then one's heart sickens, and one's tongue
curses the age into which one has survived. A few years ago,
in the Print Room of the British Museum, Mr. Laurence
Binyon showed me a very ancient little water-colour drawing.
The foreground of it was a rather steep grassy slope. At the
foot of the slope stood a single building, which I at once
recognized as St. James's Palace. Beyond the Palace were
stretches of green meadows; and far away there was just one
building—the Abbey of Westminster. And I thought how
pained the artist would have been if he had foreseen the coming
of St. James's Street. I felt sure that he, like myself, preferred
the country to any town. Yet I could not find it in my heart
to deplore the making of that steep little street, destined to be
so full of character and history. I could only regret that my
favourite street was being steadily degraded, year after year,
by the constructive vandals. There are no actual skyscrapers
in it, as yet. But already the Palace cuts a poor figure. And the
lovely façade of Boodle's is sadly squat. And a certain little old
but ever young shop that stands somewhere between those two
is hardly visible to the naked eye. I would affectionately name
it, were I not so anxious to obey the B.B.C.'s admirable ban on
that greatest of all modern pests, the advertiser.

Regent Street, Nash's masterpiece, which is mourned so bitterly by so many people, was never very dear to my heart, even before the days when Norman Shaw's pseudo-Florentine fortress suddenly sprang up and ruined the scale of its quadrant and all the rest of it. Its tone was always rather vulgar. It was never anything but a happy hunting-ground for ardent shoppers. Nothing but shopping had ever happened in it. But it was a noble design. And when its wide road and pavements were empty in the dawn, and its level copings were pale against the smokeless sky, the great long strong curve of the smooth-faced houses had a beauty that I shall not forget. I conceive that the pretentious chaos now reigning in its stead must in the quiet magic of the dawn be especially nasty.

It was the Squares, that particular glory of London, that I loved best of all. Their green centres have not yet been built over, for some reason. I look with pleasure at their surviving grass and trees. But I try not to see from the corners of my eyes what has happened to their architecture. St. James's Square, the finest of them all, has been wrecked utterly. Berkeley Square, which was a good second, has suffered a like fate. So has Portman Square. Dear little Kensington Square has been saved, by the obstinacy of some enlightened tenants, from the clutches of Mammon. Bedford Square is intact, as yet. Let us be thankful, before it is too late, for much of Blooms-bury. The London University is about to play the deuce there. I suppose the Inns of Court, those four sanctuaries of civilization, are safe in the adroit hands of the lawyers. Parliament will not be able to betray *them,* as she has betrayed that other sanctuary, the Adelphi.

I revisit England and London at intervals of two or three years; and every time I find that the havoc that has been wrought in my absence is more than ever extensive. How do I contrive to bear it? Let me reveal that secret. As I go my rounds, I imagine that the present is the past. I imagine myself

a man of the twenty-first century, a person with an historic
sense, whose prayer that he should behold the London of a
hundred years ago has been granted. And my heart is thrilled
with rapture. Look! There's a horse drawing a cart! And
look! There's a quite small house—a lovely little thing that
looks as though it had been built by the hand of man, and as
though a man might quite pleasantly live in it. It has a chimney, with smoke coming out of it. And there's a coal-heaver.
And there's—it must be—it *is*—a muffin-man!

By such devices of make-believe do I somewhat console and
brace myself. But there is always a deadweight of sadness in
me. Selfish sadness: I ought to keep my pity for the young
people who never saw what I have seen, who will live to see
what I shall not see—future great vistas of more and more
commercialism, more machinery, more standardization, more
nullity.

I warned you that I was going to be depressing. I wish I
hadn't kept my word. I might well have broken it on an
evening so soon after Christmas, so soon before the New Year.
Forget this talk. Or at any rate discount it. Remember that
after all I'm an old fogey—and perhaps rather an old fool. And
let me assure you that I'm cheerful company enough whenever
I'm not in London and not thinking of London. And now I'm
just off to the country. I have arranged to be driven straight
from Broadcasting House to Paddington. I shall *just* catch the
train.—I wish you all a very happy New Year—somewhere in
the country.—I hope I haven't advertised Paddington.—Ladies
and Gentlemen, goodnight.

A Small Boy Seeing Giants

Ladies and Gentlemen, The title that has just been announced
to you is perhaps rather cryptic. And as I am not a young poet,
and have not that lovely modesty which forbids the young poet
to think that his meaning could matter twopence to anybody
on this earth, I hasten to explain that the Small Boy is myself—
or rather *was* myself, half a century ago; and that the Giants
were some more or less elderly Liberal or Conservative
gentlemen who governed England in those days. They were
my great hobby. I might almost say that they were my
passion. I hadn't the honour of knowing any of them personally. But I knew them all by sight. And it was always with
rapture that I saw them.

In my earlier years, soldiers had monopolized the romantic
side of me. Although, like all my coevals, I wore a sailor suit,
my heart was with the land forces; insomuch that I insisted on
wearing also, out of doors, a belt with a sword attached to it,
and on my breast a medal which, though it had merely the
Crystal Palace embossed on it, I associated with the march to
Kandahar. I used to watch with emotion the sentries changing
guard outside Kensington Palace; and it was my purpose to
be one of them hereafter. Meanwhile I made many feeble little
drawings of them, which I coloured strongly. But somehow,
mysteriously, when I was eight years old or so, the soldiery
was eclipsed for me by the constabulary. Somehow the scarlet
and the bearskins began to thrill me less than the austere
costume and calling of the Metropolitan Police. Once in every
two hours a policeman came, on his beat, past the house of my

parents. At the window of the dining-room I would await his coming, punctually behold him with profound interest, and watch him out of sight. It was not the daffodils that marked for me the coming of the season of Spring. It was the fact that policemen suddenly wore short tunics with steel buttons. It was not the fall of the leaf nor the swallows' flight that signalled Autumn to me. It was the fact that policemen were wearing long thick frock-coats with buttons of copper. But even more than in the day-time did policemen arrest me, as it were, in the watches of the night. The dark lantern was the truly great, the irresistible thing about them. More than once, from the window of my night-nursery, I had seen that lantern flashed at opposite front doors and through area-railings. My paintings of policemen were mostly nocturnes—a dim, helmeted figure with a long white ray of light. Although I possessed, of course, a dark lantern of my own, and used it much, I preferred my occasional glimpses of the genuine article, and looked forward impatiently to being a member of the Force. But the young are faithless. By the time I was eleven years old I despised the Force. I was interested only in politicians—in Statesmen, as they were called at that time.

I had already, for some years, been aware of them. I had seen them, two-dimensionally and on a small scale, every Wednesday, in the pages of *Punch*, and had in a remote and tepid way revered them. I had not thought of them as actual, live men. Rather, they were, as portrayed in the cartoons of the great John Tenniel, nobly mythical to me. Sometimes they wore togas; but more often they wore chitons and breast-plates, and were wielding or brandishing swords. Their shins were protected by greaves, and their calves were immensely muscular; and in the matter of biceps they were unsurpassable. They were Ajaxes and Hectors and Achilleses. Now and then they rose to greater heights, becoming Herculeses, Vulcans, Marses and the like. *Punch* was firmly Gladstonian in its politics; and therefore the Prime Minister was always more muscular than any of his enemies, redoubtable though they too were; and the attitudes that he struck were more striking than theirs. I didn't quite like this. For my father was a Conservative, and so, accordingly, was I. I wished—though I didn't care enough to pray—for the downfall of Gladstone. Some time in the year 1883 I read a speech delivered in the House of Commons by Lord Randolph Churchill. I felt that here was the man to compass the downfall; for he was so very rude. Even the best-behaved little boys rejoice in the rudeness of other people. Lord Randolph's rudeness in a good cause refreshed my young heart greatly; nor ever did his future speeches disappoint me. But, much though I delighted in him, I didn't quite think of him as an actual person. I thought of him as Phaëton. Tenniel—or was it Linley Sambourne?—had depicted him as Phaëton, standing ready on the ground while old Sir Stafford Northcote (the leader of the Opposition, here depicted as Phoebus Apollo) was driving the chariot of the sun. I resented the cartoonist's analogy. But the physical image abode with me.

It was the London Stereoscopic Company that first opened my eyes to the fact that Churchill and Gladstone, Northcote and Harcourt, Chamberlain, Hartington and all those others were actual, mortal, modern men. Not until I was nearly twelve did I inspect that great long double window on the eastern side of Regent Street, famous for its galaxy of photographs of eminent personages. The place of honour was accorded of course to members of the Royal Family. But precedence over Archbishops and Bishops, Generals, Admirals, Poets, Actors and Actresses, was taken by the Statesmen, as we no longer call them. Not even to Lord Tennyson and Sir Garnet Wolseley and Mr. Henry Irving and Miss Connie Gilchrist was accorded such prominence as to the least of these. For these were giants in those days. They were not perhaps

Gods, but they certainly were Titans, in the public eye. And here they all were in *my* eye, tailored and hosier'd as men. With luck, I might some day see one of them in the street. I studied the portraits keenly. I fixed the features in my mind. I stayed there long. And on my way home I saw a man who was unmistakably—Mr. Childers. To you, Ladies and Gentlemen, I suppose his name means nothing. But he was at that time Chancellor of the Exchequer. It was a great, a throbbing moment.

Of Mr. Childers I made several drawings—very unpromising little drawings—when I reached my home. And thereafter, in the course of my holidays from school, I drew many of his colleagues. When a Cabinet Council was to be held, the fact was usually announced by the morning papers of that day. And there at the hour appointed, there on the pavement of Downing Street, opposite to No. 10, would be I, awaiting breathlessly the advent of the Giants. The greatest and most awful of them all would of course be invisible. Mr. Gladstone was somewhere behind those brown brick walls. But the others would be vouchsafed to me, one of them coming perhaps from the direction of Parliament Street, another from the courtyard of the Government Offices behind me, another up the flight of steps from St. James's Park. They are dead, one and all of them. Most of them died very many years ago. While I stood staring at them, Mr. Asquith was unknown to them: he was just a barrister in fairly good practice. The present Father of the House of Commons, Mr. Lloyd George, was a young solicitor, roaming nightly with bare feet and dreamful eyes along the clouded ridges of the Welsh mountains and hailing the roseate dawn. Mr. Baldwin was at Harrow. A quite recent President of the Oxford Union, Mr. George Nathaniel Curzon, was travelling observantly in the waste spaces of Siam and of Korea. Mr. Edward Carson was just beginning to make a name for himself in the Irish police-courts. Mr. Austen Chamberlain was at Trinity College, Cambridge. Mr. Neville Chamberlain was at Rugby. Mr. Winston Churchill was a pugnacious and not very happy little boy at a preparatory school. Many, many years were to elapse before Mr. Duff Cooper and Mr. Anthony Eden, Mr. Harold Nicolson and Mr. A. P. Herbert, were summoned forth from among the infinite ranks of the unborn. I am what the writers of obituary notices call 'an interesting link with the past'.

I wish I could have foreseen the future. Had I done so—had I known how exactly, how furtively like one another our rulers would try to look—I should have revelled even more than I did revel at the sight of those men of 1884. Visually, they let themselves go, without self-consciousness or fear. Each one of them was a law unto himself. Some of them—Lord Kimberley for example, and Mr. Dodson—had beards without moustaches. Some of them were clean-shaven. One of them, Mr. Shaw-Lefevre, had always what looked like a four days' growth of beard. Lord Hartington's beard and moustache were far longer than Sir Charles Dilke's. Mr. Joseph Chamberlain was content with small side-whiskers. Sir William Harcourt had a 'Newgate frill'. So had Lord Northbrook, who wore, however and moreover, a becoming tuft on the chin. The wide, pale, pleasantly roguish face of old Lord Granville was framed in masses of silvery curls. Some wore their hair long, others short. Some of them dressed badly, others—in an off-hand way—well. To none of them except Chamberlain and Dilke, those two harbingers of another age, would one have applied the epithet *neat*. Believe me, they offered no end of latitude to the limner.

Spiritually, nevertheless, they bore strong likenesses to one another. Barring the two harbingers, and barring of course Mr. Gladstone, who was a creature apart, not to be fitted into any category whatsoever, they were authentic Whigs, one and all; eighteenth-century men, despite their date. Some of them were old enough to have dined, often, at Holland House. Not one of them, I feel sure, had failed to breakfast frequently with Mr. Samuel Rogers. The new Government Offices were still new to them, and I expect they admired those buildings greatly. They remembered the time when Downing Street had lodging houses in it, and a tavern or two, and a milliner's shop— things inconsonant with the affairs of a great nation. I daresay they regretted that Nos. 10 and 11 had not been demolished and rebuilt in the grandiose modern fashion. What charm would the Eighteenth Century have had for gentlemen who were a part of it? The love of by-gone things is a quite recent growth—due mainly to the fact that we have fallen on evil times. If we could all of us follow Mr. H. G. Wells's good example, dismiss the present from our minds, and fix our eyes steadfastly on the future, then we could share his wholesome contempt for the past. But we can't. We are morbid. I, perhaps, more so than most of us. Some weeks ago, as I was passing through St. James's Park, I looked up towards the street that I had so fondly haunted in my childhood—the street of the Giants. I ascended the steps to it and stood again before No. 10, gazing. 'This sweet corner' Horace Walpole had called it in a letter written by him therefrom to Sir Horace Mann. 'Sweet' is a trivial epithet, but one must remember that Horace's father, Sir Robert, had no preceding Giant in that corner: only a little of history had been made there as yet; the rest was to come. I gazed at the house of Pitt and Palmerston, Disraeli, Gladstone, and all those others; at the narrow front-door, with the unassuming fanlight above it; at the lantern in the traceries of the wrought-iron 'overthrow' beneath which so many Giants had stepped so long before I was born. And then my eye was attracted by a grey-blue placard in one of the two hall-windows. I crossed the road to read it . . .

A Small Boy Seeing Giants

Garden Party
Mrs. Stanley Baldwin
At Home
at No. 10, Downing Street
in aid of
The Safer Motherhood Appeal
Tuesday July 14
when the world's greatest
male ensemble of 35 performers
The Don Cossack Choir
with their famous conductor
Serge Jaroff
will make their one appearance in London this season
Tickets £2. 2. 0.

These words I read with surprise, but with entire sympathy. Here was an excellent cause to support, a very good use for the old garden to be put to. Had I been rich enough, I would have bought a ticket. But I rather wondered what Horace Walpole would have had to say in the matter. Something supercilious, something flippant, I am afraid. He was rather inhuman.

I wished I could see again those old Gladstonian figures—and the Salisburyans who succeeded to them in '85: the distinguished and formidable figure of Sir Michael Hicks-Beach; the distinguished and venerable figure of Lord John Manners, that last survivor of the Young England movement, whom Miss Charlotte Brontë, when as a young man he visited Haworth parsonage, had thought so handsome; above all, the distinguished and attractive figure of Lord Randolph, my chosen hero. He seemed, in some ways, always rather out of the picture. He seemed young for Downing Street, and had the air of a man of fashion rather than of affairs. He alone wore a moustache without beard or whiskers—an arrangement suggestive of levity. His was the only top hat that was ironed,

329

and it was ironed to the utmost lustre. He alone smoked cigarettes, and he smoked them through a very long amber mouthpiece. He, and only he, sometimes wore a buttonhole. Sometimes he looked as happy and insouciant as Mr. Gladstone's young disciple, Lord Rosebery; at other times, and oftener, he looked as tragically sad as did Lord Rosebery in later years. Very different though the two men were in character, they had points in common. The gods had bestowed on both of them shining gifts of mind and of speech, and had foredoomed them both to fail irretrievably.

There is much to be said for failure. It is more interesting than success. Rosebery and Randolph Churchill are, among the office-holders of their generation, the only two that still hold our attention and stir our curiosity. Lord Salisbury, their elder contemporary, is a noble, a monumental figure which does not detain us. It may be that if the veteran Mr. Gladstone had carried Home Rule he would be rather less detentive than he now is. For some time after his death we tended to depreciate him. Three or four years ago I was amused by a conversation between two political ladies of fashion, one an Asquithian Liberal, the other a Tory. The Liberal one, after having spoken of Mr. Gladstone with enthusiasm, said, 'But of course people only talk of Dizzy now. Gladstone's forgotten.' The Tory one said, 'Oh—I thought he was rather comin' in again, dear?' She was right. Mr. Gladstone is once more with us. Here he is, the mystical realist. Dizzy, the sceptical idealist, is rather further away. Dizzy is, of course—Dizzy always was—irresistible. His novels, his phrases, some of his speeches even, can still delight us deeply. His imagination and his wit are glorious, as was his patience. But he lacks something. In the last year of his life, speaking to one of the members of the Fourth Party, he said, 'I fully appreciate your feelings, but you must stick to Northcote. He represents the respectability of the Party. I wholly sympathize with you all, because *I* was never respectable.' Nor has he become so. We can revel in him; but we cannot respect him. There is something unreal, something absurd about him. In this unrestful and threatened age of the world's history we are moved to hanker after the moral force and fervour, and the endless vitality of Gladstone. We want a Gladstone *de nos jours*.

I saw him only three times. Once from the Strangers' Gallery in the House of Commons, early in 1885; and then and there, for the first and last time, I also heard him. He was merely answering a question about procedure, but he spoke for not less than a couple of minutes, in low tones, leaning far forward, with hands outspread upon the table, and ever turning from side to side and around, envisaging the whole assembly. Though I regarded him as a great power for evil, he fascinated, he won me. The second time was year or so later. I was one of the crowd that assembled in Parliament Square when he was about to introduce the first Home Rule Bill. There were boos among the cheers as he drove past, beside his wife, in an open landau, gravely bowing, his great dark eyes very wide open in his ivory-white old face. I was not among the booers. I cheered—in spite of myself—wildly. The third time, I was an undergraduate, standing on the steps outside the Sheldonian Theatre, in which building Mr. Gladstone, after long absence from Oxford, was to lecture on the Homeric poems. The Vice-Chancellor's brougham punctually arrived, and out of it stepped the Vice-Chancellor and, in his D.C.L. robes, Mr. Gladstone, bareheaded, amidst a tumultuous welcome. He ascended the steps, dark-eyed, white-faced, smiling; very old, but stalwart; he turned, stood, bowed slowly, deeply, from side to side, to the crowd below. He had bowed to many crowds, in his day, but never to one that loved him more than this one. I associate him always with Oxford.

And it was with Oxford—more, even, than with Scotland, I think—that he especially associated himself. When he lay dying, the Hebdomadal Council sent to him a message of regard and affection. 'To this,' says his biographer, John Morley, 'he listened most attentively and over it brooded long, then he dictated to his youngest daughter sentence by sentence his reply: "There is no expression of Christian sympathy that I could value more than that of the ancient University of Oxford, the God-fearing and God-sustaining University of Oxford. I served her, perhaps mistakenly, but to the best of my ability. My most earnest prayers are with her to the uttermost and to the last." '

These are grand words. With them let me close my discourse. I said at the outset that I was an interesting link with the past. Perhaps that was begging the question. I claim merely that I am a link with the past. If I have bored you, forgive me. And be of good cheer. This is the last time that I shall have the honour of addressing you, for the present. I am going to Italy, to my home, and shall not soon be here again. And so I wish you not only Goodnight, but also Goodbye.

The Top Hat

'What is that?' the very young will ask; and their parents, ever quick to correct, will say to them, 'You mean, What *was* it?' For it is, of course, very definitely, a thing of the past; almost a museum piece. Indeed, some parents, those who are less than middle-aged, may not even have heard of it. I plead guilty to finding in the past a charm which the present lacks for me. I hasten to say, however, that this charm is slight in comparison with that which the future would have for me if I were youngish, for (I gather from many publicists) the future, the post-bellum period, is to be perfectly splendid: new men, new ideas, new policies, new cosmic outlooks, new hills and valleys, new Old Masters, new fathers and mothers, new wines, new Old Moore's Almanacs, new everything. But I, alas, shan't live to see much, or perhaps anything, of all that. And I fondly strain my time-dimmed eyes towards that backward horizon whereon stands the top hat, a black but shining old monument.

Just *how* old, I can't say. I do but know that it had been erected already in the later days of Charles James Fox. He wears a top hat in that fine portrait of him sitting in his garden, immensely corpulent, but still full of energy and animation, of benignity and genius. He wears it pushed cheerfully back from his brow, and it looks rather odd in relation to his knee-breeches: a queer blend of the new and the old century. It is a beaver hat, of course. The silken kind was a Victorian discovery. But I think that had I been in that garden when that portrait was in the making I should have been shocked that the sitter was not wearing a gold-laced tricorn; for even in those days I should not have been a great approver of current things. Fox himself, no doubt, was very proud of the new headgear. Perhaps he himself invented it? Had he not, a few years before, said in writing to a friend about the fall of the Bastille, 'How much the greatest thing it is in history! and how much the best!'? Strange that a hat that was to symbolize all that was most static and most reputable may have been designed by a man so dangerous!

I imagine that the Whigs, who in all things followed the beloved Charles like sheep, were soon enthusiastic wearers of the top hat, while the Tories looked on it with frigid horror and would have none of it. But very soon, long before the dreadful Reform Bill, they themselves were wearing it, sullenly perhaps, but without protest. It had imposed itself upon them, with a mysterious and inexorable power that was somehow latent in it. It had ceased to be a sign of the times. It had become a natural phenomenon. It seemed to be even a part of the human body. Not merely did one hunt in it, as one still does: one fished, one skated, one played cricket in it. One wore it throughout debates in the Houses of Parliament, taking it off (with a wrench) only when one rose to orate, and resuming it (with a sigh of relief) as soon as ever one had said one's say. At routs and receptions, however great the crush, one carried it in one's hand all the time—and one must have been glad when, some time in the 'sixties, somebody invented the crush-hat, the gibus, which could be held under the arm, inobtrusively saving the situation. One kept it on one's head, even while eating luncheon in one's club. I don't think there are any clubs now where this custom survives. But it did survive in quite recent years at the 'In and Out', magically wafting any guest into a past age. Until quite lately, in theatres or opera houses, when you went out to smoke in the foyer, you always took your hat with you lest some evil thing should befall you. And when you paid an 'afternoon call' (a habit not then extinct) you would rather have died than not appear before your hostess hat in hand—and gloves there too. These things you presently placed upon the floor beside your chair, where she could still see them, symbols of good breeding and reassuring proclamations of the fact that you were only a visitor and hadn't come to abide with her for ever.

On Sundays the top hat acquired an even sacred significance. When a family entered the family pew, the father, instead of kneeling down with his wife and children for some moments, merely sat forward and said his silent prayer into his hat. This always puzzled me. I did not grasp the underlying theory that a prayer offered through that medium was likely to be the more acceptable.

On Sundays at Oxford—I was going to use again the adverb 'recently', but though the time when I was a freshman seems to me only yesterday, it is now just half a century ago—there were still some undergraduates who honoured the day with top hats and frock-coats. And no undergraduate who, in defiance of proctorial regulations, dared to pay a flying visit to London, would have dared to do so without those urban insignia, though they invited detection on the way to the railway station. One bespoke a cab on the eve of the adventure, and on the morning of it one instructed the cabman to drive to the station very quickly; and on the platform, if one espied a donnish-looking man, one tried to look very old and irreproachable. A motor-car would have been a great convenience. But motor-cars were not yet. And the top hats which in later days they, as it were, bashed in, and the accompanying frock-coats which, so to speak, they ran over, were still vitally necessary to any young gentleman with any self-respect and respect for London.

Or, for that matter, to any decently modest young gentleman who didn't want to be stared at. In London even the crossing sweepers mostly wore top hats. The 'old-clo'-men,' those hoarsely vocal perambulants, went even further: they wore three, one rammed down on another, in token, I suppose, of big business. The policemen had indeed long ago taken to helmets—not, I am sure, of their own accord, but because some Home Secretary had thought they would look more frightening. There was only one other civilian body of men that did not follow the all-prevailing fashion: nearly all the actors wore billicocks. The comedians tended to wear brown ones, the tragedians black ones; and those tragedians who were Bohemian in their way of life were apt to prefer sombreros. The actor-manager attended rehearsals in a top hat; and a top hat could be worn also by any actor who had played leading parts in other theatres, and very careful was such an one to wear it, to the envy of less illustrious members of the cast. I always wished those others would combine to break loose and fly in the face of immemorial etiquette, boldly encylindered. But they never fulfilled my hope. Nowadays, I suppose, not even the most eminent and responsible of actors rehearses in anything but what (heaven knows why) is called a trilby. Alas, the Spirit of the Age is one that levels down, not up.

Bank-messengers, Westminster boys, the porter at either end of such places as the Albany or Palace Gardens Terrace, are faithful among the few. And there is of course the occasional, the spasmodic fidelity of men going to weddings or funerals, or (in peace time) to Ascot or the Eton and Harrow match. My heart is gladdened at sight of these? At the risk of seeming querulous, I protest that it isn't. The males of the Latin races are far less self-conscious than we, far more adaptable in the matter of costume. Carnival time in any French or Italian city is a very good time indeed. The revellers do revel in their fantastic attire, are urged up by it to the height of high spirits. But among my memories none is drearier than that of the Fancy Dress Balls which used to be given in Covent Garden Opera House. The women seemed happy enough, but the men

—how woebegone! how deeply ashamed of themselves! The street acrobats of my childhood, in their spangles and pink tights, acquitted themselves quite gaily throughout their professional somersaults and other feats. But when they finished, when they fared along the pavements to their next pitch, what shuffling figures of embarrassment they did cut, to be sure! Not less awfully abashed by their own appearance are the gentlemen going their way to and from weddings or any other of those functions which involve what has become, quite obviously, fancy dress.

Perhaps after the present war the top hat will never reappear at any function whatsoever, even on the head of the eldest man. Perhaps it will be used as a flower-pot in the home, filled with earth and nourishing the bulb of a hyacinth or other domestic flower. I hope, in the goodness of my heart, the housemaid will not handle it untenderly, and will brush it the right way. For it is very sensitive. Its sensibility was ever one of its great charms. It alone among hats had a sort of soul. If one treated it well, one wasn't sure it didn't love one. It wasn't as expressive as one's dog, yet it had an air of quiet devotion and humble comradeship. It had also, like one's cat, a great dignity of its own. And it was a creature of many moods. On dull cloudy days itself was dull, but when the sun was brightly shining, it became radiant. If it was out in a downpour of rain, without an umbrella, it suffered greatly: it was afflicted with a sort of black and blue rash, most distressing to behold, and had to be nursed back to health with tender and unremitting care. Nature herself was the best nurse, however, during the early stages of the malady. The patient was best left to grow quite dry by action of the air, before being ever so gently brushed with the softest of brushes. Gradually it became convalescent, and seemed to smile up at you while it was rubbed slowly with a piece of silk. And anon it was well enough to be ironed. When I was very young I used to have my hat ironed periodically at my hatter's, like other young men. Rather a fascinating process to watch!—the expert swiftness and sureness of it, the immense change wrought with a violent celerity that seemed dangerous and yet did no harm. But in later times I would not entrust my dumb friend to hireling hands howsoever trustworthy, and he almost spoke his gratitude to me when I purchased an iron of the kind required—or rather two irons, a wide one for shaft and crown, a narrow one for brim—and tentatively ironed him myself. At first my 'prentice hand was slow and faulty, and I never did quite master the art of swirling the curves of the iron with perfect symmetry around the crown. I must confess also that more than once, in the early days, I miscalculated the temperature of the iron and did grievous hurt to my friend—hurt so grievous that though he mutely assured me that it was no matter, and implored me not to abandon him, I had to secure a successor instantly.

But, as I look back across the gulf that lies between me and those Victorian and Edwardian years, I feel that I may justly claim to have deserved the affection my hats had for me. And I hope that my young readers will not scoff—though I fear they will—at the fullness with which that feeling was reciprocated by me.

Lytton Strachey

One day in the springtime of 1912—a date not long ago in
point of time, but infinitely long ago in point of the changes that
Europe has suffered since then—I was lunching at the Savile
Club. I had been living for two years in Italy; and there were
some faces new to me. There was one that interested me very
much; an emaciated face of ivory whiteness, above a long
square-cut auburn beard, and below a head of very long sleek
dark brown hair. The nose was nothing if not aquiline, and
Nature had chiselled it with great delicacy. The eyes, behind a
pair of gold-rimmed spectacles, eyes of an inquirer and a
cogitator, were large and brown and luminous. The man to
whom they belonged must, I judged, though he sat stooping
low down over his table, be extremely tall. He wore a jacket
of brown velveteen, a soft shirt, and a dark red tie. I greatly
wondered who he was. He looked rather like one of the Twelve
Apostles, and I decided that he resembled especially the
doubting one, Thomas, who was also called Didymus. I
learned from a friend who came in and joined me at my table
that he was one of the Stracheys: Lytton Strachey; a Cambridge man; rather an authority on French literature; had
written a book on French Literature in some series or other;
book said to be very good. 'But why,' my friend asked, 'should
he dress like that?' Well, we members of the Savile, Civil
Servants, men of letters, clergymen, scientists, doctors and so
on, were clad respectably, passably, decently, but no more than
that. And 'Hang it all,' I said, 'why *shouldn't* he dress like
that? He's the best-dressed man in the room!'

Soon afterwards I returned to Italy, and his image faded from my mind. Two years later I was back in England, but did not again see him, and his image remained in abeyance. But it instantly and vividly recurred to me when, in 1917, I was told by Desmond MacCarthy that a friend of his, Lytton Strachey, was writing a book about some of the Victorians; that these rather horrified the author, but that the book was sure to be a good one; and that I, though I didn't share the horror, would be sure to like it. A few months later I had the pleasure of meeting this man at dinner in the house of a gifted lady; and though I had no separate dialogue with him in the course of the meal, and though he seemed shy of general conversation, I was impressed by his mild dignity and benign good manners. Early in the following spring Desmond's prophecy that I would like the book was more than fulfilled.

I did far more than like it, I rejoiced in it. I can, if you will let me, lay claim to one little modest negative virtue. I have always been free from envy. In the year 1900 I had been considered a rather clever and amusing young man, but I felt no pang whatsoever at finding myself cut out at my own game by a sudden new-comer, named G. K. Chesterton, who was obviously far more amusing than I, and obviously a man of genius into the bargain. In 1918 I was young no longer, and I think I amused people less than I had. I had subsided into sober irony. Well, here was an ironist of an order far superior to mine. And here was a delicately effulgent master, a perfect master, of English prose. And in my joy there lurked no asp of satisfaction that here was not, in my opinion, a man of genius. Very exquisite literary artists seldom are men of genius. Genius tends to be careless in its strength. Genius is, by the nature of it, always in rather a hurry. Genius can't be bothered about perfection. Each of the four essays in *Eminent Victorians* was, as a work of art, perfect.

I ventured to send, I could not forbear to send, to Mr.

Strachey a reasoned letter of thanks and congratulations, by which he seemed to be pleased. But it was not until the spring of 1921 that I saw him again. I had reverted to Italy soon after the Armistice, and when he mentioned to me in a letter that he was engaged upon the theme of Queen Victoria, I immediately drew—for this time his image had not lapsed from my mind's eye—a caricature of him in his royal connexion. This drawing with others of other people, I presently brought with me to England, for exhibition; but I wished to verify Strachey's image, and wrote to tell him so, and he was so good-natured as to call on me at my hotel in order that I might professionally stare at him. He was no longer velveteen-jacketed, he was dressed now in a worldlier manner, which, I told him, seemed to me less characteristic, and he willingly agreed that he should remain velveteen-jacketed in my drawing. A few days later, his mother invited me to luncheon. She was old and almost blind, but immensely vivacious, and a very fount of wit, and with her I felt as though I were in the presence of Mme. du Deffand; and I knew very surely from whom her son derived some, at least, of the quality of his work.

Thenceforward, whenever I was in London, I met him pretty often, for he was held in great request by many hostesses in that city. He remained as shy of general talk as he had been when first I met him. He had *not* inherited his mother's forthgivingness. He asserted himself only when he was turned to and asked for his opinion. This he would offer with great concision. He never enlarged on it. Dr. Jowett was a little before my time, but the quality of his sayings, the rarity and the brevity of them, their startlingness, and the small high voice in which they were piped, were of course familiar to me by hearsay; and Lytton Strachey's reminded me of them. Let me quote one instance. A new book by another, a rather younger but more precocious, writer of great brilliance, my friend Philip Guedalla, had just been published. Mr. Philip Morrell

said he had just been reading it, and, turning to Lytton
Strachey, said, 'He seems to be a sort of disciple of *yours*,
Lytton.' 'Oh,' piped Lytton, 'I thought I was a disciple of his?
He began before me.' I say 'piped' for that was what, in my
hearing, he always did. And I was much interested by the
statement of Mr. Leonard Woolf, who of course knew him very
well and for a very long time, that in intimate conversation he
would speak in a deep strong voice. I should like to have had
the surprise of hearing that. I should like to have known well a
man whose work has given me such deep and abiding pleasure.
Some of you whom I am addressing in the University that
nurtured him may have known him very well indeed, and I
wish *you* were telling *me* about him instead of politely listening
to my vague personal impression of him. Perhaps you will
take me aside and do so when this lecture is over? But I fear
you will be too tired. I shall have to await the publication of his
Life and Letters.

In his lifetime his work was cordially acclaimed. He was
fortunate, I think, in that the Great War (as we impresciently
called it) had been going on for two and a half years before the
publication of *Eminent Victorians*. In war, inevitably, rightly,
voices are loud; and war, even when all the omens are propitious to our own cause, is a tragic, a painfully astringent
theme. And thus the sound of a quiet voice suddenly discours-
ing on well-remembered figures that had flourished in halcyon
years not long gone by was bound to give us something very
like the sense of relief that is ours in escaping from the din and
crush of a metropolis to some dear little old familiar country-
side. Strachey's publishers too were fortunate in that his book
was promptly praised in the course of a lecture on biography
by a man of high standing. English readers are ever instantly
impressionable by Prime Ministers. Mr. Gladstone had made
the fortune of *Robert Elsmere*. Quite recently Lord Baldwin
did like service to the work of Mary Webb. In the meantime

Mr. Asquith had set the name of Lytton Strachey on the lips of all men. And Strachey's future books were by way of being what I believe is technically called 'best sellers'. But, as you know, great acclaim brings great reaction. Anatole France (with whose spirit Strachey had so much in common) was unassailably the Grand Old Man of French literature, and his funeral, with all the statesmen and other dignitaries of Paris and of the provinces following the bier along the crowd-lined roads to Père Lachaise, was a great and moving occasion, almost on the very morrow of which Paris began to ring with denunciations and contempt of the departed. We are not so quick as the Latin races, and are milder. We did not revile Tennyson or Swinburne, Meredith or Henry James, directly after burial. But we did have fairly prompt and fairly strong doubts about them, and were somewhat embarrassed by the great impression they had made on us; and if we did not succeed in forgetting them we spoke coldly of them. Of all great modern writers Thomas Hardy is, I think, the only one to whom death has not brought disparagement in the interval that elapses before the justice of Time shows men in their true proportions. Well, Lytton Strachey was not a great writer, not a great man, and not old enough to have become a Grand Old Man. But his gifts and his repute amply sufficed to ensure reaction against him very soon after the breath was out of his body. I think it was Ben Jonson who spoke of 'the backward kick of the dull ass's hoof.' That is not a pretty expression. But it is neither silly nor vulgar. The vulgar term, 'a debunker,' the term that the average writer or talker cursorily applies to Strachey, is not only vulgar, it is also silly.

That he was not a hero-worshipper, or even a very gallant heroine-worshipper, may be readily conceded. Also, he was perhaps not a very warm-hearted man. (As to that, I really don't know.) Assuredly he was not an artificer and purveyor of plaster saints or angels. He was intensely concerned with the ramifications of human character, and greatly amused by them. He had a very independent mind, and was an egoist in so far as he liked finding things out for himself and using his own judgment on what he found. Perfect justice is a divine attribute. Lytton Strachey, being a human being, had it not. He had, like the rest of us, imperfect sympathies. Great strength of character, keen practical sense and efficiency, for example, did not cause his heart to glow so much as one might wish they had. They seemed rather to give him a slight chill. Though he recognized the greatness of Florence Nightingale, the necessary grit that was at the core of it rather jarred on him; while its absence from the character of Sidney Herbert gave great tenderness to his portrait of that statesman. Nor did his love of exercising his own judgment move him to dissent from that of Purcell, the biographer of Cardinal Manning. He was essentially, congenitally, a Newman man. Who among us isn't? But I think his preference rather blinded him to the fair amount of grit that was latent in the delicacy, the poetry of that great priest and greater writer. In the character of Dr. Arnold there was such a wealth of grit, and a strenuousness so terrific, that one may rather wonder how Strachey could bear to think of him and write of him. The portrait fails, I think, because it is composed throughout in a vein of sheer mockery. It is the only work of his that does not seek, does not hesitate, does not penetrate, and is definitely unfair. It is the only work of his that might, so far as it goes, justify the application to him of that term which shall not again soil my lips and afflict your ears.

The vein of mockery was very strong in him certainly, and constantly asserted itself in his writings. A satirist he was not. Mockery is a light and lambent, rather irresponsible thing. '*On se moque de ce qu'on aime*' is a true saying. Strachey was always ready to mock what he loved. In mockery there is no malice. In satire there may be plenty of it. Pope was full of it.

But he was rather an exception. Your satirist is mostly a robust fellow, as was Aristophanes, as were Juvenal and Swift; a fellow laying about him lustily, for the purpose of hurting, of injuring people who, in his opinion, ought to be hurt and injured. He may, like Aristophanes, have an abundant, a glorious gift for mockery. But fundamentally he is grim. He is grimly concerned with what he hates in the age to which he belongs. I do not remember having found anywhere in the works of Lytton Strachey one passing reference to any current event. He was quite definitely, and quite impenitently, what in current jargon is called an escapist.

Need we be angry? It takes all kinds to make a world, or even to make a national literature. Even for spirits less fastidious than Strachey's, there is, even at the best of times, a great charm in the past. Time, that sedulous artist, has been at work on it, selecting and rejecting with great tact. The past is a work of art, free from irrelevancies and loose ends. There are, for our vision, comparatively few people in it, and all of them are interesting people. The dullards have all disappeared —all but those whose dullness was so pronounced as to be in itself for us an amusing virtue. And in the past there is so blessedly nothing for us to worry about. Everything is settled. There's nothing to be done about it—nothing but to contemplate it and blandly form theories about this or that aspect of it. Strachey was by temperament an Eighteenth Century man. In the Age of Reason, and of Wit too, he felt far more at home than in the aftermath of the Industrial Revolution, and in the first fine careless rapture of the Internal Combustion Engine. Even we, in spite of our coarseness, deplore these great phenomena, and wish they had never happened, and grieve that mankind will not in any foreseeable future be able to shake them off and be quit of them. Strachey, like the good Eighteenth Century Englishman that he was, had close contacts with France. Indeed I feel that he was even more at ease in French than in English literature and life. It was in that handbook on French literature that he made his début. In the volume entitled *Books and Characters* (published in 1922) and in his last work, *Portraits in Miniature* (1931), there is constant truancy to France. Racine, Voltaire, Rousseau, Mme. de Sévigné, the Abbé Morellet, Mme. du Deffand, the Président de Brosses—with all of these he is on terms of cosiest intimacy. To our native Victorians he was rather in the relation of a visitor, an inquirer, an inquisitor. I don't think he was—as Desmond MacCarthy had gathered from him that he was—'horrified' by them. He disliked the nineteenth century in comparison with its forerunner, but it appealed to him far more than could the twentieth. Machinery, science and applied science, had not yet got a really firm grip on England, and moreover, in spite of one Reform Bill after another, government was still oligarchic. Inequality flourished almost as much as ever. Barriers were almost as ever high. The seeds of standardization and of mass-production had not been even sown. Life was full of salient variety, of idiosyncrasy, of oddity, of character, character untrammelled. Giles Lytton Strachey (I feel that I ought to have said this at the outset) was born on March the first, 1880. And therefore when, in his maturity, he began to write about the Victorians he was old enough to know his way about and among them, having been nurtured among elders to whom they were familiar; and he was young enough to feel far away from them, to be curious about them, to be wondering at them greatly. The immediate past, the time that one almost belongs to—almost but not quite—is peculiarly tantalizing. Perhaps Strachey was rather ashamed of the hold the Victorians had on him in virtue of their proximity. And perhaps it was for this reason, and to shake off these insidious rivals to his dear ones of the Eighteenth Century, or perhaps it was merely in a sudden spirit of adventure, that he plunged off into the court of Queen

Elizabeth. Anyway it was a brave thing to do. *Elizabeth and Essex* (published in 1928) is a finely constructed work, but seems to me to be essentially guesswork. A very robustious, slapdash writer might convince me that he was in close touch with the souls of those beings whose actions and motives are to me as mysterious as those of wild animals in an impenetrable jungle. You rightly infer that I am *not* a Sixteenth Century man. And I make so bold as to say 'Neither was Lytton Strachey.'

'A finely constructed work' I have said. But what work of Lytton Strachey's, large or small, was not admirably firm in structure?—*totus, teres atque rotundus.* I make no apology for that tag: it is so often forgotten by gifted authors. Let us not ignore the virtue of form in literature. It is the goblet for the wine. Be the wine never so good, is not our enjoyment of it diminished if the hospitable vintner pours it forth to be lapped up by us from the ground with our tongues? Improvisation is the essence of good talk. Heaven defend us from the talker who doles out things prepared for us! But let heaven not less defend us from the beautifully spontaneous writer who puts his trust in the inspiration of the moment!—unless indeed he be a man of genius, of genius that creates for him a rough but sufficing form in his wild career. No writer need despise literary form as something artificial and unworthy of him. Nature herself, with her flowers and her trees, with many of her hills and streams and valleys, even with some of her human beings, is an ardent and unashamed formalist. I would advise any young writer—or any middle-aged or old one who may be needing advice—to think out carefully, before he begins his novel, or biography, or essay, or what not, the shape that it should have. I would say to him—quoting another excellent Horatian tag—*Respice finem.* Let him before he begins know just how he is going to end. And I would, at the risk of boring him, insist that the beginning is not less important than the end, and that what comes between them is no less important

than they. In journalism, I have often been told, the first
sentence is the thing that matters most. Grip the reader's
attention, and all will be well. I am not sure that this is so.
Not long before the outbreak of war, when paper was very
plentiful, I saw in an evening paper a signed article about Karl
Marx. The first sentence was as follows: 'Deep down in a
grave at Highgate the corpse of Karl Marx lies rotting.' So
far, so good. But what followed was a quite mild and well-
reasoned depreciation of that writer's doctrines. The average
reader, the man in the street, had been gripped only to be disappointed. Well, literature is not read in the street. Streets
are not what they were when Thomas Macaulay would walk
from the Albany to Clapham Common reading Sophocles all
the way. Literature is read in homes only, and I fancy that in
those quiet surroundings the reader of it should at the outset
be rather invited, engaged, allured, than gripped. Indeed, I
think you will find that in all periods good poets or writers of
prose have, whether in long or in short works, made quiet
beginnings. Quiet endings, too. The reader, they have all
instinctively felt, should be lifted gently out of himself, and
borne up and up, and along, and in due course be set down
gently, to remember his adventure.

Strachey, certainly, had this good instinct, and obeyed it
always. James Boswell, describing the conversation of
members of The Club, recorded the delight of watching
Edmund Burke 'winding himself like a serpent into his
subject'. Even so was Strachey wont to wind himself into his
subject—and eventually out of it—suavely. Let me quote, as
an instance, the opening and the closing words of the essay on
the Abbé Morellet (a disciple of Diderot, a favoured friend of
Madame Helvétius, and at one time a quite well-treated
prisoner in the Bastille):

'Talleyrand once remarked that only those who had lived in
France before the Revolution had really experienced *la douceur*

de vivre. The Abbé Morellet would have agreed with him. Born in 1727 at Lyons, the son of a small paper merchant, how was it possible, in that age of caste and privilege, that André Morellet should have known anything of life but what was hard, dull, and insignificant?

Then comes the tale of the Abbé's career, beautifully told, and concluding with this picture of his old age, when he used to sit dozing by the fire in the drawing-room of young Madame de Rémusat:

'He was treated with great respect by everybody; even the First Consul was flattering; even the Emperor was polite, and made him a Senator. Then the Emperor disappeared, and a Bourbon ruled on the throne of his fathers. With that tenacity of life which seems to have been the portion of the creatures of the eighteenth century, Morellet continued in this world until his ninety-second year. But this world was no longer what it used to be: something had gone wrong. Those agitations, those arrangements and rearrangements, they seemed hardly worth attending to. One might as well doze. All his young friends were very kind certainly, but did they understand? How could they? What had been their experience of life? As for him, ah! *he* had listened to Diderot—used to sit for hours talking in the Tuileries Gardens with D'Alembert and Mademoiselle de Lespinasse—mentioned by Voltaire—spent half a life-time at Auteuil with dear Madame Helvétius—imprisoned in the Bastille . . . he nodded. Yes! *He* had known *la douceur de vivre*.'

Exquisitely beautiful, that diminuendo, is it not? And as tender as it is profound. I have said that Strachey was not, for aught I knew, a warm-hearted man. A tender-hearted man he assuredly was.

As biographer, he had, besides his gift for construction, the advantage of a splendid gift for narrative. He was a masterly teller of tales, long or short, tragic or comic. He could, as it were, *see* the thing he had to tell, *see* the people concerned in it, see them outwardly and inwardly, and make us share gratefully his vision. Who could have made so much as he of such things as the adventures of 'the boy Jones' in Buckingham Palace, of the inception and the building of the Albert Memorial, of Mr. Gorham's vicissitudes in the Court of Arches and the Judicial Committee of the Privy Council? As the finest example of his narrative gift—I had almost said his dramatic gift—I would choose perhaps his treatment of what led to the tragedy of the dereliction and death of General Gordon. The tremendous tale, charged with the strangely diverse characters of the eminent men involved in it—Gladstone, Hartington, Baring, and Gordon himself—is told with the subtlest strength, oscillating steadily, with the swing of a pendulum, between Downing Street and the Soudan. For a while we are in one place, then we are with equal vividness in the other, alternately, repeatedly; and great is the cumulative effect of this prolonged strophe and antistrophe. To those of you who are, as I am, fond of thrills, but have never read these pages, I would say earnestly, 'Read these pages.'

The element of criticism was implicit, and often explicit, in all Lytton Strachey's biographical work. From time to time he indulged in criticism undiluted. As a literary critic alone he would have been worthy to be remembered. The best kind of critic—the helpfully interpretative, the almost creative critic—is very passive before he becomes active. Such an one was Strachey. With an intellect of steely quality there was combined in him a deep sensibility and receptivity. He had felt before he thought. And two at least of his critical works—his long essay on Racine, and his Leslie Stephen Lecture on Pope—happened to be of cardinal, of crucial effect. Racine had never had high repute upon these shores; and the Romantic Movement had reduced Pope to a small shadow among our own poets. It was Strachey's silver trumpet that woke the young men of two decades ago to high appreciation of those two worthies. And by the way, literature apart, aren't there in the Elysian Fields two other worthies who have reason to be grateful to the supposed inconoclast?—Queen Victoria and the Prince Consort? The Prince in his life-time had never been popular; and after Sir Theodore Martin's saccharine biography he had become a veritable mock. I never heard a kind word for him. The Queen, who in my childhood and youth had been not only revered but worshipped, was, soon after her death, no longer in public favour. Her faults had become known, and her virtues were unheeded. This is not so now; and is not so by reason of Lytton Strachey's fully judicial presentment of her with all the faults over which her virtues so very much preponderated. And it is, by the same token, through him that we know the Prince not as just dreadfully admirable, but as someone to be loved and to be sorry for.

But after all—and perhaps you are saying 'Oh, if only it *were* all!'—it is as a writer, in the strict sense, as a user of that very beautiful medium, the English language, that I would especially extol Lytton Strachey. There is such a word as *prosaist*. It is a word that we never use; whereas *prosateur* is not seldom on the lips of Frenchmen, and is spoken in a very serious tone, a tone as serious as that in which we use the word *poet*. Frenchmen are keenly aware of the virtues of prose, and we, not being so, have accepted the idea that French prose is superior to ours. Undoubtedly, the general level of it is so. The average Frenchman writes better prose than the average Englishman. His medium is a language whose greatly prevailing Latinity makes it far more lucid than ours. It is, moreover, a language that has been by authority kept free from corruption. We have had no Richelieu, and if we had we would not, in our sturdy independence, have bowed down to the mandarins of his creation. Our prosaists, to achieve lucidity and euphony, have

to do a good deal of filtration on the way. I remember Lytton
Strachey once said to me, in reference to this need, that he
wished he were a Frenchman, writing in French. I rather
shocked him by saying 'Oh, any fool can write good French
prose.' But truth is in itself so good a thing that one may be
pardoned for exaggerating it every now and then. Good
English is, I am sure, far less easy to write than good French;
and *'pour être difficile la tâche n'est que plus glorieuse'*; and
difficulties surmounted (though only had they not been
surmounted would the reader be conscious of them) do somehow, I am convinced, enrich the texture of good writing. The
English language, being part Latin, part Saxon, is, in my
rough insular opinion, an even finer medium than the French
one. Latin is, one might say, its bony structure, Saxon its
flesh and blood. And of these two Latin is perhaps the more
important. A skeleton by itself is a noble thing, whereas an
inchoate mass of flesh and blood is not. A writer who has not
in boyhood been well-grounded in Latin is at a grievous disadvantage. However keen a natural instinct he may have for
writing, he will diffuse, he will be sloppy, as was, for example,
D. H. Lawrence, whose prose was so dangerous a model for
young admirers of his philosophy. The Latin element, on the
other hand, should not have too strong a hold on a writer, leading him to over-great austerity and nobility, even to aridity, as
happened so often in the seventeenth and eighteenth centuries.
In the best writing neither element prevails. The two merge
indistinguishably in each other.

To single Lytton Strachey out as a born writer would be to
offend a great number of people. For there is a very widespread and comfortable belief that we are all of us born writers.
Not long ago I heard that agile and mellifluous quodlibetarian,
Dr. Joad, saying in answer to a questioner who wanted to
write good letters, that anybody could write good letters: one
had but to think out clearly what one wanted to say, and then

set it down in the simplest terms. And a few weeks later, when the writing of books was under discussion, he said that the writers who thought most about how they should write were the hardest to read; and again he seemed to think lucidity all-sufficing. I admit that Herbert Spencer had also, many years ago, seemed to think so, and said so. But I maintain that had he not thought so, had Nature at the outset endowed him fully with a gift for writing, we should all of us be now reading him with greater zest and constancy than we do. A true gift for writing, though in spite of the telephone we all do still write letters sometimes, and though authors of books are more than ever numerous, is not widely bestowed. Nor is a true gift for painting, or for playing the violin; and of that we are somehow aware. We do not say to a violinist 'Just think out clearly what you want to express and then go straight ahead. Never mind how you handle your bow,' nor to a painter, 'Got your subject and your scheme of colour in your head all right, eh? Then don't bother about how you lay your paints on, dear old boy.' Let us not make similar remarks to writers. I am willing to concede that in the eighteen-nineties perhaps rather too much thought was given to *manner* in literature. The young men of that decade were perhaps over-influenced by the example of such elders as Walter Pater and Robert Louis Stevenson, over-fond of unusual words and peculiar cadences. Preciosity is a fault on the right side; but it is a fault. A venial one? Yes, in Pater, the essayist. But not in Stevenson, the novelist, when he was telling a straightforward story and wishing to give the reader an illusion of reality. From such books as *Treasure Island* and *The Master of Ballantrae* I have never for one moment had that illusion, have been too acutely and delightedly conscious of the technical graces and ingenuities of the author. When Stevenson did not aim at realism, and was entirely oblivious of Sir Walter Scott, and was giving rein to his own riotous sense of fantasy, as in

The New Arabian Nights, or *The Dynamiter*, or *The Wrong Box*, the jewelled elaboration of the manner becomes an integral part of the fun, and keeps us laughing the more irresistibly and the more loudly. These books are, I think, far and away his best—the most characteristic of himself, of his true and magical self. I have always regretted that Maurice Hewlett, one of the lights of the 'nineties and of later years, was not a humourist and wished to illude us with his tales; for his preciosity was fatal to his wish. Besides, it was a robust preciosity; and that is unnatural, is a contradiction in terms.

I conceive that had Lytton Strachey been a young man in those 'nineties, and not the merely growing boy that he was in most of them, he might have inclined to preciosity. Of this you will find no jot in his prose. His manner, though classical, is entirely natural, and rather shy. He makes no attempt to dazzle. He is not even afraid of clichés. He can be very homely. When he is narrating something humdrum he is quite congruously pedestrian; though even then felicities are apt to come shining forth by the way; as, for instance, in his account of how the young Queen Victoria's popularity was restored by the happiness of her marriage.

'The middle classes, in particular, were pleased. They liked a love-match; they liked a household in which they seemed to see reflected, as in some resplendent looking-glass, the ideal image of the very lives they lived themselves. Their own existences, less exalted, but oh! so soothingly similar, acquired an added excellence, an added succulence, from the early hours, the regularity, the plain tuckers, the round games, the roast beef and Yorkshire pudding of Osborne.'

His manner is infinitely flexible, in accord to every variation of whatever his theme may be. Consider the differences between his ways of writing about Lord Melbourne, Lord Palmerston, Mr. Disraeli, and Mr. Gladstone. His manner seems to bring us into the very presence of these widely disparate Premiers. Note the mellow and leisurely benignity of the cadences in which he writes of Lord Melbourne—'the autumn rose,' as he called him. Note the sharp brisk straightforward buoyancy of the writing whenever Lord Palmerston appears; and the elaborate Oriental richness of manner when Mr. Disraeli is on the scene. And does not all the subtlety of Mr. Gladstone confront us when we are asked, 'What, then, was the truth? In the physical universe there are no chimeras. But man is more various than nature; was Mr. Gladstone perhaps a chimera of the spirit? Did his very essence lie in the confusion of incompatibles? His very essence? It eludes the hand that grasps it. One is baffled, as his political opponents were fifty years ago. The soft serpent coils harden into quick strength that has vanished, leaving only emptiness and perplexity behind.' I can't help repeating to you the first words of that last sentence. 'The soft serpent coils harden into quick strength that has vanished.' Was ever speed so well suggested as in those eleven words?—words of a born writer, and a taker, we may be sure, of infinite pains.

If I were asked what seemed to me the paramount quality of Lytton Strachey's prose, I should reply, in one word, Beauty. That is perhaps a rather old-fashioned word, a word jarring to young writers, and to young painters or musicians, and by them associated with folly, with vanity and frivolity. To me it is still a noble word, and I fancy it will some day come back into fashion. I believe that the quality it connotes is essential to all the arts. The stress and strain, the uncertainty of life in the past thirty years has not, I think, been favourable to the arts, though in those years a great deal of admirable work has of course been done (mostly, alas, by men of maturish years). Nor do I suppose that in my time, or until long after my time, will very propitious conditions supervene. There is a spate of planning for the future of many things. Perhaps some people are at this moment strenuously planning for the future of the arts. But I doubt whether in the equalitarian era for which we are heading—the era in which we shall have built Jerusalem on England's smooth and asphalt land—the art of literature, which throve so finely and so continuously from Elizabethan to paulo-post-Victorian days, will have a wonderful renascence. We are told on high authority, from both sides of the Atlantic, that the present century is to be the Century of the Common Man. We are all of us to go down on our knees and clasp our hands and raise our eyes and worship the Common Man. I am not a learned theologian, but I think I am right in saying that this religion has at least the hall-mark of novelty—has never before been propagated, even in the East, from which so many religions have sprung. Well, I am an old man, and old men are not ready converts to new religions. This one does not stir my soul. I take some comfort in the fact that its propagators do not seek to bind us to it for ever. '*This*,' they say, 'is to be the Century of the Common Man.' I like to think that on the morning of January the first, in the year 2000, mankind will be free to unclasp its hands and rise from its knees and look about it for some other, and perhaps more rational, form of faith. I like also to think that in the meantime, in the great pale platitude of the meantime, there will be, as hitherto, a few discriminating readers of things written in past times; people likely to read, and likely to revel in, the works of Lytton Strachey. After all, it is always by the devotion of a few only that good books become classics.

I don't know whether it is 'in order' to dedicate a Rede Lecture to anybody. If it is, I would like to dedicate this one to the memory of Lytton Strachey. I am always very proud that he dedicated one of his books, his last one, to me. Forgive me for boasting that he said 'with gratitude and admiration.' To him I dedicate this lecture with far greater gratitude than ever he can have felt to me, and with far deeper admiration than ever he can have had for anything of mine.

THE REDE LECTURE, 1943

H. B. Irving as a Young Man

Ladies and Gentlemen, Almost forty years ago I wrote, but didn't publish, a few little essays about meetings with interesting contemporaries of mine. One of these essays was about my two first meetings with H. B. Irving—Harry Irving, the elder son of Sir Henry, and father of Mr. Laurence Irving, whose biography of Sir Henry is assuredly the vividest and best that any actor has ever had.

This little essay I will now read to you.

In the autumn of 1890 I was a freshman at Merton College, Oxford. I was a year younger than most of the other freshmen, and was young even for my age. Except in my very last term at school I had been wearing Eton collars. I was not yet accustomed to collars that stood up. I was a child. Not so, far from so, in his third year at New College, was Harry Irving.

It was young George Bancroft who presented me to him. He too, in his way, seemed to me very wonderful. He was so finished and formed—so perfect a little man of the world; a perfect miniature, both in face and in costume, of his father, Sir Squire Bancroft. But he did not frighten me. His eyes had the famous twinkle of his mother's, and they had twinkled very kindly on me when he came to call on me and to invite me to breakfast with him on the following Sunday. He was a Brasenose man, was in his third year, and had lodgings in St. Giles. 'I'll ask Harry Irving and some other fellows,' he said, in quite a casual tone.

Two or three of the other fellows were already there when I arrived; and two or three others followed. I was presented to

358

them all. They seemed very tall and easy and important, and I thought it impossible that they would remember me if they saw me again. George Bancroft wore a smoking-jacket with quilted facings of blue silk. This summed up for me the possibilities of adult grandeur and emancipation. It was the symbol of all that a Sunday morning at school was not. Yet anon it was to be as naught in my eyes—it and the man in it, and all those other men. For anon the door flew open: in, with the bent strut of his father, came H. B. Irving.

As he crossed the threshold, he said in a deep voice, 'Ha!' He clapped a hand on Bancroft's shoulder, rather in the manner of a very eminent detective arresting a very unimportant thief. Then, with that hand still on that shoulder, he distributed nods and 'Ha!'s among the company—the company of 'supers'. His gaze alighted on *me*.

'This,' said Bancroft (with the pride of a 'super' who has a line to speak), 'is Mr. Beerbohm, of Merton.'

'Ha!' He had a way of looking at one through his pince-nez, less intimidating only than a way he had of looking at one *over* his pince-nez. 'Ha!' he repeated. And then, 'A brother of Beerbohm Tree, aren't you?'

'A half-brother,' I said faintly.

'Ha!'

It was as though he had said 'That may or may not be an extenuating circumstance, I will consider it.'

We were to have breakfast downstairs. Bancroft led the way. The others instinctively let Irving go out next. I felt I was almost on terms of equality with these others now, and found myself talking quite glibly to one of them on the way down.

Our host was at the head of the table—topographically. But spiritually and truly, and to all intents and purposes, the head of any table at which H. B. Irving seated himself was just where H. B. Irving sat. I do not remember much that he said;

he may not even have said much; but his manner was such that anything said by him had at the moment the effect of a Standard Work condensed by him for the occasion. The name of a well-known public man was mentioned by somebody. Irving seemed for a moment to search his memory. 'I once met him at supper,' he said, 'at my father's.' Just that. No more. But it somehow—by some miracle of cadence and glance and eye-brow—implied an adverse and irrevocable judgment. That well-known man had been paraded, inspected, seen through, dismissed: the less said about him the better. And moreover, as I was to find, there always was in H. B. Irving's way of saying 'my father' something which brought to bear on one suddenly and personally the full weight of the Lyceum tradition. True, he always carried that weight around with him, as it were, but it seemed to come down on one with special force whenever 'my father' was mentioned.

It was as 'Young Irving' that he was always spoken of by the undergraduates at large. The adjective seemed rather ill-chosen, but it implied no disrespect. As was Old Irving's fame in Great Britain and America, so was Young Irving's in Oxford. In the year before I matriculated he had appeared as King John in Shakespeare's play, and had been highly praised by the many critics who travelled down from London to see him. If not perhaps one of the most eloquent speakers at the Union, he was certainly the most impressive. He had made a special study, too, of Judge Jeffreys, and had read a paper about him to more than one Essay Society. And he was a student of Criminology, and was to practise at the Criminal Bar when he 'went down'. Walking up the High, 'Look,' one undergraduate would say to another, 'there goes Young Irving,' and in Hall that evening he would say 'I saw Young Irving in the High to-day.' Young Irving's rooms were in Radcliffe Square, and it was natural that he should pass often up and down the High on his way to and from them; but the sight of him was never taken as a matter of course. It was always something to have just seen him. And oh—to have just met him at breakfast! I wonder to how many of my fellow-freshmen at Merton did I in the course of that memorable Sunday say, as lightly as I could, 'I met Young Irving at breakfast this morning.'

I knew now, after this face-to-face meeting, that the lightness of Bancroft's 'Harry Irving and some other fellows' had been a histrionic assumption. I hoped I was carrying off my own assumption equally well. I tried to make my eyes twinkle in the Bancroft manner. But I think they were yet obviously the eyes of a child who had been frightened.

What a terror to witnesses was lost by Young Irving's abandonment of the Law! True, the days of Sergeant Parry and Sergeant Ballantyne were no more. The tone of the Old Bailey had already been dulcified to that pitch of suavity and ruth which is the key-note of our modern life. Young Irving would have somewhat restored the fine old traditions, showing even from under his stuff-gown the ermine of Judge Jeffreys. Perhaps, ere the time came for him to exchange stuff for silk, he would have mellowed. For he did within a few years delightfully mellow; and it may be not really so wonderful as I like to think—not such a sign of later powers developed in myself—that I achieved the habit of calling him 'Harry'. But not at Oxford did the mellowing process begin. And when, one day, I received an invitation to lunch in Radcliffe Square, I quaked as at the service of a writ, and was gratified as by a royal command.

The summons was for the following day. I read it several times. Then I leaned out from my ground-floor window, deeply inhaling. A fellow-freshman was crossing the quadrangle. I greeted him: 'Can you lunch with me to-morrow? Oh no, by-the-by, not to-morrow: to-morrow I've got to lunch with Young Irving. The day *after* to-morrow?'

Within an hour or so, by repetition of this formula, I had

accumulated quite a large party for the day after to-morrow. I forget whether it went off well. I remember only the previous day.

It had not struck me that Irving and I might be alone. Else, I might hardly have dared to accept. Down went my heart like lead in water when, punctually presenting myself on the threshold of his room, I saw, together with my vision of his back awfully silhouetted against the bow-window, covers laid for two. Covers? I knew that I could not hide under my plate.

Probably I uttered a cough, for I remember the suddenness with which the silhouette veered round and said 'Ha!' to me.

I daresay that you, like me, often at important junctures think suddenly of some outrageous thing that you *might* do, and of the appalling results there would be if you did it—results so appalling that for an instant, in your horror, you feel that you actually *have* done the thing. There was for me a gruesome instant in which I felt that I had actually said 'Ha!' back to Irving.

The relief of finding that I had not done so seemed to inspire me with a sort of jaunty confidence. I found myself quite articulate—indeed, fluent! At school I had been thought clever. 'Has natural abilities of a rare order'—this phrase from a form-master's Report came floating into my brain. Why should I not impress myself on Irving to-day as a man with abilities of a rare order? He seemed to be inclined to draw me out. Let him be astonished with the draft. Let him get more than he bargained for. I thought of David and Goliath. But—what if Goliath had looked at David over his pince-nez as Irving looked at me over his? I felt that what I babbled was in no way remarkable. I felt I had no abilities of *any* order. That form-master had been a fool. So was I. Already, though luncheon had hardly begun, I was seen through, over that pince-nez. I was asked many questions, to which I gave the feeblest and most rambling answers, foreseeing all the while one question which especially I dreaded. Perhaps, thought I, hoping against hope, this question would not be put. But at the end of the meal came a silence which I knew could terminate in only one way. Irving had risen from the table and offered me a cigar. Never having smoked a cigar, I took a cigarette. Irving cut and lit a cigar for himself, motioned me to an armchair, flung himself on the sofa, propped his elbow on the back of it, propped his brow on his hand, and over his pince-nez looked at me. 'And what,' he asked, 'are you going to do in after-life?'

'Well,' I said—and the poor monosyllable came out as a polysyllabic bleat, 'we-e-e-e-ell,' after which the other poor words came out in three separate gasps sped by a weak smile— 'as a matter of fact I'm—I'm thinking of—being called to the Bar.'

And these words, at the very moment of utterance, became untrue. I *had*, up to that moment, vaguely destined myself for the Bar. But in expressing to Irving this ambition, I saw the full absurdity of it and for good and all dropped it before he had time to say (as he did with more than his usual gravity say) 'Ha!' My weak smile, my gasps, the blush burning my brow, had forced this plain moral on me: I was *not* for the Forum. I suppose that in any case I would have discovered this truth for myself fairly soon; but the fact remains that I discovered it then and there by stress of Irving's presence. I did not let him know this. I was too proud to say, 'But please, Sir, I've just changed my mind, I'm not for the Forum—oh no, Sir! The Forum's for you, Sir!' Indeed, I rather resented his power over me; and so glad, presently, was I to be out on the doorstep in Radcliffe Square that I not merely could have danced: I did, actually, dance. . . . I was only a child, remember.

(*Written* 1914)

The Happy Hypocrite

1

None, it is said, of all who revelled with the Regent, was half so wicked as Lord George Hell. I will not trouble my little readers with a long recital of his great naughtiness. But it were well they should know that he was greedy, destructive, and disobedient. I am afraid there is no doubt that he often sat up at Carlton House until long after bedtime, playing at games, and that he generally ate and drank far more than was good for him. His fondness for fine clothes was such that he used to dress on week-days quite as gorgeously as good people dress on Sundays. He was thirty-five years old and a great grief to his parents.

And the worst of it was that he set such a bad example to others. Never, never did he try to conceal his wrongdoing; so that, in time, every one knew how horrid he was. In fact, I think he was proud of being horrid. Captain Tarleton, in his account of *Contemporary Bucks*, suggested that his Lordship's great Candour was a virtue and should incline us to forgive some of his abominable faults. But, painful as it is to me to dissent from any opinion expressed by one who is now dead, I hold that Candour is good only when it reveals good actions or good sentiments, and that when it reveals evil, itself is evil, even also.

Lord George Hell did, at last, atone for all his faults, in a way that was never revealed to the world during his lifetime. The reason of his strange and sudden disappearance from that social sphere in which he had so long moved, and never moved again, I will unfold. My little readers will then, I think, acknowledge that any angry judgment they may have passed upon him must be reconsidered and, maybe, withdrawn. I will leave his Lordship in their hands. But my plea for him will not be based upon that Candour of his, which some of his friends so much admired. There were, yes! some so weak and so wayward as to think it a fine thing to have an historic title and no scruples. 'Here comes George Hell,' they would say. 'How wicked my Lord is looking!' *Noblesse oblige*, you see, and so an aristocrat should be very careful of his good name. Anonymous naughtiness does little harm.

It is pleasant to record that many persons were inobnoxious to the magic of his title and disapproved of him so strongly that, whenever he entered a room where they happened to be, they would make straight for the door and watch him very severely through the keyhole. Every morning, when he strolled up Piccadilly, they crossed over to the other side in a compact body, leaving him to the companionship of his bad companions on that which is still called the 'shady side'. Lord George – .... – was quite indifferent to this demonstration. Indeed, he seemed wholly hardened, and when ladies gathered up their skirts as they passed him, he would lightly appraise their ankles.

I am glad I never saw his Lordship. They say he was rather like Caligula, with a dash of Sir John Falstaff, and that sometimes on wintry mornings in St James's Street young children would hush their prattle and cling in disconsolate terror to their nurses' skirts, as they saw him come (that vast and fearful gentleman!) with the east wind ruffling the rotund surface of his beaver, ruffling the fur about his neck and wrists, and striking the purple complexion of his cheeks to a still deeper purple. 'King Bogey' they called him in the nurseries. In the hours when they too were naughty, their nurses would predict his advent down the chimney or from the linen-press, and then they always 'behaved'. So that, you see, even the unrighteous are a power for good, in the hands of nurses.

It is true that his Lordship was a non-smoker —a negative virtue, certainly, and due, even that, I fear, to the fashion of the day—but there the list of his good qualities comes to an abrupt conclusion. He loved with an insatiable love the town and the pleasures of the town, whilst the ennobling influences of our English lakes were quite unknown to him. He used to boast that he had not seen a buttercup for twenty years, and once he called the country 'a Fool's Paradise.' London was the only place marked on the map of his mind. London gave him all he wished for. Is it not extraordinary to think that he had never spent a happy day nor a day of any kind in Follard Chase, that desirable mansion in Herts, which he had won from Sir Follard Follard, by a chuck of the dice, at Boodle's, on his seventeenth birthday? Always cynical and unkind, he had refused to give the broken baronet his 'revenge'. Always unkind and insolent, he had offered to install him in the lodge— an offer which was, after a little hesitation, accepted. 'On my soul, the man's place is a sinecure,' Lord George would say; 'he never has to open the gate to me.'[1] So rust had covered the great iron gates of Follard Chase, and moss had covered its paths. The deer browsed upon its terraces. There were only wild flowers anywhere. Deep down among the weeds and water-lilies of the little stone-rimmed pond he had looked down upon, lay the marble faun, as he had fallen.

Of all the sins of his Lordship's life surely not one was more wanton than his neglect of Follard Chase. Some whispered (not did he ever trouble to deny) that he had won it by foul means, by loaded dice. Indeed no card-player in St James's cheated more persistently than he. As he was rich and had no wife and family to support, and as his luck was always capital, I can offer no excuse for his conduct. At Carlton House,

1. *Lord Coleraine's Correspondence,* page 101.

in the presence of many bishops and cabinet ministers, he once dunned the Regent most arrogantly for 5,000 guineas out of which he had cheated him some months before, and went so far as to declare that he would not leave the house till he got it; whereupon His Royal Highness, with that unfailing tact for which he was ever famous, invited him to stay there as a guest; which, in fact, Lord George did, for several months. After this, we can hardly be surprised when we read that he 'seldom sat down to the fashionable game of Limbo with less than four, and sometimes with *as many as seven* aces up his sleeve.'1 We can only wonder that he was tolerated at all.

At Garble's, that nightly resort of titled rips and roysterers, he usually spent the early hours of his evenings. Round the illuminated garden, with La Gambogi, the dancer, on his arm, and a Bacchic retinue at his heels, he would amble leisurely, clad in Georgian costume, which was not then, of course, fancy dress, as it is now.2 Now and again, in the midst of his noisy talk, he would crack a joke of the period, or break into a sentimental ballad, dance a little, or pick a quarrel. When he tired of such fooling, he would proceed to his box in the tiny alfresco theatre and patronize the jugglers, pugilists, play-actors, and whatever eccentric persons happened to be performing there.

The stars were splendid and the moon as beautiful as a great camelia, one night in May, as his Lordship laid his arms upon the cushioned ledge of his box and watched the antics of the Merry Dwarf, a little, curly-headed creature,

1. *Contemporary Bucks*, vol. i, page 73.
2. It would seem, however, that, on special occasions, his Lordship indulged in odd costumes. 'I have seen him,' says Captain Tarleton (vol. i, p. 69), 'attired as a French clown, as a sailor, or in the crimson hose of a Sicilian grandee – *peu beau spectacle*. He never disguised his face, whatever his costume, however.'

whose *début* it was. Certainly Garble had found a novelty. Lord George led the applause, and the Dwarf finished his frisking with a pretty song about lovers. Nor was this all. Feats of archery were to follow. In a moment the Dwarf reappeared with a small, gilded bow in his hand and a quiver-full of arrows slung at his shoulder. Hither and thither he shot these vibrant arrows, very precisely, several into the bark of the acacias that grew about the overt stage, several into the fluted columns of the boxes, two or three to the stars. The audience was delighted. '*Bravo! Bravo Sagittaro!*' murmured Lord George, in the language, of La Gambogi, who was at his side. Finally, the waxen figure of a man was carried on by an assistant and propped against the trunk of a tree. A scarf was tied across the eyes of the Merry Dwarf, who stood in a remote corner of the stage. *Bravo* indeed! For the shaft had pierced the waxen figure through the heart, or just where the heart would have been if the figure had been human and not waxen.

Lord George called for port and champagne and beckoned the bowing homuncule to his box, that he might compliment him on his skill and pledge him in a bumper of the grape.

'On my soul, you have a genius for the bow,' his Lordship cried with florid condescension. 'Come and sit by me; but first let me present you to my divine companion the Signora Gambogi—Virgo and Saggittarius, egad! You may have met on the Zodiac.'

'Indeed, I met the Signora many years ago,' the Dwarf replied, with a low bow. 'But not on the Zodiac, and the Signora perhaps forgets me.'

At this speech the Signora flushed angrily, for she was indeed no longer young, and the Dwarf had a childish face. She thought he mocked her; her eyes flashed. Lord George's twinkled rather maliciously.

'Great is the experience of youth,' he laughed. 'Pray, are you stricken with more than twenty summers?'

'With more than I can count,' said the Dwarf. 'To the health of your Lordship!' and he drained his long glass of wine. Lord George replenished it, and asked by what means or miracle he had acquired his mastery of the bow.

'By long practice,' the little thing rejoined; 'long practice on human creatures.' And he nodded his curls mysteriously.

'On my heart, you are a dangerous box-mate.'

'Your Lordship were certainly a good target.'

Little liking this joke at his bulk, which really rivalled the Regent's, Lord George turned brusquely in his chair and fixed his eyes upon the stage. This time it was the Gambogi who laughed.

A new operette, *The Fair Captive of Samarcand*, was being enacted, and the frequenters of Garble's were all curious to behold the *debutante*, Jenny Mere, who was said to be both pretty and talented. These predictions were surely fulfilled, when the captive peeped from the window of her wooden turret. She looked so pale under her blue turban. Her eyes were dark with fear; her parted lips did not seem capable of speech. 'Is it that she is frightened of us?' the audience wondered. 'Or of the flashing scimitar of Aphoschaz, the cruel father who holds her captive?' So they gave her loud applause, and when at length she jumped down, to be caught in the arms of her gallant lover, Nissarah, and, throwing aside her Eastern draperies, did a simple dance in the convention of Columbine, their delight was quite unbounded. She was very young and did not dance very well, it is true, but they forgave her that. And when she turned in the dance and saw her father with his scimitar, their hearts beat swiftly for her. Nor were all eyes tearless when she pleaded with him for her life.

Strangely absorbed, quite callous of his two companions, Lord George gazed over the footlights. He seemed as one who is in a trance. Of a sudden, something shot sharp into his heart. In pain he sprang to his feet and, as he turned, he seemed to see a winged and laughing child, in whose hand was a bow, fly swiftly away into the darkness. At his side was the Dwarf's chair. It was empty. Only La Gambogi was with him, and her dark face was like the face of a fury.

Presently he sank back into his chair, holding one hand to his heart, that still throbbed from the strange transfixion. He breathed very painfully and seemed scarce conscious of his surroundings. But La Gambogi knew he would pay no more homage to her now, for that the love of Jenny Mere had come into his heart.

When the operette was over, his love-sick Lordship snatched up his cloak and went away without one word to the lady at his side. Rudely he brushed aside Count Karoloff and Mr. FitzClarence, with whom he had arranged to play hazard. Of his comrades, his cynicism, his reckless scorn—of all the material of his existence—he was oblivious now. He had no time for penitence or diffident delay. He only knew that he must kneel at the feet of Jenny Mere and ask her to be his wife.

'Miss Mere,' said Garble, 'is in her room, resuming her ordinary attire. If you Lordship deign to await the conclusion of her humble toilet, it shall be my privilege to present her to your Lordship. Even now, indeed, I hear her footfall on the stair.'

Lord George uncovered his head and with one hand nervously smoothed his rebellious wig.

'Miss Mere, come hither,' said Garble. 'This is my Lord George Hell, that you have pleased whom by your poor efforts this night will ever be the prime gratification of your passage through the roseat realms of art.'

Little Miss Mere, who had never seen a lord, except in fancy or in dreams, curtseyed shyly and hung her head. With a loud crash, Lord George fell on his knees. The manager was greatly surprised, the girl greatly embarrassed. Yet neither of them laughed, for sincerity dignified his posture and sent eloquence from his lips.

'Miss Mere,' he cried, 'give ear, I pray you, to my poor words, nor spurn me in misprision from the pedestal of your Beauty, Genius, and Virtue. All too conscious, alas! of my presumption in the same, I yet abase myself before you as a suitor for your adorable Hand. I grop under the shadow of your raven Locks. I am dazzled in the light of those translucent Orbs, your Eyes. In the intolerable Whirlwind of your Fame I faint and am afraid.'

'Sir——' the girl began, simply.

'Say "My Lord," ' said Garble solemnly.

'My Lord, I thank you for your words. They are beautiful But indeed, indeed, I can never be your bride.'

Lord George hid his face in his hands.

'Child,' said Mr. Garble, 'let not the sun rise ere you have retracted those wicked words.'

'My wealth, my rank, my irremediable love for you, I throw them at your feet,' Lord George cried piteously. 'I would wait an hour, a week, a lustre, even a decade, did you but bid me hope!'

'I can never be your wife,' she said, slowly. 'I can never be the wife of any man whose face is not saintly. Your face, my Lord, mirrors, it may be, true love for me, but it is even as a mirror long tarnished by the reflection of this world's vanity. It is even as a tarnished mirror. Do not kneel to me, for I am poor and humble. I was not made for such impetuous wooing. Kneel, if you please, to some greater, gayer lady. As for my love, it is my own, nor can it be ever torn from me, but given, as true love must needs be given, freely. Ah, rise from your knees. That man, whose face is wonderful as are the faces of the saints, to him I will give my true love.'

371

Miss Mere, though visibly affected, had spoken this speech
with a gesture and elocution so superb, that Mr. Garble could
not help applauding, deeply though he regretted her attitude
towards his honoured patron. As for Lord George, he was
immobile as a stricken oak. With a sweet look of pity, Miss
Mere went her way, and Mr. Garble, with some solicitude,
helped his Lordship to rise from his knees. Out into the night,
without a word, his Lordship went. Above him the stars were
still splendid. They seemed to mock the festoons of little lamps,
dim now and guttering, in the garden of Garble's. What should
he do? No thoughts came; only his heart burnt hotly. He stood
on the brim of Garble's lake, shallow and artificial as his past
had been. Two swans slept on its surface. The moon shone
strangely upon their white, twisted necks. Should he drown
himself? There was no one in the garden to prevent him, and
in the morning they would find him floating there, one of the
noblest of love's victims. The garden would be closed in the
evening. There would be no performance in the little theatre.
It might be that Jenny Mere would mourn him. 'Life is a prison,
without bars,' he murmured, as he walked away.

All night long he strode, knowing not wither, through the
mysterious streets and squares of London. The watchmen, to
whom his figure was familiar, gripped their staves at his
approach, for they had old reason to fear his wild and riotous
habits. He did not heed them. Through that dim conflict
between darkness and day, which is ever waged silently over
our sleep, Lord George strode on in the deep absorption of his
love and of his despair. At dawn he found himself on the
outskirts of a little wood in Kensington. A rabbit rushed past
him through the dew. Birds were fluttering in the branches.
The leaves were tremulous with the presage of day, and the
air was full of the sweet scent of hyacinths.

How cool the country was! It seemed to cool the feverish
maladies of his soul and conscrate his love. In the fair light

of the dawn he began to shape the means of winning Jenny
Mere, that he had conceived in the desperate hours of the night.
Soon an old woodman passed by, and, with rough courtesy,
showed him the path that would lead him quickest to the town.
He was loth to leave the wood. With Jenny, he thought, he
would live always in the country. And he picked a posy of
wild flowers for her.

His *rentrée* into the still silent town strengthened his
Arcadian resolves. He, who had seen the town so often in its
hours of sleep, had never noticed how sinister its whole aspect
was. In its narrow streets the white houses rose on either side
of him like cliffs of chalk. He turned swiftly along the unswept
pavement. How had he loved this city of evil secrets?

At last he came to St. James's Square, to the hateful door
of his own house. Shadows lay like memories in every corner
of the dim hall. Through the window of his room, a sunbeam
slanted across his smooth white bed, and fell ghastly on the
ashen grate.

2

It was a bright morning in Old Bond Street, and fat little
Mr. Aeneas, the fashionable mask-maker, was sunning himself
at the door of his shop. His window was lined as usual with all
kinds of masks—beautiful masks with pink cheeks, and absurd
masks with protuberant chins; curious .... copied from
old tragic models; masks of paper for children, of fine silk
for ladies, and of leather for working men; bearded or beardless,
gilded or waxen (most of them, indeed, were waxen), big
or little masks. And in the middle of this vain galaxy hung
the presentment of a Cyclops' face, carved cunningly of gold,
with a great sapphire in its brow.

The sun gleamed brightly on the window and on the bald head and varnished shoes of fat little Mr. Aeneas. It was too early for any customers to come, and Mr. Aeneas seemed to be greatly enjoying his leisure in the fresh air. He smiled complacently as he stood there, and well he might, for he was a great artist and was patronized by several crowned heads and not a few of the nobility. Only the evening before, Mr. Brummell had come into his shop and ordered a light summer mask, wishing to evade for a time the jealous vigilance of Lady Otterton. It pleased Mr. Aeneas to think that his art made him the recipient of so many high secrets. He smiled as he thought of the titled spendthrifts who, at this moment, *perdus* behind his masterpieces, passed unscathed among their creditors. He was the secular confessor of his day, always able to gave absolution. A unique position!

The street was as quiet as a village street. At an open window over the way, a handsome lady, wrapped in a muslin *peignoir*, sat sipping her cup of chocolate. It was La Signora Gambogi, and Mr. Aeneas made her many elaborate bows. This morning, however, her thoughts seemed far away, and she did not notice the little man's polite efforts. Nettled at her negligence, Mr. Aeneas was on the point of retiring into his shop, when he saw Lord George Hell hastening up the street, with a posy of wild flowers in his hand.

'His Lordship is up betimes!' he said to himself. 'An early visit to La Signora, I suppose.'

Not so, however. His Lordship came straight towards the mask-shop. Once he glanced up at La Signora's window and looked deeply annoyed when he saw her sitting there. He came quickly into the shop.

'I want the mask of a saint,' he said.

'Mask of a saint, my Lord? Certainly!' said Mr. Aeneas, briskly. 'With or without halo? His Grace the Bishop of St. Aldred's always wears his with a halo. Your Lordship does not wish for a halo? Certainly! If your Lordship will allow me to take his measurement——'

'I must have the mask to-day,' Lord George said. 'Have you none ready-made?'

'Ah I see. Required for immediate wear,' murmured Mr. Aeneas, dubiously. 'You see, your Lordship takes a rather large size.' And he looked at the floor.

'Julius!' he cried suddenly to his assistant, who was putting the finishing touches to a mask of Barbarossa which the young king of Zürremburg was to wear at his coronation the following week. 'Julius! Do you remember the saint's mask we made for Mr. Ripsby, a couple of years ago?'

'Yes, sir,' said the boy. 'It's stored upstairs.'

'I thought so,' replied Mr. Aeneas. 'Mr. Ripsby only had it on hire. Step upstairs, Julius, and bring it down. I fancy it is just what your Lordship would wish. Spiritual, yet handsome.'

'Is it a mask that is even a mirror of true love?' Lord George asked, gravely.

'It was made precisely as such,' the mask-maker answered. 'In fact it was made for Mr. Ripsby to wear at his silver wedding and was very highly praised by the relatives of Mrs. Ripsby. Will your Lordship step into my little room?'

So Mr. Aeneas led the way to his parlour behind the shop. He was elated by the distinguished acquisition to his *clientèle*, for hitherto Lord George had never patronized his business. He bustled round his parlour and insisted that his Lordship should take a chair and a pinch from his snuff-box, while the saint's mask was being found.

Lord George's eye travelled along the rows of framed letters from great personages, which lined the walls. He did not see them though, for he was calculating the chances that La Gambogi had not observed him as he entered the mask-shop. He had comedown so early that he had thought she would still

375

be abed. That sinister old proverb, *La jalouse se lève de bonne heure,* rose in his memory. His eye fell unconsciously on a large, round mask made of dull silver, with the features of a human face traced over its surface in faint filigree.

'Your Lordship wonders what mask that is?' chirped Mr. Aeneas tapping the thing with one of his little finger-nails.

'What is that mask?' Lord George murmured, absently.

'I ought not to divulge, my Lord,' said the mask-maker. 'But I know your Lordship would respect a professional secret, a secret of which I am pardonably proud. This,' he said 'is a mask for the sun-god, Apollo, whom heaven bless!'

'You astound me,' said Lord George.

'Of no less a person, I do assure you. When Jupiter, his father, made him lord of the day, Apollo craved that he might sometimes see the doings of mankind in the hours of night-time. Jupiter granted so reasonable a request, and when next Apollo had passed over the sky and hidden in the sea, and darkness had fallen on all the world, he raised his head above the waters that he might watch the doings of mankind in the hours of night-time. But,' Mr. Aeneas added, with a smile, 'his bright countenance made light all the darkness. Men rose from their couches or from their revels, wondering that day was so soon come, and went to their work. And Apollo sank weeping into the sea. "Surely," he cried, "it is a bitter thing that I alone, of all the gods, may not watch the world in the hours of night-time. For in those hours, as I am told, men are even as gods are. They spill the wine and are wreathed with roses. Their daughters dance in the light of torches. They laugh to the sound of flutes. On their long couches they lie down at last, and sleep comes to kiss their eyelids. None of these things may I see. Wherefore the brightness of my beauty is even as a curse to me, and I would put it from me." And as he wept, Vulcan said to him, "I am not the least cunning of the gods, not the least pitiful. Do not weep, for I

will give you that which shall end your sorrow. Nor need
you put from you the brightness of your beauty." And Vulcan
made a mask of dull silver and fastened it across his brother's
face. And that night, thus masked, the sun-god rose from the
sea and watched the doings of mankind in the night-time.
Nor any longer were men abashed by his bright beauty, for it
was hidden by the mask of silver. Those whom he had so often
seen haggard over their daily tasks, he saw feasting now
and wreathed with red roses. He heard them laugh to the
sound of flutes, as their daughters danced in the red light of
torches. And when at length they lay down upon their soft
couches and sleep kissed their eyelids, he sank back into the
sea and hid his mask under a little rock in the bed of the sea.
Nor have men ever known that Apollo watches them often
in the night-time, but fancied it to be some pale goddess.'

'I myself have always thought it was Diana,' said Lord
George Hell.

'An error, my Lord!' said Mr. Aeneas, with a smile. '*Ecce
signum*!' And he tapped the mask of dull silver.

'Strange!' said his Lordship. 'And pray how comes it that
Apollo has ordered of *you* this new mask?'

'He has always worn twelve new masks every year, inasmuch as no mask can endure for many nights the near brightness of his face, before which even a mask of the best and
purest silver soon tarnishes and wears away. Centuries ago,
Vulcan tired of making so many masks. And so Apollo sent
Mercury down to Athens, to the shop of Phoron, a Phoenician
mask-maker of great skill. Phoron made Apollo's masks for
many years, and every month Mercury came to his shop for a
new one. When Phoron died, another artist was chosen, and,
when he died, another, and so on through all the ages of the
world. Conceive, my Lord, my pride and pleasure when
Mercury flew into my shop, one night last year, and made me
Apollo's warrant-holder. It is the highest privilege that any

mask-maker can desire. And when I die,' said Mr. Aeneas, with some emotion, 'Mercury will confer my post upon another.'

'And do they pay you for your labour?' Lord George asked.

Mr. Aeneas drew himself up to his full height, such as it was. 'In Olympus, my Lord,' he said, 'they have no currency. For any mask-maker, so high a privilege is its own reward. Yet the sun-god is generous. He shines more brightly into my shop than into any other. Nor does he suffer his rays to melt any waxen mask made by me, until its wearer doff it and it be done with.'

At this moment Julius came in with the Ripsby mask. 'I must ask your Lordship's pardon for having kept you so long,' pleaded Mr. Aeneas. 'But I have a large store of old masks and they are imperfectly catalogued.'

It certainly was a beautiful mask, with its smooth pink cheeks and devotional brows. It was made of the finest wax. Lord George took it gingerly in his hands and tried it on his face. It fitted *à merveille*.

'Is the expression exactly as your Lordship would wish?' asked Mr. Aeneas.

Lord George laid it on the table and studied it intently. 'I wish it were more as a perfect mirror of true love,' he said at length. 'It is too calm, too contemplative.'

'Easily remedied!' said Mr. Aeneas. Selecting a fine pencil, he deftly drew the eyebrows closer to each other. With a brush steeped in some scarlet pigment, he put a fuller curve upon the lips. And behold! it was the mask of a saint who loves dearly. Lord George's heart throbbed with pleasure.

'And for how long does your Lordship wish to wear it?' asked Mr. Aeneas.

'I must wear it until I die,' replied Lord George.

'Kindly be seated then, I pray,' rejoined the little man. 'For

I must apply the mask with great care. Julius, you will assist me!'

So, while Julius heated the inner side of the waxen mask over a little lamp, Mr. Aeneas stood over Lord George gently smearing his features with some sweet-scented pomade. Then he took the mask and powdered its inner side, quite soft and warm now, with a fluffy puff. 'Keep quite still, for one instant,' he said, and clapped the mask firmly on his Lordship's up-turned face. So soon as he was sure of its perfect adhesion, he took from his assistant's hand a silver file and a little wooden spatula, with which he proceeded to pare down the edge of the mask, where it joined the neck and ears. At length, all traces of the 'join' were obliterated. It remained only to arrange the curls of the lordly wig over the waxen brow.

The diguise was done. When Lord George looked through the eyelets of his mask into the mirror that was placed in his hand, he saw a face that was saintly, itself a mirror of true love. How wonderful it was! He felt his past was a dream. He felt he was a new man indeed. His voice went strangely through the mask's parted lips, as he thanked Mr. Aeneas.

'Proud to have served your Lordship,' said that little worthy, pocketing his fee of fifty guineas, while he bowed his customer out.

When he reached the street, Lord George nearly uttered a curse through those sainted lips of his. For there, right in his way stood La Gambogi, with a small pink parasol. She laid her hand upon his sleeve and called him softly by his name. He passed her by without a word. Again she confronted him.

'I cannot let go so handsome a lover,' she laughed, 'even though he spurn me! Do not spurn me, George. Give me your posy of wild flowers. Why, you never looked so lovingly at me in all your life!'

'Madam,' said Lord George, sternly, 'I have not the honour to know you.' And he passed on.

The lady gazed after her lost lover with the blackest hatred in her eyes. Presently she beckoned across the road to a certain spy.

And the spy followed him.

3

Lord George, greatly agitated, had turned into Picacdilly. It was horrible to have met this garish embodiment of his past on the very theshold of his fair future. The mask-maker's elevating talk about the gods, followed by the initiative ceremony of his saintly mask, had driven all discordant memories from his love-thoughts of Jenny Mere. And then to be met by La Gambogi! It might be that, after his stern words, she would not seek to cross his path again. Surely she would not seek to mar his sacred love. Yet, he knew her dark Italian nature, her passion of revenge. What was the line in Virgil? *Spretaeque*—something. Who knew but that somehow, sooner or later, she might come between him and his love?

He was about to pass Lord Barrymore's mansion. Count Karoloff and Mr. FitzClarence were lounging in one of the lower windows. Would they know him behind his mask? Thank God! they did not. They merely laughed as he went by, and Mr. FitzClarence cried in a mocking voice, 'Sing us a hymn, Mr. Whatever-your-saint's-name is!' The mask, then at least, was perfect. Jenny Mere would not know him. He need fear no one but La Gambogi. But would not she betray his secret? He sighed.

That night he was going to visit Garble's and to declare his love to the little actress. He never doubted that she would love him for his saintly face. Had she not said, 'That man whose face is wonderful as are the faces of the saints, to him I will give my true love'? She could not say now that his face was as a tarnished mirror of love. She would smile on him. She would be his bride. But would La Gambogi be at Garble's?

The operette would not be over before ten that night. The clock in Hyde Park Gate told him it was not yet ten—ten of the morning. Twelve whole hours to wait before he could fall at Jenny's feet! 'I cannot spend that time in this place of memories, he thought. So he hailed a yellow cabriolet and bade the jarvey drive him out to the village of Kensington.

When they came to the little wood where he had been but a few hours ago, Lord George dismissed the jarvey. The sun, that had risen as he stood there thinking of Jenny, shone down on his altered face, but, though it shone very fiercely, it did not melt his waxen features. The old woodman, who had shown him his way, passed by under a load of faggots and did not know him. He wandered among the trees. It was a lovely wood.

Presently he came to the bank of that tiny stream, the Ken, which still flowed there in those days. On the moss of its bank he lay down and let its water ripple over his hand. Some bright pebble glistened under the surface, and, as he peered down at it, he saw in the stream the reflection of his mask. A great shame filled him that he should so cheat the girl he loved. Behind that fair mask there would still be the evil face that had repelled her. Could he be so base as to decoy her into love of that most ingenious deception? He was filled with a great pity for her, with a hatred of himself. And yet, he argued, was the mask indeed a mean trick? Surely it was a secret symbol of his true repentance and of his true love. His face was evil, because his life had been evil. He had seen a gracious girl, and of a sudden his very soul had changed. His face alone was the same as it had been. It was not just that his face should be evil still.

There was the faint sound of someone sighing, Lord George looked up, and there, on the further bank, stood Jenny Mere, watching him. As their eyes met, she blushed and hung her head. She looked like nothing but a tall child as she stood there with her straight limp frock of lilac cotton and her sunburnt straw bonnet. He dared not speak; he could only gaze at her.

Suddenly there perched astride the bough of a tree, at her side, that winged and laughing child in whose hand was a bow. Before Lord George could warn her, an arrow had flashed down and vanished in her heart, and Cupid had flown away.

No cry of pain did she utter, but stretched out her arms to her lover, with a glad smile. He leapt quite lightly over the little stream and knelt at her feet. It seemed more fitting that he should kneel before the gracious thing he was unworthy of. But she, knowing only that his face was as the face of a great saint, bent over him and touched him with her hand.

'Surely,' she said, 'you are that good man for whom I have waited. Therefore do not kneel to me, but rise and suffer me to kiss your hand. For my love of you is lowly, and my heart is all yours.'

But he answered, looking up into her fond eyes, 'Nay, you are a queen, and I must needs kneel in your presence.'

But she shook her head wistfully, and she knelt down, also, in her tremulous ecstasy, before him. And as they knelt, the one to the other, the tears came into her eyes, and he kissed her. Though the lips that he pressed to her lips were only waxen, he thrilled with happiness, in that mimic kiss. He held her close to him in his arms, and they were silent in the sacredness of their love.

From his breast he took the posy of wild flowers that he had gathered.

'They are for you,' he whispered. 'I gathered them for you hours ago, in this wood. See! They are not withered.'

But she was perpelexed by his words and said to him, blushing, 'How was it for me that you gathered them, though you had never seen me?'

'I gathered them for you,' he answered, 'knowing I should

382

soon see you. How was it that you, who had never seen me, yet waited for me?'

'I waited, knowing I should see you at last.' And she kissed the posy and put it at her breast.

And they rose from their knees and went into the wood, walking hand in hand. As they went, he asked the names of the flowers that grew under their feet. 'These are primroses,' she would say. 'Did you not know? And these are ladies'-feet, and these forget-me-nots. And that white flower climbing up the trunks of the trees and trailing down so prettily from the branches, is called Astyanax. These little yellow things are buttercups. Did you not know?' And she laughed.

'I know the names of none of the flowers,' he said.

She looked up into his face and said timidly, 'Is it worldly and wrong of me to have loved the flowers? Ought I to have thought more of those higher things that are unseen?'

His heart smote him. He could not answer her simplicity.

'Surely the flowers are good, and did you not gather this posy for me?' she pleaded. 'But if you do not love them, I must not. And I will try to forget their names. For I must try to be like you in all things.'

'Love the flowers always,' he said. 'And teach me to love them.'

So she told him all about the flowers, how some grew very slowly and others bloomed in a night; how clever the convolvulus was at climbing, and how shy violets were, and why honeycups had folded petals. She told him of the birds, too, that sang in the wood, how she knew them all by their voices. 'That is a chaffinch singing. Listen!' she said. And she tried to imitate its note, that her lover might remember. All the birds, according to her, were good, except the cuckoo, and whenever she heard him sing she would stop her ears, lest she should forgive him for robbing the nests. 'Every day,' she said, 'I have come to the wood, because I was lonely, and it seemed to pity me. But now I have you. And it is glad!'

She clung closer to his arm, and he kissed her. She pushed back her straw bonnet, so that it dangled from her neck by its ribands, and laid her little head against his shoulder. For a while he forgot his treachery to her, thinking only of his love and her love. Suddenly she said to him, 'Will you try not to be angry with me, if I tell you something? It is something that will seem dreadful to you.'

'*Pauvrette*,' he answered, 'you cannot have anything very dreadful to tell.'

'I am very poor,' she said, 'and every night I dance in a theatre. It is the only thing I can do to earn my bread. Do you despise me because I dance?' She looked up shyly at him and saw that his face was full of love for her and not angry.

'Do you like dancing?' he asked.

'I hate it,' she answered, quickly. 'I hate it indeed. Yet— to-night, alas! I must dance again in the theatre.'

'You need never dance again,' said her lover. 'I am rich and I will pay them to release you. You shall dance only for me. Sweetheart, it cannot be much more than noon. Let us go into the town, while there is time, and you shall be made my bride, and I your bridegroom, this very day. Why should you and I be lonely?'

'I do not know,' she said.

So they walked back through the wood, taking a narrow path which Jenny said would lead them quickest to the village. And, as they went, they came to a tiny cottage, with a garden that was full of flowers. The old woodman was leaning over its paling, and he nodded to them as they passed.

'I often used to envy the woodman,' said Jenny, 'living in that dear little cottage.'

'Let us live there, then.' said Lord George. And he went back and asked the old man if he were not unhappy, living there alone.

' 'Tis a poor life here for me,' the old man answered. 'No folk come to the wood except little children, now and again, to play, or lovers like you. But they seldom notice me. And in winter I am alone with Jack Frost! Old men love merrier company than that. Oh! I shall die in the snow with my faggots on my back. A poor life here!'

'I will give you gold for your cottage and whatever is in it, and then you can go and live happily in the town,' Lord George said. And he took from his coat a note for two hundred guineas, and held it across the palings.

'Lovers are poor foolish derry-docks,' the old man muttered. 'But I thank you kindly, Sir. This little sum will keep me cosy, as long as I last. Come into the cottage as soon as can be. It's a lonely place and does my heart good to depart from it.'

'We are going to be married this afternoon, in the town,' said Lord George. 'We will come straight back to our home.'

'May you be happy,' replied the woodman. 'You'll find me gone when you come.'

And the lovers thanked him and went their way.

'Are you very rich?' Jenny asked. 'Ought you to have bought the cottage for that great price?'

'Would you love me as much if I were quite poor, little Jenny?' he asked her, after a pause.

'I did not know you were rich when I saw you across the stream,' she said.

And in his heart Lord George made a good resolve. He would put away from him all his worldly possessions. All the money that he had won at the clubs, fairly or foully, all that hideous accretion of gold guineas, he would distribute among the comrades he had impoverished. As he walked, with the sweet and trustful girl at his side, the vague record of his infamy assailed him, and a look of pain shot behind his smooth mask. He would atone. He would shun no sacrifice that might cleanse his soul. All his fortune he would put from him. Follard

Chase he would give back to Sir Follard. He would sell his house in St. James's Square. He would keep some little part of his patrimony, enough for him in the wood with Jenny, but no more.

'I shall be quite poor, Jenny!' he said.

And they talked of the things that lovers love to talk of, how happy they would be together and how economical. As they were passing Herbert's pastry shop, which as my little readers know, still stands in Kensington, Jenny looked up rather wistfully into her lover's ascetic face.

'Should you think me greedy,' she asked him, 'if I wanted a bun? They have beautiful buns here!'

Buns! The simple word started latent memories of his childhood. Jenny was only a child after all. Buns! He had forgotten what they were like. And as they looked at the piles of variegated cakes in the window, he said to her, 'Which are buns, Jenny? I should like to have one, too.'

'I am almost afraid of you,' she said. 'You must despise me so. Are you so good that you deny yourself all the vanity and pleasure that most people love? It is wonderful not to know what buns are! The round, brown, shiny cakes, with little raisins in them, are buns.'

So he bought two beautiful buns, and they sat together in the shop, eating them. Jenny bit hers rather diffidently, but was reassured when he said that they must have buns very often in the cottage. Yes! he, the famous toper and *gourmet* of St. James's, relished this homely fare, as it passed through the insensible lips of his mask to the palate. He seemed to rise, from the consumption of his bun, a better man.

But there was no time to lose now. It was already past two o'clock. So he got a chaise from the inn opposite the pastry-shop, and they were swiftly driven to Doctor's Commons. There he purchased a special licence. When the clerk asked him to write his name upon it, he hesitated. What name should he assume? Under a mask he had wooed this girl, under an unreal name he must make her his bride. He loathed himself for a trickster. He had vilely stolen from her the love she would not give him. Even now, should he not confess himself the man whose face had frightened her, and go his way? And yet, surely, it was not just that he, whose soul was transfigured, should bear his old name, Surely George Hell was dead, and his name had died with him. So he dipped a pen in the ink and wrote 'George Heaven,' for want of a better name. And Jenny wrote 'Jenny Mere' beneath it.

An hour later they were married according to the simple rites of a dear little registry-office in Covent Garden.

And in the cool evening they went home.

4

In the cottage that had been the woodman's they had a wonderful honeymoon. No king and queen in any palace of gold were happier than they. For them their tiny cottage was a palace, and the flowers that filled the garden were their courtiers. Long and careless and full of kisses were the days of their reign.

Sometimes, indeed, strange dreams troubled Lord George's sleep. Once he dreamed that he stood knocking and knocking at the great door of a castle. It was a bitter night. The frost enveloped him. No one came. Presently he heard a footstep in the hall beyond, and a pair of frightened eyes peered at him through the grill. Jenny was scanning his face. She would not open to him. With tears and wild words he besought her, but she would not open to him. Then, very stealthily he crept round the castle and found a small casement in the wall. It was open. He climbed swiftly, quietly, through it, In the darkness of the room someone ran to him and kissed him gladly.

It was Jenny. With a cry of joy and shame he awoke. By his side lay Jenny, sleeping like a little child.

After all, what was a dream to him? It could not mar the reality of his daily happiness. He cherished his true penitence for the evil he had done in the past. The past! That was indeed the only unreal thing that lingered in his life. Every day its substance dwindled, grew fainter, yet as he lived his rustic honeymoon. Had he not utterly put it from him? Had he not, a few hours after his marriage, written to his lawyer, declaring solemnly that he, Lord George Hell, had forsworn the world, that he was where no man would find him, that he desired all his worldly goods to be distributed, thus and thus, among these and those of his companions? By this testament he had verily atoned for the wrong he had done, had made himself dead indeed to the world.

No address had he written upon this document. Though its injunctions were final and binding, it could betray no clue to his hiding-place. For the rest, no one would care to seek him out. He, who had done no good to human creature, would pass unmourned out of memory. The clubs, doubtless, would laugh and puzzle over his strange recantations, envious of whomever he had enriched. They would say 'twas a good riddance of a rogue, and soon forget him.1 But she, whose prime patron he had been, who had loved him in her vile

1. I would refer my little readers once more to the pages o^f *Contemporary Bucks*, where Captain Tarleton speculates upon the sudden disappearance of Lord George Hell and describes its effect on the town. 'No even the shrewdest,' says he, 'even gave a guess that would throw a ray of revealing light on the *disparition* of this profligate man. It was supposed that he carried off with him a little dancer from Garble's, at which *haunt of pleasantry* he was certainly on the night he vanished, and whither the young lady never returned again. Garble declared he had been compensated for her perfidy, but that he was sure she had not succumbed to his Lordship, having in fact rejected him soundly. Did his Lordship, say the cronies, take his life – and hers? *Il n'y a pas d'épreuve.* The

fashion, La Gambogi, would she forget him easily, like the rest? As the sweet days went by, her spectre, also, grew fainter and less formidable. She knew his mask indeed, but how should she find him in the cottage near Kensington? *Devia dulcedo latebrarum!* He was safe-hidden with his bride. As for the Italian, she might search and search—or had forgotten him, in the arms of another lover.

Yes! Few and faint became the blemishes of his honeymoon. At first he had felt that his waxen mask, though it had been the means of his happiness, was rather a barrier 'twixt him and his bride. Though it was sweet to kiss her through it, to look at her through it with loving eyes, yet there were times when it incommoded him with its mockery. Could he put it from him! Yet that, of course, could not be. He must wear it all his life. And so, as days went by, he grew reconciled to his mask. No longer did he feel it jarring on his face. It seemed to become a very part of him, and, for all its rigid material, it did forsooth express the one emotion that filled him, true love. The face for whose sake Jenny gave him her heart could not but be dear to this George Heaven, also.

Every day chastened him with its joy. They lived a very simple life, he and Jenny. They rose betimes, like the birds,

---

most astonishing matter is that the runaway should have written out a complete will, restoring all money he had won at cards, etc. etc. This certainly corroborates the opinion that he was seized with a sudden repentance and fled over the seas to a foreign monastery, where he died at last in *religious silence.* That's as it may, but many a spendthrift found his pocket clinking with guineas, a not unpleasant sound, I declare. The Regent himself was benefited by the odd will, and old Sir Follard Follard found himself once more in the ancestral home he had forfeited. As for Lord George's mansion in St James's Square, that was sold with all its appurtenances, and the money fetched by the sale, no bagatelle, was given to various good objects, according to my Lord's stated wishes. Well, many of us blessed his name – we had cursed it often enough. Peace to his ashes, in whatever urn they may be resting, on the billows of whatever ocean they float!'

for whose goodness they both had so sincere a love. Bread and honey and little strawberries were their morning fare, and in the evening they had seed-cake and dewberry wine. Jenny herself made the wine, and her husband drank it, in strict moderation, never more than two glasses. He thought it tasted far better than the Regent's cherry brandy, or the Tokay at Brooks's. Of these treasured topes he had indeed, nearly forgotten the taste. The wine made from wild berries by his little bride was august enough for his palate. Sometimes, after they had dined thus, he would play the flute to her upon the moonlit lawn, or tell her of the great daisy-chain he was going to make for her on the morrow, or sit silently by her side, listening to the nightingale, till bedtime. So admirably simple were their days.

5

One morning, as he was helping Jenny to water the flowers, he said to her suddenly, 'Sweetheart, we had forgotten!'

'What was there we should forget?' asked Jenny, looking up from her task.

' 'Tis the mensiversary of our wedding,' her husband answered gravely. 'We must not let it pass without some celebration.'

'No indeed,' she said, 'we must not. What shall we do?'

Between them they decided upon an unusual feast. They would go into the village and buy a bag of beautiful buns and eat them in the afternoon. So soon, then, as all the flowers were watered, they set forth to Herbert's shop, bought the buns and returned home in very high spirits, George bearing a paper bag that held no less than twelve of the wholesome delicacies. Under the plane-tree on the lawn Jenny sat her down, and George stretched himself at her feet. They were loth to enjoy their feast too soon. They dallied in childish anticipation. On the little rustic table Jenny built up the buns, one above another, till they looked like a tall pagoda. When very gingerly, she had crowned the structure with the twelfth bun, her husband looking on with admiration, she clapped her hands and danced about it. She laughed so loudly (for, though she was only sixteen years old, she had a great sense of humour) that the table shook, and alas! the pagoda tottered and fell to the lawn. Swift as a kitten, Jenny chased the buns, as they rolled, hither and thither, over the grass, catching them deftly with her hand. Then she came back, flushed and merry under her tumbled hair, with her arm full of buns. She began to put them back in the paper bag.

'Dear husband,' she said, looking down to him, 'why do you not smile at my folly? Your grave face rebukes me. Smile, or I shall think I vex you. Please smile a little.'

But the mask could not smile, of course. It was made for a mirror of true love, and it was grave and immobile. 'I am very much amused, dear,' he said, 'at the fall of the buns, but my lips will not curve to a smile. Love of you has bound them in spell.'

'But I can laugh, though I love you. I do not understand.' And she wondered. He took her hand in his his and stroked it gently, wishing it were possible to smile. Some day, perhaps, she would tire of this monotonous gravity, this rigid sweetness. It was not strange that she should long for a little facial expression. They sat silently.

'Jenny, what is it?' he whispered suddenly. For Jenny, with wide-open eyes, was gazing over his head, across the lawn. 'Why do you look frightened?'

'There is a strange woman smiling at me across the palings,' she said. 'I do not know her.'

Her husband's heart sank. Somehow, he dared not turn his head to the intruder.

'She is nodding to me,' said Jenny. 'I think she is foreign, for she has an evil face.'

'Do not notice her,' he whispered. 'Does she look evil?'

'Very evil and very dark. She has a pink parasol. Her teeth are like ivory.'

'Do not notice her. Think! It is the mensiversary of our wedding dear!'

'I wish she would not smile at me. Her eyes are like bright blots of ink.'

'Let us eat out beautiful buns!'

'Oh, she is coming in!' George heard the latch of the gate jar. 'Forbid her to come in!' whispered Jenny. 'I am afraid! He heard the jar of heels on the gravel path. Yet he dared not turn. Only he clasped Jenny's hand more tightly, as he waited for the voice. It was La Gambogi's.

'Pray, pray, pardon me! I could not mistake the back of so old a friend.'

With the courage of despair, George turned and faced the woman.

'Even,' she smiled, 'though his face has changed marvellously.'

'Madam,' he said, rising to his full height and stepping between her and his bride, 'begone, I command you, from this garden. I do not see what good is to be served by the renewal of our acquaintance.'

'Acquaintance!' murmured La Gambogi, with an arch of her beetle-brows. 'Surely we were friends, rather, nor is my esteem for you so dead that I would crave estrangement.'

'Madam,' rejoined Lord George, with a tremor in his voice, 'you see me happy, living very peacefully with my bride——'

'To whom, I beseech you, old friend, present me.'

'I would not,' he said hotly, 'desecrate her sweet name by speaking it with so infamous a name as yours.'

'Your choler hurts me, old friend,' said La Gambogi,

sinking composedly upon the garden seat and smoothing the silk of her skirts.

'Jenny,' said George, 'then do you retire, pending this lady's departure, to the cottage,' But Jenny clung to his arm. 'I were less frightened at your side,' she whispered. 'Do not send me away!'

'Suffer her pretty presence,' said La Gambogi. 'Indeed I am come this long way from the heart of the town, that I may see her, no less than you, George. My wish is only to befriend her. Why should she not set you a mannerly example, giving me welcome? Come and sit by me, little bride, for I have things to tell you. Though you reject my friendship, give me, at least, the slight courtesy of audience. I will not detain you overlong, will be gone very soon. Are you expecting guests, George? *On dirait une masque champêtre!*' She eyed the couple critically. 'Your wife's mask,' she said, 'is even better than yours.'

'What does she mean?' whispered Jenny. 'Oh, send her away!'

'Serpent,' was all George could say, 'crawl from our Eden, ere you poison with your venom its fairest denizen.'

La Gambogi rose. 'Even *my* pride,' she cried passionately, 'knows certain bounds. I have been forbearing, but even in *my* zeal for friendship I will not be called "serpent." I will indeed be gone from this rude place. Yet ere I go, there is a boon I will deign to beg. Show me, oh, show me but once again, the dear face I have so often caressed, the lips that were dear to me!'

George started back.

'What does she mean?' whispered Jenny.

'In memory of our old friendship,' continued La Gambogi, 'grant me this piteous favour. Show me your own face but for one instant, and I vow that I will never again remind you that I live. Intercede for me, little bride. Bid him unmask for me. You have more authority over him than I. Doff his mask with your own uxorious fingers.'

'What does she mean?' was the refrain of poor Jenny.

'If,' said George, gazing sternly at his traitress, 'you do not go now, of your own will, I must drive you, man though I am, violently from the garden.'

'Doff your mask and I am gone.'

George made a step of menace towards her.

'False saint!' she shrieked, 'then *I* will unmask you.'

Like a panther she sprang upon him and clawed at his waxen cheeks. Jenny fell back, mute with terror. Vainly did George try to free himself from his assailant, who writhed round and round him, clawing, clawing at what Jenny fancied to be his face. With a wild cry, Jenny fell upon the furious creature and tried, with all her childish strength, to release her dear one. The combatives swayed to and fro, a revulsive trinity. There was a loud pop, as though some great cork had been withdrawn, and La Gambogi recoiled. She had torn away the mask. It lay before her upon the lawn, upturned to the sky.

George stood motionless. La Gambogi stared up into his face, and her dark flush died swiftly away. For there, staring back at her, was the man she had unmasked, but lo! his face was even as his mask had been. Line for line, feature for feature, it was the same. 'Twas a saint's face.

'Madam,' he said, in the calm voice of despair, 'your cheek may well blanch, when you regard the ruin you have brought upon me. Nevertheless do I pardon you. The gods have avenged through you, the imposture I wrought upon one who was dear to me. For that unpardonable sin I am punished. As for my poor bride, whose love I stole by the means of that waxen semblance, of her I cannot ask pardon. Ah, Jenny, Jenny, do not look at me. Turn your eyes from the foul reality that I dissembled.' He shuddered and hid his face in his hands. 'Do not look at me. I will go from the garden. Nor will I ever curse you with the odious spectacle of my face. Forget me, forget me.'

But, as he turned to go, Jenny laid her hands upon his wrists and besought him that he would look at her. 'For indeed,' she said, 'I am bewildered by your strange words. Why did you woo me under a mask? And why do you imagine I could love you less dearly, seeing your own face?'

He looked into her eyes. On their violet surface he saw the tiny reflection of his own face. He was filled with joy and wonder.

'Surely,' said Jenny, 'your face is even dearer to me, even fairer, than the semblance that hid it and deceived me. I am not angry. 'Twas well that you veiled from me the full glory of your face, for indeed I wa not worthy to behold it too soon. But I am your wife now. Let me look always at your own face. Let the time of my probation be over. Kiss me with your own lips.'

So he took her in his arms, as though she had been a little child, and kissed her with his own lips. She put her arms round his neck, and he was happier than he had ever been. They were alone in the garden now. Nor lay the mask any longer upon the lawn, for the sun had melted it.

NEW YORK INSTITUTE
OF TECHNOLOGY LIBRARY